CCNP Routing and Switching SWITCH 300-115 Official Cert Guide

David Hucaby

Copyright © 2015 Pearson Education, Inc.

Published by:
Cisco Press
800 East 96th Street
Indianapolis, IN 46240 USA

Printed in the United States of America

Second Printing: April 2015

Library of Congress Control Number: 2014954903

ISBN-13: 978-1-58720-560-6

ISBN-10: 1-58720-560-2

Warning and Disclaimer

This book is designed to provide information about the Cisco CCNP SWITCH exam (300-115). Every effort has been made to make this book as complete and as accurate as possible, but no warranty or fitness is implied.

The information is provided on an "as is" basis. The authors, Cisco Press, and Cisco Systems, Inc. shall have neither liability nor responsibility to any person or entity with respect to any loss or damages arising from the information contained in this book or from the use of the discs or programs that may accompany it.

The opinions expressed in this book belong to the author and are not necessarily those of Cisco Systems, Inc.

Trademark Acknowledgments

All terms mentioned in this book that are known to be trademarks or service marks have been appropriately capitalized. Cisco Press or Cisco Systems, Inc., cannot attest to the accuracy of this information. Use of a term in this book should not be regarded as affecting the validity of any trademark or service mark.

Special Sales

For information about buying this title in bulk quantities, or for special sales opportunities (which may include electronic versions; custom cover designs; and content particular to your business, training goals, marketing focus, or branding interests), please contact our corporate sales department at corpsales@pearsoned.com or (800) 382-3419.

For government sales inquiries, please contact governmentsales@pearsoned.com.

For questions about sales outside the U.S., please contact international@pearsoned.com.

Feedback Information

At Cisco Press, our goal is to create in-depth technical books of the highest quality and value. Each book is crafted with care and precision, undergoing rigorous development that involves the unique expertise of members from the professional technical community.

Readers' feedback is a natural continuation of this process. If you have any comments regarding how we could improve the quality of this book, or otherwise alter it to better suit your needs, you can contact us through email at feedback@ciscopress.com. Please make sure to include the book title and ISBN in your message.

We greatly appreciate your assistance.

Publisher: Paul Boger

Associate Publisher: Dave Dusthimer

Business Operation Manager, Cisco Press: Jan Cornelssen

Executive Editor: Brett Bartow

Managing Editor: Sandra Schroeder

Senior Development Editor: Christopher Cleveland

Project Editor: Seth Kerney

Copy Editor: Keith Cline

Technical Editors: Joe Harris, Geoff Tagg

Editorial Assistant: Vanessa Evans

Book Designer: Mark Shirar

Composition: Bronkella Publishing

Indexer: Johnna Vanhoose Dinse

Proofreader: Debbie Williams

Americas Headquarters
Cisco Systems, Inc.
San Jose, CA

Asia Pacific Headquarters
Cisco Systems (USA) Pte. Ltd.
Singapore

Europe Headquarters
Cisco Systems International BV
Amsterdam, The Netherlands

Cisco has more than 200 offices worldwide. Addresses, phone numbers, and fax numbers are listed on the Cisco Website at **www.cisco.com/go/offices**.

About the Author

David Hucaby, CCIE No. 4594, is a lead network engineer for the University of Kentucky, where he works with a large healthcare network based on the Cisco product lines. David holds bachelor's and master's degrees in electrical engineering from the University of Kentucky. He is the author of several Cisco Press titles, including *CCNA Wireless Cert Guide, Cisco ASA, PIX, and FWSM Firewall Handbook,* Second Edition; *Cisco Firewall Video Mentor;* and *Cisco LAN Switching Video Mentor.* David lives in Kentucky with his wife, Marci, and two daughters.

About the Technical Reviewers

Joe Harris, CCIE No. 6200 (R/S, Security & SP), is a triple CCIE working for Cisco as a Consulting Systems Engineer with their SP organization, where he specializes in security and data center technologies. With more than 16 years of extensive experience focusing on advanced technologies within the IP arena, Joe has been primarily focused on supporting some of Cisco's large service provider accounts, in addition to local government and federal agencies. Joe holds a bachelor of science degree from Louisiana Tech University and resides with his wife and two children in Frisco, Texas.

Geoff Tagg is based in Oxford in the United Kingdom, where he runs a networking consulting business. Geoff has worked with clients ranging from small UK businesses to large multinationals and service providers for many years, combining implementation with onsite training. He is currently working with a large international organization in Italy, but is also a course author for Learning Tree International and Professor of Networking at Oxford Brookes University. Over the past 30 years, Geoff has worked with most major networking technologies, developing a specific expertise in secure, converged network infrastructures based largely on Cisco hardware. Before that, he accumulated 15 years in systems programming and operations management. Geoff lives with his wife Christine, and family, where he finds the combination of work, family, and garden a continuing, but exciting, challenge.

Dedications

As always, this book is dedicated to the most important people in my life: my wife, Marci, and my two daughters, Lauren and Kara. Their love, encouragement, and support carry me along. I'm so grateful to God, who gives endurance and encouragement (Romans 15:5), and who has allowed me to work on projects like this.

Acknowledgments

It has been my great pleasure to work on another Cisco Press project. I enjoy the networking field very much, and technical writing even more. And more than that, I'm thankful for the joy and inner peace that Jesus Christ gives, making everything more abundant.

Technical writing may be hard work, but I'm finding that it's also quite fun because I'm working with very good friends at Cisco Press. Even after nearly 15 years, I still get to work with Brett Bartow and Chris Cleveland, the finest editors I know.

I am very grateful for the insight, suggestions, and helpful comments that Geoff Tagg and Joe Harris contributed. Their knowledge and attention to detail helped make this a more well-rounded book and me a more educated author.

Contents at a Glance

Introduction   xxiv

Part I   **Designing Campus Networks**

Chapter 1   Enterprise Campus Network Design   3

Chapter 2   Switch Operation   29

Chapter 3   Switch Port Configuration   55

Part II   **Building a Campus Network**

Chapter 4   VLANs and Trunks   89

Chapter 5   VLAN Trunking Protocol   123

Part III   **Working with Redundant Links**

Chapter 6   Traditional Spanning Tree Protocol   147

Chapter 7   Spanning-Tree Configuration   177

Chapter 8   Protecting the Spanning Tree Protocol Topology   203

Chapter 9   Advanced Spanning Tree Protocol   219

Chapter 10   Aggregating Switch Links   241

Part IV   **Multilayer Switching**

Chapter 11   Multilayer Switching   265

Chapter 12   Configuring DHCP   289

Part V   **Monitoring Campus Networks**

Chapter 13   Logging Switch Activity   305

Chapter 14   Managing Switches with SNMP   321

Chapter 15   Monitoring Performance with IP SLA   333

Chapter 16   Using Port Mirroring to Monitor Traffic   349

Part VI   **Implementing High Availability**

Chapter 17   Understanding High Availability   365

Chapter 18   Layer 3 High Availability   381

Part VII   Securing Switched Networks

Chapter 19   Securing Switch Access   411

Chapter 20   Securing VLANs   431

Chapter 21   Preventing Spoofing Attacks   449

Chapter 22   Managing Switch Users   461

Part VIII   Final Preparation

Chapter 23   Final Preparation   475

Part IX   Appendixes

Appendix A   Answers to the "Do I Know This Already?" Quizzes   481

Appendix B   Exam Updates   489

              Glossary   493

              Index   504

CD-Only Appendixes

Appendix C   Memory Tables

Appendix D   Memory Table Answer Key

Appendix E   Study Planner

Contents

Introduction   xxiv

Part I   **Designing Campus Networks**

Chapter 1   **Enterprise Campus Network Design   3**

"Do I Know This Already?" Quiz   3

Foundation Topics   7

Hierarchical Network Design   7

   Predictable Network Model   9

   Access Layer   12

   Distribution Layer   12

   Core Layer   12

Modular Network Design   13

   Sizing a Switch Block   16

   Switch Block Redundancy   18

   Network Core   20

   Collapsed Core   23

   Core Size in a Campus Network   24

   Cisco Products in a Hierarchical Network Design   24

Exam Preparation Tasks   27

Review All Key Topics   27

Complete Tables and Lists from Memory   27

Define Key Terms   27

Chapter 2   **Switch Operation   29**

"Do I Know This Already?" Quiz   29

Foundation Topics   32

Layer 2 Switch Operation   32

   Transparent Bridging   32

   Follow That Frame!   35

Multilayer Switch Operation   36

   Types of Multilayer Switching   36

   Follow That Packet!   37

   Multilayer Switching Exceptions   39

Tables Used in Switching   40

   Content-Addressable Memory   40

   Ternary Content-Addressable Memory   41

   TCAM Structure   42

   TCAM Example   43

   Port Operations in TCAM   44

Managing Switching Tables   45

CAM Table Operation   45

TCAM Operation   48

Managing Switching Table Sizes   49

Exam Preparation Tasks   52

Review All Key Topics   52

Complete Tables and Lists from Memory   52

Define Key Terms   52

Use Command Reference to Check Your Memory   52

Chapter 3   Switch Port Configuration   55

"Do I Know This Already?" Quiz   55

Foundation Topics   59

Ethernet Concepts   59

Ethernet Overview   59

Scaling Ethernet   60

Fast Ethernet   60

Gigabit Ethernet   61

10-Gigabit Ethernet   62

Beyond 10-Gigabit Ethernet   63

Duplex Operation over Ethernet Links   63

Connecting Switches and Devices   65

Ethernet Port Cables and Connectors   65

Switch Port Configuration   66

Selecting Ports to Configure   66

Identifying Ports   68

Port Speed   68

Port Duplex Mode   69

Managing Error Conditions on a Switch Port   69

Detecting Error Conditions   69

Automatically Recover from Error Conditions   70

Enable and Use the Switch Port   71

Troubleshooting Port Connectivity   71

Looking for the Port State   71

Looking for Speed and Duplex Mismatches   72

Discovering Connected Devices   73

Cisco Discovery Protocol   73

Link Layer Discovery Protocol   75

Using Power over Ethernet   77

How PoE Works   78

Detecting a Powered Device   79

Configuring PoE   80

Verifying PoE   81

Exam Preparation Tasks   84

Review All Key Topics   84

Complete Tables and Lists from Memory   84

Define Key Terms   84

Use Command Reference to Check Your Memory   85

Part II   Building a Campus Network

Chapter 4   VLANs and Trunks   89

"Do I Know This Already?" Quiz   89

Foundation Topics   95

Virtual LANs   95

VLAN Membership   96

Static VLANs   96

Configuring Static VLANs   97

Dynamic VLANs   99

Deploying VLANs   99

End-to-End VLANs   100

Local VLANs   101

VLAN Trunks   101

VLAN Frame Identification   103

Inter-Switch Link Protocol   103

IEEE 802.1Q Protocol   104

Dynamic Trunking Protocol   105

VLAN Trunk Configuration   106

Configuring a VLAN Trunk   106

Trunk Configuration Example   108

Troubleshooting VLANs and Trunks   110

Voice VLANs   112

Voice VLAN Configuration   113

Verifying Voice VLAN Operation   115

Wireless VLANs   117

Exam Preparation Tasks   119

Review All Key Topics   119

Complete Tables and Lists from Memory   119

Define Key Terms   119

Use Command Reference to Check Your Memory   119

Chapter 5   VLAN Trunking Protocol   123

"Do I Know This Already?" Quiz   123

Foundation Topics   127

VLAN Trunking Protocol   127

VTP Domains   127

VTP Modes   127

VTP Advertisements   128

VTP Synchronization   131

VTP Configuration   132

Configuring the VTP Version   133

Configuring a VTP Management Domain   134

Configuring the VTP Mode   135

VTP Configuration Example   136

VTP Status   137

VTP Pruning   138

Enabling VTP Pruning   140

Troubleshooting VTP   141

Exam Preparation Tasks   143

Review All Key Topics   143

Complete Tables and Lists from Memory   143

Define Key Terms   143

Use Command Reference to Check Your Memory   143

Part III   Working with Redundant Links

Chapter 6   Traditional Spanning Tree Protocol   147

"Do I Know This Already?" Quiz   147

Foundation Topics   151

IEEE 802.1D Overview   151

Bridging Loops   151

Preventing Loops with Spanning Tree Protocol   154

Spanning-Tree Communication: Bridge Protocol Data Units   155

Electing a Root Bridge   156

Electing Root Ports   158

Electing Designated Ports   160

STP States   162

STP Timers   165

Topology Changes   167

Direct Topology Changes   168

Indirect Topology Changes   169

Insignificant Topology Changes   171

Types of STP   172

Common Spanning Tree   173

Per-VLAN Spanning Tree   173

Per-VLAN Spanning Tree Plus   173

Exam Preparation Tasks   175

Review All Key Topics   175

Complete Tables and Lists from Memory   175

Define Key Terms   175

Chapter 7   Spanning-Tree Configuration   177

"Do I Know This Already?" Quiz   177

Foundation Topics   181

STP Root Bridge   181

Root Bridge Placement   181

Root Bridge Configuration   184

Tuning the Root Path Cost   188

Tuning the Port ID   190

Tuning Spanning-Tree Convergence   191

Modifying STP Timers   191

Manually Configuring STP Timers   192

Automatically Configuring STP Timers   192

Redundant Link Convergence   194

PortFast: Access Layer Nodes   194

UplinkFast: Access Layer Uplinks   196

BackboneFast: Redundant Backbone Paths   197

Monitoring STP   199

Exam Preparation Tasks   200

Review All Key Topics   200

Complete Tables and Lists from Memory   200

Define Key Terms   200

Use Command Reference to Check Your Memory   200

Chapter 8   **Protecting the Spanning Tree Protocol Topology   203**

"Do I Know This Already?" Quiz   203

Foundation Topics   207

Protecting Against Unexpected BPDUs   207

Root Guard   207

BPDU Guard   208

Protecting Against Sudden Loss of BPDUs   210

Loop Guard   210

UDLD   211

Using BPDU Filtering to Disable STP on a Port   213

Troubleshooting STP Protection   214

Exam Preparation Tasks   215

Review All Key Topics   215

Complete Tables and Lists from Memory   215

Define Key Terms   215

Use Command Reference to Check Your Memory   215

Chapter 9   **Advanced Spanning Tree Protocol   219**

"Do I Know This Already?" Quiz   219

Foundation Topics   223

Rapid Spanning Tree Protocol   223

RSTP Port Behavior   223

BPDUs in RSTP   224

RSTP Convergence   225

Port Types   226

Synchronization   227

Topology Changes and RSTP   229

RSTP Configuration   229

Rapid Per-VLAN Spanning Tree Protocol   230

Multiple Spanning Tree Protocol   231

MST Overview   233

MST Regions   233

Spanning-Tree Instances Within MST   234

IST Instances   234

MST Instances   235

MST Configuration   236

Exam Preparation Tasks   238

Review All Key Topics   238

Complete Tables and Lists from Memory   238

Define Key Terms   239

Use Command Reference to Check Your Memory   239

Chapter 10   Aggregating Switch Links   241

"Do I Know This Already?" Quiz   241

Foundation Topics   245

Switch Port Aggregation with EtherChannel   245

   Bundling Ports with EtherChannel   247

   Distributing Traffic in EtherChannel   247

   Configuring EtherChannel Load Balancing   249

EtherChannel Negotiation Protocols   251

   Port Aggregation Protocol   252

   Link Aggregation Control Protocol   252

EtherChannel Configuration   253

   Configuring a PAgP EtherChannel   253

   Configuring a LACP EtherChannel   254

   Avoiding Misconfiguration with EtherChannel Guard   255

Troubleshooting an EtherChannel   257

Exam Preparation Tasks   261

Review All Key Topics   261

Complete Tables and Lists from Memory   261

Define Key Terms   261

Command Reference to Check Your Memory   261

Part IV   Multilayer Switching

Chapter 11   Multilayer Switching   265

"Do I Know This Already?" Quiz   265

Foundation Topics   268

Inter-VLAN Routing   268

   Types of Interfaces   268

   Configuring Inter-VLAN Routing   269

   Layer 2 Port Configuration   270

   Layer 3 Port Configuration   270

   SVI Port Configuration   271

   Multilayer Switching with CEF   272

   Traditional MLS Overview   272

   CEF Overview   272

   Forwarding Information Base   273

Adjacency Table   276

Packet Rewrite   279

Configuring CEF   280

Verifying Multilayer Switching   280

Verifying Inter-VLAN Routing   280

Verifying CEF   283

Exam Preparation Tasks   285

Review All Key Topics   285

Complete Tables and Lists from Memory   285

Define Key Terms   285

Use Command Reference to Check Your Memory   285

Chapter 12   Configuring DHCP   289

"Do I Know This Already?" Quiz   289

Foundation Topics   292

Using DHCP with a Multilayer Switch   292

Configuring an IPv4 DHCP Server   293

Configuring a Manual Address Binding   294

Configuring DHCP Options   296

Configuring a DHCP Relay   296

Configuring DHCP to Support IPv6   297

Stateless Autoconfiguration   298

DHCPv6   298

DHCPv6 Lite   299

Configuring a DHCPv6 Relay Agent   300

Verifying IPv6 DHCP Operation   300

Exam Preparation Tasks   301

Review All Key Topics   301

Complete Tables and Lists from Memory   301

Define Key Terms   301

Use Command Reference to Check Your Memory   301

Part V   Monitoring Campus Networks

Chapter 13   Logging Switch Activity   305

"Do I Know This Already?" Quiz   305

Foundation Topics   308

Syslog Messages 308

    Logging to the Switch Console 310

    Logging to the Internal Buffer 310

    Logging to a Remote Syslog Server 311

Adding Time Stamps to Syslog Messages 312

    Setting the Internal System Clock 312

    Using NTP to Synchronize with an External Time Source 313

    Securing NTP 316

    Using SNTP to Synchronize Time 316

    Adding Time Stamps to Logging Messages 317

Exam Preparation Tasks 318

Review All Key Topics 318

Complete Tables and Lists from Memory 318

Define Key Terms 318

Use Command Reference to Check Your Memory 318

Chapter 14   **Managing Switches with SNMP**   **321**

"Do I Know This Already?" Quiz 321

Foundation Topics 324

SNMP Overview 324

Configuring SNMP 326

    Configuring SNMPv1 327

    Configuring SNMPv2C 327

    Configuring SNMPv3 328

Exam Preparation Tasks 330

Review All Key Topics 330

Complete Tables and Lists from Memory 330

Define Key Terms 330

Use Command Reference to Check Your Memory 330

Chapter 15   **Monitoring Performance with IP SLA**   **333**

"Do I Know This Already?" Quiz 333

Foundation Topics 336

IP SLA Overview 336

Configuring IP SLA 338

Using IP SLA 341

Exam Preparation Tasks 345

Review All Key Topics 345

Complete Tables and Lists from Memory 345

Define Key Terms   345

Use Command Reference to Check Your Memory   345

Chapter 16   Using Port Mirroring to Monitor Traffic   349

"Do I Know This Already?" Quiz   349

Foundation Topics   352

Using Local SPAN   352

Local SPAN Configuration   354

Remote SPAN   356

Remote SPAN Configuration   357

Managing SPAN Sessions   359

Exam Preparation Tasks   361

Review All Key Topics   361

Complete Tables and Lists from Memory   361

Define Key Terms   361

Use Command Reference to Check Your Memory   361

Part VI   Implementing High Availability

Chapter 17   Understanding High Availability   365

"Do I Know This Already?" Quiz   365

Foundation Topics   368

Leveraging Logical Switches   368

StackWise   371

Virtual Switching System   372

Supervisor and Route Processor Redundancy   373

Redundant Switch Supervisors   373

Configuring the Redundancy Mode   374

Configuring Supervisor Synchronization   376

Nonstop Forwarding   377

Exam Preparation Tasks   378

Review All Key Topics   378

Complete Tables and Lists from Memory   378

Define Key Terms   378

Use Command Reference to Check Your Memory   378

Chapter 18   Layer 3 High Availability   381

"Do I Know This Already?" Quiz   381

Foundation Topics   384

Packet-Forwarding Review   384

Hot Standby Router Protocol   385

   HSRP Router Election   386

   Plain-Text HSRP Authentication   388

   MD5 Authentication   388

   Conceding the Election   389

   HSRP Gateway Addressing   390

   Load Balancing with HSRP   391

Virtual Router Redundancy Protocol   394

Gateway Load Balancing Protocol   397

   Active Virtual Gateway   397

   Active Virtual Forwarder   398

   GLBP Load Balancing   400

   Enabling GLBP   400

Verifying Gateway Redundancy   405

Exam Preparation Tasks   406

Review All Key Topics   406

Complete Tables and Lists from Memory   406

Define Key Terms   406

Use Command Reference to Check Your Memory   406

Part VII   **Securing Switched Networks**

Chapter 19   **Securing Switch Access   411**

"Do I Know This Already?" Quiz   411

Foundation Topics   415

Port Security   415

Port-Based Authentication   418

   802.1X Configuration   419

   802.1X Port-Based Authentication Example   420

Using Storm Control   421

Best Practices for Securing Switches   423

Exam Preparation Tasks   428

Review All Key Topics   428

Complete Tables and Lists from Memory   428

Define Key Terms   428

Use Command Reference to Check Your Memory   428

Chapter 20   Securing VLANs   431

"Do I Know This Already?" Quiz   431

Foundation Topics   435

VLAN Access Lists   435

  VACL Configuration   435

Private VLANs   436

  Private VLAN Configuration   438

  Configure the Private VLANs   438

  Associate Ports with Private VLANs   439

  Associate Secondary VLANs to a Primary VLAN SVI   440

Securing VLAN Trunks   441

  Switch Spoofing   441

  VLAN Hopping   443

Exam Preparation Tasks   446

Review All Key Topics   446

Complete Tables and Lists from Memory   446

Define Key Terms   446

Use Command Reference to Check Your Memory   446

Chapter 21   Preventing Spoofing Attacks   449

"Do I Know This Already?" Quiz   449

Foundation Topics   451

DHCP Snooping   451

IP Source Guard   453

Dynamic ARP Inspection   455

Exam Preparation Tasks   458

Review All Key Topics   458

Complete Tables and Lists from Memory   458

Define Key Terms   458

Use Command Reference to Check Your Memory   458

Chapter 22   Managing Switch Users   461

"Do I Know This Already?" Quiz   461

Foundation Topics   464

Configuring Authentication   465

Configuring Authorization   468

Configuring Accounting   469

Exam Preparation Tasks   471

Review All Key Topics   471

Complete Tables and Lists from Memory   471

Define Key Terms   471

Use Command Reference to Check Your Memory   471

Part VIII   Final Preparation

Chapter 23   Final Preparation   475

Tools for Final Preparation   475

Exam Engine and Questions on the CD   475

Install the Exam Engine   476

Activate and Download the Practice Exam   476

Activating Other Exams   477

Premium Edition   477

The Cisco Learning Network   477

Memory Tables   477

Chapter-Ending Review Tools   478

Study Plan   478

Recall the Facts   478

Practice Configurations   478

Using the Exam Engine   479

Part IX   Appendixes

Appendix A   Answers to the "Do I Know This Already?" Quizzes   481

Appendix B   Exam Updates   489

Always Get the Latest at the Companion Website   489

Technical Content   490

Glossary   493

Index   504

CD-Only Appendixes

Appendix C   Memory Tables

Appendix D   Memory Table Answer Key

Appendix E   Study Planner

Command Syntax Conventions

The conventions used to present command syntax in this book are the same conventions used in the IOS Command Reference. The Command Reference describes these conventions as follows:

- **Boldface** indicates commands and keywords that are entered literally as shown. In actual configuration examples and output (not general command syntax), boldface indicates commands that are manually input by the user (such as a **show** command).

- *Italic* indicates arguments for which you supply actual values.

- Vertical bars (|) separate alternative, mutually exclusive elements.

- Square brackets ([ ]) indicate an optional element.

- Braces ({ }) indicate a required choice.

- Braces within brackets ([{ }]) indicate a required choice within an optional element.

Introduction

This book focuses on one major goal: to help you prepare to pass the SWITCH exam (300-115). To help you prepare, this book achieves other useful goals as well: It explains a wide range of networking topics, shows how to configure those features on Cisco switches, and explains how to determine whether the features are working. As a result, you can also use this book as a general reference as you work with switched networks in your job. The main motivation for this book and the Cisco Press Certification Guide series is to help you pass the SWITCH exam.

The rest of this introduction focuses on two topics: the SWITCH exam and a description of this book.

The CCNP SWITCH Exam

Professional certifications have been an important part of the computing industry for many years and will continue to become more important. Many reasons exist for these certifications, but the most popularly cited reason is that of credibility. All other considerations held equal, the certified employee/consultant/job candidate is considered more valuable than one who is not.

Cisco offers four levels of routing and switching certification, each with an increasing level of proficiency: Entry, Associate, Professional, and Expert. These are commonly known by their acronyms CCENT (Cisco Certified Entry Networking Technician), CCNA (Cisco Certified Network Associate), CCNP (Cisco Certified Network Professional), and CCIE (Cisco Certified Internetworking Expert). There are others, too, but this book focuses on the certifications for enterprise networks.

Cisco first announced its initial Professional level certifications in 1998 with the CCNP Routing and Switching certification. To become certified, you must pass exams on a series of CCNP topics, including the SWITCH, ROUTE, and TSHOOT exams. For most exams, Cisco does not publish the scores needed for passing. You need to take the exam to find that out for yourself.

To see the most current requirements for the CCNP Routing and Switching certification, go to http://www.cisco.com/go/ccnp, and look for the 300-115 SWITCH exam (*Implementing IP Switched Networks, SWITCH v2.0*). There you can find out other exam details such as an exam blueprint, which contains a list of exam topics. You will also learn how to register for an exam.

Also, you can go to the Cisco Learning Network website at http://www.cisco.com/go/learnnetspace to find exam information, learning tools, and forums in which you can communicate with others and learn more about this and other Cisco exams.

The SWITCH exam topics are grouped into three broad categories:

■   Layer 2 Technologies

■   Infrastructure Security

■   Infrastructure Services

Table I-1 lists the exam topics, along with the part of this book where the topic is covered. The list of topics is accurate, as of the time this book was printed.

Table I-1 *SWITCH Exam 300-115 Topics*

Exam Topic	Book Part
Layer 2 Technologies	
Configure and Verify Switch Administration	I
Configure and Verify Layer 2 Protocols	I, III
Configure and Verify VLANs	II
Configure and Verify Trunking	II
Configure and Verify EtherChannels	III
Configure and Verify Spanning Tree	III
Configure and Verify Other LAN Switching Technologies	V
Describe Chassis Virtualization and Aggregation Technologies	VI
Infrastructure Security	
Configure and Verify Switch Security Features	VII
Describe Device Security Using Cisco IOS AAA with TACACS+ and RADIUS	VII
Infrastructure Services	
Configure and Verify First-Hop Redundancy Protocols	VI

How to Take the SWITCH Exam

As of the publication of this book, Cisco exclusively uses testing vendor Pearson Vue (http://www.vue.com) for delivery of all Cisco career certification exams. To register, go to http://www.vue.com, establish a login, and register for the 300-115 SWITCH exam. You also need to choose a testing center near your home.

Format of the CCNP SWITCH Exam

The SWITCH exam follows the same general format as the other Cisco exams. When you get to the testing center and check in, the proctor will give you some general instructions and then take you into a quiet room with a PC. When you're at the PC, you have a few things to do before the timer starts on your exam. For instance, you can take a sample quiz, just to get accustomed to the PC and to the testing engine.

When you start the exam, you will be asked a series of questions. Answer a question, and then move on to the next question. The exam engine does not let you go back and change the answers you entered on previous questions.

The exam questions can be in any of the following formats:

- Multiple choice (MC)

- Testlet

- Drag-and-drop (DND)

- Simulated lab (sim)

- Simlet

The first three types of questions are relatively common in many testing environments. The MC format simply requires that you point and click on a circle (that is, a radio button) beside the correct answer for a single-answer question or on squares (that is, check boxes) beside the correct answers for a multi-answer question. Cisco traditionally tells you how many answers you need to choose, and the testing software prevents you from choosing too many answers. Testlets are questions with one general scenario, with multiple MC questions about the overall scenario. DND questions require you to left-click and hold a mouse button, move an object (for example, a text box) to another area on the screen, and release the mouse button to place the object somewhere else-typically into a list. For some questions, as an example, you might need to put a list of five things into the proper order to get the whole question correct.

The last two types both use a network simulator to ask questions. Interestingly, the two types actually allow Cisco to assess two very different skills. First, sim questions generally describe a problem, and your task is to configure one or more routers/switches to fix the problem. The exam then grades the question based on the configuration you changed or added. The simlet questions may well be the most difficult style of question on the exams. Simlet questions also use a network simulator, but instead of answering the question by changing the configuration, the question includes one or more multiple choice questions. The questions require that you use the simulator to examine the current behavior of a network, interpreting the output of any show commands that you can remember to answer the question. Although sim questions require you to troubleshoot problems related to a configuration, simlets require you to both analyze working networks and networks with problems, correlating show command output with your knowledge of networking theory and configuration commands.

The Cisco Learning Network (http://learningnetwork.cisco.com) website has tools that let you experience the environment and see how each of these question types work. The environment should be the same as when you passed CCNA (a prerequisite for CCNP and CCDP).

CCNP SWITCH 300-115 Official Certification Guide

The most important and somewhat obvious objective of this book is to help you pass the Cisco CCNP SWITCH exam (Exam 300-115). While you are learning about topics that can help you pass the SWITCH exam, you will also become much more knowledgeable about how to do your job. Although this book and the accompanying CD have many exam preparation tasks and example test questions, the method in which they are used is not to simply make you memorize as many questions and answers as you possibly can.

The methodology of this book helps you discover the exam topics about which you need more review, fully understand and remember exam topic details, and prove to yourself that you have retained your knowledge of those topics. So this book helps you pass not by memorization, but by helping you truly learn and understand the topics. The SWITCH exam is just one of the foundation topics in the CCNP Routing and Switching certification, and the knowledge contained within is vitally important to consider yourself a truly skilled routing and switching engineer or specialist.

The strategy you use to prepare for the SWITCH exam might differ slightly from strategies used by other readers, mainly based on the skills, knowledge, and experience you already have obtained. For instance, if you have attended the SWITCH course, you might take a different approach than someone who learned switching through on-the-job training. Regardless of the strategy you use or the background you have, this book is designed to help you get to the point where you can pass the exam with the least amount of time required.

Book Features and Exam Preparation Methods

This book uses several key methodologies to help you discover the exam topics on which you need more review, to help you fully understand and remember those details, and to help you prove to yourself that you have retained your knowledge of those topics.

The book includes many features that provide different ways to study and prepare yourself for the exam. If you understand a topic when you read it, but do not study it any further, you will probably not be ready to pass the exam with confidence. The features included in this book give you tools that help you determine what you know, review what you know, better learn what you don't know, and be well prepared for the exam. These tools include the following:

- **"Do I Know This Already?" quizzes:** Each chapter begins with a quiz that helps you determine the amount of time you need to spend studying that chapter.

- **Foundation topics:** These are the core sections of each chapter. They explain the protocols, concepts, and configuration for the topics in that chapter.

- **Exam preparation tasks:** The "Exam Preparation Tasks" section lists a series of study activities that should be done after reading the "Foundation Topics" section. Each chapter includes the activities that make the most sense for studying the topics in that chapter. The activities include the following:

  - **Key Topics Review:** The Key Topic icon is shown next to the most important items in the "Foundation Topics" section of the chapter. The Key Topics Review activity lists the key topics from the chapter, and page number. Although the contents of the entire chapter could be on the exam, you should definitely know the information listed in each key topic. Review these topics carefully.

- **Memory tables:** To help you exercise your memory and memorize some lists of facts, many of the more important lists and tables from the chapter are included in a document on the CD. This document lists only partial information, allowing you to complete the table or list. CD-only Appendix C holds the incomplete tables, and Appendix D includes the completed tables from which you can check your work.

- **Definition of key terms:** Although Cisco exams might be unlikely to ask a question such as "Define this term," the SWITCH exam requires that you learn and know a lot of networking terminology. This section lists some of the most important terms from the chapter, asking you to write a short definition and compare your answer to the glossary on the enclosed CD.

- **CD-based practice exam:** The companion CD contains an exam engine, including a bank of multiple-choice questions. You can use the practice exams to get a feel for the actual exam content and to gauge your knowledge of switching topics.

How This Book is Organized

Although this book can be read cover to cover, it is designed to be flexible and allow you to easily move between chapters and sections of chapters to focus on specific material. The chapters can be covered in any order, although some chapters are related and build upon each other. If you do intend to read them all, the order in the book is an excellent sequence to use.

This book contains 23 chapters, plus appendixes. The book organizes switching topics into nine major parts. The following list outlines the major part organization of this book.

- **Part I: Designing Campus Networks**

  - **Chapter 1, "Enterprise Campus Network Design":** This chapter covers different campus network models, hierarchical network design, and how to design, size, and scale a campus network using a modular approach.

  - **Chapter 2, "Switch Operation":** This chapter covers Layer 2 and multilayer switch operation, how various content-addressable memory (CAM) and ternary content-addressable memory (TCAM) tables are used to make switching decisions, and how to monitor these tables to aid in troubleshooting.

  - **Chapter 3, "Switch Port Configuration":** This chapter covers basic Ethernet concepts, how to use scalable Ethernet, how to connect switches and devices together, and how to verify switch port operation to aid in troubleshooting.

- **Part II: Building a Campus Network**

  - **Chapter 4, "VLANs and Trunks":** This chapter covers basic VLAN concepts, how to transport multiple VLANs over single links, how to configure VLAN trunks, and how to verify VLAN and trunk operation.

  - **Chapter 5, "VLAN Trunking Protocol":** This chapter covers VLAN management using VTP, VTP configuration, traffic management through VTP pruning, and how to verify VTP operation.

- Part III: Working with Redundant Links

  - **Chapter 6, "Traditional Spanning Tree Protocol"**: This chapter covers IEEE 802.1D Spanning Tree Protocol (STP) and gives an overview of the other STP types that might be running on a switch.

  - **Chapter 7, "Spanning-Tree Configuration"**: This chapter covers the STP root bridge, how to customize the STP topology, how to tune STP convergence, redundant link convergence, and how to verify STP operation.

  - **Chapter 8, "Protecting the Spanning Tree Protocol Topology"**: This chapter covers protecting the STP topology using Root Guard, BPDU Guard, and Loop Guard, and also how to use BPDU filtering and how to verify that these STP protection mechanisms are functioning properly.

  - **Chapter 9, "Advanced Spanning Tree Protocol"**: This chapter covers Rapid Spanning Tree Protocol (RSTP) for Rapid PVST+ and Multiple Spanning Tree (MST) Protocol.

  - **Chapter 10, "Aggregating Switch Links"**: This chapter covers switch port aggregation with EtherChannel, EtherChannel negotiation protocols, EtherChannel configuration, and how to verify EtherChannel operation.

- Part IV: Multilayer Switching

  - **Chapter 11, "Multilayer Switching"**: This chapter covers inter-VLAN routing, multilayer switching with Cisco Express Forwarding (CEF), and how to verify that multilayer switching is functioning properly.

  - **Chapter 12, "Configuring DHCP"**: This chapter discusses ways to configure a switch to relay Dynamic Host Configuration Protocol (DHCP) requests or to act as a DHCP server to local client devices.

- Part V: Monitoring Campus Networks

  - **Chapter 13, "Logging Switch Activity"**: This chapter explains how to configure a switch to generate logging information and how to correlate logging messages with accurate timestamps.

  - **Chapter 14, "Managing Switches with SNMP"**: This chapter discusses SNMP and how you can use it to monitor and manage switches in a network.

  - **Chapter 15, "Monitoring Performance with IP SLA"**: This chapter explains how to leverage IP SLA probes to measure network performance against expected service level agreement parameters.

  - **Chapter 16, "Using Port Mirroring to Monitor Traffic"**: This chapter covers methods you can use to mirror or copy switched traffic to a destination where it can be collected and analyzed.

- Part VI: Implementing High Availability

  - **Chapter 17, "Understanding High Availability"**: This chapter discusses ways that multiple physical switches can be connected or configured together to operate as one logical switch, increasing availability.

  - **Chapter 18, "Layer 3 High Availability"**: This chapter covers providing redundant router or gateway addresses on Catalyst switches and verifying that redundancy is functioning properly.

- **Part VII: Securing Switched Networks**

  - **Chapter 19, "Securing Switch Access":** This chapter covers port security using MAC addresses, port-based security using IEEE 802.1X, storm control to reduce traffic storms, and best practices for securing switches.

  - **Chapter 20, "Securing VLANs":** This chapter covers how to control traffic within a VLAN using access lists, implementing private VLANs, and best practices for securing trunk links.

  - **Chapter 21, "Preventing Spoofing Attacks":** This chapter explains features like DHCP snooping, IP Source Guard, and dynamic ARP inspection, which you can leverage to prevent network attacks that use spoofed information to gain a foothold.

  - **Chapter 22, "Managing Switch Users":** This chapter covers switch authentication, authorization, and accounting (AAA)—mechanisms that control who can access a switch and what they can do on the switch, as well as provide a record of what occurred.

- **Part VIII: Final Preparation**

  - **Chapter 23, "Final Preparation":** This chapter explains how to use the practice exam CD to enhance your study, along with a basic study plan.

- **Part IX: Appendixes**

  - **Appendix A:** This appendix contains answers to the "Do I Know This Already" quizzes.

  - **Appendix B:** This appendix tells you how to find any updates, should there be changes to the exam.

  - **Glossary:** The glossary contains definitions for all the terms listed in the "Define Key Terms" sections at the conclusions of Chapters 1 through 22.

In addition, you can find the following appendixes on the CD that is included with this book:

- **Appendix C, "Memory Tables":** This appendix holds the key tables and lists from each chapter with some of the content removed. You can print this appendix, and as a memory exercise, complete the tables and lists. The goal is to help you memorize facts that can be useful on the exams.

- **Appendix D, "Memory Table Answer Key":** This appendix contains the answer key for the exercises in Appendix D.

- **Appendix E, "Study Planner,"** is a spreadsheet with major study milestones, where you can track your progress through your study.

For More Information

If you have any comments about the book, you can submit those via http://www.ciscopress.com. Just go to the website, select Contact Us, and type your message.

Cisco might make changes that affect the SWITCH exam from time to time. You should always check http://www.cisco.com/go/ccnp for the latest details.

This chapter covers the following topics that you need to master for the CCNP SWITCH exam:

■ **Hierarchical Network Design:** This section details a three-layer hierarchical structure of campus network designs.

■ **Modular Network Design:** This section covers the process of designing a campus network, based on breaking it into functional modules. You also learn how to size and scale the modules in a design.

CHAPTER 1

Enterprise Campus Network Design

This chapter presents a logical design process that you can use to build a new switched campus network or to modify and improve an existing network. Networks can be designed in layers using a set of building blocks that can organize and streamline even a large, complex campus network. These building blocks can then be placed using several campus design models to provide maximum efficiency, functionality, and scalability.

"Do I Know This Already?" Quiz

The "Do I Know This Already?" quiz allows you to assess whether you should read this entire chapter thoroughly or jump to the "Exam Preparation Tasks" section. If you are in doubt based on your answers to these questions or your own assessment of your knowledge of the topics, read the entire chapter. Table 1-1 outlines the major headings in this chapter and the "Do I Know This Already?" quiz questions that go with them. You can find the answers in Appendix A, "Answers to the 'Do I Know This Already?' Quizzes."

Table 1-1 *"Do I Know This Already?" Foundation Topics Section-to-Question Mapping*

Foundation Topics Section	Questions Covered in This Section
Hierarchical Network Design	1–10
Modular Network Design	11–17

1. Where does a collision domain exist in a switched network?

   a. On a single switch port

   b. Across all switch ports

   c. On a single VLAN

   d. Across all VLANs

2. Where does a broadcast domain exist in a switched network?

   a. On a single switch port

   b. Across all switch ports

   c. On a single VLAN

   d. Across all VLANs

3. What is a VLAN primarily used for?

   a. To segment a collision domain

   b. To segment a broadcast domain

   c. To segment an autonomous system

   d. To segment a spanning-tree domain

4. How many layers are recommended in the hierarchical campus network design model?

   a. 1

   b. 2

   c. 3

   d. 4

   e. 7

5. What is the purpose of breaking a campus network into a hierarchical design?

   a. To facilitate documentation

   b. To follow political or organizational policies

   c. To make the network predictable and scalable

   d. To make the network more redundant and secure

6. End-user PCs should be connected into which of the following hierarchical layers?

   a. Distribution layer

   b. Common layer

   c. Access layer

   d. Core layer

7. In which OSI layer should devices in the distribution layer typically operate?

   a. Layer 1

   b. Layer 2

   c. Layer 3

   d. Layer 4

8. A hierarchical network's distribution layer aggregates which of the following?

   a. Core switches

   b. Broadcast domains

   c. Routing updates

   d. Access layer switches

9. In the core layer of a hierarchical network, which of the following are aggregated?

    a. Routing tables

    b. Packet filters

    c. Distribution switches

    d. Access layer switches

10. In a properly designed hierarchical network, a broadcast from one PC is confined to which one of the following?

    a. One access layer switch port

    b. One access layer switch

    c. One switch block

    d. The entire campus network

11. Which one or more of the following are the components of a typical switch block?

    a. Access layer switches

    b. Distribution layer switches

    c. Core layer switches

    d. E-commerce servers

    e. Service provider switches

12. Which of the following are common types of core, or backbone, designs? (Choose all that apply.)

    a. Collapsed core

    b. Loop-free core

    c. Dual core

    d. Layered core

    e. Multinode core

13. What is the maximum number of access layer switches that can connect into a single distribution layer switch?

    a. 1

    b. 2

    c. Limited only by the number of ports on the access layer switch

    d. Limited only by the number of ports on the distribution layer switch

    e. Unlimited

14. A switch block should be sized according to which two of the following parameters? (Choose all that apply.)

   a. The number of access layer users

   b. A maximum of 250 access layer users

   c. A study of the traffic patterns and flows

   d. The amount of rack space available

   e. The number of servers accessed by users

15. What evidence can be seen when a switch block is too large? (Choose all that apply.)

   a. IP address space is exhausted.

   b. You run out of access layer switch ports.

   c. Broadcast traffic becomes excessive.

   d. Traffic is throttled at the distribution layer switches.

   e. Network congestion occurs.

16. How many distribution switches should be built into each switch block?

   a. 1

   b. 2

   c. 4

   d. 8

17. Which are the most important aspects to consider when designing the core layer in a large network? (Choose all that apply.)

   a. Low cost

   b. Switches that can efficiently forward traffic, even when every uplink is at 100 percent capacity

   c. High port density of high-speed ports

   d. A low number of Layer 3 routing peers

Foundation Topics

Hierarchical Network Design

A campus network is an enterprise network consisting of many LANs in one or more buildings, all connected and all usually in the same geographic area. A company typically owns the entire campus network and the physical wiring. Campus networks commonly consist of wired Ethernet LANs and shared wireless LANs.

An understanding of traffic flow is a vital part of the campus network design. You might be able to leverage high-speed LAN technologies and "throw bandwidth" at a network to improve traffic movement. However, the emphasis should be on providing an overall design that is tuned to known, studied, or predicted traffic flows. The network traffic can then be effectively moved and managed, and you can scale the campus network to support future needs.

As a starting point, consider the simple network shown in Figure 1-1. A collection of PCs, printers, and servers are all connected to the same network segment and use the 192.168.1.0 subnet. All devices on this network segment must share the available bandwidth.

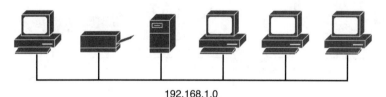

192.168.1.0

Figure 1-1 *Simple Shared Ethernet Network*

Recall that if two or more hosts try to transmit at the same time on a shared network, their frames will collide and interfere. When collisions occur, all hosts must become silent and wait to retransmit their data. The boundary around such a shared network is called a *collision domain*. In Figure 1-1, the entire shared segment represents one collision domain.

A network segment with six hosts might not seem crowded. Suppose the segment contains hundreds of hosts instead. Now the network might not perform very well if many of the hosts are competing to use the shared media. Through network segmentation, you can reduce the number of stations on a segment. This, in turn, reduces the size of the collision domain and lowers the probability of collisions because fewer stations will try to transmit at a given time.

Broadcast traffic can also present a performance problem on a Layer 2 network because all broadcast frames flood to reach all hosts on a network segment. If the segment is large, the broadcast traffic can grow in proportion and monopolize the available bandwidth. In addition, all hosts on the segment must listen to and process every broadcast frame. To contain broadcast traffic, the idea is to provide a barrier at the edge of a LAN segment so that broadcasts cannot pass or be forwarded outward. The extent of a Layer 2 network, where a broadcast frame can reach, is known as a *broadcast domain.*

To limit the size of a collision domain, you can connect smaller numbers of hosts to individual switch interfaces. Ideally, each host should connect to a dedicated switch interface so that they can operate in full-duplex mode, preventing collisions altogether. Switch interfaces do not propagate collisions, so each interface becomes its own collision domain—even if several interfaces belong to a common VLAN.

In contrast, when broadcast traffic is forwarded, it is flooded across switch interface boundaries. In fact, broadcast frames will reach every switch interface in a VLAN. In other words, a VLAN defines the extent of a broadcast domain. To reduce the size of a broadcast domain, you can segment a network or break it up into smaller Layer 2 VLANs. The smaller VLANs must be connected by a Layer 3 device, such as a router or a multilayer switch, as shown in Figure 1-2. The simple network of Figure 1-1 now has two segments or VLANs interconnected by Switch A, a multilayer switch. A Layer 3 device cannot propagate a collision condition from one segment to another, and it will not forward broadcasts between segments.

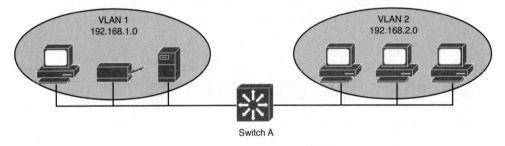

Figure 1-2   *Example of Network Segmentation*

The network might continue to grow as more users and devices are added to it. Switch A has a limited number of ports, so it cannot directly connect to every device. Instead, the network segments can be grown by adding a new switch to each, as shown in Figure 1-3.

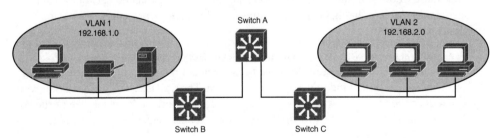

Figure 1-3   *Expanding a Segmented Network*

Switch B aggregates traffic to and from VLAN 1, while Switch C aggregates VLAN 2. As the network continues to grow, more VLANs can be added to support additional applications or user communities. As an example, Figure 1-4 shows how Voice over IP (VoIP) has been implemented by placing IP phones into two new VLANs (10 and 20). The same two aggregating switches can easily support the new VLANs.

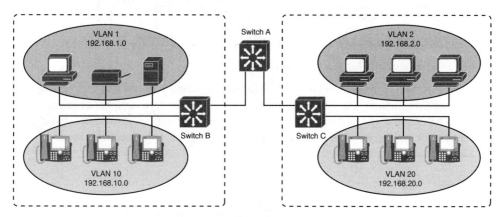

Figure 1-4   *Network Growth Through New VLANs*

Predictable Network Model

Ideally, you should design a network with a predictable behavior in mind to offer low maintenance and high availability. For example, a campus network needs to recover from failures and topology changes quickly and in a predetermined manner. You should scale the network to easily support future expansions and upgrades. With a wide variety of multiprotocol and multicast traffic, the network should be capable of efficiently connecting users with the resources they need, regardless of location.

In other words, design the network around traffic flows rather than a particular type of traffic. Ideally, the network should be arranged so that all end users are located at a consistent distance from the resources they need to use. If one user at one corner of the network passes through two switches to reach an email server, any other user at any other location in the network should also require two switch hops for email service.

Cisco has refined a hierarchical approach to network design that enables network designers to organize the network into distinct layers of devices. The resulting network is efficient, intelligent, scalable, and easily managed.

Figure 1-4 can be redrawn to emphasize the hierarchy that is emerging. In Figure 1-5, two layers become apparent: the access layer, where switches are placed closest to the end users; and the distribution layer, where access layer switches are aggregated.

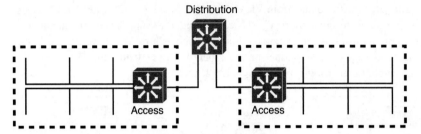

Figure 1-5   *Two-Layer Network Hierarchy Emerges*

As the network continues to grow with more buildings, more floors, and larger groups of users, the number of access switches increases. As a result, the number of distribution switches increases. Now things have scaled to the point where the distribution switches need to be aggregated. This is done by adding a third layer to the hierarchy, the *core layer*, as shown in Figure 1-6.

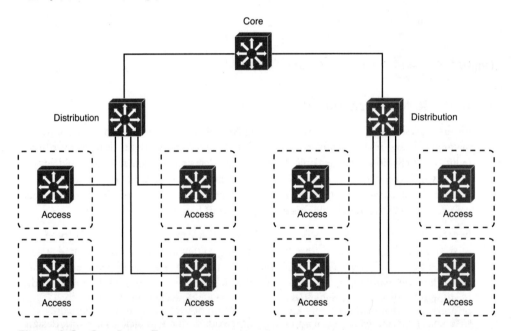

Figure 1-6   *Core Layer Emerges*

Traffic flows in a campus network can be classified as three types, based on where the network service or resource is located in relation to the end user. Figure 1-7 illustrates the flow types between a PC and some file servers, along with three different paths the traffic might take through the three layers of a network. Table 1-2 also lists the types and the extent of the campus network that is crossed going from any user to the service.

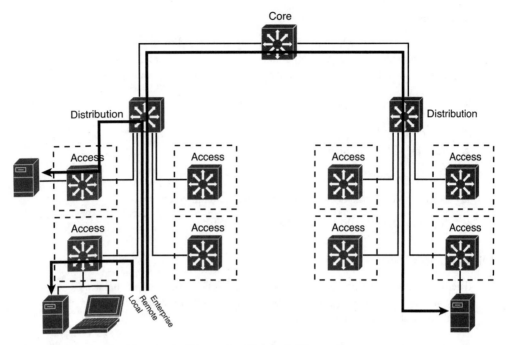

Figure 1-7 *Traffic Flow Paths Through a Network Hierarchy*

Table 1-2 *Types of Network Services*

Service Type	Location of Service	Extent of Traffic Flow
Local	Same segment/VLAN as user	Access layer only
Remote	Different segment/VLAN as user	Access to distribution layers
Enterprise	Central to all campus users	Access to distribution to core layers

Notice how easily the traffic paths can be described. Regardless of where the user is located, the traffic path always begins at the access layer and progresses into the distribution and perhaps into the core layers. Even a path between two users at opposite ends of the network becomes a consistent and predictable access > distribution > core > distribution > access layer.

Each layer has attributes that provide both physical and logical network functions at the appropriate point in the campus network. Understanding each layer and its functions or limitations is important to properly apply the layer in the design process.

Access Layer

The access layer exists where the end users are connected to the network. Access switches usually provide Layer 2 (VLAN) connectivity between users. Devices in this layer, sometimes called building access switches, should have the following capabilities:

- Low cost per switch port

- High port density

- Scalable uplinks to higher layers

- High availability

- Ability to converge network services (that is, data, voice, video)

- Security features and quality of service (QoS)

Distribution Layer

The distribution layer provides interconnection between the campus network's access and core layers. Devices in this layer, sometimes called building *distribution switches*, should have the following capabilities:

- Aggregation of multiple access layer switches

- High Layer 3 routing throughput for packet handling

- Security and policy-based connectivity functions

- QoS features

- Scalable and redundant high-speed links to the core and access layers

In the distribution layer, uplinks from all access layer devices are aggregated, or come together. The distribution layer switches must be capable of processing the total volume of traffic from all the connected devices. These switches should have a high port density of high-speed links to support the collection of access layer switches.

VLANs and broadcast domains converge at the distribution layer, requiring routing, filtering, and security. The switches at this layer also must be capable of routing packets with high throughput.

Notice that the distribution layer usually is a Layer 3 boundary, where routing meets the VLANs of the access layer.

Core Layer

A campus network's core layer provides connectivity between all distribution layer devices. The core, sometimes referred to as the backbone, must be capable of switching traffic as efficiently as possible. Core switches should have the following attributes:

- Very high Layer 3 routing throughput

- No costly or unnecessary packet manipulations (access lists, packet filtering)

- Redundancy and resilience for high availability

- Advanced QoS functions

Devices in a campus network's core layer or backbone should be optimized for high-performance switching. Because the core layer must handle large amounts of campus-wide data, the core layer should be designed with simplicity and efficiency in mind.

Although campus network design is presented as a three-layer approach (access, distribution, and core layers), the hierarchy can be collapsed or simplified in certain cases. For example, small or medium-size campus networks might not have the size or volume requirements that would require the functions of all three layers. In that case, you could combine the distribution and core layers for simplicity and cost savings. When the distribution and core layers are combined into a single layer of switches, a *collapsed core* network results.

Modular Network Design

Designing a new network that has a hierarchy with three layers is fairly straightforward. You can also migrate an existing network into a hierarchical design. The resulting network is organized, efficient, and predictable. However, a simple hierarchical design does not address other best practices like redundancy, in the case where a switch or a link fails, or scalability, when large additions to the network need to be added.

Consider the hierarchical network shown in the left portion of Figure 1-8. Each layer of the network is connected to the adjacent layer by single links. If a link fails, a significant portion of the network will become isolated. In addition, the access layer switches are aggregated into a single distribution layer switch. If that switch fails, all the users will become isolated.

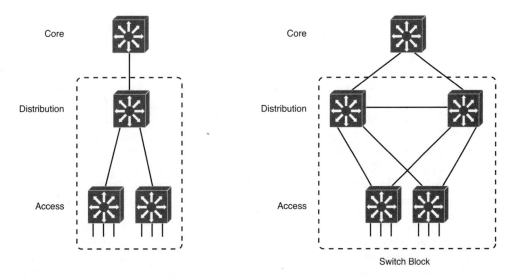

Figure 1-8 *Improving Availability in the Distribution and Access Layers*

To mitigate a potential distribution switch failure, you can add a second, redundant distribution switch. To mitigate a potential link failure, you can add redundant links from each access layer switch to each distribution switch. These improvements are shown on the right in Figure 1-8.

One weakness is still present in the redundant design of Figure 1-8: The core layer has only one switch. If that core switch fails, users in the access layer will still be able to communicate with each other. However, they will not be able to reach other areas of the network, such as a data center, the Internet, and so on. To mitigate the effects of a core switch failure, you can add a second, redundant core switch, as shown in Figure 1-9. Redundant links should also be added between each distribution layer switch and each core layer switch.

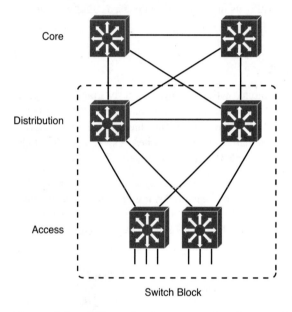

Figure 1-9 *Fully Redundant Hierarchical Network Design*

The redundancy needed for the small network shown in Figure 1-9 is fairly straightforward. As the network grows and more redundant switches and redundant links are added into the design, the design can become confusing. For example, suppose many more access layer switches need to be added to the network of Figure 1-9 because several departments of users have moved into the building or into an adjacent building. Should the new access layer switches be dual-connected into the same two distribution switches? Should new distribution switches be added, too? If so, should each of the distribution switches be connected to every other distribution *and* every other core switch, creating a fully meshed network?

Figure 1-10 shows one possible network design that might result. With so many interconnecting links between switches, it becomes a "brain-buster" exercise to figure out where VLANs are trunked, what the spanning-tree topologies look like, which links should have Layer 3 connectivity, and so on. Users might have connectivity through this network, but it might not be clear how they are actually working or what has gone wrong if they are not working. This network looks more like a spider's web than an organized, streamlined design.

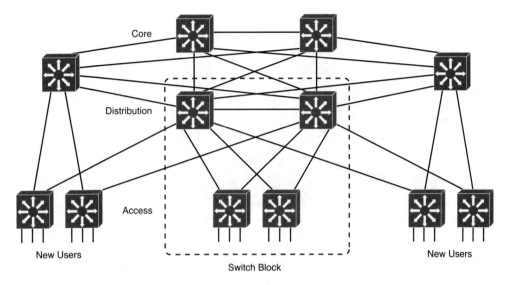

Figure 1-10 *Network Growth in a Disorganized Fashion*

To maintain organization, simplicity, and predictability, you can design a campus network in a logical manner, using a modular approach. In this approach, each layer of the hierarchical network model can be broken into basic functional units. These units, or modules, can then be sized appropriately and connected, while allowing for future scalability and expansion.

You can divide enterprise campus networks into the following basic elements or building blocks:

■ **Switch block:** A group of access layer switches, together with their distribution switches. This is also called an *access distribution block*, named for the two switch layers that it contains. The dashed rectangle in Figures 1-8 through 1-10 represent typical switch blocks.

■ **Core:** The campus network's backbone, which connects all switch blocks.

Other related elements can exist. Although these elements do not contribute to the campus network's overall function, they can be designed separately and added to the network design. For example, a data center containing enterprise resources or services can have its own access and distribution layer switches, forming a switch block that connects into the core layer. In fact, if the data center is very large, it might have its own core switches, too, which connect into the normal campus core. Recall how a campus network is divided into access, distribution, and core layers. The switch block contains switching devices from the access and distribution layers. The switch block then connects into the core layer, providing end-to-end connectivity across the campus. As the network grows, you can add new access layer switches by connecting them into an existing pair of distribution switches, as shown in Figure 1-11. You could also add a completely new access distribution switch block that contains the areas of new growth, as shown in Figure 1-12.

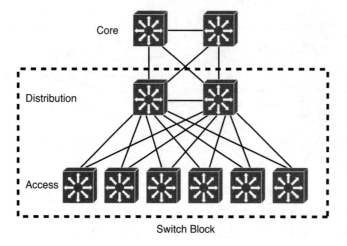

Figure 1-11 *Network Growth by Adding Access Switches to a Switch Block*

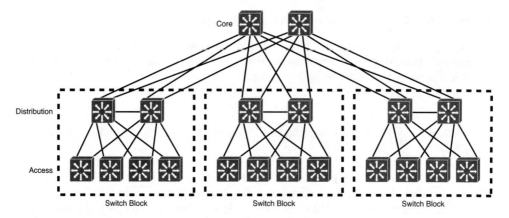

Figure 1-12 *Network Growth by Adding New Switch Blocks*

Sizing a Switch Block

Containing access and distribution layer devices, the switch block is simple in concept. You should consider several factors, however, to determine an appropriate size for the switch block. The range of available switch devices makes the switch block size very flexible. At the access layer, switch selection is usually based on port density or the number of connected users.

The distribution layer must be sized according to the number of access layer switches that are aggregated or brought into a distribution device. Consider the following factors:

- Traffic types and patterns

- Amount of Layer 3 switching capacity at the distribution layer

- Total number of users connected to the access layer switches

- Geographic boundaries of subnets or VLANs

Designing a switch block based solely on the number of users or stations contained within the block is usually inaccurate. Usually, no more than 2000 users should be placed within a single switch block. Although this is useful for initially estimating a switch block's size, this idea doesn't take into account the many dynamic processes that occur on a functioning network.

Instead, switch block size should be based primarily on the following:

- Traffic types and behavior

- Size and number of common workgroups

Because of the dynamic nature of networks, you can size a switch block too large to handle the load that is placed on it. Also, the number of users and applications on a network tends to grow over time. A provision to break up or downsize a switch block might be necessary as time passes. Again, base these decisions on the actual traffic flows and patterns present in the switch block. You can estimate, model, or measure these parameters with network-analysis applications and tools.

Note The actual network-analysis process is beyond the scope of this book. Traffic estimation, modeling, and measurement are complex procedures, each requiring its own dedicated analysis tool.

Generally, a switch block is too large if the following conditions are observed:

- The routers (multilayer switches) at the distribution layer become traffic bottlenecks. This congestion could be because of the volume of inter-VLAN traffic, intensive CPU processing, or switching times required by policy or security functions (access lists, queuing, and so on).

- Broadcast or multicast traffic slows the switches in the switch block. Broadcast and multicast traffic must be replicated and forwarded out many ports simultaneously. This process requires some overhead in the multilayer switch, which can become too great if significant traffic volumes are present.

Switch Block Redundancy

In any network design, the potential always exists for some component to fail. For example, if an electrical circuit breaker is tripped or shuts off, a switch might lose power. A better design is to use a switch that has two independent power supplies. Each power supply could be connected to two power sources so that one source is always likely to be available to power the switch. In a similar manner, a single switch might have an internal problem that causes it to fail. A single link might go down because a media module fails, a fiber-optic cable gets cut, and so on. To design a more resilient network, you can implement most of the components in redundant pairs.

Key Topic

A switch block consists of two distribution switches that aggregate one or more access layer switches. Each access layer switch should have a pair of uplinks—one connecting to each distribution switch. The physical cabling is easy to draw, but the logical connectivity is not always obvious. For example, Figure 1-13 shows a switch block that has a single VLAN A that spans multiple access switches. You might find this where there are several separate physical switch chassis in an access layer room, or where two nearby communications rooms share a common VLAN. Notice from the shading how the single VLAN spans across every switch (both access and distribution) and across every link connecting the switches. This is necessary for the VLAN to be present on both access switches and to have redundant uplinks for high availability.

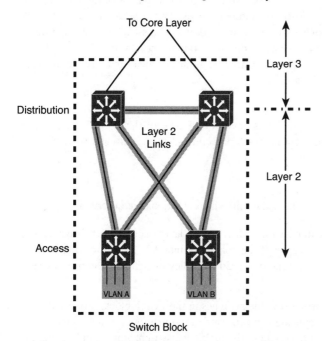

Figure 1-13   *A Redundant Switch Block Design*

Although this design works, it is not optimal. VLAN A must be carried over every possible link within the block to span both access switches. Both distribution switches must also support VLAN A because they provide the Layer 3 router function for all hosts on the VLAN. The two distribution switches can use one of several redundant gateway protocols to provide an active IP gateway and a standby gateway at all times. These protocols require Layer 2 connectivity between the distribution switches and are discussed in Chapter 18, "Layer 3 High Availability."

Notice how the shaded links connect to form two triangular loops. Layer 2 networks cannot remain stable or usable if loops are allowed to form, so some mechanism must be used to detect the loops and keep the topology loop free.

In addition, the looped topology makes the entire switch block a single failure domain. If a host in VLAN A misbehaves or generates a tremendous amount of broadcast traffic, all the switches and links in the switch block could be negatively impacted.

A better design works toward keeping the switch block inherently free of Layer 2 loops. As Figure 1-14 shows, a loop-free switch block requires a unique VLAN on each access switch. In other words, VLANs are not permitted to span across multiple access switches. The extent of each VLAN, as shown by the shaded areas, becomes a *V* shape rather than a closed triangular loop.

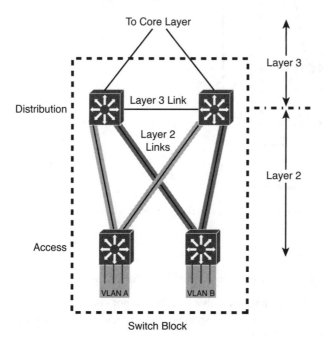

Figure 1-14   *Best Practice Loop-Free Switch Block Topology*

Key Topic

The boundary between Layers 2 and 3 remains the same. All Layer 2 connectivity is contained within the access layer, and the distribution layer has only Layer 3 links. Without any potential Layer 2 loops, the switch block can become much more stable and much less reliant on any mechanisms to detect and prevent loops. Also, because each access switch has two dedicated paths into the distribution layer, both links can be fully utilized with traffic load balanced across them. In turn, each Layer 3 distribution switch can load balance traffic over its redundant links into the core layer using routing protocols.

It is also possible to push the Layer 3 boundary from the distribution layer down into the access layer, as long as the access switches can support routing functions. Figure 1-15 illustrates this design. Because Layer 3 links are used throughout the switch block, network stability is offered through the fast convergence of routing protocols and updates. Routing can also load balance packets across the redundant uplinks, making full use of every available link between the network layers.

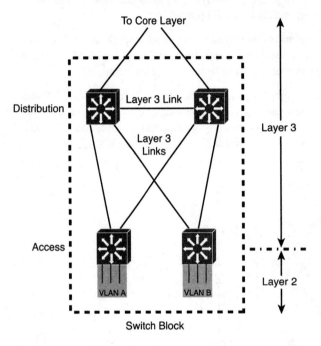

Figure 1-15 *A Completely Routed Switch Block*

You should become familiar with a few best practices that can help with a redundant hierarchical network design:

■   Design each layer with pairs of switches.

■   Connect each switch to the next higher layer with two links for redundancy.

■   Connect each pair of distribution switches with a link, but do not connect the access layer switches to each other (unless the access switches support some other means to function as one logical stack or chassis).

■   Do not extend VLANs beyond distribution switches. The distribution layer should always be the boundary of VLANs, subnets, and broadcasts. Although Layer 2 switches can extend VLANs to other switches and other layers of the hierarchy, this activity is discouraged. VLAN traffic should not traverse the network core.

Network Core

A core layer is required to connect two or more switch blocks in a campus network. Because all traffic passing to and from all switch blocks must cross the core, the core layer must be as efficient and resilient as possible. The core is the campus network's basic foundation and carries much more traffic than any other switch block.

Recall that both the distribution and core layers provide Layer 3 functionality. Preferably, the links between distribution and core layer switches should be Layer 3 routed interfaces. You can also use Layer 2 links that carry a small VLAN bounded by the two switches. In the latter case, a Layer 3 switch virtual interface (SVI) is used to provide routing within each small VLAN.

The links between layers should be designed to carry the amount of traffic load handled by the distribution switches, at a minimum. The links between core switches should be of sufficient size to carry the aggregate amount of traffic coming into one of the core switches. Consider the average link utilization, but allow for future growth. An Ethernet core allows simple and scalable upgrades of magnitude; consider the progression from Gigabit Ethernet to 10-Gigabit Ethernet (10GE), and so on.

A core should consist of two multilayer switches that connect two or more switch blocks in a redundant fashion. A redundant core is sometimes called a *dual core* because it is usually built from two identical switches. Figure 1-16 illustrates the core. Notice that this core appears as an independent module and is not merged into any other block or layer.

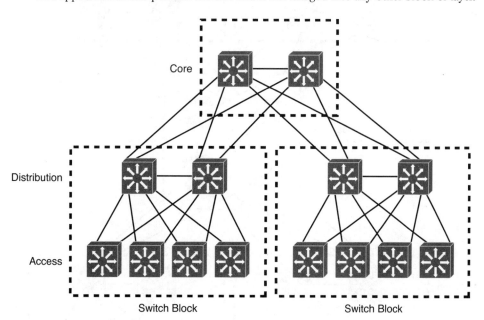

Figure 1-16 *A Redundant Core Layer*

Redundant links connect each switch block's distribution layer portion to each of the dual core switches. The two core switches connect by a common link.

With a redundant core, each distribution switch has two equal-cost paths into the core, allowing the available bandwidth of both paths to be used simultaneously. Both paths remain active because the distribution and core layers use Layer 3 devices that can manage equal-cost paths in routing tables. The routing protocol in use determines the availability or loss of a neighboring Layer 3 device. If one switch fails, the routing protocol reroutes traffic using an alternative path through the remaining redundant switch.

If the campus network continues to grow to the point that it spans two large buildings or two large locations, the core layer can be replicated, as shown in Figure 1-17. Notice how the two-node redundant core has been expanded to include four core switches. This is known as a *multinode core*. Each of the four core switches is connected to the other core switches to form a fully meshed core layer.

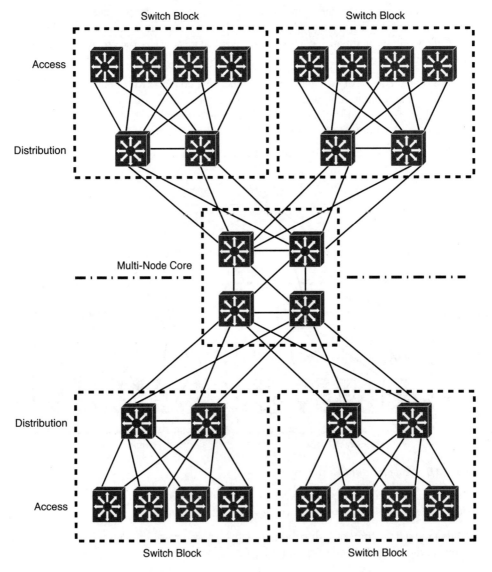

Figure 1-17   *Using a Multi-Node Core in a Very Large Campus Network*

Even though the multinode core is fully meshed, the campus network is still divided across the two pairs of core switches. Each switch block has redundant connections to only one core pair—not to all of the core switches.

Collapsed Core

Should all networks have a distinct redundant core layer? Perhaps not, in smaller campus networks, where the cost and scalability of a separate core layer is not warranted. A *collapsed core block* is one in which the hierarchy's core layer is collapsed into the distribution layer. Here, both distribution and core functions are provided within the same switch devices.

Figure 1-18 shows the basic collapsed core design. Although the distribution and core layer functions are performed in the same device, keeping these functions distinct and properly designed is important. Note also that the collapsed core is not an independent building block but is integrated into the distribution layer of the individual standalone switch blocks.

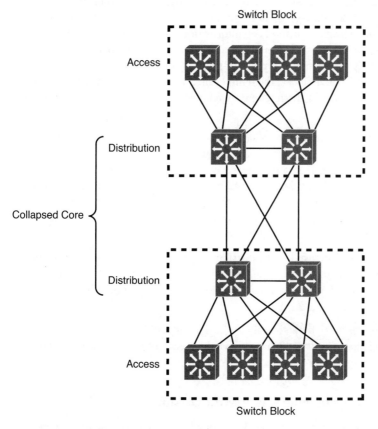

Figure 1-18   *A Collapsed Core Network Design*

In the collapsed core design, each access layer switch has a redundant link to each distribution layer switch. All Layer 3 subnets present in the access layer terminate at the distribution switches' Layer 3 ports, as in the basic switch block design. The distribution switches connect to each other with redundant links, completing a path to use during a failure.

Core Size in a Campus Network

The core layer is made up of redundant switches and is bounded and isolated by Layer 3 devices. Routing protocols determine paths and maintain the core's operation. As with any network, you must pay some attention to the overall design of the routers and routing protocols in the network. Because routing protocols propagate updates throughout the network, network topologies might be undergoing change. The network's size (the number of routers) then affects routing protocol performance as updates are exchanged and network convergence takes place.

Although the network shown previously in Figure 1-16 might look small, with only two switch blocks of two Layer 3 switches (route processors within the distribution layer switches) each, large campus networks can have many switch blocks connected into the core. If you think of each multilayer switch as a router, you will recall that each route processor must communicate with and keep information about each of its directly connected peers. Most routing protocols have practical limits on the number of peer routers that can be directly connected on a point-to-point or multiaccess link. In a network with a large number of switch blocks, the number of connected routers can grow quite large. Should you be concerned about a core switch peering with too many distribution switches?

No, because the actual number of directly connected peers is quite small, regardless of the campus network size. Access layer VLANs terminate at the distribution layer switches (unless the access layer is configured for Layer 3 operation). The only peering routers at that boundary are pairs of distribution switches, each providing routing redundancy for each of the access layer VLAN subnets. At the distribution and core boundary, each distribution switch connects to only two core switches over Layer 3 switch interfaces. Therefore, only pairs of router peers are formed.

When multilayer switches are used in the distribution and core layers, the routing protocols running in both layers regard each pair of redundant links between layers as equal-cost paths. Traffic is routed across both links in a load-sharing fashion, utilizing the bandwidth of both.

One final core layer design point is to scale the core switches to match the incoming load. At a minimum, each core switch must handle switching each of its incoming distribution links at 100 percent capacity.

Cisco Products in a Hierarchical Network Design

Before delving into the design practices needed to build a hierarchical campus network, you should have some idea of the actual devices that you can place at each layer. Cisco has switching products tailored for layer functionality and for the size of the campus network.

For the purposes of this discussion, a large campus can be considered to span across many buildings. A medium campus might make use of one or several buildings, and a small campus might have only a single building.

Choose your Cisco products based on the functionality that is expected at each layer of a small, medium, or large campus. Do not get lost in the details of the tables. Rather, try to understand which switch fits into which layer for a given network size.

In the access layer, high port density, Power over Ethernet (PoE), and low cost are usually desirable. The Catalyst 2960-X, 3650, and 3850 switches provide 48 ports each. Like switch models can be connected to form a single logical switch when a greater number of ports is needed. The Catalyst 4500E is a single-switch chassis that can be populated with a variety of line cards. It also offers a choice of redundant supervisor modules that offer redundancy and even the ability to perform software upgrades with no impact to the production network. Table 1-3 describes some Cisco switch platforms that are commonly used in the access layer.

Table 1-3 *Common Access Layer Switch Platforms*

	Catalyst Model	Max Port Density	Uplinks	Max Backplane	Other Features
	2960-X	384 (Up to 8 48-port switches in a stack)	2 10GE or 4 1 Gigabit Ethernet per switch	80 Gbps	RIP, OSPF available for routed access layer; PoE+
	3650	432 (Up to 9 48-port switches in a stack)	2 Gigabit Ethernet or 4 10GE	160 Gbps	Full-featured routing available, integrated wireless controller, PoE+
	3850	432 (Up to 9 48-port switches in a stack)	4 Gigabit Ethernet, 4 10GE	480 Gbps	Full-featured routing available, integrated wireless controller, PoE+, UPoE
	4500E	384 (Up to 8 48-port modules per chassis)	Up to 12-port 10GE per module	928 Gbps	Dual supervisors, full-featured routing available, integrated wireless controller, PoE+, UPoE

The distribution and core layers are very similar in function and switching features. Generally, these layers require high Layer 3 switching throughput and a high density of high-bandwidth optical media. Cisco offers the Catalyst 3750-X, 4500-X, 4500E, and 6800, as summarized in Table 1-4.

Table 1-4   *Common Distribution and Core Layer Switch Platforms*

	Catalyst Model	Max Port Density	Max Backplane	Other Features
	4500-X	80 10GE	1.6 Tbps	Dual-chassis Virtual Switching System (VSS) redundancy
	4500E	96 10GE or 384 Gigabit Ethernet	928 Gbps	Dual supervisors
	6807-XL	40 40Gbps, 160 Gigabit Ethernet, 480 Gigabit Ethernet	22.8 Tbps	Dual supervisor, dual-chassis VSS redundancy

Exam Preparation Tasks

Review All Key Topics

Review the most important topics in the chapter, noted with the Key Topic icon in the outer margin of the page. Table 1-5 lists a reference of these key topics and the page numbers on which each is found.

Key Topic

Table 1-5 *Key Topics for Chapter 1*

Key Topic Element	Description	Page Number
Paragraph	Describes the Cisco hierarchical network design principles	9
Paragraph	Describes the access layer	12
Paragraph	Describes the distribution layer	12
Paragraph	Describes the core layer	12
Paragraph	Explains modular network design using switch blocks	15
Paragraph	Discusses the pitfalls of letting VLANs span access layer switches	18
Paragraph	Discusses two best practice designs for switch block redundancy	19
Paragraph	Explains a redundant core design	21

Complete Tables and Lists from Memory

There are no memory tables in this chapter.

Define Key Terms

Define the following key terms from this chapter, and check your answers in the glossary:

hierarchical network design, access layer, distribution layer, core layer, switch block, collapsed core, dual core

This chapter covers the following topics that you need to master for the CCNP SWITCH exam:

- **Layer 2 Switch Operation:** This section describes the functionality of a switch that forwards Ethernet frames.

- **Multilayer Switch Operation:** This section describes the mechanisms that forward packets at OSI Layers 3 and 4.

- **Tables Used in Switching:** This section explains how tables of information and computation are used to make switching decisions. Coverage focuses on the content-addressable memory table involved in Layer 2 forwarding, and the ternary content-addressable memory used in packet-handling decisions at Layers 2 through 4.

- **Managing Switching Tables:** This section reviews the Catalyst commands that you can use to configure and monitor the switching tables and memory. You will find these commands useful when troubleshooting or tracing the sources of data or problems in a switched network.

CHAPTER 2

Switch Operation

To have a good understanding of the many features that you can configure on a Catalyst switch, you first should understand the fundamentals of the switching function.

This chapter serves as a primer, describing how an Ethernet switch works. It presents Layer 2 forwarding, along with the hardware functions that make forwarding possible. Multilayer switching is also explained. A considerable portion of the chapter deals with the memory architecture that performs switching at Layers 3 and 4 both flexibly and efficiently. This chapter also provides a brief overview of useful switching table management commands.

"Do I Know This Already?" Quiz

The "Do I Know This Already?" quiz allows you to assess whether you should read this entire chapter thoroughly or jump to the "Exam Preparation Tasks" section. If you are in doubt based on your answers to these questions or your own assessment of your knowledge of the topics, read the entire chapter. Table 2-1 outlines the major headings in this chapter and the "Do I Know This Already?" quiz questions that go with them. You can find the answers in Appendix A, "Answers to the 'Do I Know This Already?' Quizzes."

Table 2-1 *"Do I Know This Already?" Foundation Topics Section-to-Question Mapping*

Foundation Topics Section	Questions Covered in This Section
Layer 2 Switch Operation	1–5
Multilayer Switch Operation	6–9
Switching Tables	10–11
Troubleshooting Switching Tables	12

1. Which of the following devices performs transparent bridging?

    a. Ethernet hub

    b. Layer 2 switch

    c. Layer 3 switch

    d. Router

2. When a PC is connected to a Layer 2 switch port, how far does the collision domain spread?

   a. No collision domain exists.

   b. One switch port.

   c. One VLAN.

   d. All ports on the switch.

3. What information is used to forward frames in a Layer 2 switch?

   a. Source MAC address

   b. Destination MAC address

   c. Source switch port

   d. IP addresses

4. What does a switch do if a MAC address cannot be found in the CAM table?

   a. The frame is forwarded to the default port.

   b. The switch generates an ARP request for the address.

   c. The switch floods the frame out all ports (except the receiving port).

   d. The switch drops the frame.

5. In a Catalyst switch, frames can be filtered with access lists for security and QoS purposes. This filtering occurs according to which of the following?

   a. Before a CAM table lookup

   b. After a CAM table lookup

   c. Simultaneously with a CAM table lookup

   d. According to how the access lists are configured

6. Access list contents can be merged into which of the following?

   a. CAM table

   b. TCAM table

   c. FIB table

   d. ARP table

7. Multilayer switches using CEF are based on which of these techniques?

   a. Route caching

   b. NetFlow switching

   c. Topology-based switching

   d. Demand-based switching

8. Which answer describes multilayer switching with CEF?

   a. The first packet is routed and then the flow is cached.

   b. The switch supervisor CPU forwards each packet.

   c. The switching hardware learns station addresses and builds a routing database.

   d. A single database of routing information is built for the switching hardware.

9. In a switch, frames are placed in which buffer after forwarding decisions are made?

   a. Ingress queues

   b. Egress queues

   c. CAM table

   d. TCAM

10. What size are the mask and pattern fields in a TCAM entry?

   a. 64 bits

   b. 128 bits

   c. 134 bits

   d. 168 bits

11. Access list rules are compiled as TCAM entries. When a packet is matched against an access list, in what order are the TCAM entries evaluated?

   a. Sequentially in the order of the original access list.

   b. Numerically by the access list number.

   c. Alphabetically by the access list name.

   d. All entries are evaluated in parallel.

12. Which Catalyst IOS command can you use to display the addresses in the CAM table?

   a. show cam

   b. show mac address-table

   c. show mac

   d. show cam address-table

Foundation Topics

Layer 2 Switch Operation

Consider a simple network that is built around many hosts that all share the same available bandwidth. This is known as a *shared media network* and was used in early legacy LANs made up of Ethernet hubs. The carrier sense multiple access collision detect (CSMA/CD) scheme determines when a device can transmit data on the shared LAN.

When more than one host tries to talk at one time, a collision occurs, and everyone must back off and wait to talk again. This forces every host to operate in half-duplex mode, by either talking or listening at any given time. In addition, when one host sends a frame, all connected hosts hear it. When one host generates a frame with errors, everyone hears that, too. This type of LAN is a *collision domain* because all device transmissions are susceptible to collisions.

An Ethernet switch operates at OSI Layer 2, making decisions about forwarding frames based on the destination MAC addresses found within the frames. This means that the Ethernet media is no longer shared among connected devices. Instead, at its most basic level, an Ethernet switch provides isolation between connected hosts in several ways:

- The collision domain's scope is severely limited. On each switch port, the collision domain consists of the switch port itself and the devices directly connected to that port—either a single host or, if a shared-media hub is connected, the set of hosts connected to the hub.

- Host connections can operate in full-duplex mode because there is no contention on the media. Hosts can talk *and* listen at the same time.

- Bandwidth is no longer shared. Instead, each switch port offers dedicated bandwidth across a switching fabric to another switch port. (These frame forwarding paths change dynamically.)

- Errors in frames are not propagated. Each frame received on a switch port is checked for errors. Good frames are regenerated when they are forwarded or transmitted. This is known as *store-and-forward* switching technology: Packets are received, stored for inspection, and then forwarded.

- You can limit broadcast traffic to a volume threshold.

- Other types of intelligent filtering or forwarding become possible.

Transparent Bridging

A Layer 2 switch is basically a multiport transparent bridge, where each switch port is its own Ethernet LAN segment, isolated from the others. Frame forwarding is based completely on the MAC addresses contained in each frame, such that the switch will not forward a frame unless it knows the destination's location. (When the switch does not know where the destination is, it makes some safe assumptions.) Figure 2-1 shows the progression from a two-port to a multiport transparent bridge, and then to a Layer 2 switch.

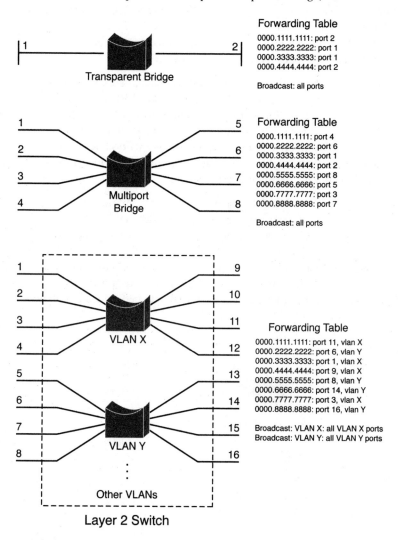

Forwarding Table

0000.1111.1111: port 2
0000.2222.2222: port 1
0000.3333.3333: port 1
0000.4444.4444: port 2

Broadcast: all ports

Forwarding Table

0000.1111.1111: port 4
0000.2222.2222: port 6
0000.3333.3333: port 1
0000.4444.4444: port 2
0000.5555.5555: port 8
0000.6666.6666: port 5
0000.7777.7777: port 3
0000.8888.8888: port 7

Broadcast: all ports

Forwarding Table

0000.1111.1111: port 11, vlan X
0000.2222.2222: port 6, vlan Y
0000.3333.3333: port 1, vlan X
0000.4444.4444: port 9, vlan X
0000.5555.5555: port 8, vlan Y
0000.6666.6666: port 14, vlan Y
0000.7777.7777: port 3, vlan X
0000.8888.8888: port 16, vlan Y

Broadcast: VLAN X: all VLAN X ports
Broadcast: VLAN Y: all VLAN Y ports

Figure 2-1 *A Comparison of Transparent Bridges and Switches*

The entire process of forwarding Ethernet frames then becomes figuring out what MAC addresses connect to which switch ports. For example, the Layer 2 switch in Figure 2-1 knows that the device using MAC address 0000.5555.5555 is located on switch port 8, which is assigned to VLAN Y. It also knows that frames arriving on VLAN Y and destined for the broadcast MAC address must be flooded out all ports that are assigned to VLAN Y.

A switch either must be told explicitly where hosts are located or must learn this information for itself. You can configure MAC address locations through a switch's command-line interface, but this quickly gets cumbersome when there are many stations on the network or when stations move around from one switch port to another.

To dynamically learn about station locations, a switch listens to incoming frames and keeps a table of address information. In Figure 2-1, this information is kept in a forwarding table. As a frame is received on a switch port, the switch inspects the source MAC address. If that address is not in the address table already, the MAC address, switch port, and virtual LAN (VLAN) on which it arrived are recorded in the table. Learning the address locations of the incoming packets is easy and straightforward.

Incoming frames also include the destination MAC address. Again, the switch looks up this address in the address table, hoping to find the switch port and VLAN where the destination address is attached. If it is found, the frame can be forwarded out the corresponding switch port. If the address is not found in the table, the switch must take more drastic action: The frame is forwarded in a "best effort" fashion by flooding it out all switch ports assigned to the source VLAN. This is known as *unknown unicast flooding*, because the location of the unicast destination is unknown.

Figure 2-2 illustrates this process, using only a single VLAN for simplification. Suppose, for instance, that a packet arrives on switch port 3, containing destination MAC address 0000.aaaa.aaaa. The switch looks for that MAC address in its forwarding table, but is unable to find a matching entry. The switch then floods copies of the packet out every other port that is assigned to port 3's VLAN, to increase the likelihood that 0000.aaaa. aaaa will eventually receive the packet that is destined for it. If the destination is the broadcast MAC address, the switch knows that the frame should be flooded out all ports on the VLAN.

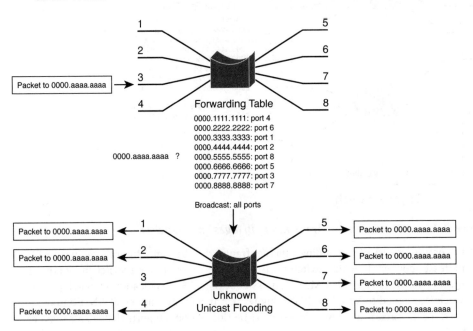

Figure 2-2 *Unknown Unicast Flooding*

A switch constantly listens to incoming frames on each of its ports, learning source MAC addresses. However, be aware that the learning process is allowed only when the

Spanning Tree Protocol (STP) algorithm has decided that a port is stable for normal use. STP is concerned only with maintaining a loop-free network, where frames will not be forwarded recursively. If a loop formed, a flooded frame could follow the looped path, where it would be flooded again and again. STP is covered in greater detail in Chapters 6, "Traditional Spanning Tree Protocol," through 9, "Advanced Spanning Tree Protocol."

In a similar manner, frames containing a broadcast or multicast destination address are also flooded. These destination addresses are not unknown—the switch knows them well because they use standardized address values. For example, the Ethernet broadcast address is always ffff.ffff.ffff, IPv4 multicast addresses always begin with 01xx.xxxx. xxxx, and IPv6 multicast addresses begin with 3333.xxxx.xxxx. These addresses are destined for multiple locations, so they must be flooded by definition. In the case of multicast addresses, flooding is performed by default unless more specific recipient locations have been learned.

Follow That Frame!

You should have a basic understanding of the operations that a frame undergoes as it passes through a Layer 2 switch. This helps you get a firm grasp on how to configure the switch for complex functions. Figure 2-3 shows a typical Layer 2 Catalyst switch and the decision processes that take place to forward each frame.

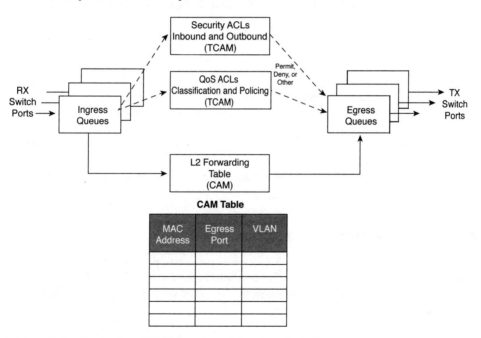

Figure 2-3   *Operations Within a Layer 2 Catalyst Switch*

When a frame arrives at a switch port, it is placed into one of the port's ingress queues. The queues each can contain frames to be forwarded, with each queue having a different priority or service level. The switch port then can be fine-tuned so that important frames get processed and forwarded before less-important frames. This can prevent time-critical data from being "lost in the shuffle" during a flurry of incoming traffic.

As the ingress queues are serviced and a frame is pulled off, the switch must figure out not only *where* to forward the frame, but also *whether* it should be forwarded and *how*. Three fundamental decisions must be made: one concerned with finding the egress switch port, and two concerned with forwarding policies. All these decisions are made *simultaneously* by independent portions of switching hardware and can be described as follows:

- **L2 forwarding table:** The frame's destination MAC address is used as an index, or key, into the content-addressable memory (CAM), or address, table. If the address is found, the egress switch port and the appropriate VLAN ID are read from the table. (If the address is not found, the frame is marked for flooding so that it is forwarded out every switch port in the VLAN.)

- **Security ACLs:** Access control lists (ACLs) can be used to identify frames according to their MAC addresses, protocol types (for non-IP frames), IP addresses, protocols, and Layer 4 port numbers. The ternary content-addressable memory (TCAM) contains ACLs in a compiled form so that a decision can be made on whether to forward a frame in a single table lookup.

- **QoS ACLs:** Other ACLs can classify incoming frames according to quality of service (QoS) parameters, to police or control the rate of traffic flows, and to mark QoS parameters in outbound frames. The TCAM is also used to make these decisions in a single table lookup.

The CAM and TCAM tables are discussed in greater detail in the "Content-Addressable Memory" and "Ternary Content-Addressable Memory" sections, later in this chapter. After the CAM and TCAM table lookups have occurred, the frame is placed into the appropriate egress queue on the appropriate outbound switch port. The egress queue is determined by QoS values either contained in the frame or passed along with the frame. Like the ingress queues, the egress queues are serviced according to importance or time criticality; higher priority frames are sent out without being delayed by other outbound traffic.

Multilayer Switch Operation

Many Cisco Catalyst switches can also forward frames based on Layers 3 and 4 information contained in packets. This is known as *multilayer switching* (MLS). Naturally, Layer 2 switching is performed at the same time because even the higher-layer encapsulations still are contained in Ethernet frames.

Types of Multilayer Switching

Catalyst switches have supported two basic generations or types of MLS: route caching (first-generation MLS) and topology based (second-generation MLS). This section presents an overview of both, although only the second generation is supported in the Cisco

IOS Software-based switch families, such as the Catalyst 2960, 3750, 4500, and 6500. You should understand the two types and the differences between them:

■ **Route caching:** The first generation of MLS, requiring a route processor (RP) and a switch engine (SE). The RP must process a traffic flow's first packet to determine the destination. The SE listens to the first packet and to the resulting destination, and then sets up a "shortcut" entry in its MLS cache. The SE forwards subsequent packets belonging to the same traffic flow based on shortcut entries in its cache.

This type of MLS also is known by the names *NetFlow LAN switching*, *flow-based* or *demand-based switching*, and *route once, switch many*. The RP must examine each new traffic flow and set up shortcut entries for the SE. Even if this method isn't used to forward packets in Cisco IOS–based Catalyst switches, the technique can still be used to generate traffic flow information and statistics.

■ **Topology based:** The second generation of MLS, utilizing specialized hardware, is also organized with distinct RP and SE functions. The RP uses Layer 3 routing information to build and prepopulate a single database of the entire known network topology. This database becomes an efficient table lookup in hardware, and is consulted so that packets can be forwarded at high rates by the SE. The longest match found in the database is used as the correct Layer 3 destination. As the routing topology changes over time, the database contained in the hardware can be updated dynamically with no performance penalty.

This type of MLS is known as *Cisco Express Forwarding* (CEF). A routing process running on the switch downloads the current routing table database into the Forwarding Information Base (FIB) area of hardware. CEF is discussed in greater detail in Chapter 11, "Multilayer Switching."

Tip   Although the RP and SE functions within a multilayer switch do interact, they can operate independently, as if they are on different "planes." The control plane of a switch includes the RP and any process that runs to control or manage the switch, whereas the data plane exists in the SE, where data is forwarded.

Follow That Packet!

The path that a Layer 3 packet follows through a multilayer switch is similar to that of a Layer 2 switch. Obviously, some means of making a Layer 3 forwarding decision must be added. Beyond that, several, sometimes unexpected, things can happen to packets as they are forwarded. Figure 2-4 shows a typical multilayer switch and the decision processes that must occur. Packets arriving on a switch port are placed in the appropriate ingress queue, just as in a Layer 2 switch.

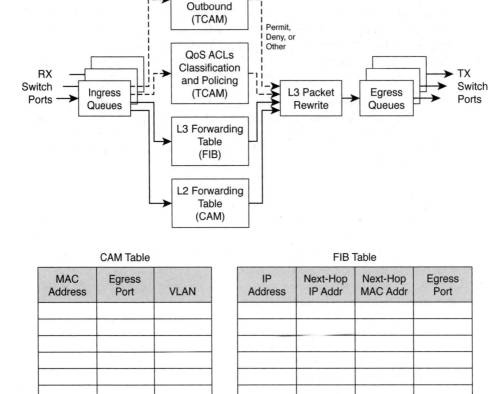

Figure 2-4   *Operations Within a Multilayer Catalyst Switch*

Each packet is pulled off an ingress queue and inspected for both Layer 2 and Layer 3 destination addresses. Now, the decision of *where* to forward the packet is based on two address tables, whereas the decision of *how* to forward the packet still is based on access list results.

All the multilayer switching decisions are performed simultaneously in hardware, using the following functions:

- **L2 forwarding table:** The destination MAC address is used as an index into the CAM table. If the frame contains a Layer 3 packet that needs to be forwarded from one subnet to another, the destination MAC address will contain the address of a Layer 3 port on the switch itself. In this case, the CAM table results are used only to decide that the frame should be processed at Layer 3.

- **L3 forwarding table:** The FIB table is consulted, using the destination IP address as an index. The longest match in the table is found (both address and mask), and the resulting next-hop Layer 3 address is obtained. The FIB also contains each next-hop router's Layer 2 MAC address and the egress switch port (and VLAN ID) so that further table lookups are not necessary.

- **Security ACLs:** Inbound and outbound access lists are compiled into TCAM entries so that decisions of whether to forward a packet can be determined as a single table lookup.

- **QoS ACLs:** Packet classification, policing, and marking all can be performed as single table lookups in the QoS TCAM.

As with Layer 2 switching, the packet finally must be placed in the appropriate egress queue on the appropriate egress switch port.

During the multilayer switching process, some portions of the frame must be modified or rewritten, just as any router would do. For example, the destination MAC address in the inbound frame contains the address of the next-hop destination, which is the ingress Layer 3 interface on the multilayer switch. Once the FIB table is consulted, the next-hop router IP and MAC addresses are found.

The next-hop Layer 2 address must be put into the frame in place of the original destination address (the multilayer switch). The frame's Layer 2 source address also must become that of the multilayer switch's egress interface before the frame is sent on to the next hop. As any good router must do, the time-to-live (TTL) value in the Layer 3 packet must be decremented by one.

Because the contents of the Layer 3 packet (the TTL value) have changed, the Layer 3 header checksum must be recalculated. And because both Layers 2 and 3 contents have changed, the Layer 2 checksum must be recalculated. In other words, the entire Ethernet frame must be rewritten before it goes into the egress queue. This also is accomplished efficiently in hardware.

Multilayer Switching Exceptions

To forward packets using the simultaneous decision processes described in the preceding section, the packet must be "MLS ready" and must require no additional decisions. For example, CEF can directly forward most IP and IPv6 packets between hosts. This occurs when the source and destination addresses (both MAC and IP) are already known and no other IP parameters must be manipulated.

Other packets cannot be directly forwarded by CEF and must be handled in more detail. This is done by a quick inspection during the forwarding decisions. If a packet meets criteria such as the following, it is flagged for further processing and sent or "punted" to the switch CPU for *process switching*:

- ARP requests and replies

- IP packets requiring a response from a router (TTL has expired, maximum transmission unit [MTU] is exceeded, fragmentation is needed, and so on)

- IP broadcasts that will be relayed as unicast (Dynamic Host Configuration Protocol [DHCP] requests, IP helper-address functions)

- Routing protocol updates

- Cisco Discovery Protocol (CDP) packets

- Packets needing encryption

- Packets triggering Network Address Translation (NAT)

- Legacy multiprotocol packets (IPX, AppleTalk, and so on)

As you might expect, packets that are punted to the CPU cannot be forwarded as efficiently as ones that can be forwarded in hardware directly. The additional processing takes additional time and consumes CPU resources. Ideally, all packets should be forwarded in hardware, but that is not always possible.

Tables Used in Switching

Catalyst switches maintain several types of tables to be used in the switching process. The tables are tailored for Layer 2 switching or MLS and are kept in very fast memory so that many fields within a frame or packet can be compared in parallel.

Content-Addressable Memory

All Catalyst switch models use a CAM table for Layer 2 switching. As frames arrive on switch ports, the source MAC addresses are learned and recorded in the CAM table. The port of arrival and the VLAN both are recorded in the table, along with a time stamp. If a MAC address learned on one switch port has moved to a different port, the MAC address and time stamp are recorded for the most recent arrival port. Then, the previous entry is deleted. If a MAC address is found already present in the table for the correct arrival port, only its time stamp is updated.

Switches generally have large CAM tables so that many addresses can be looked up for frame forwarding. However, there is not enough table space to hold every possible address on large networks. To manage the CAM table space, *stale entries* (addresses that have not been heard from for a period of time) are aged out. By default, idle CAM table entries are kept for 300 seconds before they are deleted. You can change the default setting using the following configuration command:

```
Switch(config)# mac address-table aging-time seconds
```

By default, MAC addresses are learned dynamically from incoming frames. You also can configure static CAM table entries that contain MAC addresses that might not be learned otherwise. To do this, use the following configuration command:

```
Switch(config)# mac address-table static mac-address vlan vlan-id interface type
    mod/num
```

Note   You should be aware that there is a slight discrepancy in the CAM table command syntax. Until Catalyst IOS version 12.1(11)EA1, the syntax for CAM table commands used the keywords **mac-address-table**. In more recent Cisco IOS versions, the syntax has changed to use the keywords **mac address-table** (first hyphen omitted). The Catalyst 4500 and 6500 IOS Software are exceptions, however, and continue to use the **mac-address-table** keyword form. Many switch platforms support either syntax to ease the transition.

Exactly what happens when a host's MAC address is learned on one switch port, and then the host moves so that it appears on a different switch port? Ordinarily, the host's original CAM table entry would have to age out after 300 seconds, while its address was learned on the new port. To avoid having duplicate CAM table entries during that time, a switch purges any existing entries for a MAC address that has just been learned on a different switch port. This is a safe assumption because MAC addresses are unique, and a single host should never be seen on more than one switch port unless problems exist in the network. If a switch notices that a MAC address is being learned on alternating switch ports, it generates an error message that flags the MAC address as "flapping" between interfaces.

Ternary Content-Addressable Memory

In traditional routing, ACLs can match, filter, or control specific traffic. Access lists are made up of one or more access control entities (ACEs) or matching statements that are evaluated in sequential order. Evaluating an access list can take up additional time, adding to the latency of forwarding packets.

In multilayer switches, however, all the matching process that ACLs provide is implemented in hardware called a TCAM. With a TCAM, a packet can be evaluated against an entire access list within a single table lookup. Most switches have multiple TCAMs so that both inbound and outbound security and QoS ACLs can be evaluated simultaneously, or entirely in parallel with a Layer 2 or Layer 3 forwarding decision.

The Catalyst IOS Software has two components that are part of the TCAM operation:

- **Feature Manager (FM):** After an access list has been created or configured, the Feature Manager software compiles, or merges, the ACEs into entries in the TCAM table. The TCAM then can be consulted at full frame-forwarding speed.

- **Switching Database Manager (SDM):** On some Catalyst switch models, the TCAM is partitioned into several areas that support different functions. The SDM software configures or tunes the TCAM partitions, if needed, to provide ample space for specific switching functions. (The TCAM is fixed on Catalyst 4500 and 6500 platforms and cannot be repartitioned.)

TCAM Structure

The TCAM is an extension of the CAM table concept. Recall that a CAM table takes in an index or key value (usually a MAC address) and looks up the resulting value (usually a switch port or VLAN ID). Table lookup is fast and always based on an exact key match consisting of binary numbers made up of two possible values: 0 and 1 bits.

TCAM also uses a table-lookup operation but is greatly enhanced to allow a more abstract operation. For example, binary values (0s and 1s) make up a key into the table, but a mask value also is used to decide which bits of the key are actually relevant. This effectively makes a key consisting of three input values: 0, 1, and X (do not care) bit values—a threefold or *ternary* combination.

TCAM entries are composed of Value, Mask, and Result (VMR) combinations. Fields from frame or packet headers are fed into the TCAM, where they are matched against the value and mask pairs to yield a result. As a quick reference, these can be described as follows:

■ **Values** are always 134-bit quantities, consisting of source and destination addresses and other relevant protocol information—all patterns to be matched. The information concatenated to form the value depends on the type of access list, as shown in Table 2-2. Values in the TCAM come directly from any address, port, or other protocol information given in an ACE, up to a maximum of 134 bits.

Table 2-2   *TCAM Value Pattern Components*

Access List Type	Value and Mask Components (Number of Bits)
Ethernet	Source MAC (48), destination MAC (48), EtherType (16)
ICMP	Source IP (32), destination IP (32), protocol (16), ICMP code (8), ICMP type (4), IP type of service (ToS) (8)
Extended IP using TCP/UDP	Source IP (32), destination IP (32), protocol (16), IP ToS (8), source port (16), source operator (4), destination port (16), destination operator (4)
Other IP	Source IP (32), destination IP (32), protocol (16), IP ToS (8)
IGMP	Source IP (32), destination IP (32), protocol (16), IP ToS (8), IGMP message type (8)

■ **Masks** are also 134-bit quantities, in exactly the same format, or bit order, as the values. Masks select only the value bits of interest; a mask bit is set to mark a value bit to be exactly matched or is not set to mark a value bit that does not matter. The masks used in the TCAM stem from address or bit masks in ACEs.

■ **Results** are numeric values that represent what action to take after the TCAM lookup occurs. Whereas traditional access lists offer only a permit or deny result, TCAM lookups offer a number of possible results or actions. For example, the result can be a permit or deny decision, an index value to a QoS policer, a pointer to a next-hop routing table, and so on.

Note   This section discusses TCAM from an IPv4 perspective. When a dual IPv4-IPv6 SDM template is used, the TCAM becomes more limited in size. Because IPv6 addresses are 128 bits in length, some address compression must be used to store them in TCAM entries.

The TCAM is always organized by masks, where each unique mask has eight value patterns associated with it. For example, the Catalyst 6500 TCAM (one for security ACLs and one for QoS ACLs) holds up to 4096 masks and 32,768 value patterns. The trick is that each of the mask-value pairs is evaluated simultaneously, or in parallel, revealing the best or longest match in a single table lookup.

TCAM Example

Figure 2-5 shows how the TCAM is built and used. This is a simple example and might or might not be identical to the results that the Feature Manager produces because the ACEs might need to be optimized or rewritten to achieve certain TCAM algorithm requirements.

```
access-list 100 permit tcp host 192.168.199.14 10.41.0.0 0.0.255.255 eq telnet
access-list 100 permit ip any 192.168.100.0 0.0.0.255
access-list 100 deny udp any 192.168.5.0 0.0.0.255 gt 1024
access-list 100 deny udp any 192.168.199.0 0.0.0.255 range 1024 2047
```

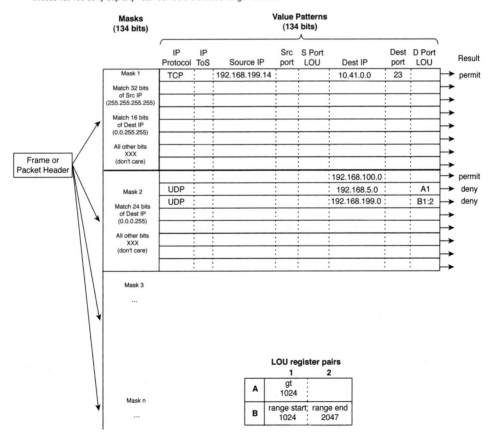

Figure 2-5   *How an Access List Is Merged into TCAM*

The sample access list 100 (extended IP) is configured and merged into TCAM entries. First, the mask values must be identified in the access list. When an address value and a corresponding address mask are specified in an ACE, those mask bits must be set for matching. All other mask bits can remain in the "do not care" state because they will not be used.

The access list contains only three unique masks: one that matches all 32 bits of the source IP address (found with an address mask of 0.0.0.0 or the keyword **host**), one that matches 16 bits of the destination address (found with an address mask of 0.0.255.255), and one that matches only 24 bits of the destination address (found with an address mask of 0.0.0.255). The keyword **any** in the ACEs means "match anything" or "do not care."

The three unique masks are placed into the TCAM. Then, for each mask, all possible value patterns are identified. For example, a 32-bit source IP mask (Mask 1) can be found only in ACEs with a source IP address of 192.168.199.14 and a destination of 10.41.0.0. (The rest of Mask 1 is the destination address mask 0.0.255.255.) Those address values are placed into the first value pattern slot associated with Mask 1. Mask 2 (0.0.255.255) has three value patterns: destination addresses 192.168.100.0, 192.168.5.0, and 192.168.199.0. Each of these is placed in the three pattern positions of Mask 2. This process continues until all ACEs have been merged.

When a mask's eighth pattern position has been filled, the next pattern with the same mask must be placed under a new mask in the table. A bit of a balancing act occurs to try to fit all ACEs into the available mask and pattern entries without an overflow.

Port Operations in TCAM

You might have noticed that matching strictly based on values and masks covers only ACE statements that involve exact matches (either the **eq** port operation keyword or no Layer 4 port operations). For example, ACEs such as the following involve specific address values, address masks, and port numbers:

```
access-list test permit ip 192.168.254.0 0.0.0.255 any
access-list test permit tcp any host 192.168.199.10 eq www
```

What about ACEs that use port operators, where a comparison must be made? Consider the following:

```
access-list test permit udp any host 192.168.199.50 gt 1024
access-list test permit tcp any any range 2000 2002
```

A simple logical operation between a mask and a pattern cannot generate the desired result. The TCAM also provides a mechanism for performing a Layer 4 operation or comparison, also done during the single table lookup. If an ACE has a port operator, such as **gt**, **lt**, **neq**, or **range**, the Feature Manager software compiles the TCAM entry to include the use of the operator and the operand in a logical operation unit (LOU) register. Only a limited number of LOUs are available in the TCAM. If there are more ACEs with comparison operators than there are LOUs, the Feature Manager must break up the ACEs into multiple ACEs with only regular matching (using the **eq** operator).

In Figure 2-5, two ACEs require a Layer 4 operation:

■   One that checks for UDP destination ports greater than 1024

■   One that looks for the UDP destination port range 1024 to 2047

The Feature Manager checks all ACEs for Layer 4 operation and places these into LOU register pairs. These can be loaded with operations, independent of any other ACE parameters. The LOU contents can be reused if other ACEs need the same comparisons and values. After the LOUs are loaded, they are referenced in the TCAM entries that need them. This is shown by LOUs A1 and the B1:2 pair. A finite number (actually, a rather small number) of LOUs are available in the TCAM, so the Feature Manager software must use them carefully.

Managing Switching Tables

You can display or query the switching tables to verify the information that the switch has learned. As well, you might want to check the tables to find out on which switch port a specific MAC address has been learned. You can also manage the size of the various switching tables to optimize performance.

CAM Table Operation

To view the contents of the CAM table, you can use the following form of the **show mac address-table** EXEC command:

```
Switch# show mac address-table dynamic [address mac-address | interface type
mod/num | vlan vlan-id]
```

The entries that have been learned dynamically will be shown. You can add the **address** keyword to specify a single MAC address, or the **interface** or **vlan** keyword to see addresses that have been learned on a specific interface or VLAN.

For example, assume that you need to find the learned location of the host with MAC address 0050.8b11.54da. The **show mac address-table dynamic address 0050.8b11.54da** command might produce the output in Example 2-1.

Example 2-1   *Determining Host Location by MAC Address*

```
Switch# show mac address-table dynamic address 0050.8b11.54da
          Mac Address Table
-------------------------------------------------


Vlan    Mac Address       Type       Ports
----    -----------       ----       -----
  54    0050.8b11.54da    DYNAMIC    Gi1/0/1
Total Mac Addresses for this criterion: 1
Switch#
```

From this output, you can see that the host is somehow connected to interface Gigabit Ethernet 1/0/1, on VLAN 54.

> **Tip**   If your Catalyst IOS switch is not accepting commands of the form **mac address-table,** try adding a hyphen between the keywords. For example, the Catalyst 4500 and 6500 most likely will accept **show mac-address-table** instead.

Suppose that this same command produced no output, showing nothing about the interface and VLAN where the MAC address is found. What might that mean? Either the host has not sent a frame that the switch can use for learning its location, or something odd is going on. Perhaps the host is using two network interface cards (NICs) to load balance traffic; one NIC is only receiving traffic, whereas the other is only sending. Therefore, the switch never hears and learns the receiving-only NIC address.

To see all the MAC addresses that are currently found on interface Gigabit Ethernet 1/0/29, you could use the **show mac address-table dynamic interface gig1/0/29** command. The output shown in Example 2-2 indicates that only one host has been learned on the interface. Perhaps only a single PC connects to that interface.

Example 2-2   *Determining Hosts Active on an Interface*

```
Switch# show mac address-table dynamic interface gigabitethernet1/0/29
          Mac Address Table
-------------------------------------------------


Vlan    Mac Address      Type        Ports
----    -----------      ----        -----
 537    0013.7297.3d4b   DYNAMIC     Gi1/0/29
Total Mac Addresses for this criterion: 1
Switch#
```

However, suppose the same command is used to check interface Gigabit Ethernet 1/1/1. The output shown in Example 2-3 lists many MAC addresses—all found on a single interface. How can so many addresses be learned on one switch interface? This interface must lead to another switch or another part of the network where other devices are located. As frames have been received on Gigabit Ethernet 1/1/1, coming from the other devices, the local switch has added the source MAC addresses into its CAM table.

Example 2-3   *Finding Many Hosts on an Interface*

```
Switch# show mac address-table dynamic interface gig1/1/1
          Mac Address Table
-------------------------------------------------


Vlan    Mac Address      Type        Ports
```

```
----     -----------     ----     -----
580     0000.0c07.ac01   DYNAMIC   Gi1/1/1
580     0007.0e0b.f918   DYNAMIC   Gi1/1/1
580     000f.1f78.1094   DYNAMIC   Gi1/1/1
580     0011.43ac.b083   DYNAMIC   Gi1/1/1
580     0011.bb2d.3f6e   DYNAMIC   Gi1/1/1
580     0014.6a86.1f1e   DYNAMIC   Gi1/1/1
580     0014.6a86.1f3d   DYNAMIC   Gi1/1/1
580     0014.6a86.1f3f   DYNAMIC   Gi1/1/1
580     0014.6a86.1f47   DYNAMIC   Gi1/1/1
—More—
```

Tip   Often, you need to know where a user with a certain MAC address is connected. In
a large network, discerning at which switch and switch port a MAC address can be found
might be difficult. Start at the network's center, or core, and display the CAM table entry
for the user's MAC address. Look at the switch port shown in the entry and find the neighboring switch connected to that port using CDP neighbor information. Then move to that
switch and repeat the CAM table query process. Keep moving from switch to switch until
you reach the edge of the network where the MAC address physically connects.

To see the CAM table's size, use the **show mac address-table count** command, as shown
in Example 2-4. MAC address totals are shown for each active VLAN on the switch, as
well as the total number of spaces remaining in the CAM table. This can give you a good
idea of the size of the CAM table and how many hosts are using the network.

Example 2-4   *Checking the Size of the CAM Table*

```
Switch# show mac address-table count
Mac Entries for Vlan 1:
--------------------------
Dynamic Address Count  : 0
Static  Address Count  : 0
Total Mac Addresses    : 0


Mac Entries for Vlan 2:
--------------------------
Dynamic Address Count  : 89
Static  Address Count  : 0
Total Mac Addresses    : 89


Mac Entries for Vlan 580:
--------------------------
Dynamic Address Count  : 244
Static  Address Count  : 0
```

```
Total Mac Addresses    : 244


Total Mac Address Space Available: 5791
Switch#
```

CAM table entries can be cleared manually, if needed, by using the following EXEC command:

```
Switch# clear mac address-table dynamic [address mac-address | interface type
mod/num | vlan vlan-id]
```

TCAM Operation

The TCAM in a switch is more or less self-sufficient. Access lists are compiled or merged automatically into the TCAM, so there is nothing to configure. The only concept you need to be aware of is how the TCAM resources are being used. You can use the **show platform tcam utilization** EXEC command shown in Example 2-5 to get an idea of the TCAM utilization. Compare the Used number of entries to the Max value.

Example 2-5 *Displaying TCAM Utilization*

```
Switch# show platform tcam utilization
CAM Utilization for ASIC# 0                     Max              Used
                                           Masks/Values      Masks/Values
   Unicast mac addresses:                   6364/6364          311/311
   IPv4 IGMP groups + multicast routes:     1120/1120           8/8
   IPv4 unicast directly-connected routes:  6144/6144           0/0
   IPv4 unicast indirectly-connected routes: 2048/2048          28/28
   IPv4 policy based routing aces:           452/452           12/12
   IPv4 qos aces:                            512/512           21/21
   IPv4 security aces:                       964/964           33/33


Note: Allocation of TCAM entries per feature uses
a complex algorithm. The above information is meant
to provide an abstract view of the current TCAM utilization
Switch#
```

TCAMs have a limited number of usable mask, value pattern, and LOU entries. If access lists grow to be large or many Layer 4 operations are needed, the TCAM tables and registers can overflow. If that happens while you are configuring an ACL, the switch will generate syslog messages that flag the TCAM overflow situation as it tries to compile the ACL into TCAM entries.

Managing Switching Table Sizes

High-end Cisco switches are designed for efficient multilayer switching at any location within a network. For example, the versatile Catalyst 4500 and 6500 models can be used equally well in the core, distribution, or access layer because their hardware contains ample switching engines and table space for any application. Other models, such as the 2960, 3750, and 3850, have a fixed architecture with limited switching table space. The CAM, FIB, and other tables must all share resources; for one table to grow larger, the others must grow smaller.

Fortunately, you can select a preferred type of switching that, in turn, affects the relative size of the switching tables. To excel at Layer 2 switching, the CAM table should increase in size, whereas the FIB or routing table space should decrease. If a switch is used to route traffic, its FIB table space should grow and its CAM table should shrink.

The SDM manages the memory partitions in a switch. You can display the current partition preference and a breakdown of table sizes with the following EXEC command:

```
Switch# show sdm prefer
```

Example 2-6 shows that the switch is operating with the "desktop default" memory template, which is tailored for the access layer. According to the numbers, the desktop default template provides a balanced mix of Layer 2 (unicast MAC addresses, or the CAM table) and Layer 3 (IPv4 unicast routes, or the FIB table), in addition to IPv4 ACLs, and some minimal support for IPv6.

Example 2-6 *Displaying the Current SDM Template*

```
Switch# show sdm prefer
 The current template is "desktop default" template.
 The selected template optimizes the resources in
 the switch to support this level of features for
 8 routed interfaces and 1024 VLANs.

   number of unicast mac addresses:                6K
   number of IPv4 IGMP groups + multicast routes:  1K
   number of IPv4 unicast routes:                  8K
     number of directly-connected IPv4 hosts:      6K
     number of indirect IPv4 routes:               2K
   number of IPv6 multicast groups:                64
   number of directly-connected IPv6 addresses:    74
   number of indirect IPv6 unicast routes:         32
   number of IPv4 policy based routing aces:       0
   number of IPv4/MAC qos aces:                    0.5K
   number of IPv4/MAC security aces:               0.875k
   number of IPv6 policy based routing aces:       0
   number of IPv6 qos aces:                        0
   number of IPv6 security aces:                   60
 Switch#
```

You can configure a switch to operate based on other SDM templates by using the following global configuration command:

```
Switch(config)# sdm prefer template
```

The switch must then be rebooted for the new template to take effect. Tables 2-3 and 2-4 list the template types along with the number of entries allowed in each memory partition. The two shaded rows represent the CAM and FIB table spaces. To get a feel for the SDM templates, notice which function is favored in each of the template types. The unicast MAC addresses and unicast routes rows are highlighted as examples.

Do not worry about memorizing the tables and their contents; instead, you should know how to display the current template and how to configure a new one.

Table 2-3   *IPv4 SDM Templates and Memory Partitions*

Memory Partition	SDM Template Type Keyword			
	default	access	vlan	routing
Unicast MAC Addresses	6 K	4 K	12 K	3 K
IPv4 IGMP Groups + Multicast Routes	1 K	1 K	1 K	1 K
IPv4 Unicast Routes	8 K	6 K	0	11 K
Directly Connected IPv4 Hosts	6 K	4 K	0	3 K
Indirect IPv4 Routes	2 K	2 K	0	8 K
IPv4 Policy-Based Routing ACEs	0	0.5 K	0	0.5 K
IPv4/MAC QoS ACEs	0.5 K	0.5 K	0.5 K	0.375 K
IPv4/MAC Security ACEs	1 K	2 K	1 K	1 K
VLANs	1 K	1 K	1 K	1 K

Table 2-4   *Dual IPv4-IPv6 SDM Templates and Memory Partitions*

Memory Partition	SDM Template Type Keyword			
	dual-ipv4-and-ipv6			indirect-ipv4-and-ipv6
	default	vlan	routing	
Unicast MAC Addresses	2 K	8 K	1.5 K	2 K
IPv4 IGMP Groups + Multicast Routes	1 K	1 K IGMP0 multicast	1 K	1 K
IPv4 Unicast Routes	3 K	0	2.7 K	4 K
Directly Connected IPv4 Hosts	2 K	0	1.5 K	2 K

Memory Partition	SDM Template Type Keyword			
	dual-ipv4-and-ipv6			indirect-ipv4-and-ipv6
	default	vlan	routing	
Indirect IPv4 Routes	1 K	0	1.2 K	2 K
IPv6 Multicast Groups	1 K	1 K	1 K	1 K
Directly Connected IPv6 Addresses	2 K	0	1.5 K	2 K
Indirect IPv6 Unicast Routes	1 K	0.125 K	1.25 K	3 K
IPv4 Policy-Based Routing ACEs	0	0	0.25 K	0.125 K
IPv4/MAC QoS ACEs	0.5 K	0.5 K	0.5 K	0.5 K
IPv4/MAC Security ACEs	1 K	1 K	0..5 K	0.625 K
IPv6 Policy-Based Routing ACEs	0	0	0.25 K	0.125 K
IPv6 QoS ACEs	0.5 K	0.5 K	0.5 K	0.125 K
IPv6 Security ACEs	0.5 K	0.5 K	0.5 K	0.125 K

Exam Preparation Tasks

Review All Key Topics

Review the most important topics in the chapter, noted with the Key Topic icon in the outer margin of the page. Table 2-5 lists a reference of these key topics and the page numbers on which each is found.

Key
Topic

Table 2-5 *Key Topics for Chapter 2*

Key Topic Element	Description	Page Number
Paragraph	Discusses collision domain	32
Paragraph	Discusses flooding and unknown unicast flooding	34
List	Describes topology-based switching	37
Paragraph	Discusses the CAM table	40
Paragraph	Explains TCAM operation	43

Complete Tables and Lists from Memory

There are no memory tables in this chapter.

Define Key Terms

Define the following key terms from this chapter, and check your answers in the glossary:

collision domain, flooding, unknown unicast flooding, CEF, FIB, CAM, TCAM, SDM

Use Command Reference to Check Your Memory

This section includes the most important configuration and EXEC commands covered in this chapter. It might not be necessary to memorize the complete syntax of every command, but you should remember the basic keywords that are needed.

To test your memory of the CAM-related commands, cover the right side of Table 2-6 with a piece of paper, read the description on the left side, and then see how much of the command you can remember.

Remember that the CCNP exam focuses on practical or hands-on skills that are used by a networking professional. For most of the skills covered in this chapter, remember that the commands always involve the keywords **mac address-table**.

Table 2-6   *Commands Used to Monitor and Manipulate the CAM Table*

Task	Command
Find the location of a specific MAC address.	**show mac address-table dynamic address** *mac-address*
Display all MAC addresses learned on a specific interface.	**show mac address-table dynamic interface** *type number*
Display the current CAM table size.	**show mac address-table count**
Enter a static CAM table entry.	**mac address-table static** *mac-address* **vlan** *vlan-id* {**drop** | **interface** *type number*}
Clear a CAM entry.	**clear mac address-table dynamic** [**address** *mac-address* | **interface** *type number* | **vlan** *vlan-id*]
Display TCAM utilization.	**show platform tcam utilization**
Display the current memory template.	**show sdm prefer**
Configure a preferred memory template.	**sdm prefer** *template*

This chapter covers the following topics that you need to master for the CCNP SWITCH exam:

■ **Ethernet Concepts:** This section discusses the concepts and technology behind various forms of Ethernet media.

■ **Connecting Switches and Devices:** This section discusses the physical cabling and connectivity used with Catalyst switches.

■ **Switch Port Configuration:** This section covers the configuration steps and commands needed to use Ethernet, Fast Ethernet, and Gigabit and 10-Gigabit Ethernet switch ports in a network.

■ **Discovering Connected Devices:** This section explains the protocols that can be used to automatically discover other devices that are connected to a Catalyst switch.

■ **Using Power over Ethernet:** This section discusses how a Catalyst switch can provide power to operate devices such as wireless access points and Cisco IP phones.

CHAPTER 3

Switch Port Configuration

This chapter presents the various Ethernet network technologies used to establish switched connections within the campus network. You can connect a switch to an end device such as a PC or to another switch. The chapter also details the switch commands required for configuring and troubleshooting Ethernet LAN ports.

"Do I Know This Already?" Quiz

The "Do I Know This Already?" quiz allows you to assess whether you should read this entire chapter thoroughly or jump to the "Exam Preparation Tasks" section. If you are in doubt based on your answers to these questions or your own assessment of your knowledge of the topics, read the entire chapter. Table 3-1 outlines the major headings in this chapter and the "Do I Know This Already?" quiz questions that go with them. You can find the answers in Appendix A, "Answers to the 'Do I Know This Already?' Quizzes."

Table 3-1 *"Do I Know This Already?" Foundation Topics Section-to-Question Mapping*

Foundation Topics Section	Questions Covered in This Section
Ethernet Concepts	1–6
Connecting Switches and Devices	7
Switch Port Configuration	8–10
Discovering Connected Devices	11–12
Using Power over Ethernet	13–14

1. What does the IEEE 802.3 standard define?

   a. Spanning Tree Protocol

   b. Token Ring

   c. Ethernet

   d. Switched Ethernet

2. At what layer are traditional 10-Mbps Ethernet, Fast Ethernet, and Gigabit Ethernet the same?

    a. Layer 1

    b. Layer 2

    c. Layer 3

    d. Layer 4

3. At what layer are traditional 10-Mbps Ethernet, Fast Ethernet, and Gigabit Ethernet different?

    a. Layer 1

    b. Layer 2

    c. Layer 3

    d. Layer 4

4. What is the maximum cable distance for an Ethernet, Fast Ethernet, and Gigabit Ethernet connection over unshielded twisted pair cabling?

    a. 100 feet

    b. 100 m

    c. 328 m

    d. 500 m

5. Ethernet autonegotiation determines which of the following?

    a. Spanning-tree mode

    b. Duplex mode

    c. Quality of service mode

    d. MAC address learning

    e. Device discovery

6. Which of the following cannot be automatically determined and set if the far end of a connection does not support autonegotiation?

    a. Link speed

    b. Link duplex mode

    c. Link media type

    d. MAC address

7. Which of these is not a standard type of gigabit interface converter (GBIC) or small form factor pluggable (SFP) module?

   a. 1000BASE-LX/LH

   b. 1000BASE-T

   c. 1000BASE-FX

   d. 1000BASE-ZX

8. Assume that you have just entered the **configure terminal** command. You want to configure the speed and duplex of the first 10/100/1000 twisted-pair Ethernet interface on the first Cisco Catalyst switch stack member to 1-Gbps full-duplex mode. Which one of these commands should you enter first?

   a. speed 1000 mbps

   b. speed 1000

   c. interface gigabitethernet 1/0/1

   d. interface gigabit ethernet 1/0/1

   e. duplex full

9. If a switch port is in the errdisable state, what is the first thing you should do?

   a. Reload the switch.

   b. Use the **clear errdisable port** command.

   c. Use the **shut and no shut interface-configuration** commands.

   d. Determine the cause of the problem.

10. Which of the following **show interface** output information can you use to diagnose a switch port problem?

   a. Port state

   b. Port speed

   c. Input errors

   d. Collisions

   e. All answers are correct

11. Which one of the following is a standards-based protocol that can be used to discover and collect information about connected devices?

   a. CDP

   b. STP

   c. ICMP

   d. LLDP

12. Which one of the following statements is true about a Catalyst switch?

    a. Neither CDP nor LLDP are enabled by default.

    b. CDP is enabled and LLDP is disabled by default.

    c. CDP is disabled and LLDP is enabled by default.

    d. Both CDP and LLDP are enabled by default.

13. For a Catalyst switch to offer Power over Ethernet to a device, what must occur?

    a. Nothing; power always is enabled on a port.

    b. The switch must detect that the device needs inline power.

    c. The device must send a CDP message asking for power.

    d. The device must send an LLDP message asking for power.

    e. The switch is configured to turn on power to the port.

14. Which one of these commands can enable Power over Ethernet to a switch interface?

    a. inline power enable

    b. inline power on

    c. power inline on

    d. power inline auto

Foundation Topics

Ethernet Concepts

This section reviews the varieties of Ethernet and their application in a campus network. The bandwidth requirements for a network segment are determined by the types of applications in use, the traffic flows within the network, and the size of the user community served. Ethernet scales to support increasing bandwidths; the Ethernet medium should be chosen to match the need at each point in the campus network. As network bandwidth requirements grow, you can scale the links between access, distribution, and core layers to match the load.

Ethernet Overview

Ethernet is a LAN technology based on the Institute of Electrical and Electronics Engineers (IEEE) 802.3 standard. Ethernet offers a specific bandwidth between end users. In its most basic form, Ethernet is a shared medium that becomes both a collision and a broadcast domain. As the number of users on the shared media increases, so does the probability that a user is trying to transmit data at any given time. When one user transmits at about the same time as another, a *collision* occurs. In other words, both users cannot transmit data at the same time if they both are sharing the same network media.

Ethernet is based on the carrier sense multiple access collision detect (CSMA/CD) technology, which requires that transmitting stations back off for a random period of time when a collision occurs. If a station must wait its turn to transmit, it cannot transmit and receive at the same time. This is called *half-duplex* operation.

The more crowded an Ethernet segment becomes, the number of stations likely to be transmitting at a given time increases. Imagine standing in a crowded room trying to tell a story. Instead of attempting to talk over the crowd, you stop and politely wait while other people talk. The more people there are in the room, the more difficult talking becomes. Likewise, as an Ethernet segment becomes more crowded, it becomes more inefficient.

Ethernet switching addresses this problem by breaking a shared segment up into many individual segments. An Ethernet switch can allocate a dedicated amount of bandwidth to each of its interfaces or ports. The resulting increased network performance occurs by reducing the number of users connected to an Ethernet segment. In effect, collisions are less probable and the collision domain is reduced in size. Ideally, each switch port is connected to only one end user, which in turn, limits the collision domain to that single switch port.

Because switched Ethernet can remove the possibility of collisions, stations do not have to listen to each other to take a turn transmitting on the wire. Instead, stations can operate in full-duplex mode—transmitting and receiving simultaneously. Full-duplex mode further increases network performance by effectively doubling the net throughput on each switch port.

Scaling Ethernet

The original Ethernet standard was based on a bandwidth of 10 Mbps per network segment. Over time, networking technology has evolved to offer higher amounts of bandwidth. Instead of requiring campuses to invest in a completely new technology to leverage ever increasing bandwidth, the networking industry has developed higher-speed generations of Ethernet that are based on existing Ethernet standards.

Typically, each generation of Ethernet offers a ten-fold bandwidth improvement. Even so, the Ethernet cabling schemes, CSMA/CD operation, and all upper-layer protocol operations are maintained with each generation. The net result is the same data link Media Access Control (MAC) layer (OSI Layer 2) merged with a new physical layer (OSI Layer 1). Table 3-2 lists several generations and bandwidths that are included in the IEEE 802.3 standard.

Table 3-2 *Generations of Ethernet*

Ethernet Technology	Segment Bandwidth
Ethernet	10 Mbps
Fast Ethernet	100 Mbps
Gigabit Ethernet	1 Gbps
10-Gigabit Ethernet	10 Gbps
40-Gigabit Ethernet	40 Gbps
100-Gigabit Ethernet	100 Gbps

The following sections provide a brief overview of the successive Ethernet technologies and their cabling requirements.

Fast Ethernet

Fast Ethernet supports a maximum of 100 Mbps untwisted pair (UTP) or fiber-optic cabling. Table 3-3 lists the specifications for Fast Ethernet that define the media types and distances. Notice that UTP cabling is limited to 100 meters, which is identical to the original 10 Mbps Ethernet.

Table 3-3 *Cabling Specifications for Fast Ethernet*

Technology	Wiring Type	Pairs	Cable Length
100BASE-TX	EIA/TIA Category 5 UTP	2	100 m
100BASE-T2	EIA/TIA Category 3, 4, 5 UTP	2	100 m
100BASE-T4	EIA/TIA Category 3, 4, 5 UTP	4	100 m

Technology	Wiring Type	Pairs	Cable Length
100BASE-FX	Multimode fiber (MMF); 62.5-micron core, 125-micron outer cladding (62.5/125)	1	400 m half duplex or 2000 m full duplex
	Single-mode fiber (SMF)	1	10 km

Cisco provides one additional capability to Fast Ethernet, which allows several Fast Ethernet links to be bundled together for increased throughput. Fast EtherChannel (FEC) allows two to eight full-duplex Fast Ethernet links to act as a single physical link, for 400- to 1600-Mbps duplex bandwidth. This technology is described in greater detail in Chapter 10, "Aggregating Switch Links."

Gigabit Ethernet

Key Topic

You can scale a Fast Ethernet network by an additional order of magnitude with Gigabit Ethernet (which supports 1000 Mbps or 1 Gbps) using the same IEEE 802.3 Ethernet frame format as before. However, the physical layer has been modified to increase data-transmission speeds. Two technologies were merged to gain the benefits of each: the IEEE 802.3 Ethernet standard and the American National Standards Institute (ANSI) X3T11 Fibre Channel. IEEE 802.3 provided the foundation of frame format, CSMA/CD, full duplex, and other Ethernet characteristics. Fibre Channel provided a base of high-speed application-specific integrated circuits (ASICs), optical components, and encoding/decoding and serialization mechanisms.

Gigabit Ethernet supports several cabling types, referred to as 1000BASE-X. Table 3-4 lists the cabling specifications for each type.

Table 3-4 *Gigabit Ethernet Cabling and Distance Limitations*

GE Type	Wiring Type	Pairs	Cable Length
1000BASE-CX	Shielded twisted pair (STP)	1	25 m
1000BASE-T	EIA/TIA Category 5 UTP	4	100 m
1000BASE-SX	Multimode fiber (MMF) with 62.5-micron core; 850-nm laser	1	275 m
	MMF with 50-micron core; 850-nm laser	1	550 m
1000BASE-LX/LH	MMF with 62.5-micron core; 1300-nm laser	1	550 m
	MMF with 50-micron core; 1300-nm laser	1	550 m
	SMF with 9-micron core; 1300-nm laser	1	10 km
1000BASE-ZX	SMF with 9-micron core; 1550-nm laser	1	70 km
	SMF with 8-micron core; 1550-nm laser	1	100 km

Most Gigabit Ethernet switch ports used between switches are fixed at 1000 Mbps. However, other switch ports can support a fallback to Fast or Legacy Ethernet speeds. The "Gigabit over copper" solution that the 1000BASE-T media provides can be autonegotiated between end nodes to use the highest common speed—10 Mbps, 100 Mbps, or 1000 Mbps. These ports are often called *10/100/1000 ports* to denote the triple speed.

Cisco has extended the concept of Fast EtherChannel to bundle several Gigabit Ethernet links to act as a single physical connection. With Gigabit EtherChannel (GEC), two to eight full-duplex Gigabit Ethernet connections can be aggregated, for a single logical link of up to 16-Gbps throughput. Link aggregation and the EtherChannel technology are described further in Chapter 6.

10-Gigabit Ethernet

To meet the demand for aggregating many Gigabit Ethernet links over a single connection, 10-Gigabit Ethernet was developed. Again, the Layer 2 characteristics of Ethernet have been preserved; the familiar 802.3 frame format and size, along with the MAC protocol, remain unchanged.

The 10-Gigabit Ethernet, also known as *10GE*, and the IEEE 802.3ae standard differ from their predecessors only at the physical layer (PHY); 10GE operates only at full duplex. The standard defines several different transceivers that can be used as Physical Media Dependent (PMD) interfaces. These are classified into the following:

- **LAN PHY:** Interconnects switches in a campus network, predominantly in the core layer

- **WAN PHY:** Interfaces with existing synchronous optical network (SONET) or synchronous digital hierarchy (SDH) networks that were typically found in metropolitan-area networks (MAN)

The PMD interfaces also have a common labeling scheme, much as Gigabit Ethernet does. Whereas Gigabit Ethernet uses 1000BASE-X to indicate the media type, 10-Gigabit Ethernet uses 10GBASE-X. Table 3-5 lists the different PMDs defined in the standard, along with the type of fiber and distance limitations. All the fiber-optic PMDs can be used as either a LAN or a WAN PHY, except for the 10GBASE-LX4, which is only a LAN PHY. Be aware that the extra-long wavelength PMDs carry a significantly greater expense than the others.

Table 3-5   *10-Gigabit Ethernet PMD Types and Characteristics*

PMD Type*	Fiber Medium	Maximum Distance
10GBASE-SR/SW (850 nm serial)	MMF: 50 micron	66m
	MMF: 50 micron (2GHz* km modal bandwidth)	300m
	MMF: 62.5 micron	33m

PMD Type*	Fiber Medium	Maximum Distance
10GBASE-LR/LW (1310 nm serial)	SMF: 9 micron	10 km
10GBASE-ER/EW(1550 nm serial)	SMF: 9 micron	40 km
10GBASE-LX4/LW4 (1310 nm WWDM)	MMF: 50 micron	300 m
	MMF: 62.5 micron	300 m
	SMF: 9 micron	10 km
10GBASE-CX4	Copper: CX4 with Infiniband connectors	15 m

Transceiver types are denoted by a two-letter suffix. The first letter specifies the wavelength used: S = short, L = long, E = extra-long wavelength. The second letter specifies the PHY type: R = LAN PHY, W = WAN PHY. For LX4 and LW4, L refers to a long wavelength, X and W refer to the coding used, and 4 refers to the number of wavelengths transmitted. WWDM is wide-wavelength division multiplexing.

Cisco Catalyst switches supported 10-Gigabit Ethernet PMDs in the form of XENPAK, X2, and SFP+ transceivers. Generally, the X2 form factor is smaller than the XENPAK, and the SFP+ is smaller still, allowing more port density on a switch module.

For the most current switch compatibility listing, refer to the "Cisco 10-Gigabit Ethernet Transceiver Modules Compatibility Matrix" document at http://www.cisco.com/en/US/docs/interfaces_modules/transceiver_modules/compatibility/matrix/OL_6974.html.

Beyond 10-Gigabit Ethernet

With 10-Gigabit Ethernet links extending further toward the access layer, even higher bandwidth is needed to aggregate traffic in the distribution and core layers, as well as in the data center. Some Catalyst switches now offer 40-Gigabit Ethernet and 100-Gigabit Ethernet capabilities.

You have already learned that Ethernet bandwidth increases ten-fold with each new generation. For example, it is easy to see the progression from 1 Gbps to 10 Gbps to 100 Gbps, but 40 Gbps might seem like an odd multiple. The 40-Gigabit Ethernet standard bonds four individual 10-Gigabit Ethernet fiber optic links together using a single QSFP+ (quad SFP+) media module. 100 Gigabit Ethernet uses similar schemes to bond multiple channels or "lanes" together to leverage much greater bandwidth. In fact, both 40 and 100 Gigabit Ethernet are defined by the same 802.3ba standard.

Tip   40- and 100-Gigabit Ethernet are beyond the scope of the CCNP SWITCH course and exam.

Duplex Operation over Ethernet Links

Recall that when multiple devices share an Ethernet segment, they must cooperate with each other by not transmitting at the same time. This half-duplex mode of communication also means that a device cannot transmit and receive at the same time. To maximize the use of a segment, only two devices should be connected to it so that each one can transmit and receive simultaneously. The natural progression to full-duplex operation effectively doubles a link's throughput.

This maximum throughput is possible only when one device (a workstation, server, router, or another switch) is connected directly to a switch port. In addition, the devices at each end of the link must both support full-duplex operation, allowing each to transmit at will without having to detect and recover from collisions.

The Fast Ethernet and Gigabit Ethernet specifications offer backward compatibility to support the lower Ethernet speeds. In the case of 100BASE-TX, switch ports often are called "10/100" ports, to denote the dual speed. Twisted pair Gigabit Ethernet ports support all three 10/100/1000 speeds. To provide support for alternate speeds, the two devices at each end of a network connection automatically can negotiate link capabilities so that they both can operate at a maximum common level. This negotiation involves detecting and selecting the highest physical layer technology (available bandwidth) and half-duplex or full-duplex operation. To properly negotiate a connection, *both* ends should be configured for autonegotiation.

Key Topic

The link speed is determined by electrical signaling so that either end of a link can determine what speed the other end is trying to use. If both ends of the link are configured to autonegotiate, they will use the highest speed that is common to them.

A link's duplex mode, however, is negotiated through an exchange of information. This means that for one end to successfully autonegotiate the duplex mode, the other end also must be set to autonegotiate. Otherwise, one end never will see duplex information from the other end and won't be capable of determining the correct mode to use. If duplex autonegotiation fails, a switch port always falls back to its default setting—half-duplex—because it offers the safety of collision detection.

> **Tip**   Beware of a duplex mismatch when both ends of a link are not set for autonegotiation. During a mismatch, one end uses full duplex while the other end uses half duplex. The result is that the half-duplex station will detect a collision when both ends transmit; it will back off appropriately. The full-duplex station, however, will assume that it has the right to transmit at any time. It will not stop and wait for any reason. This can cause errors on the link and poor response times between the stations.

Autonegotiation selects port speed and duplex mode according to a series of priorities. If both devices can support more than one speed, they will agree to use the highest speed available. Likewise, full-duplex mode will be chosen over half-duplex. As an example, if two devices can support 10/100/1000, both devices will select 1000 (1 Gbps) with full-duplex, if possible.

To ensure proper configuration at both ends of a link, Cisco recommends that the appropriate values for transmission speed and duplex mode be configured manually on switch ports. This precludes any possibility that one end of the link will change its settings, resulting in an unusable connection. If you manually set the switch port, do not forget to manually set the device on the other end of the link accordingly. Otherwise, a speed or duplex mismatch between the two devices might occur.

Tip   Speed and duplex mode can be configured or negotiated only on switch ports that support twisted-pair cabling. Fixed speed Gigabit and 10-Gigabit Ethernet ports always use full-duplex mode.

Connecting Switches and Devices

Switch deployment in a network involves two steps: physical connectivity and switch configuration. This section describes the connections and cabling requirements for devices in a switched network.

Ethernet Port Cables and Connectors

Catalyst switches support a variety of network connections, including all forms of Ethernet. In addition, Catalyst switches support several types of cabling, including UTP and optical fiber.

All Catalyst switch families support 10/100/1000 autosensing for Gigabit Ethernet. These ports use RJ-45 connectors on UTP cabling to complete the connections. UTP cabling is arranged so that RJ-45 pins 1 and 2, 3 and 6, 4 and 5, and 7 and 8 form four twisted pairs. These pairs connect straight through to the far end.

Gigabit Ethernet connections take a different approach by providing modular connectivity options. Catalyst switch ports have standardized rectangular openings that can accept small form factor pluggable (SFP) modules. The SFP modules provide the media personality for the port so that various cable media can connect. In this way, the switch chassis is completely modular and requires no major change to accept a new media type. Instead, the appropriate module is hot-swappable and is plugged into the switch to support the new media. SFP modules can use LC and MT-RJ fiber-optic and RJ-45 UTP connectors and are available for the following Gigabit Ethernet media:

- **1000BASE-SX:** Short-wavelength connectivity using SC fiber connectors and MMF for distances up to 550 m (1804 feet).

- **1000BASE-LX/LH:** Long-wavelength/long-haul connectivity using SC fiber connectors and either MMF or single-mode fiber (SMF); MMF can be used for distances up to 550 m (1804 feet), and SMF can be used for distances up to 10 km (32,810 feet). MMF requires a special mode-conditioning cable for fiber distances less than 100 m (328 feet) or greater than 300 m (984 feet). This keeps the GBIC from overdriving the far-end receiver on a short cable and lessens the effect of differential mode delay on a long cable.

■ **1000BASE-ZX:** Extended-distance connectivity using SC fiber connectors and SMF; works for distances up to 70 km, and even to 100 km when used with premium-grade SMF.

■ **1000BASE-T:** Sports an RJ-45 connector for fixed-speed four-pair UTP cabling; works for distances up to 100 m (328 feet).

10-Gigabit Ethernet switch ports support the following rectangular X2 and SFP+ media modules:

■ **10GBASE-CX4:** Copper connectivity up to 15 m

■ **10GBASE-SR:** Short-reach connectivity using 62.5 or 50 micron MMF for distances up to 33 m or 300 m, respectively

■ **10GBASE-LRM:** Long-reach multimode connectivity using 62.5 or 50 micron MMF for distances up to 220 m

■ **10GBASE-LX4:** Provides connectivity using 62.5 or 50 micron MMF for distances up to 300 m

■ **10GBASE-LR:** Long-reach connectivity using SMF for distances up to 10 km

■ **10GBASE-ER:** Extended-reach connectivity using SMF for distances up to 40 km

40- and 100-Gigabit Ethernet both use unique fiber optical modules that leverage multiple fibers simultaneously. These technologies are beyond the scope of the SWITCH exam.

> **Caution**   The fiber-based modules could produce invisible laser radiation from the transmit connector. Therefore, always keep unused connectors covered with the rubber plugs, and do not ever look directly into the connectors.

Switch Port Configuration

You can configure the individual ports on a switch with various information and settings, as detailed in the following sections.

Selecting Ports to Configure

Before you can modify port settings, you must select one or more switch ports. Even though they have traditionally been called *ports*, Catalyst switches running the Cisco IOS Software refer to them as *interfaces*.

To select a single switch port, enter the following command in global configuration mode:

```
Switch(config)# interface type member/module/number
```

A physical port is identified by its Ethernet type (**fastethernet, gigabitethernet, tengiga-bitethernet**), the stack member or chassis slot number, the module where it is located, and the port number within the module. Most switches do not have individual modules within each stack member or chassis, so the module number is usually 0. As an example, the Gigabit Ethernet port numbered 14 on the first switch in a stack is selected for configuration using the following command:

```
Switch(config)# interface gigabitethernet 1/0/14
```

Naturally, you can select and configure multiple interfaces in this fashion, one at a time. If you need to make many configuration changes for each interface in a 48-port switch or in several switches in a stack, however, this can get very tedious. The Catalyst IOS Software also allows multiple interfaces to be selected in a single pass through the **interface range** configuration command. After you select the range, any interface configuration commands entered are applied to each of the interfaces in the range.

To select several arbitrary ports for a common configuration setting, you can identify them as a "range" entered as a list. All port numbers and the commas that separate them must be separated with spaces. Use the following command in global configuration mode:

```
Switch(config)# interface range type member/module/number [, type member/module/
number ...]
```

For example, to select interfaces Gigabit Ethernet 1/0/3, 1/0/7, 1/0/9, and 1/0/48 for configuration, you could use this command:

```
Switch(config)# interface range gigabitethernet 1/0/3 , gigabitethernet 1/0/7,
gigabitethernet 1/0/9 , gigabitethernet 1/0/48
```

You also can select a continuous range of ports, from a beginning interface number to an ending interface number. Enter the interface type, stack member, and module, followed by the beginning and ending port number separated by a dash with spaces. Use this command in global configuration mode:

```
Switch(config)# interface range type member/module/first-number - last-number
```

For example, you could select all 48 Gigabit Ethernet interfaces on switch stack member 1 with the following command:

```
Switch(config)# interface range gigabitethernet 1/0/1 - 48
```

Finally, you sometimes need to make configuration changes to several groups or ranges of ports at the same time. You can define a macro that contains a list of interfaces or ranges of interfaces or both. Then, you can invoke the interface-range macro just before configuring the port settings. This applies the port settings to each interface that is identified by the macro. The steps for defining and applying this macro are as follows:

Step 1.   Define the macro name and specify as many lists and ranges of interfaces as needed. The command syntax is open ended but follows the list and range syntax of the interface range commands defined previously:

```
Switch(config)# define interface-range macro-name type member/module/
number [,   type member/module/ number ...] [type member/module/first-
number - last-number] [...]
```

Step 2.   Invoke the macro called *macro-name* just as you would with a regular interface, just before entering any interface-configuration commands:

```
Switch(config)# interface range macro macro-name
```

Suppose, for example, that you need to configure Gigabit Ethernet 2/0/1, 2/0/3 through
2/0/5, 3/0/1, 3/0/10, and 3/0/32 through 3/0/48 with a set of identical interface configurations. You could use the following commands to define and apply a macro, respectively:

```
Switch(config)# define interface-range MyGroup gig 2/0/1 , gig 2/0/3 - 2/0/5 , gig
3/0/1 , gig 3/0/10, gig 3/0/32 - 3/0/48
Switch(config)# interface range macro MyGroup
```

Remember to surround any commas and hyphens with spaces when you enter **interface
range** commands.

Identifying Ports

You can add a text description to a switch port's configuration to help identify it. This
description is meant as a comment field only, as a record of port use or other unique
information. The port description is included when displaying the switch configuration
and interface information.

To assign a comment or description to a port, enter the following command in interface
configuration mode:

```
Switch(config-if)# description description-string
```

The description string can have embedded spaces between words, if needed. To remove a
description, use the no description interface-configuration command.

As an example, interface Gigabit Ethernet 2/0/11 is labeled with "Printer in Bldg A,
room 213":

```
Switch(config)# interface gigabitethernet 2/0/11
Switch(config-if)# description Printer in Bldg A, room 213
```

Port Speed

You can assign a specific speed to multiple-speed switch ports through interface configuration commands. Use the **speed** command to set a speed of 10, 100, 1000, or
Autonegotiate (the default).

> **Note**   If a 10/100 or a 10/100/1000 port is assigned a speed of Auto, both its speed and
> duplex mode will be negotiated.

To specify the port speed on a particular Ethernet port, use the following interface-configuration command:

```
Switch(config-if)# speed {10 | 100 | 1000 | auto}
```

Port Duplex Mode

You also can assign a specific duplex mode to Ethernet-based switch ports. A port can operate in half-duplex, full-duplex, or autonegotiated mode. Autonegotiation is allowed only on UTP 10/100 and 10/100/1000 ports. In this mode, the port participates in a negotiation by attempting full-duplex operation first and then half-duplex operation if full-duplex operation is not successful. The autonegotiation process repeats whenever the link status changes. Be sure to set both ends of a link to the same speed and duplex settings to eliminate any chance that the two ends will be mismatched.

To set the link mode on a switch port, enter the following command in interface configuration mode:

```
Switch(config-if)# duplex {auto | full | half}
```

For instance, you could use the commands in Example 3-1 to configure 10/100/1000 interfaces Gigabit Ethernet 3/0/1 for autonegotiation and 3/0/2 for 100-Mbps full duplex (no autonegotiation).

Example 3-1 *Configuring the Link Mode on a Switch Port*

```
Switch(config)# interface gigabitethernet 3/0/1
Switch(config-if)# speed auto
Switch(config-if)# duplex auto
Switch(config-if)# interface gigabitethernet 3/0/2
Switch(config-if)# speed 100
Switch(config-if)# duplex full
```

Managing Error Conditions on a Switch Port

A network-management application can be used to detect a serious error condition on a switch port. A switch can be polled periodically so that its port error counters can be examined to see whether an error condition has occurred. If so, an alert can be issued so that someone can take action to correct the problem.

Catalyst switches can detect error conditions automatically, without any further help. If a serious error occurs on a switch port, that port can be shut down automatically until someone manually enables the port again, or until a predetermined time has elapsed.

Detecting Error Conditions

By default, a Catalyst switch detects an error condition on every switch port for every possible cause. If an error condition is detected, the switch port is put into the "errdisable" state and is disabled. You can tune this behavior on a global basis so that only certain causes trigger any port being disabled. Use the following command in global configuration mode, where the **no** keyword is added to disable the specified cause:

```
Switch(config)# [no] errdisable detect cause [all | cause-name]
```

You can repeat this command to enable or disable more than one cause. One of the following triggers the errdisable state:

- **all:** Detects every possible cause

- **arp-inspection:** Detects errors with dynamic ARP inspection

- **bpduguard:** Detects when a spanning-tree bridge protocol data unit (BPDU) is received on a port configured for STP PortFast

- **dhcp-rate-limit:** Detects an error with DHCP snooping

- **dtp-flap:** Detects when trunking encapsulation is changing from one type to another

- **gbic-invalid:** Detects the presence of an invalid GBIC or SFP module

- **inline-power:** Detects an error with offering PoE inline power

- **l2ptguard:** Detects an error with Layer 2 Protocol Tunneling

- **link-flap:** Detects when the port link state is "flapping" between the up and down states

- **loopback:** Detects when an interface has been looped back

- **pagp-flap:** Detects when an EtherChannel bundle's ports no longer have consistent configurations

- **pppoe-ia-rate-limit:** Detects errors with PPPoE Intermediate Agent rate limiting

- **psecure-violation:** Detects conditions that trigger port security configured on a port

- **psp:** Detects an error related to protocol storm protection

- **security-violation:** Detects errors related to 802.1X security

- **sfp-config-mismatch:** Detects errors related to SFP configuration mismatches

- **small-frame:** Detects errors when VLAN-tagged packets are too small and arrive above a certain rate

- **storm-control:** Detects when a storm control theshhold has been exceeded on a port

- **udld:** Detects when a link is seen to be unidirectional (data passing in only one direction)

Automatically Recover from Error Conditions

By default, ports put into the errdisable state must be re-enabled manually. This is done by issuing the **shutdown** command in interface configuration mode, followed by the **no shutdown** command. Before you reenable a port from the errdisable condition, you should always determine the cause of the problem so that the errdisable condition does not occur again.

You can decide to have a switch automatically reenable an errdisabled port if it is more important to keep the link up until the problem can be resolved. To automatically reenable an errdisabled port, you first must specify the errdisable causes that can be reenabled. Use the following command in global configuration mode, with a *cause-name* from the preceding list:

```
Switch(config)# errdisable recovery cause [all | cause-name]
```

If any errdisable causes are configured for automatic recovery, the errdisabled port stays down for 300 seconds (5 minutes), by default. To change the recovery timer, use the following command in global configuration mode:

```
Switch(config)# errdisable recovery interval seconds
```

You can set the interval from 30 to 86,400 seconds (24 hours).

For example, you could use the following commands to configure all switch ports to be reenabled automatically in 1 hour after a PoE error has been detected:

```
Switch(config)# errdisable recovery cause inline-power
Switch(config)# errdisable recovery interval 3600
```

Remember that the errdisable causes and automatic recovery are configured globally; the settings apply to all switch ports.

Enable and Use the Switch Port

If the port is not enabled or activated automatically, use **the no shutdown** interface-configuration command. To view a port's current speed and duplex state, use the **show interfaces** command. You can see a brief summary of all interface states with the **show interfaces status** command.

Troubleshooting Port Connectivity

Suppose that you are experiencing problems with a switch port. How would you troubleshoot it? The following sections cover a few common troubleshooting techniques.

Looking for the Port State

Use the **show interfaces** EXEC command to see complete information about the switch port. The port's current state is given in the first line of output, as in Example 3-2.

Example 3-2 *Determining Port State Information*

```
Switch# show interfaces gigabitethernet 1/0/1
GigabitEthernet1/0/1 is up, line protocol is up
  Hardware is Gigabit Ethernet, address is 0009.b7ee.9801 (bia 0009.b7ee.9801)
  MTU 1500 bytes, BW 10000 Kbit, DLY 1000 usec,
     reliability 255/255, txload 1/255, rxload 1/255
```

The first up tells the state of the port's physical or data link layer. If this is shown as down, the link is physically disconnected or a link cannot be detected. The second state, given as line protocol is up, shows the Layer 2 status. If the state is given as err-disabled, the switch has detected a serious error condition on this port and has automatically disabled it.

To quickly see a list of states for all switch ports, use the **show interface status** EXEC command. Likewise, you can see a list of all ports in the errdisable state (and the cause) by using the **show interface status err-disabled** EXEC command.

Looking for Speed and Duplex Mismatches

Key Topic

If a user notices slow response time or low throughput on a 10/100 or 10/100/1000 switch port, the problem could be a mismatch of the port speed or duplex mode between the switch and the host. This is particularly common when one end of the link is set to autonegotiate the link settings and the other end is not.

Use the **show interface** command for a specific interface and look for any error counts that are greater than 0. For example, in the following output in Example 3-3, the switch port is set to autonegotiate the speed and duplex mode. It has decided on 100 Mbps at half duplex. Notice that there are many *runts* (packets that were truncated before they were fully received) and input errors. These are symptoms that a setting mismatch exists between the two ends of the link.

Example 3-3 *Determining Link Speed and Duplex Mode*

```
Switch# show interfaces gigabitethernet 1/0/13
GigabitEthernet1/0/13 is up, line protocol is up
  Hardware is Gigabit Ethernet, address is 00d0.589c.3e8d (bia 00d0.589c.3e8d)
  MTU 1500 bytes, BW 1000000 Kbit, DLY 10 usec,
     reliability 255/255, txload 1/255, rxload 1/255
  Encapsulation ARPA, loopback not set
  Keepalive not set
  Auto-duplex (Half), Auto Speed (100), media type is 10/100/1000BaseTX
ARP type: ARPA, ARP
    Timeout 04:00:00
 Last input never, output 00:00:01, output hang never
  Last clearing of "show interface" counters never
  Queueing strategy: fifo
  Output queue 0/40, 0 drops; input queue 0/75, 0 drops
  5 minute input rate 0 bits/sec, 0 packets/sec
  5 minute output rate 81000 bits/sec, 49 packets/sec
     500867 packets input, 89215950 bytes
     Received 12912 broadcasts, 374879 runts, 0 giants, 0 throttles
     374879 input errors, 0 CRC, 0 frame, 0 overrun, 0 ignored
     0 watchdog, 0 multicast
     0 input packets with dribble condition detected
     89672388 packets output, 2205443729 bytes, 0 underruns
```

```
0 output errors, 0 collisions, 3 interface resets
0 babbles, 0 late collision, 0 deferred
0 lost carrier, 0 no carrier
0 output buffer failures, 0 output buffers swapped out
```

Because this port is autonegotiating the link speed, it must have detected an electrical signal that indicated 100 Mbps in common with the host. However, the host most likely was configured for 100 Mbps at full duplex (not autonegotiating). The switch was incapable of exchanging duplex information, so it fell back to its default of half duplex. Again, always make sure both ends of a connection are set to the same speed and duplex mode.

Discovering Connected Devices

Suppose that you have two switches and connect a cable between them. Through your knowledge of the physical cabling, you know that the switches are connected and that they are directly connected neighbors. If you are not onsite with the equipment, you might not have an easy way to discover or verify how the switches are connected or even if they are connected at all. This situation might grow even more frustrating in a large network with many devices, except that you have a couple of handy discovery tools at your disposal. A switch can also leverage the discovery tools to learn about connected devices and their power requirements.

Cisco Discovery Protocol

The Cisco Discovery Protocol (CDP) is designed as an automated method for Cisco devices to advertise their existence to other neighboring devices. CDP is a Cisco proprietary protocol, so it is not always compatible with equipment from other manufacturers. CDP works in only one direction; advertisements are sent at regular intervals toward any listening device, but nothing is expected in return.

Key Topic

CDP advertisements are sent at the data link layer (Layer 2) so that neighboring devices can receive and understand them regardless of what upper layer protocol is in use on an interface. The advertisements are not meant to be routed or forwarded on through a network. Rather, they are received and processed by only directly connected neighbors.

Cisco devices such as routers and switches have CDP enabled by default. CDP advertisements are sent out every active interface at 60-second intervals. You can use the following command to display information about CDP advertisements that have been received by a switch:

```
Switch(config)# show cdp neighbors [type member/module/number] [detail]
```

The **show cdp neighbors** command will display a summary of CDP neighbors that have been discovered on all switch ports, as shown in Example 3-4. Switch1 has received advertisements from three other devices (a switch, a wireless access point, and an IP phone) that are connected to local interfaces. The Cisco device platform model is displayed, along with the port identifier on the connected device.

Example 3-4   *Output from the* **show cdp neighbors** *Command*

```
Switch1# show cdp neighbors
Capability Codes: R - Router, T - Trans Bridge, B - Source Route Bridge
                  S - Switch, H - Host, I - IGMP, r - Repeater, P - Phone,
                  D - Remote, C - CVTA, M - Two-port Mac Relay


Device ID         Local Intrfce   Holdtme    Capability  Platform   Port ID
Switch2           Gig 1/0/24      178              S I    WS-C3750E  Gig 2/0/24
APb838.6181.0664  Gig 1/0/23      137              R T    AIR-CAP37  Gig 0.1
SEP2893FEA2E7F4   Gig 1/0/22      159              H P M  IP Phone   Port 1
Switch1#
```

If there are many discovered neighbors, you can specify the local switch interface where a single device is connected. For example, the **show cdp neighbors gig1/0/24** command would display only the CDP entry for Switch 2.

To see all of the CDP information received in an advertisement, add the **detail** keyword. Example 3-5 lists details learned about the CDP neighbor on interface Gigabit Ethernet 1/0/22, which is a Cisco IP phone. Notice that you find out useful information such as the software release, the neighbor's duplex mode, and power requirements that have been negotiated.

Example 3-5   *Displaying Detailed CDP Neighbor Information*

```
Switch1# show cdp neighbors gig1/0/22 detail
-------------------------
Device ID: SEP2893FEA2E7F4
Entry address(es):
  IP address: 10.120.48.177
Platform: Cisco IP Phone 7942,  Capabilities: Host Phone Two-port Mac Relay
Interface: GigabitEthernet2/0/7,  Port ID (outgoing port): Port 1
Holdtime : 131 sec
Second Port Status: Down
Version :
SCCP42.9-3-1-1S
advertisement version: 2
Duplex: full
Power drawn: 6.300 Watts
Power request id: 59380, Power management id: 3
Power request levels are:6300 0 0 0 0
Management address(es):
Switch1#
```

Although CDP is enabled by default, you disable it globally with the **no cdp run** command or reenable it with the **cdp run** global configuration command. Sometimes for security reasons, you might want to disable CDP advertisements on an individual interface so that devices (and people) on the other end of a switch port cannot learn about your switch. You can control CDP operation with the following interface configuration command:

```
Switch(config)# interface type member/module/number
Switch(config-if)# [no] cdp enable
```

Link Layer Discovery Protocol

The Link Layer Discovery Protocol (LLDP) is similar to CDP, but is based on the IEEE 802.1ab standard. As a result, LLDP works in multivendor networks. It is also extensible because information is advertised by grouping attributes into Type-Length-Value (TLV) structures. For example, a device can advertise its system name with one TLV, its management address in another TLV, its port description in another TLV, its power requirements in another TLV, and so on. The LLDP advertisement then becomes a chain of various TLVs that can be interpreted by the receiving device.

LLDP also supports additional TLVs that are unique to audio-visual devices such as VoIP phones. The LLDP Media Endpoint Device (LLDP-MED) TLVs carry useful device information like a network policy with VLAN numbers and quality of service information needed for voice traffic, power management, inventory management, and physical location data.

LLDP supports the LLDP-MED TLVs by default, but it cannot send both basic and MED TLVs simultaneously on a switch port. Instead, LLDP sends only the basic TLVs to connected devices. If a switch receives LLDP-MED TLVs from a device, it will begin sending LLDP-MED TLVs back to the device.

Key Topic

By default, LLDP is globally disabled on a Catalyst switch. To see if it is currently running or not, use the **show lldp** command. You can enable or disable LLDP with the **lldp run** and **no lldp run** global configuration commands, respectively.

Use the following command to display information about LLDP advertisements that have been received by a switch.

```
Switch(config)# show lldp neighbors [type member/module/number] [detail]
```

Use the **show lldp neighbors** command to see a summary of neighbors that have been discovered. Example 3-6 lists the same three neighboring devices that were discovered with CDP in Example 3-4.

Example 3-6 *Output from the* **show lldp neighbors** *Command*

```
Switch1# show lldp neighbors
Capability codes:
    (R) Router, (B) Bridge, (T) Telephone, (C) DOCSIS Cable Device
    (W) WLAN Access Point, (P) Repeater, (S) Station, (O) Other
Device ID          Local Intf     Hold-time  Capability     Port ID
Switch2            Gi1/0/24       113        B              Gi2/0/24
APb838             Gi1/0/23       91         B,R            Gi0
SEP2893FEA2E7F4    Gi1/0/22       180        B,T            2893FEA2E7F4:P1
Total entries displayed: 2
Switch1#
```

You can specify a switch interface to display the LLDP neighbor discovered there. Add the **detail** keyword to see all of the information about a neighbor. Example 3-7 lists the detailed information about the Cisco IP phone that is connected to interface Gigabit Ethernet 1/0/22. Notice that the bottom portion of the output contains parameters that were advertised in the LLDP-MED TLVs, such as the phone's VLAN, quality of service, power configuration, and location.

Example 3-7 *Displaying Detailed LLDP Neighbor Information*

```
Switch1# show lldp neighbors gig1/0/22 detail
------------------------------------------------
Chassis id: 10.120.48.177
Port id: 2893FEA2E7F4:P1
Port Description: SW PORT
System Name: SEP2893FEA2E7F4.voice.uky.edu
System Description:
Cisco IP Phone 7942G,V6, SCCP42.9-3-1-1S
Time remaining: 124 seconds
System Capabilities: B,T
Enabled Capabilities: B,T
Management Addresses:
    IP: 10.120.48.177
Auto Negotiation - supported, enabled
Physical media capabilities:
    1000baseT(HD)
    1000baseX(FD)
    Symm, Asym Pause(FD)
    Symm Pause(FD)
Media Attachment Unit type: 16
Vlan ID: - not advertised


MED Information:
    MED Codes:
          (NP) Network Policy, (LI) Location Identification
          (PS) Power Source Entity, (PD) Power Device
          (IN) Inventory


    H/W revision: 6
    F/W revision: tnp42.8-3-1-21a.bin
    S/W revision: SCCP42.9-3-1-1S
    Serial number: FCH1414A0BA
    Manufacturer: Cisco Systems, Inc.
    Model: CP-7942G
    Capabilities: NP, PD, IN
    Device type: Endpoint Class III
    Network Policy(Voice): VLAN 837, tagged, Layer-2 priority: 5, DSCP: 46
    Network Policy(Voice Signal): VLAN 837, tagged, Layer-2 priority: 4, DSCP: 32
```

```
        PD device, Power source: Unknown, Power Priority: Unknown, Wattage: 6.3
        Location - not advertised


Total entries displayed: 1
Switch1#
```

Once LLDP is enabled, advertisements are sent and received on every switch interface. You can control LLDP operation on an interface with the following command.

```
Switch(config-if)# [no] lldp {receive | transmit}
```

> **Tip**   Why should you choose to use LLDP over CDP? LLDP is standards-based so devices from different vendors can discover each other. Switches that use LLDP can also collect detailed location information from connected devices that can be exported to a Cisco Management Services Engine (MSE). The MSE offers a location service to track devices as they join and leave a network and change locations.

Using Power over Ethernet

A Cisco wireless access point or a Cisco IP phone is like any other node on the network; it must have power to operate. Power can come from the following three sources, as illustrated in Figure 3-1.

1. An external AC adapter connected directly to the device

2. A power injector, which connects to AC power near an Ethernet switch and provides DC power over the network data cable

3. A switch capable of providing DC Power over Ethernet (PoE) over the network data cable

The external AC adapter plugs into a normal AC wall outlet and provides 48V DC to the device. These adapters, commonly called *wall warts*, are handy if no other power source is available. However, if a power failure occurs in the room or outlet where the adapter is located, the powered device will fail.

As an alternative, you can connect a regular data switch port to a power injector, which injects DC power onto the network cable leading to the powered device. The power injector lets you use the network cabling for both power and data, but requires a connection to a normal AC power source. Typically, a power injector is connected to AC power in a wiring closet close to the switch. One pitfall of using power injectors is that you need one injector and one AC power outlet *per switch port*!

Key Topic

A more elegant solution is available as inline power or Power over Ethernet (PoE). Here, a 48V DC supply is provided to a device over the same unshielded twisted-pair cable that is used for Ethernet connectivity. The DC power source is the Catalyst switch itself. No other power source is needed unless an AC adapter is required as a redundant source.

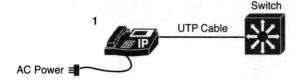

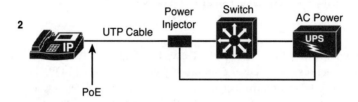

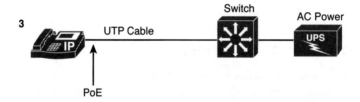

Figure 3-1   *Methods to Supply Power to a Networked Device*

PoE has the benefit that it can be managed, monitored, and offered only to a known device. In fact, this capability is not limited to Cisco devices—any device that can request and use inline power in a compatible manner can be used. Otherwise, if a non-powered device such as a normal PC is plugged into the same switch port, the switch will not offer power to it.

In a best practice design, the Catalyst switch should be connected to an uninterruptible power supply (UPS) so that it continues to receive and offer power even if the regular AC source fails. This allows an IP phone or other powered device to be available for use even during a power failure.

How PoE Works

A Catalyst switch can offer power over its Ethernet ports only if it is designed to do so. It must have one or more power supplies that are rated for the additional load that will be offered to the connected devices. PoE is available on many Cisco Catalyst switch platforms.

Several methods provide PoE to connected devices, as listed in Table 3-6. Cisco Inline Power (ILP) is a proprietary method that was developed before the IEEE standards. The

802.3af and 802.3at standards offer vendor interoperability, as well as power at varying capacities. Cisco Universal PoE (UPoE) is a proprietary method to deliver high capacity power to devices beyond that of 802.3at.

Table 3-6 *PoE Methods*

Method	Common Name	Power Offered
Cisco Inline Power	ILP	7W
IEEE 802.3af	PoE	15.4W
IEEE 802.3at	PoE+	25.5W
Cisco Universal PoE	UPoE	60W

Detecting a Powered Device

A switch always keeps the power disabled when a switch port is down; however, the switch must continually try to detect whether a powered device is connected to a port. If it is, the switch must begin providing power so that the device can initialize and become operational. Only then will the Ethernet link be established.

The switch begins by supplying a small voltage across the transmit and receive pairs of the copper twisted-pair connection. It then can measure the resistance across the pairs to detect whether current is being drawn by the device. For example, if a 25K ohm resistance is measured, a powered device is indeed present.

The switch also can apply several predetermined voltages to test for corresponding resistance values. These values are applied by the powered device to indicate which of the five PoE power classes it belongs to. Knowing this, the switch can begin allocating the appropriate maximum power needed by the device. Table 3-7 lists the power classes.

Key
Topic

Table 3-7 *PoE Power Classes*

Power Class	Maximum Power Offered at 48V DC
0 (default)	15.4W
1	4.0W
2	7.0W
3	15.4W
4 (802.3at)	Up to 30W

The default class 0 is used if either the switch or the powered device does not support or does not attempt the optional power class discovery. Class 4 represents the highest power range (up to 30W) that can be offered to a device.

Normally, a switch will offer a maximum of 15.4W per port. Once the switch begins offering power on the port, the device can power up all or a portion of its circuitry. If additional power is needed, the device can inform the switch through CDP or LLDP advertisements and request up to the full 30W allowed for PoE class 4.

On a Catalyst switch that can support the Cisco proprietary UPoE feature, a powered device can request more than 30W of power. The device can use special TLVs with either CDP or LLDP to request UPoE up to a maximum of 60W. At press time, only the Catalyst 4500 offers UPoE.

Configuring PoE

PoE configuration is fairly straightforward. By default, each switch port can automatically detect the presence of a PoE-capable device before applying power. You can configure how the switch will handle PoE with the following interface configuration command:

```
Switch(config-if)# power inline {auto | static} [max milliwatts]
```

With the **auto** keyword, the connected device can request power through CDP or LLDP and the switch will attempt to deliver it, up to a default maximum of 30W—as long as there is enough power available from the switch's power supply. You can use the **static** keyword instead, to preallocate a fixed amount of power to a device.

Add the **max** keyword to specify a maximum amount of power to offer on the interface, regardless of what the device requests. Specify the maximum power with a value from 4000 to 30000 milliwatts (4 to 30W). The maximum value you choose should be more than you expect the connected device to use, but not set to the maximum possible.

In Example 3-8, interface Gigabit Ethernet 1/0/1 has been configured for PoE auto mode with a maximum power of 6 watts (6000 milliwatts). Unfortunately, the connected device would like to use 15.4W; as a result, the switch rejects the power request and keeps the device in a not-connected state. The request-reject cycle continues at regular intervals until the PoE maximum is set to a sufficient value.

Example 3-8   *Setting a Maximum PoE Limit on a Switch Port*

```
Switch(config)# interface gigabitethernet1/0/1
Switch(config-if)# power inline auto max 6000
Switch(config-if)#
Mar 30 02:36:21.269: %ILPOWER-7-DETECT: Interface Gi1/0/1: Power Device detected:
IEEE PD
Mar 30 02:36:21.269: %ILPOWER-5-ILPOWER_POWER_DENY: Interface Gi1/0/1: inline power
denied. Reason: Insufficient total available power
Mar 30 02:36:37.073: %ILPOWER-7-DETECT: Interface Gi1/0/1: Power Device detected:
IEEE PD
Mar 30 02:36:37.073: %ILPOWER-5-ILPOWER_POWER_DENY: Interface Gi1/0/1: inline power
denied. Reason: Insufficient total available power
Switch(config-if)#
Switch(config-if)# power inline auto max 15400
Switch(config-if)#
```

```
Switch(config-if)#
Mar 30 01:38:37.034: %ILPOWER-5-POWER_GRANTED: Interface Gi1/0/1: Power granted
Mar 30 01:38:41.513: %LINK-3-UPDOWN: Interface GigabitEthernet1/0/1, changed state
to up
Mar 30 01:38:42.520: %LINEPROTO-5-UPDOWN: Line protocol on Interface GigabitEther-
net1/0/1, changed state to up
Mar 30 01:39:09.540: %LINEPROTO-5-UPDOWN: Line protocol on Interface Vlan1, changed
state to up
```

To disable PoE on a switch interface, use the following interface configuration command:

```
Switch(config-if)# power inline never
```

Power never will be offered and powered devices never will be detected on that port.

Verifying PoE

As you manage a PoE switch, be mindful of its power capacity. The power supply installed in the switch must provide power for the switch electronics, as well as any connected PoE devices. It is quite possible that the power supply is not rated to offer the maximum power on every switch port. Make sure that the maximum power configured on each switch port represents a reasonable value expected for the connected device. You should also make sure that the total power that can possibly be used by all connected devices does not exceed the total power available from the power supply.

You might be tempted to leave a switch with its default configuration, using auto-discovery of PoE devices on every port, with a generous maximum power level. In that way, the switch should be able to power devices as they are connected, with no further intervention from you. However, suppose that more and more PoE devices are connected to the switch over time. Some of them may be newer models that require greater amounts of power to operate. Without keeping a close watch on the switch's power budget, you might end up with more demand for power than the switch can supply. Once that occurs, the best outcome is that some devices will not receive power; the worst outcome is that the power supply might be damaged.

To monitor the power budget, you can use the following command:

```
Switch# show power inline
```

With no other options, **show power inline** displays a list of switch ports and their current states. Example 3-9 lists the inline power status for all interfaces on a switch.

Example 3-9   *Displaying Switch Port PoE Status*

```
Switch1# show power inline
Module    Available    Used     Remaining
          (Watts)      (Watts)  (Watts)
------    ---------    -------- ---------
1         710.0        110.4    599.6
```

Interface	Admin	Oper	Power (Watts)	Device	Class	Max
Gi1/0/1	auto	on	6.3	IP Phone 7910	n/a	30.0
Gi1/0/2	auto	on	6.3	IP Phone 7912	n/a	30.0
Gi1/0/3	auto	off	0.0	n/a	n/a	30.0
Gi1/0/4	auto	off	0.0	n/a	n/a	30.0
Gi1/0/5	auto	on	6.3	IP Phone 7910	n/a	30.0
Gi1/0/6	auto	off	0.0	n/a	n/a	30.0
Gi1/0/7	auto	on	6.3	IP Phone 7910	n/a	30.0
Gi1/0/8	auto	on	6.3	IP Phone 7910	n/a	30.0
Gi1/0/9	auto	on	6.3	IP Phone 7910	n/a	30.0
Gi1/0/10	auto	on	6.3	IP Phone 7942	2	30.0
Gi1/0/11	auto	off	0.0	n/a	n/a	30.0
Gi1/0/12	auto	on	16.8	AIR-CAP3702I-A-K9	4	30.0
Gi1/0/13	auto	on	16.8	AIR-CAP3702I-A-K9	4	30.0
Gi1/0/14	auto	on	16.8	AIR-CAP3702I-A-K9	4	30.0
Gi1/0/15	auto	on	16.8	AIR-CAP3702I-A-K9	4	30.0
Gi1/0/16	auto	on	4.0	Ieee PD	1	30.0
Gi1/0/17	auto	on	4.0	Ieee PD	1	30.0
Gi1/0/18	auto	off	0.0	n/a	n/a	30.0

Notice that the first few lines display information about the current power budget. The switch has 710.0W available for PoE; 110.4W are used, leaving 599.6W for additional PoE use.

Switch ports are listed with the following columns:

- **Interface:** The interface number

- **Admin:** The administrative PoE state; autodiscover, on, or off

- **Oper:** The operational state; on, off, or errdisable

- **Power** (*watts*): The actual amount of power being drawn by the device, measured in real-time by power measurement circuitry

- **Device:** The device model or type, determined by CDP or LLDP

- **Class:** The IEEE PoE class **number**

- **Max:** The maximum allowed power draw on the port

In Example 3-9, all switch ports have defaulted to a maximum allowed power of 30W. Suppose that PoE devices were connected to every one of the 48 ports and each device required the full 30W. The total power needed would be 1440W—much greater than the 710W available. Even at 15.4W per port, the power supply would still be oversubscribed. As a best practice, you should configure each port's maximum power to a reasonable value that won't overwhelm the switch.

You can use the following commands to focus on the PoE activity on a specific switch stack member or a specific interface, respectively:

```
Switch# show power inline [module member] [detail]
Switch# show power inline [type member/module/number] [detail]
```

Example 3-10 provides some sample output from the latter command, with and without the **detail** keyword.

Example 3-10   *Displaying Detailed PoE Information*

```
Switch1# show power inline gigabitethernet1/0/5
Interface Admin  Oper        Power   Device              Class Max
                             (Watts)

--------- ------ ----------- ------- ------------------- ----- ----

Gi1/0/5   auto   on          16.8    AIR-CAP3702I-A-K9   4     30.0


Interface  AdminPowerMax    AdminConsumption
           (Watts)          (Watts)
---------- ---------------  --------------------

Gi1/0/5             30.0                30.0
Switch1#
Switch1# show power inline gigabitethernet1/0/5 detail
 Interface: Gi1/0/5
 Inline Power Mode: auto
 Operational status: on
 Device Detected: no
 Device Type: cisco AIR-CAP3702I-
 IEEE Class: 4
 Discovery mechanism used/configured: Unknown
 Police: off
 Power Allocated
 Admin Value: 30.0
 Power drawn from the source: 16.8
 Power available to the device: 16.8

 Actual consumption
 Measured at the port: 6.2
 Maximum Power drawn by the device since powered on: 9.2

 Absent Counter: 0
 Over Current Counter: 0
 Short Current Counter: 0
 Invalid Signature Counter: 0
 Power Denied Counter: 0
Switch1#
```

Exam Preparation Tasks

Review All Key Topics

Review the most important topics in the chapter, noted with the Key Topic icon in the outer margin of the page. Table 3-8 lists a reference of these key topics and the page numbers on which each is found.

Table 3-8   *Key Topics for Chapter 3*

Key Topic Element	Description	Page Number
Paragraph	Describes the characteristics of Ethernet switching	59
Paragraph	Discusses Ethernet scaling	61
Paragraph	Covers 10-Gigabit Ethernet	62
Paragraph	Explains Ethernet autonegotiation	64
Paragraph	Covers interface selection for configuration	66
Paragraph	Explains how to configure the port speed	68
Paragraph	Explains how to configure the port duplex mode	69
Paragraph	Explains how to configure port error detection	69
Paragraph	Explains how to verify the port state	71
Paragraph	Explains how to verify port speed and duplex mode	72
Paragraph	Covers CDP neighbor discovery	73
Paragraph	Covers LLDP neighbor discovery	75
Paragraph	Describes Power over Ethernet for Cisco IP phones	77
Table 3-7	Lists IEEE 802.3af PoE device classes	79

Complete Tables and Lists from Memory

There are no memory tables in this chapter.

Define Key Terms

Define the following key terms from this chapter, and check your answers in the glossary:

CSMA/CD, duplex mode, autonegotiation, duplex mismatch, IEEE 802.3, CDP, LLDP, TLV, Power over Ethernet (PoE), power class

Use Command Reference to Check Your Memory

This section includes the most important configuration and EXEC commands covered in this chapter. It might not be necessary to memorize the complete syntax of every command, but you should remember the basic keywords that are needed.

To test your memory of the port configuration commands, cover the right side of Tables 3-9 through 3-11 with a piece of paper, read the description on the left side, and then see how much of the command you can remember.

Remember that the CCNP exam focuses on practical or hands-on skills that are used by a networking professional. Therefore, you should remember the commands needed to configure and test a switch interface.

Table 3-9   *Switch Port Configuration Commands*

Task	Command Syntax
Select a port.	Switch(config)# **interface** *type member/module/number*
Select multiple ports.	Switch(config)# **interface range** *type member/module/ number* [, *type member/module/number ...*]
	or
	Switch(config)# **interface range** *type member/module/ first-number – last-number*
Define an interface macro.	Switch(config)# **define interface-range** *macro-name type member/module/number* [, *type member/module/ number ...*] [*type member/module/first-number – last-number*] [...]
	Switch(config)# **interface range macro** *macro-name*
Identify port.	Switch(config-if)# **description** *description-string*
Set port speed.	Switch(config-if)# **speed {10	100	1000	auto}**
Set port mode.	Switch(config-if)# **duplex {auto	full	half}**
Detect port error conditions.	Switch(config-if)# **errdisable detect cause [all |** *cause-name*]
Automatically recover from errdisable.	Switch(config-if)# **errdisable recovery cause [all |** *cause-name*]
	Switch(config-if)# **errdisable recovery interval** *seconds*
Manually recover from errdisable.	Switch(config-if)# **shutdown**
	Switch(config-if)# **no shutdown**
Display ports in errdisable state	Switch(config)# **show interface status err-disabled**

Table 3-10   *Neighbor Discovery Commands*

Task	Command Syntax
Display CDP neighbor information.	Switch# **show cdp neighbors** [*type member/ module/number*] [**detail**]
Control CDP operation globally.	Switch(config)# **[no] cdp run**
Control CDP operation on an interface.	Switch(config-if)# **[no] cdp enable**
Display LLDP neighbor information.	Switch(config)# **show lldp neighbors** [*type member/module/number*] [**detail**]
Control LLDP operation globally.	Switch(config)# **[no] lldp run**
Control LLDP operation on an interface.	Switch(config-if)# **[no] lldp {receive | transmit}**

Table 3-11   *Power over Ethernet Commands*

Task	Command Syntax
Set PoE behavior.	Switch(config-if)# **power inline {auto | static}** [**max** *milliwatts*]
Disable PoE on a switch port	Switch(config-if)# **power inline never**
Display PoE status.	Switch# **show power inline** [*type member/ mod/num*] [**detail**]

This chapter covers the following topics that you need to master for the CCNP SWITCH exam:

- **Virtual LANs:** This section reviews VLANs, VLAN membership, and VLAN configuration on a Catalyst switch.

- **VLAN Trunks:** This section covers transporting multiple VLANs over single links and VLAN trunking with Ethernet.

- **VLAN Trunk Configuration:** This section outlines the Catalyst switch commands that configure VLAN trunks.

- **Troubleshooting VLANs and Trunks:** This section provides commands to use when a VLAN or trunk is not operating properly.

- **Voice VLANs:** This section describes the basic configuration needed to support Cisco IP phones and Voice over IP traffic.

- **Wireless VLANs:** This section provides an overview of switch port configuration to support Cisco wireless access points in the access layer.

CHAPTER 4

VLANs and Trunks

Switched campus networks can be broken up into distinct broadcast domains or virtual LANs (VLANs). A flat network topology, or a network with a single broadcast domain, can be simple to implement and manage. However, flat network topology is not scalable. Instead, the campus can be divided into segments using VLANs, while Layer 3 routing protocols manage inter-VLAN communication.

This chapter details the process of defining common workgroups within a group of switches. It covers switch configuration for VLANs, along with the method of identifying and transporting VLANs on various types of links.

"Do I Know This Already?" Quiz

The "Do I Know This Already?" quiz allows you to assess whether you should read this entire chapter thoroughly or jump to the "Exam Preparation Tasks" section. If you are in doubt based on your answers to these questions or your own assessment of your knowledge of the topics, read the entire chapter. Table 4-1 outlines the major headings in this chapter and the "Do I Know This Already?" quiz questions that go with them. You can find the answers in Appendix A, "Answers to the 'Do I Know This Already?' Quizzes."

Table 4-1 *"Do I Know This Already?" Foundation Topics Section-to-Question Mapping*

Foundation Topics Section	Questions Covered in This Section
Virtual LANs	1–4
VLAN TrunksVLAN Trunk Configuration	5–12
Troubleshooting VLANs and Trunks	13–14
Voice VLANs	15-17
Wireless VLANs	18

1. A VLAN is which of the following?

   a. Collision domain

   b. Spanning-tree domain

   c. Broadcast domain

   d. VTP domain

2. Switches provide VLAN connectivity at which layer of the OSI model?

   a. Layer 1

   b. Layer 2

   c. Layer 3

   d. Layer 4

3. Which one of the following switch functions is needed to pass data between two PCs, each connected to a different VLAN?

   a. Layer 2 switch

   b. Layer 3 switch

   c. Trunk

   d. Tunnel

4. Which Catalyst IOS switch command is used to assign a port to a VLAN?

   a. access vlan *vlan-id*

   b. switchport access vlan *vlan-id*

   c. vlan *vlan-id*

   d. set port vlan *vlan-id*

5. Which of the following is a standardized method of trunk encapsulation?

   a. 802.1d

   b. 802.1Q

   c. 802.3z

   d. 802.1a

6. What is the Cisco proprietary method for trunk encapsulation?

   a. CDP

   b. EIGRP

   c. ISL

   d. DSL

7. Which of these protocols dynamically negotiates trunking parameters?

   a. PAgP

   b. STP

   c. CDP

   d. DTP

8. How many different VLANs can an 802.1Q trunk support?

    a. 256

    b. 1024

    c. 4096

    d. 32,768

    e. 65,536

9. Which of the following incorrectly describes a native VLAN?

    a. Frames are untagged on an 802.1Q trunk.

    b. Frames are untagged on an ISL trunk.

    c. Frames can be interpreted by a nontrunking host.

    d. The native VLAN can be configured for each trunking port.

10. If two switches each support all types of trunk encapsulation on a link between them, which one will be negotiated?

    a. ISL

    b. 802.1Q

    c. DTP

    d. VTP

11. Which VLANs are allowed on a trunk link by default?

    a. None

    b. Only the native VLAN

    c. All active VLANs

    d. Only negotiated VLANs

12. Which command configures a switch port to form a trunk without using negotiation?

    a. switchport mode trunk

    b. switchport mode trunk nonegotiate

    c. switchport mode dynamic auto

    d. switchport mode dynamic desirable

13. Two hosts are connected to switch interfaces Gigabit Ethernet 1/0/1 and 1/0/33, but they cannot communicate with each other. Their IP addresses are in the 192.168.10.0/24 subnet, which is carried over VLAN 10. The **show vlan id 10** command generates the following output:

```
Switch# show vlan id 10
VLAN Name                             Status    Ports
---- -------------------------------- --------- ----------------------------
Users                                 active    Gi1/0/1, Gi1/0/2, Gi1/0/3,
Gi1/0/4,
Gi1/0/5, Gi1/0/6,                               Gi1/0/7, Gi1/0/8,
Gi1/0/9, Gi1/0/10,                              Gi1/0/11, Gi1/0/12,
Gi1/0/13, Gi1/0/14,                             Gi1/0/15, Gi1/0/16,
Gi1/0/17, Gi1/0/18,                             Gi1/0/19, Gi1/0/20,
Gi1/0/21, Gi1/0/22,                             Gi1/0/23, Gi1/0/25,
Gi1/0/26, Gi1/0/27,                             Gi1/0/28, Gi1/0/31,
Gi1/0/32, Gi1/0/34,                             Gi1/0/35, Gi1/0/36,
Gi1/0/37, Gi1/0/39,                             Gi1/0/40, Gi1/0/41,
Gi1/0/42, Gi1/0/43,                             Gi1/0/46
```

The hosts are known to be up and connected. Which of the following reasons might be causing the problem? (Choose all that apply.)

a. The two hosts are assigned to VLAN 1.

b. The two hosts are assigned to different VLANs.

c. Interface Gigabit Ethernet 1/0/33 is a VLAN trunk.

d. The two hosts are using unregistered MAC addresses.

14. A trunk link between two switches did not come up as expected. The configuration on Switch A is as follows:

```
Switch A# show running-config interface gigabitethernet1/0/1
interface GigabitEthernet1/0/1
  switchport trunk encapsulation dot1q
  switchport trunk allowed vlan 1-10
  switchport mode dynamic auto
  no shutdown
```

The interface configuration on Switch B is as follows:

```
Switch B# show running-config interface gigabitethernet1/0/1
interface GigabitEthernet1/0/1
  switchport trunk encapsulation dot1q
  switchport mode dynamic auto
  switchport access vlan 5
  no shutdown
```

Assuming the interfaces began with a default configuration before the commands were applied, which one of the following reasons is probably causing the problem?

a. The two switches do not have matching **switchport trunk allowed vlan** commands.

b. Neither switch has a native VLAN configured.

c. Both switches are configured in the dynamic auto mode.

d. Switch B is configured to use access VLAN 5.

15. What command configures an IP phone to use VLAN 9 for voice traffic?

a. switchport voice vlan 9

b. switchport voice-vlan 9

c. switchport voice 9

d. switchport voip 9

16. What is the default voice VLAN condition for a switch port?

a. switchport voice vlan 1

b. switchport voice vlan dot1p

c. switchport voice vlan untagged

d. switchport voice vlan none

17. If the following interface configuration commands have been used, what VLAN numbers will the voice and PC data be carried over, respectively?

```
interface gigabitethernet1/0/1
    switchport access vlan 10
    switchport trunk native vlan 20
    switchport voice vlan 50
    switchport mode access
```

   a. VLAN 50, VLAN 20

   b. VLAN 50, VLAN 1

   c. VLAN 1, VLAN 50

   d. VLAN 20, VLAN 50

   e. VLAN 50, VLAN 10

18. A Cisco lightweight wireless access point is connected to switch interface Gigabit Ethernet 1/0/20. Which one of the following commands enables you to configure the interface on the switch?

   a. switchport access vlan 50

   switchport mode access

   b. switchport trunk allowed vlan 1-100

   switchport mode trunk

   c. switchport ap vlan 50

   d. no switchport mode dynamic autonomous

Foundation Topics

Virtual LANs

Consider a network design that consists of Layer 2 devices only. For example, this design could be a single Ethernet segment, an Ethernet switch with many ports, or a network with several interconnected Ethernet switches. A full Layer 2-only switched network is referred to as a *flat network topology*. A flat network is a single broadcast domain, such that every connected device sees every broadcast packet that is transmitted anywhere in the network. As the number of stations on the network increases, so does the number of broadcasts.

Because of the Layer 2 foundation, flat networks cannot contain redundant paths for load balancing or fault tolerance. The reason for this is explained in Chapters 6, "Traditional Spanning Tree Protocol," through 9, "Advanced Spanning Tree Protocol." To gain any advantage from additional paths to a destination, Layer 3 routing functions must be introduced.

Key Topic

A switched environment offers the technology to overcome flat network limitations. Switched networks can be subdivided into virtual networks, or VLANs. By definition, a VLAN is a single broadcast domain. All devices connected to the VLAN receive broadcasts sent by any other VLAN members. However, devices connected to a different VLAN will not receive those same broadcasts. (Naturally, VLAN members also receive unicast packets directed toward them from other members of the same VLAN.)

A VLAN consists of hosts defined as members, communicating as a *logical* network segment. In contrast, a physical segment consists of devices that must be connected to a physical cable segment. A VLAN can have connected members located anywhere in the campus network, as long as VLAN connectivity is provided among all members. Layer 2 switches are configured with a VLAN mapping and provide the logical connectivity among the VLAN members.

Figure 4-1 shows how a VLAN can provide logical connectivity between switch ports. Two workstations on the left Catalyst switch are assigned to VLAN 1, whereas a third workstation is assigned to VLAN 100. In this example, no communication can occur between VLAN 1 and VLAN 100. VLAN 1 can also be extended into the right Catalyst switch by assigning both ends of the link between the Catalysts to VLAN 1. One workstation on the right Catalyst also is assigned to VLAN 1. Because there is end-to-end connectivity of VLAN 1, any of the workstations on VLAN 1 can communicate as if they were connected to the same physical network segment.

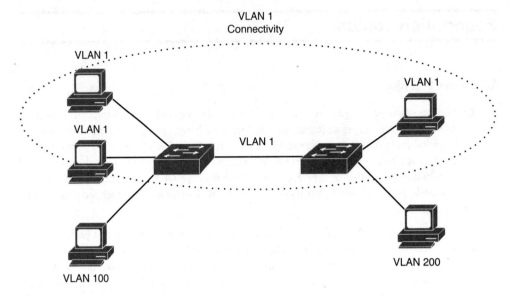

Figure 4-1 *VLAN Functionality*

VLAN Membership

When a VLAN is provided at an access layer switch, an end user must have some means of gaining membership to it. Two membership methods exist on Cisco Catalyst switches:

■ Static VLAN configuration

■ Dynamic VLAN assignment

Static VLANs

Static VLANs offer *port-based* membership, in which switch ports are assigned to specific VLANs. End-user devices become members in a VLAN based on the physical switch port to which they are connected. No handshaking or unique VLAN membership protocol is needed for the end devices; they automatically assume VLAN connectivity when they connect to a port. Normally, the end device is not even aware that the VLAN exists. The switch port and its VLAN simply are viewed and used as any other network segment, with other "locally attached" members on the wire.

Switch ports are assigned to VLANs through manual intervention and configuration, hence the static nature. Each port receives a port VLAN ID (PVID) that associates it with a VLAN number. The ports on a single switch can be assigned and grouped into many VLANs. Even though two devices are connected to the same switch, traffic will not pass between them if they are connected to ports on different VLANs. To perform this function, you could use either a Layer 3 device to route packets or an external Layer 2 device to bridge packets between the two VLANs.

The static port-to-VLAN membership is normally handled in hardware with application-specific integrated circuits (ASICs) in the switch. This membership provides good performance because all port mappings are done at the hardware level, with no complex table lookups needed.

Configuring Static VLANs

To use a VLAN, it must be created on the switch, if it does not already exist. Then, the VLAN must be assigned to specific switch ports. VLANs are always referenced by a VLAN number, which can range from 1 to 1005. VLANs 1 and 1002 through 1005 automatically are created and are set aside for special uses.

VLAN 1 is the default VLAN for every switch port. VLANs 1002 to 1005 are reserved for legacy functions related to Token Ring and FDDI switching. VLAN 1 is set to be a VLAN type of Ethernet, and have a maximum transmission unit (MTU) size of 1500 bytes.

Catalyst switches can also support extended-range VLAN numbers 1006 through 4094. With the addition of the extended-range VLANs VLAN numbers can be 1 to 4094—the same range of numbers as the IEEE 802.1Q standard. The extended range is enabled only when the switch is configured for VTP transparent mode with the **vtp mode transparent** global configuration command. This is because of limitations with VTP Versions 1 and 2. VTP Version 3 does allow extended range VLANs to be used and advertised. (VTP is covered in Chapter 5, "VLAN Trunking Protocol.")

> **Tip**   Although the extended range of VLAN numbers enables you to support more VLANs in your network, some limitations exist. For example, a switch normally maintains VLAN definitions in a special database file, separate from the switch configuration. The VLAN Trunking Protocol (VTP) uses the VLAN database so that VLAN definitions can be advertised and shared between switches over trunk links. When extended-range VLANs are created, they are not stored in the VLAN database file.
>
> Why does this matter? As long as the switch remains in VTP transparent mode, the extended VLANs can be used. However, if the switch is later configured to participate in VTP as either a server or a client, you must manually delete the extended VLANs. For any switch ports that were assigned to the extended VLANs, you must also reconfigure them for VLAN membership within the normal VLAN range.

Key Topic

To configure a VLAN, begin by defining the VLAN with the following commands in global configuration mode:

```
Switch(config)# vlan vlan-num
Switch(config-vlan)# name vlan-name
```

The VLAN numbered *vlan-num* is immediately created and stored in the database, along with a descriptive text string defined by *vlan-name* (up to 32 characters with no embedded spaces). The **name** command is optional; if it is not used, the default VLAN name is of the form VLANXXX, where XXX represents the VLAN number. If you need to include spaces to separate words in the VLAN name, use underscore characters instead.

As an example, you can use the following commands to create VLANs 2 and 101:

```
Switch(config)# vlan 2
Switch(config-vlan)# name Engineering
Switch(config-vlan)# vlan 101
Switch(config-vlan)# name Marketing
```

To delete a VLAN from the switch configuration, you can use the **no vlan** *vlan-num* command.

Next, you should assign one or more switch ports to the VLAN. Use the following configuration commands:

```
Switch(config)# interface type member/module/number
Switch(config-if)# switchport
Switch(config-if)# switchport mode access
Switch(config-if)# switchport access vlan vlan-num
```

The initial **switchport** command configures the port for Layer 2 operation. Switch ports on most Catalyst switch platforms default to Layer 2 operation. In that case, the **switchport** command will already be present in the configuration and you will not have to enter it explicitly. Otherwise, the switch will reject any Layer 2 configuration command if the port is not already configured for Layer 2 operation.

The **switchport mode access** command forces the port to be assigned to only a single VLAN, providing VLAN connectivity to the access layer or end user. The port is given a static VLAN membership by the **switchport access vlan** command. Here, the logical VLAN is referenced by the *vlan-num* setting (1 to 1005 or 1 to 4094). In Example 4-1, several switch ports are put into access mode and assigned to VLANs 2 and 101.

Example 4-1 *Assigning Switch Ports to VLANs*

```
Switch(config)# interface range gigabitethernet4/0/1 - 24
Switch(config-if)# switchport
Switch(config-if)# switchport mode access
Switch(config-if)# switchport access vlan 2
Switch(config)# interface range gigabitethernet2/0/1 - 24
Switch(config-if)# switchport
Switch(config-if)# switchport mode access
Switch(config-if)# switchport access vlan 101
Switch(config-if)# exit
Switch(config)#
```

To verify VLAN configuration, use the **show vlan** or **show vlan brief** command to output a list of all VLANs defined in the switch, along with the ports that are assigned to each

VLAN. Example 4-2 shows some sample output from the **show vlan** command, based on the configuration listed in Example 4-1.

Example 4-2   *Verifying VLAN Configuration with the show vlan Command*

```
Switch#
show vlan
VLAN Name                             Status    Ports
---- -------------------------------- ------    -------------------------------
1    default                          active    Gi1/0/1, Gi1/0/2, Gi3/0/20, Gi4/0/20
2    Engineering                      active    Gi4/0/2, Gi4/0/3, Gi4/0/4, Gi4/0/5
                                                Gi4/0/6, Gi4/0/7, Gi4/0/8, Gi4/0/9
                                                Gi4/0/10, Gi4/0/11, Gi4/0/12
101  Marketing                        active    Gi2/0/5, Gi2/0/6, Gi2/0/7, Gi2/0/8
                                                Gi2/0/9, Gi2/0/10, Gi2/0/11, Gi2/0/12
                                                Gi2/0/13, Gi2/0/14, Gi2/0/15, Gi2/0/16
                                                    Gi2/0/17, Gi2/0/18
```

Dynamic VLANs

Dynamic VLANs provide membership based on the MAC address of an end-user device, rather than the switch port where it is connected. The switch must, in effect, query a database to establish VLAN membership for the device. A network administrator also must assign the user's MAC address to a VLAN in the database of a VLAN Membership Policy Server (VMPS). Dynamic VLANs allow a great deal of flexibility and mobility for end users but require more administrative overhead.

Note   Dynamic VLANs are not covered in this text or in the SWITCH course or exam. For more information, refer to a Catalyst switch configuration guide.

Deploying VLANs

Key
Topic

To implement VLANs, you must consider the number of VLANs you need and how best to place them. As usual, the number of VLANs depends on traffic patterns, application types, segmentation of common workgroups, and network-management requirements.

An important factor to consider is the relationship between VLANs and the IP addressing schemes used. Cisco recommends a one-to-one correspondence between VLANs and IP subnets. This recommendation means that if a subnet with a 24-bit mask (255.255.255.0) is used for a VLAN, no more than 254 devices should be in the VLAN. In addition, you should not allow VLANs to extend beyond the Layer 2 domain of a distribution switch. In other words, the VLAN should stay inside a switch block and not reach across a network's core and into another switch block. The idea again is to keep broadcasts and unnecessary traffic movement out of the core block. This also limits the failure domain, or the extent of the network that would be affected if something goes wrong and the VLAN becomes saturated with traffic to the point that it is unusable.

VLANs can be scaled in the switch block by using two basic methods:

■   End-to-end VLANs

■   Local VLANs

End-to-End VLANs

End-to-end VLANs, also called campus-wide VLANs, span the entire switch fabric of a network. They seem attractive because they can support maximum flexibility and mobility of end devices. Users can be assigned to an end-to-end VLAN regardless of their physical location. As a user moves around the campus, that user's VLAN membership stays the same. This means that the VLAN must be made available at the access layer in *every* switch block. It also means that the VLAN must be made available on the network core switches too. Figure 4-2 illustrates how an end-to-end VLAN can exist in multiple locations but must be carried across multiple switch blocks and the core.

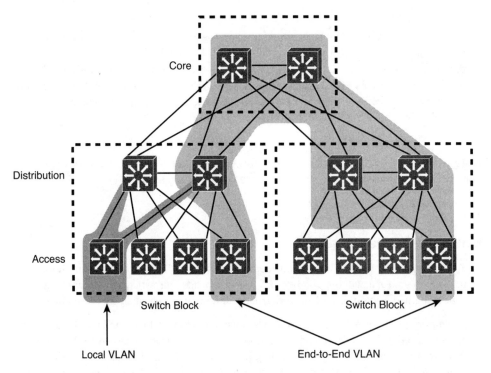

Figure 4-2   *The Extent of an End-to-End VLAN*

End-to-end VLANs should group users according to common requirements. All users in a VLAN should have roughly the same traffic flow patterns, following the 80/20 rule. Recall that this rule estimates that 80 percent of user traffic stays within the local workgroup, whereas 20 percent is destined for a remote resource in the campus network.

Although only 20 percent of the traffic in a VLAN is expected to cross the network core, end-to-end VLANs make it possible for 100 percent of the traffic within a single VLAN to cross the core.

Tip   End-to-end VLANs are not recommended in an enterprise network, unless there is a good reason. In an end-to-end VLAN, broadcast traffic is carried over from one end of the network to the other, creating the possibility for a broadcast storm or Layer 2 bridging loop to spread across the whole extent of a VLAN. This can exhaust the bandwidth of distribution and core layer links, as well as switch CPU resources. In that case, the storm or loop will have disrupted all users on the end-to-end VLAN, in addition to users on other VLANs that might be crossing the core to reach resources on the other side. When such a problem occurs, troubleshooting becomes more difficult. In other words, the risks of end-to-end VLANs outweigh the convenience and benefits.

Local VLANs

Because most enterprise networks have moved toward the 20/80 rule (where server and intranet/Internet resources are centralized), end-to-end VLANs have become cumbersome and difficult to maintain. The 20/80 rule reverses the traffic pattern of the end-to-end VLAN: Only 20 percent of traffic is local, whereas 80 percent is destined to a remote resource across the core layer. End users usually require access to central resources outside their VLAN. Users must cross into the network core more frequently to reach the centralized resources. In this type of network, VLANs should be designed to contain user communities based on geographic boundaries, with little regard to the amount of traffic leaving the VLAN.

Local or geographic VLANs range in size from a single switch in a wiring closet to an entire building. Arranging VLANs in this fashion enables the Layer 3 function in the campus network to intelligently handle the inter-VLAN traffic loads, where traffic passes into the core. This scenario provides maximum availability by using multiple paths to destinations, maximum scalability by keeping the VLAN within a switch block, and maximum manageability.

Figure 4-2 shows a local VLAN. Notice how it is limited to a single switch block, creating a very small failure domain in comparison to the end-to-end VLAN. As a best practice, you should always try to build local VLANs and keep them bounded inside a single switch block.

VLAN Trunks

At the access layer, end-user devices usually connect to switch ports that provide simple connectivity to a single VLAN each. The attached devices are unaware of any VLAN structure and simply attach to what appears to be a normal physical network segment. Remember, sending information from an access link on one VLAN to another VLAN is not possible without the intervention of an additional device—either a Layer 3 router or an external Layer 2 bridge connected between the VLANs.

Suppose that you have one switch that groups users together into three different VLANs. You would like to expand your one-switch network to include a second switch so that the same three VLANs exist on both switches. To bring the three VLANs from one switch to the other, you could take a brute force approach and use three separate physical links— one for each VLAN. The top half of Figure 4-3 shows how two switches might be connected in this fashion.

As VLANs are added to a network, the number of links between switches can grow quickly. A more efficient use of physical interfaces and cabling involves the use of trunking.

A *trunk link* can transport more than one VLAN through a single switch port. Trunk links are most beneficial when switches are connected to other switches or routers. A trunk link is not assigned to a specific VLAN. Instead, one, many, or all active VLANs can be transported between switches using a single physical trunk link, as shown in the bottom half of Figure 4-3.

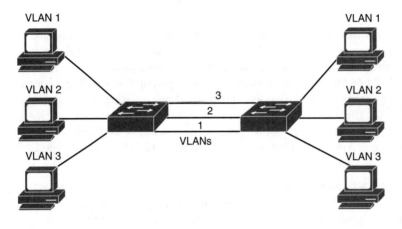

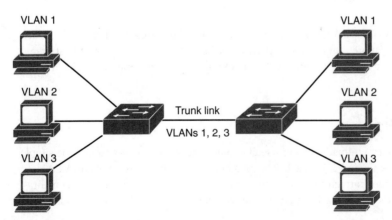

Figure 4-3 *Passing VLAN Traffic Using Single Links Versus a Trunk Link*

Cisco supports trunking on all forms of Ethernet switch links, as well as aggregated EtherChannel links. To distinguish between traffic belonging to different VLANs on a trunk link, the switch must have a method of associating each frame with the appropriate VLAN. The switches on *each end* of a trunk link must use the same method for correlating frames with VLAN numbers so that frames do not get lost as they traverse the trunk. The next section covers several available VLAN identification methods.

VLAN Frame Identification

Because a trunk link can transport many VLANs, a switch must identify frames with their respective VLANs as they are sent and received over a trunk link. Frame identification, or *tagging*, assigns a unique user-defined ID to each frame transported on a trunk link. Think of this ID as the VLAN number or VLAN "color," as if each VLAN were drawn on a network diagram in a unique color.

VLAN frame identification was developed for switched networks. As each frame is transmitted over a trunk link, a unique identifier is placed in the frame header so that the VLAN association travels with the frame itself. As the frame exits the trunk, the switch at the far end of the link examines the VLAN identifier and places the frame into the correct VLAN.

If a frame must be transported out another trunk link, the VLAN identifier simply travels along with the frame in the header. Otherwise, if the frame is destined out an access (nontrunk) link, the VLAN identifier is removed before the frame is transmitted to the destination host. Therefore, all traces of VLAN association are hidden from the end station.

VLAN identification can be performed using two methods, each using a different frame identifier mechanism:

- Inter-Switch Link (ISL) protocol

- IEEE 802.1Q protocol

These methods are described in the sections that follow.

Inter-Switch Link Protocol

The Inter-Switch Link (ISL) protocol is a Cisco-proprietary method for preserving the source VLAN identification of frames passing over a trunk link. ISL performs frame identification in Layer 2 by encapsulating the original frame between a header and a trailer. Any Cisco switch or router device configured for ISL can process and understand the ISL VLAN information.

When a frame is destined out a trunk link to another switch or router, ISL adds a 26-byte header and a 4-byte trailer to the frame. The source VLAN is identified with a 15-bit VLAN ID field in the ISL header; however, VLAN numbers are limited to a range from 1 to 4094. The trailer contains a cyclic redundancy check (CRC) value to ensure the data integrity of the new encapsulated frame. Figure 4-4 shows how Ethernet frames are encapsulated and forwarded out a trunk link.

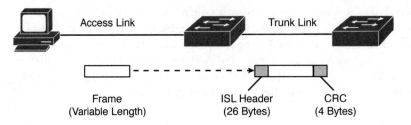

Figure 4-4 *ISL Frame Identification*

> **Tip** The ISL method of VLAN identification or trunking encapsulation no longer is supported across all Cisco Catalyst switch platforms. Even so, you should still be familiar with it and know how it compares to the standards-based IEEE 802.1Q method.

IEEE 802.1Q Protocol

The IEEE 802.1Q protocol also can carry VLAN associations over trunk links. However, this frame-identification method is standardized, allowing VLAN trunks to exist and operate between equipment from multiple vendors. You can find further information about the 802.1Q standard at http://grouper.ieee.org/groups/802/1/pages/802.1Q.html.

As with Cisco ISL, IEEE 802.1Q can be used for VLAN identification with Ethernet trunks. However, instead of encapsulating each frame with a VLAN ID header and trailer, 802.1Q embeds its tagging information within the Layer 2 frame. This method is referred to as *single tagging* or *internal tagging*.

802.1Q also introduces the concept of a *native* VLAN on a trunk. Frames belonging to this VLAN are not encapsulated with any tagging information at all, as if a trunk link was not being used. If an end station is connected to an 802.1Q trunk link, the end station can receive and understand only the native VLAN frames because they are not tagged. This provides a simple way to offer full trunk encapsulation to the devices that can understand it, while giving normal access stations some inherent connectivity over the trunk.

In an Ethernet frame, 802.1Q adds a 4-byte tag just after the Source Address field, as shown in Figure 4-5.

The first two bytes are used as a tag protocol identifier (TPID) and always have a value of 0x8100 to signify an 802.1Q tag. The remaining two bytes are used as a Tag Control Information (TCI) field. The TCI information contains a three-bit Priority field, which is used to implement class of service (CoS) functions. The last 12 bits are used as a VLAN identifier (VID) to indicate the source VLAN for the frame. The VID can have values from 0 to 4095, but VLANs 0, 1, and 4095 are reserved.

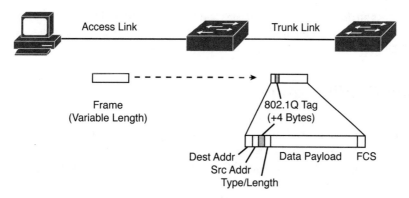

Figure 4-5 *IEEE 802.1Q Frame-Tagging Standard*

Note that both ISL and 802.1Q tagging methods have one implication—they add to the length of an existing Ethernet frame. ISL adds a total of 30 bytes to each frame, whereas 802.1Q adds 4 bytes. Because Ethernet frames cannot exceed 1518 bytes, the additional VLAN tagging information can cause the frame to become too large. Frames that barely exceed the MTU size are called *baby giant frames*. Switches usually report these frames as Ethernet errors or oversize frames.

Note   Baby giant, or oversize, frames can exceed the frame size set in various standards. To properly handle and forward them anyway, Catalyst switches use proprietary hardware with the ISL encapsulation method. In the case of 802.1Q encapsulation, switches can comply with the IEEE 802.3ac standard, which extends the maximum frame length to 1522 bytes.

Dynamic Trunking Protocol

You can manually configure trunk links on Catalyst switches for either ISL or 802.1Q mode. In addition, Cisco has implemented a proprietary, point-to-point protocol called *Dynamic Trunking Protocol* (DTP) that negotiates a common trunking mode between two switches. The negotiation covers the encapsulation (ISL or 802.1Q) and whether the link becomes a trunk at all. This allows trunk links to be used without a great deal of manual configuration or administration. The use of DTP is explained in the next section.

Tip   You should disable DTP negotiation if a switch has a trunk link connected to a nontrunking router or firewall interface because those devices cannot participate in DTP negotiation. A trunk link can be negotiated between two switches only if both switches belong to the same VLAN Trunking Protocol (VTP) management domain or if one or both switches have not defined their VTP domain (that is, the NULL domain). VTP is discussed in Chapter 5.

If the two switches are in different VTP domains and trunking is desired between them, you must set the trunk links to **on** mode or **nonegotiate** mode. This setting forces the trunk to be established. These options are explained in the next section.

VLAN Trunk Configuration

By default, all switch ports in Layer 2 mode are nontrunking and operate as access links until some intervention changes the mode. Specifically, ports actively try to become trunks as long as the far end agrees. In that case, a common encapsulation is chosen, favoring ISL if both support it. The sections that follow demonstrate the commands necessary to configure VLAN trunks.

Configuring a VLAN Trunk

Use the following commands to create a VLAN trunk link:

```
Switch(config)# interface type member/module/number
Switch(config-if)# switchport
Switch(config-if)# switchport trunk encapsulation {isl | dot1q | negotiate}
Switch(config-if)# switchport trunk native vlan vlan-id
Switch(config-if)# switchport trunk allowed vlan {vlan-list | all |
   {add | except | remove} vlan-list}
Switch(config-if)# switchport mode {trunk | dynamic {desirable | auto}}
```

A switch port must be in Layer 2 mode before it can support a trunk. To accomplish this, you use the **switchport** command with no other keywords. You then can configure the trunk encapsulation with the **switchport trunk encapsulation** command, as one of the following:

- **isl:** VLANs are tagged by encapsulating each frame using the Cisco ISL protocol.

- **dot1q:** VLANs are tagged in each frame using the IEEE 802.1Q standard protocol. The only exception is the native VLAN, which is sent normally and is not tagged.

- **negotiate (the default):** The encapsulation is negotiated to select either ISL or IEEE 802.1Q, whichever both ends of the trunk support. If both ends support both types, ISL is favored.

In the case of an IEEE 802.1Q trunk, you should configure the native VLAN with the **switchport trunk native vlan** command, identifying the untagged or native VLAN number as *vlan-id* (1 to 4094). By default, an 802.1Q trunk uses VLAN 1 as the native VLAN. In the case of an ISL trunk, using this command has no effect because ISL does not support an untagged VLAN.

The last command, **switchport trunk allowed vlan**, defines which VLANs can be trunked over the link. By default, a switch transports all active VLANs (1 to 4094) over a trunk link. An active VLAN is one that has been defined on the switch and has ports assigned to carry it.

There might be times when the trunk link should not carry all VLANs. For example, broadcasts are forwarded to every switch port on a VLAN—including a trunk link because it, too, is a member of the VLAN. If the VLAN does not extend past the far end of the trunk link, propagating broadcasts across the trunk makes no sense and only wastes trunk bandwidth.

You can tailor the list of allowed VLANs on the trunk by using the **switchport trunk allowed vlan** command with one of the following:

- *vlan-list*: An explicit list of VLAN numbers, separated by commas or dashes.

- **all:** All active VLANs (1 to 4094) will be allowed.

- **add** *vlan-list*: A list of VLAN numbers will be added to the already configured list; this is a shortcut to keep from typing a long list of numbers.

- **except** *vlan-list*: All VLANs (1 to 4094) will be allowed, except for the VLAN numbers listed; this is a shortcut to keep from typing a long list of numbers.

- **remove** *vlan-list*: A list of VLAN numbers will be removed from the already configured list; this is a shortcut to keep from typing a long list of numbers.

In the **switchport mode** command, you can set the trunking mode to any of the following:

- **trunk:** This setting places the port in permanent trunking mode. DTP is still operational, so if the far-end switch port is configured to **trunk**, **dynamic desirable**, or **dynamic auto** mode, trunking will be negotiated successfully.

  The trunk mode is usually used to establish an unconditional trunk. Therefore, the corresponding switch port at the other end of the trunk should be configured similarly. In this way, both switches always expect the trunk link to be operational without any negotiation. You also should manually configure the encapsulation mode to eliminate its negotiation.

- **dynamic desirable:** The port actively attempts to convert the link into trunking mode. In other words, it "asks" the far-end switch to bring up a trunk. If the far-end switch port is configured to **trunk**, **dynamic desirable**, or **dynamic auto** mode, trunking is negotiated successfully.

- •**dynamic auto (the default):** The port can be converted into a trunk link, but only if the far-end switch actively requests it. Therefore, if the far-end switch port is configured to **trunk** or **dynamic desirable** mode, trunking is negotiated. Because of the passive negotiation behavior, the link never becomes a trunk if both ends of the link are left to **dynamic auto**.

Tip In all these modes, DTP frames are sent out every 30 seconds to keep neighboring switch ports informed of the link's mode. On critical trunk links in a network, manually configuring the trunking mode on both ends is best so that the link never can be negotiated to any other state.

As a best practice, you should configure *both ends* of a trunk link as a fixed trunk (**switchport mode trunk**) or as an access link (**switchport mode access**), to remove any uncertainty about the link operation. In the case of a trunk, you can disable DTP completely so that the negotiation frames are not exchanged at all. To do this, add the **switchport nonegotiate** command to the interface configuration. Be aware that after DTP frames are disabled, no future negotiation is possible until this configuration is reversed.

To view the trunking status on a switch port, use the following command, as demonstrated in Example 4-3:

```
Switch# show interface type member/module/number trunk
```

Example 4-3 *Determining Switch Port Trunking Status*

```
Switch# show interface gigabitethernet 2/0/1 trunk
Port        Mode           Encapsulation  Status          Native vlan
Gi2/0/1     on             802.1q         trunking        1


Port        Vlans allowed on trunk
Gi2/0/1     1-4094


Port        Vlans allowed and active in management domain
Gi2/0/1     1-2,526,539,998


Port        Vlans in spanning tree forwarding state and not pruned
Gi2/0/1     1-2,526,539,998
```

Trunk Configuration Example

As an example of trunk configuration, consider two switches, Switch D and Switch A, which are distribution layer and access layer switches, respectively. The two switches are connected by a link between their Gigabit Ethernet 2/0/1 interfaces. This link should be configured as a trunk carrying only VLAN numbers 100 through 105, although more VLANs might exist on the switches.

The trunk link should use 802.1Q encapsulation, with VLAN 100 as the native VLAN. First, configure Switch D to actively negotiate a trunk with the far-end switch. You could use the following configuration commands on Switch D:

```
Switch-D(config)# interface gigabitethernet 2/0/1
Switch-D(config-if)# switchport
Switch-D(config-if)# switchport trunk encapsulation dot1q
```

```
Switch-D(config-if)# switchport trunk native vlan 100
Switch-D(config-if)# switchport trunk allowed vlan 100-105
Switch-D(config-if)# switchport mode dynamic desirable
```

At this point, you assume that Switch A is configured correctly, too. Now, you should try to verify that the trunk is working as expected. On Switch D, you can view the trunk status with the following command:

```
Switch-D# show interface gigabitethernet 2/0/1 trunk
Port          Mode          Encapsulation  Status        Native vlan

Gi2/0/1       desirable     802.1q         not-trunking  100
Port          Vlans allowed on trunk
Gi2/0/1       100
Port          Vlans allowed and active in management domain
Gi2/0/1       100
Port          Vlans in spanning tree forwarding state and not pruned
Gi2/0/1       none
```

To your surprise, the trunk's status is not-trunking. Next, you should verify that the physical link is up:

```
Switch-D# show interface status
Port     Name          Status        Vlan   Duplex Speed Type
Gi2/0/1                connected     100      full  1000 1000BaseSX
Gi2/0/2                notconnect    1        auto  1000 1000BaseSX
Gi2/0/3                notconnect    1        auto  1000 1000BaseSX
```

What could be preventing the trunk from being established? If Switch D is in dynamic desirable negotiation mode, it is actively asking Switch A to bring up a trunk. Obviously, Switch A must not be in agreement. The desirable mode can negotiate a trunk with all other trunking modes, so Switch A's interface must not be configured for trunking. Instead, it is most likely configured as an access port (**switchport mode access**).

Switch A can be corrected by configuring its Gigabit Ethernet 2/0/1 interface to negotiate a trunk. Switch D is in dynamic desirable mode, so Switch A could use either **trunk**, **dynamic desirable**, or **dynamic auto** mode.

Now, suppose that you realize VLAN 103 should not be passed between these switches. You can use either of the following command sequences to manually prune VLAN 103 from the trunk:

```
Switch-D(config)# interface gigabitethernet 2/0/1
Switch-D(config-if)# switchport trunk allowed vlan 100-102,104-105
```

or

```
Switch-D(config-if)# switchport trunk allowed vlan remove 103
```

In the latter case, the previous range of 100 to 105 is kept in the configuration, and only 103 is removed from the list.

When you manually prune VLANs from being allowed on a trunk, the same operation should be performed at both ends of the trunk link. Otherwise, one of the two switches still could flood broadcasts from that VLAN onto the trunk, using unnecessary bandwidth in only one direction.

For completeness, the configuration of Switch A at this point would look like the following:

```
Switch-A(config)# interface gigabitethernet 2/0/1
Switch-A(config-if)# switchport trunk encapsulation dot1q
Switch-A(config-if)# switchport trunk native vlan 100
Switch-A(config-if)# switchport trunk allowed vlan 100-105
Switch-A(config-if)# switchport trunk allowed vlan remove 103
Switch-A(config-if)# switchport mode dynamic desirable
```

Troubleshooting VLANs and Trunks

Remember that a VLAN is nothing more than a logical Layer 2 network segment that can be spread across many switches. If a PC in one location cannot communicate with a PC in another location, where both are assigned to the same IP subnet, make sure that both of their switch ports are configured for the same VLAN. If they are, examine the path between the two. Is the VLAN carried continuously along the path? If there are trunks along the way, is the VLAN being carried across the trunks?

To verify a VLAN's configuration on a switch, use the **show vlan id** *vlan-id* EXEC command, as demonstrated in Example 4-4. Make sure that the VLAN is shown to have an active status and that it has been assigned to the correct switch ports.

Example 4-4   *Verifying Switch VLAN Configuration*

```
Switch# show vlan id 2
VLAN Name                             Status    Ports
---- -------------------------------- --------- -------
2    Engineering                      active    Gi2/0/1, Gi2/0/2, Gi2/0/3, Gi2/0/4
                                                Gi4/0/2, Gi4/0/3, Gi4/0/4, Gi4/0/5
                                                Gi4/0/6, Gi4/0/7, Gi4/0/8, Gi4/0/9
                                                Gi4/0/10, Gi4/0/11, Gi4/0/12


VLAN Type  SAID       MTU   Parent RingNo BridgeNo Stp  BrdgMode Trans1 Trans2
---- ----- ---------- ----- ------- ------ -------- ---- -------- ------ -------
2    enet  100002     1500  -       -      -        -    -        0      0


Primary Secondary Type               Ports
------- --------- ------------------ ---------------------------------------------


Switch#
```

For a trunk, the following parameters must be agreeable on both ends before the trunk can operate correctly:

■ Trunking mode (unconditional trunking, negotiated, or non-negotiated).

■ Trunk encapsulation (ISL, IEEE 802.1Q, or negotiated through DTP).

■ Native VLAN. You can bring up a trunk with different native VLANs on each end; however, both switches will log error messages about the mismatch, and the potential exists that traffic will not pass correctly between the two native VLANs.

■ The native VLAN mismatch is discovered through the exchange of Cisco Discovery Protocol (CDP) or Link Layer Discovery Protocol (LLDP) messages, not through examination of the trunk itself. Also, the native VLAN is configured independently of the trunk encapsulation, so it is possible to have a native VLAN mismatch even if the ports use ISL encapsulation. In this case, the mismatch is only cosmetic and will not cause a trunking problem.

■ Allowed VLANs. By default, a trunk allows all VLANs to be transported across it. If one end of the trunk is configured to disallow a VLAN, that VLAN will not be contiguous across the trunk. A trunk link can become operational even if the list of allowed VLANs is not consistent on both ends.

Key Topic

To see a comparison of how a trunking switch port is configured versus its operational state, use the **show interface** *type member/module/number* **switchport** command, as demonstrated in Example 4-5. Look for the administrative versus operational values, respectively, to see whether the trunk is working the way you configured it.

Notice that the port has been configured to negotiate a trunk through DTP (dynamic auto), but the port is operating in the static access (nontrunking) mode. This should tell you that both ends of the link probably are configured for the auto mode so that neither will actively request a trunk.

Example 4-5 *Comparing Switch Port Trunking Configuration and Operational State*

```
Switch# show interface gigabitethernet 2/0/2 switchport
Name: Gi2/0/2
Switchport: Enabled
Administrative Mode: dynamic auto

Operational Mode: static access
Administrative Trunking Encapsulation: dot1q
Operational Trunking Encapsulation: native
Negotiation of Trunking: On
Access Mode VLAN: 1 (default)
Trunking Native Mode VLAN: 1 (default)
Administrative private-vlan host-association: none
Administrative private-vlan mapping: none
Operational private-vlan: none
Trunking VLANs Enabled: ALL
```

```
Pruning VLANs Enabled: 2-1001


Protected: false

Unknown unicast blocked: disabled

Unknown multicast blocked: disabled


Voice VLAN: none (Inactive)

Appliance trust: none

Switch#
```

For more concise information about a trunking port, you can use the **show interface** [*type member/module/number*] **trunk** command, as demonstrated in Example 4-6.

Example 4-6 *Viewing Concise Information About a Trunking Port*

```
Switch# show interface gigabitethernet 2/0/2 trunk
Port       Mode         Encapsulation  Status        Native vlan
Gi2/0/2    auto         802.1q         not-trunking  1


Port       Vlans allowed on trunk
Gi2/0/2    1


Port       Vlans allowed and active in management domain
Gi2/0/2    1


Port       Vlans in spanning tree forwarding state and not pruned
Gi2/0/2    1
Switch#
```

Again, notice that the port is in the autonegotiation mode, but it is currently not-trunking. Because the port is not-trunking, only the access VLAN (VLAN 1 in this example) is listed as allowed and active on the trunk.

To see whether and how DTP is being used on a switch, use the **show dtp** [**interface** *type member/module/number*] command. Specifying an interface shows the DTP activity in greater detail.

Voice VLANs

A Cisco IP phone provides a data connection for a user's PC, in addition to its own voice data stream. This allows a single Ethernet drop to be installed per user, even though several types of data pass over it. The IP phone also can control some aspects of how the packets (both voice and user data) are presented to the switch.

Most Cisco IP phone models contain a three-port switch, connecting to the upstream switch, the user's PC, and the internal Voice over IP (VoIP) data stream, as illustrated in Figure 4-6. The voice and user PC ports always function as access mode switch ports.

The port that connects to the upstream switch, however, can operate as an 802.1Q trunk or as an access mode (single VLAN) port.

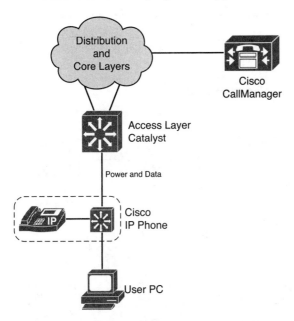

Figure 4-6 *Basic Connections to a Cisco IP Phone*

The link mode between the IP phone and the switch is negotiated; you can configure the switch to instruct the phone to use a special-case 802.1Q trunk or a single VLAN access link. With a trunk, the voice traffic can be isolated from other user data, providing security and quality of service (QoS) capabilities.

As an access link, both voice and data must be combined over the single VLAN. This simplifies other aspects of the switch configuration because a separate voice VLAN is not needed, but it could compromise the voice quality, depending on the PC application mix and traffic load.

Voice VLAN Configuration

Although you can configure the IP phone uplink as a trunk or nontrunk, the real consideration pertains to how the voice traffic will be encapsulated. The voice packets must be carried over a unique voice VLAN (known as the *voice VLAN ID* or *VVID*) or over the regular data VLAN (known as the *native VLAN* or the *port VLAN ID, PVID*). The QoS information from the voice packets also must be carried somehow.

To configure the IP phone uplink, just configure the switch port where the phone connects. The switch instructs the phone to follow the mode that is selected. In addition, the switch port does not need any special trunking configuration commands if a trunk is wanted. If an 802.1Q trunk is needed, a special-case trunk is automatically negotiated by the Dynamic Trunking Protocol (DTP) and CDP.

Use the following interface configuration command to select the voice VLAN mode that will be used:

```
Switch(config-if)# switchport voice vlan {vlan-id | dot1p | untagged | none}
```

Figure 4-7 shows the four different voice VLAN configurations. Pay particular attention to the link between the IP phone and the switch.

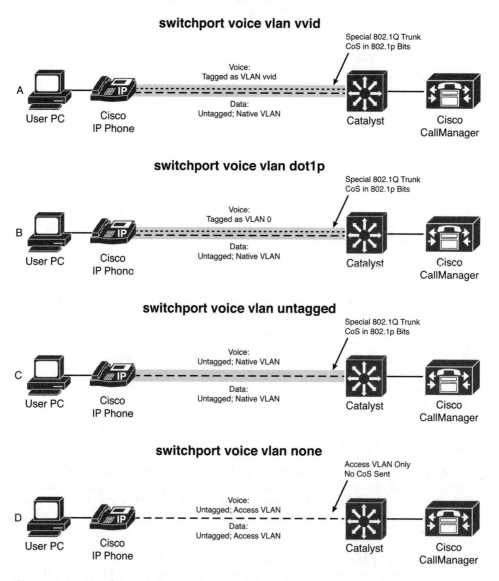

Figure 4-7 *Trunking Modes for Voice VLANs with a Cisco IP Phone*

Table 4-2 documents the four different voice VLAN configurations and how the voice and PC traffic are carried over the link between the phone and the switch.

Table 4-2 *Trunking Modes with a Cisco IP Phone*

Keyword	Representation in Figure 4-7	Trunk?	Voice Traffic	PC Traffic
vlan-id	A	Yes	VLAN vlan-id	Untagged
dot1p	B	Yes	VLAN 0	Untagged
untagged	C	Yes	Untagged	Untagged
none (default)	D	No	Access VLAN	Access VLAN

The default condition for every switch port is **none**, where a trunk is not used. All modes except for **none** use the special-case 802.1Q trunk. The only difference between the **dot1p** and **untagged** modes is the encapsulation of voice traffic. The **dot1p** mode puts the voice packets on VLAN 0, which requires a VLAN ID (not the native VLAN) but does not require a unique voice VLAN to be created. The **untagged** mode puts voice packets in the native VLAN, requiring neither a VLAN ID nor a unique voice VLAN.

The most versatile mode uses the *vlan-id*, as shown in case A in Figure 4-7. Here, voice and user data are carried over separate VLANs. Be aware that the special-case 802.1Q trunk is automatically enabled through a CDP or LLDP information exchange between the switch and the IP phone. The trunk contains only two VLANs—a voice VLAN (tagged VVID) and the data VLAN. The switch port's access VLAN is used as the data VLAN that carries packets to and from a PC that is connected to the phone's PC port.

If an IP phone is removed and a PC is connected to the same switch port, the PC still will be capable of operating because the data VLAN still will appear as the access VLAN—even though the special trunk no longer is enabled.

Verifying Voice VLAN Operation

You can verify the switch port mode (access or trunk) and the voice VLAN by using the **show interface switchport** command. As demonstrated in Example 4-7, the port is in access mode and uses access VLAN 10 and voice VLAN 110.

Example 4-7 *Verifying Switch Port Mode and Voice VLAN*

```
Switch# show interfaces gigabitethernet 1/0/1 switchport
Name: Gi1/0/1
Switchport: Enabled
Administrative Mode: dynamic auto
Operational Mode: static access
Administrative Trunking Encapsulation: negotiate
Operational Trunking Encapsulation: native
Negotiation of Trunking: On
Access Mode VLAN: 10 (VLAN0010)
Trunking Native Mode VLAN: 1 (default)
Administrative Native VLAN tagging: enabled
Voice VLAN: 110 (VoIP)
```

```
Administrative private-vlan host-association: none
Administrative private-vlan mapping: none
Administrative private-vlan trunk native VLAN: none
Administrative private-vlan trunk Native VLAN tagging: enabled
Administrative private-vlan trunk encapsulation: dot1q
Administrative private-vlan trunk normal VLANs: none
Administrative private-vlan trunk private VLANs: none
Operational private-vlan: none
Trunking VLANs Enabled: ALL
Pruning VLANs Enabled: 2-1001
Capture Mode Disabled
Capture VLANs Allowed: ALL
Protected: false
Unknown unicast blocked: disabled
Unknown multicast blocked: disabled
Appliance trust: none
Switch#
```

When the IP phone trunk is active, it is not shown in the trunking mode from any Cisco IOS Software **show** command. However, you can verify the VLANs being carried over the trunk link by looking at the Spanning Tree Protocol (STP) activity. STP runs with two instances—one for the voice VLAN and one for the data VLAN, which can be seen with the **show spanning-tree interface** command.

For example, suppose that a switch port is configured with access VLAN 10, voice VLAN 110, and native VLAN 99. Example 4-8 shows the switch port configuration and STP information when the switch port is in access mode. The access VLAN (10) is being used as the data VLAN from the IP phone.

Example 4-8 *IP Phone Trunk Configuration and STP Information*

```
Switch# show running-config interface gigabitethernet 1/0/1
interface GigabitEthernet1/0/1
 switchport trunk native vlan 99
 switchport access vlan 10
 switchport voice vlan 110
Switch# show spanning-tree interface gigabitethernet 1/0/1
Vlan            Role Sts Cost    Prio.Nbr Type
--------------- ---- --- --------- -------- --------------------------------
VLAN0010        Desg FWD 19      128.51   P2p
VLAN0110        Desg FWD 19      128.51   P2p
Switch#
```

Wireless VLANs

Cisco wireless access points (APs) are access devices that can connect to switch ports in the access layer. The switch provides connectivity between wired and wireless environments, or between VLANs and wireless LANs (WLANs). Although the SWITCH exam might not cover wireless AP support, you should become familiar with the basic concepts and know how to configure a switch port where an AP is connected.

Cisco APs can operate in one of the two following modes:

- **Autonomous mode:** The AP operates independently and directly connects VLANs to WLANs on a one-to-one basis.

- **Lightweight mode:** The AP must join and cooperate with a wireless LAN controller located elsewhere on the network. The AP connects each of its own WLANs with a VLAN connected to the controller. All of the VLAN-WLAN traffic is encapsulated and carried over a special tunnel between the AP and the controller.

Figure 4-8 illustrates the switch port configuration needed to support an AP in autonomous mode. Because the AP maps VLANs to WLANs locally, each VLAN must be transported to it over a trunk link. Suppose there are three WLANs that connect to three VLANs 10, 20, and 30. The switch port connected to the AP might be configured with the commands listed in Example 4-9.

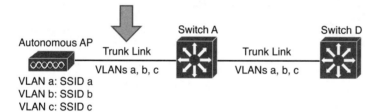

Figure 4-8   *Configuring a Switch Port to Support an Autonomous Wireless AP*

Example 4-9   *Switch Port Configuration for an Autonomous AP*

```
SwitchA(config)# interface gigabitethernet1/0/5
SwitchA(config-if)# switchport
SwitchA(config-if)# switchport trunk encapsulation dot1q
SwitchA(config-if)# switchport trunk allowed vlans 10,20,30
SwitchA(config-if)# switchport mode trunk
SwitchA(config-if)# no shutdown
```

An AP operating in lightweight mode needs a different configuration approach. Figure 4-9 shows how a lightweight AP connects to a switch port over a nontrunking access link. The AP needs a single VLAN to support IP connectivity between itself and the wireless LAN controller so that a Control and Provisioning of Wireless Access Points (CAPWAP) protocol tunnel can be built to transport wireless traffic. The VLAN used on the switch port is not related to any wireless LANs at all; the wireless VLANs terminate on the controller elsewhere in the network.

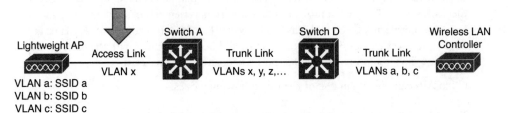

Figure 4-9   *Configuring a Switch Port to Support a Lightweight Wireless AP*

Suppose that the lightweight AP is connected to the switch port using VLAN 100. Three WLANs map to three VLANs 10, 20, and 30. The switch port can be configured using the commands listed in Example 4-10.

Example 4-10   *Switch Port Configuration for a Lightweight AP*

```
SwitchA(config)# interface gigabitethernet1/0/5
SwitchA(config-if)# switchport
SwitchA(config-if)# switchport access vlan 100
SwitchA(config-if)# switchport mode access
SwitchA(config-if)# no shutdown
```

Exam Preparation Tasks

Review All Key Topics

Review the most important topics in the chapter, noted with the Key Topic icon in the outer margin of the page. Table 4-3 lists a reference of these key topics and the page numbers on which each is found.

Key Topic

Table 4-3 *Key Topics for Chapter 4*

Key Topic Element	Description	Page Number
Paragraph	Explains VLAN characteristics	95
Paragraph	Discusses how to configure a VLAN	97
Paragraph	Discusses planning strategies for VLAN implementation	99
Paragraph	Explains the 802.1Q trunking protocol	104
Paragraph	Describes VLAN trunk link configuration	110
Paragraph	Discusses how to verify VLAN configuration	111
Paragraph	Explains how to verify that a trunk link is working properly	113

Complete Tables and Lists from Memory

There are no memory tables in this chapter.

Define Key Terms

Define the following key terms from this chapter, and check your answers in the glossary:

VLAN, broadcast domain, VLAN number, end-to-end VLAN, local VLAN, 20/80 rule, VLAN trunk, ISL, 802.1Q, DTP, native VLAN, voice VLAN

Use Command Reference to Check Your Memory

This section includes the most important configuration and EXEC commands covered in this chapter. It might not be necessary to memorize the complete syntax of every command, but you should remember the basic keywords that are needed.

To test your memory of the VLAN and trunk-related commands, cover the right side of Tables 4-4 and Table 4-5 with a piece of paper, read the description on the left side, and then see how much of the command you can remember.

Remember that the CCNP exam focuses on practical or hands-on skills that are used by a networking professional. For the skills covered in this chapter, notice that most of the commands involve the keyword **switchport**.

Table 4-4   *VLAN and Trunking Configuration Commands*

Task	Command Syntax
Create VLAN.	Switch(config)# **vlan** *vlan-num* Switch(config-vlan)# **name** *vlan-name*
Assign port to VLAN.	Switch(config)# **interface** *type member/module/number* Switch(config-if)# **switchport mode access** Switch(config-if)# **switchport access vlan** *vlan-num*
Configure trunk.	Switch(config)# **interface** *type member/module/number* Switch(config-if)# **switchport trunk encapsulation {isl | dot1q | negotiate}** Switch(config-if)# **switchport trunk native vlan** *vlan-id* Switch(config-if)# **switchport trunk allowed vlan** {*vlan-list* | **all** | {**add** | **except** | **remove**} *vlan-list*} Switch(config-if)# **switchport mode {trunk | dynamic {desirable | auto}}**
Define the trunking on a port to a Cisco IP phone.	Switch(config-if)# **switchport voice vlan** {*vlan-id* | **dot1p** | **untagged** | **none**}

Table 4-5   *VLAN and Trunking Troubleshooting Commands*

Task	Command Syntax
Verify VLAN configuration.	Switch# **show vlan id** *vlan-id* Switch# **show vlan** [**brief**]
Verify active trunk parameters.	Switch# **show interface** *type member/module/number* **trunk**
Compare trunk configuration and active parameters.	Switch# **show interface** *type member/module/number* **switchport**
Verify DTP operation.	Switch# **show dtp** [**interface** *type member/module/number*]

This chapter covers the following topics that you need to master for the CCNP SWITCH exam:

■ **VLAN Trunking Protocol:** This section presents Cisco VLAN Trunking Protocol (VTP) for VLAN management in a campus network.

■ **VTP Configuration:** This section covers the Catalyst switch commands used to configure VTP.

■ **VTP Pruning:** This section details traffic management by pruning within VTP domains, along with the commands needed for configuration.

■ **Troubleshooting VTP:** This section gives a brief summary of things to consider and commands to use when VTP is not operating properly.

CHAPTER 5

VLAN Trunking Protocol

When VLANs are defined and used on switches throughout an enterprise or campus network, the administrative overhead can easily increase. Using the VLAN Trunking Protocol (VTP) can make VLAN administration more organized and manageable. This chapter covers VTP and its configuration. A similar standards-based VLAN-management protocol for IEEE 802.1Q trunks is called *GARP VLAN Registration Protocol* (GVRP). The GARP and GVRP protocols are defined in the IEEE 802.1D and 802.1Q (clause 11) standards, respectively. At the time of this writing, GVRP was not supported in any of the Cisco Catalyst switches. Therefore, it is not covered in this text or in the SWITCH course.

"Do I Know This Already?" Quiz

The "Do I Know This Already?" quiz allows you to assess whether you should read this entire chapter thoroughly or jump to the "Exam Preparation Tasks" section. If you are in doubt based on your answers to these questions or your own assessment of your knowledge of the topics, read the entire chapter. Table 5-1 outlines the major headings in this chapter and the "Do I Know This Already?" quiz questions that go with them. You can find the answers in Appendix A, "Answers to the 'Do I Know This Already?' Quizzes."

Table 5-1 *"Do I Know This Already?" Foundation Topics Section-to-Question Mapping*

Foundation Topics Section	Questions Covered in This Section
VLAN Trunking Protocol VTP Configuration	1-9
VTP Pruning	10-11
Troubleshooting VTP	12

1. Which of the following is not a Catalyst switch VTP mode?

   a. Server

   b. Client

   c. Designated

   d. Transparent

2. A switch in VTP transparent mode can do which one of the following?

   a. Create a new VLAN

   b. Only listen to VTP advertisements

   c. Send its own VTP advertisements

   d. Cannot make VLAN configuration changes

3. Which one of the following is a valid VTP advertisement?

   a. Triggered update

   b. VLAN database

   c. Subset

   d. Domain

4. Which one of the following is needed for VTP communication?

   a. A Management VLAN

   b. A trunk link

   c. An access VLAN

   d. An IP address

5. Which one of the following VTP modes does not allow any manual VLAN configuration changes?

   a. Server

   b. Client

   c. Designated

   d. Transparent

6. Select all the parameters that decide whether to accept new VTP information.

   a. VTP priority

   b. VTP domain name

   c. Configuration revision number

   d. VTP server name

7. How many VTP management domains can a Catalyst switch participate in?

    a. 1

    b. 2

    c. Unlimited

    d. 4096

8. Which command configures a Catalyst switch for VTP client mode?

    a. set vtp mode client

    b. vtp client

    c. vtp mode client

    d. vtp client mode

9. If a VTP server is configured for VTP Version 2, what else must happen for successful VTP communication in a domain?

    a. A VTP version 2 password must be set.

    b. All other switches in the domain must be version 2 capable.

    c. All other switches must be configured for VTP version 2.

    d. The VTP configuration revision number must be reset.

10. What is the purpose of VTP pruning?

    a. Limit the number of VLANs in a domain

    b. Stop unnecessary VTP advertisements

    c. Limit the extent of broadcast traffic

    d. Limit the size of the virtual tree

11. Which VLAN number is never eligible for VTP pruning?

    a. 0

    b. 1

    c. 1000

    d. 1001

12. Which of the following might present a VTP problem?

    a. Two or more VTP servers in a domain

    b. Two servers with the same configuration revision number

    c. A server in two domains

    d. A new server with a higher configuration revision number

Foundation Topics

VLAN Trunking Protocol

As the previous chapter demonstrated, VLAN configuration and trunking on a switch or a small group of switches is fairly intuitive. Campus network environments, however, usually consist of many interconnected switches. Configuring and managing a large number of switches, VLANs, and VLAN trunks quickly can get out of control.

Cisco has developed a method to manage VLANs across the campus network. The VLAN Trunking Protocol (VTP) uses Layer 2 trunk frames to communicate VLAN information among a group of switches. VTP manages the addition, deletion, and renaming of VLANs across the network from a central point of control. Any switch participating in a VTP exchange is aware of and can use any VLAN that VTP manages.

VTP Domains

VTP is organized into *management domains*, or areas with common VLAN requirements. A switch can belong to only one VTP domain, sharing VLAN information with other switches in the domain. Switches in different VTP domains, however, do not share VTP information.

Switches in a VTP domain advertise several attributes to their domain neighbors. Each advertisement contains information about the VTP management domain, VTP revision number, known VLANs, and specific VLAN parameters. When a VLAN is added to a switch in a management domain, other switches are notified of the new VLAN through *VTP advertisements*. In this way, all switches in a domain can prepare to receive traffic on their trunk ports using the new VLAN.

VTP Modes

To participate in a VTP management domain, each switch must be configured to operate in one of several modes. The VTP mode determines how the switch processes and advertises VTP information. You can use the following modes:

- **Server mode:** VTP servers have full control over VLAN creation and modification for their domains. All VTP information is advertised to other switches in the domain, while all received VTP information is synchronized with the other switches. By default, a switch is in VTP server mode. Note that each VTP domain must have at least one server so that VLANs can be created, modified, or deleted, and VLAN information can be propagated.

- **Client mode:** VTP clients do not allow the administrator to create, change, or delete any VLANs. Instead, they listen to VTP advertisements from other switches and modify their VLAN configurations accordingly. In effect, this is a passive listening mode. Received VTP information is forwarded out trunk links to neighboring switches in the domain, so the switch also acts as a VTP relay.

- **Transparent mode:** VTP transparent switches do not participate in VTP. While in transparent mode, a switch does not advertise its own VLAN configuration, and it does not synchronize its VLAN database with received advertisements. In VTP version 1, a transparent mode switch does not even relay VTP information it receives to other switches unless its VTP domain names and VTP version numbers match those of the other switches. In VTP version 2, transparent switches do forward received VTP advertisements out of their trunk ports, acting as VTP relays. This occurs regardless of the VTP domain name setting.

- **Off mode:** Like transparent mode, switches in VTP off mode do not participate in VTP; however, VTP advertisements are not relayed at all. You can use VTP off mode to disable all VTP activity on or through a switch.

Tip   While a switch is in VTP transparent mode, it can create and delete VLANs that are local only to itself. These VLAN changes, however, are not propagated to any other switch.

VTP Advertisements

VTP has evolved over time to include three different versions. Cisco switches can support all three versions, but the versions are not fully backward compatible with each other. If a network contains switches that are running different VTP versions, you should consider how the switches will interact with their VTP information. By default, Cisco switches use VTP Version 1.

Each Cisco switch participating in VTP advertises VLANs, revision numbers, and VLAN parameters on its trunk ports to notify other switches in the management domain. VTP Versions 1 and 2 support VLAN numbers 1 to 1005, whereas only VTP Version 3 supports the full extended VLAN range 1 to 4094.

VTP advertisements are sent as multicast frames. A switch intercepts frames sent to the VTP multicast address and processes them locally. The advertisements can also be relayed or forwarded out trunk links toward neighboring switches in all VTP modes except off mode. Because all switches in a management domain learn of new VLAN configuration changes, a VLAN must be created and configured on only one VTP server switch in the domain.

By default, management domains are set to use nonsecure advertisements without a password. You can add a password to set the domain to secure mode. The same password must be configured on every switch in the domain so that all switches exchanging VTP information use identical encryption methods.

VTP switches use an index called the VTP configuration revision number to keep track of the most recent information. Every switch in a VTP domain stores the configuration revision number that it last heard from a VTP advertisement. The VTP advertisement process always starts with configuration revision number 0.

When subsequent changes are made on a VTP server, the revision number is incremented before the advertisements are sent. When listening switches (configured as members of the same VTP domain as the advertising switch) receive an advertisement with a greater revision number than is stored locally, they assume that the advertisement contains new and updated information. The advertisement is stored and overwrites any previously stored VLAN information.

VTP advertisements usually originate from server mode switches as VLAN configuration changes occur and are announced. Advertisements can also originate as requests from client mode switches that want to learn about the VTP database as they boot.

VTP advertisements can occur in three forms:

- **Summary advertisements:** VTP domain servers send summary advertisements every 300 seconds and every time a VLAN database change occurs. The summary advertisement lists information about the management domain, including VTP version, domain name, configuration revision number, time stamp, MD5 encryption hash code, and the number of subset advertisements to follow. For VLAN configuration changes, summary advertisements are followed by one or more subset advertisements with more specific VLAN configuration data. Figure 5-1 shows the summary advertisement format.

Version (1 byte)	Type (Summary Adv) (1 byte)	Number of subset advertisements to follow (1 byte)	Domain name length (1 byte)
Management Domain Name (zero-padded to 32 bytes)			
Configuration Revision Number (4 bytes)			
Updater Identity (orginating IP address: 4 bytes)			
Update Time Stamp (12 bytes)			
MD5 Digest hash code (16 bytes)			

Figure 5-1 *VTP Summary Advertisement Format*

- **Subset advertisements:** VTP domain servers send subset advertisements after a VLAN configuration change occurs. These advertisements list the specific changes that have been performed, such as creating or deleting a VLAN, suspending or activating a VLAN, changing the name of a VLAN, and changing a VLAN's maximum transmission unit (MTU). Subset advertisements can list the following VLAN parameters: status of the VLAN, VLAN type (such as Ethernet or Token Ring), MTU, length of the VLAN name, VLAN number, security association identifier (SAID) value, and VLAN name. VLANs are listed individually in sequential subset advertisements. Figure 5-2 shows the VTP subset advertisement format.

VTP Subset Advertisement

0	1	2	3
Version (1 byte)	Type (Subset Adv) (1 byte)	Subset sequence number (1 byte)	Domain name length (1 byte)
Management Domain Name (zero-padded to 32 bytes)			
Configuration Revision Number (4 bytes)			
VLAN Info Field 1 (see below)			
VLAN Info Field ...			
VLAN Info Field N			

VTP VLAN Info Field

0	1	2	3
Info Length	VLAN Status	VLAN Type	VLAN Name Length
VLAN ID		MTU Size	
802.10 SAID			
VLAN Name (padded with zeros to multiple of 4 bytes)			

Figure 5-2 *VTP Subset Advertisement and VLAN Info Field Formats*

■ **Advertisement requests from clients:** A VTP client can request any VLAN information it lacks. For example, a client switch might be reset and have its VLAN database cleared, and its VTP domain membership might be changed, or it might hear a VTP summary advertisement with a higher revision number than it currently has. After a client advertisement request, the VTP domain servers respond with summary and subset advertisements to bring it up to date. Figure 5-3 shows the advertisement request format.

0	1	2	3
Version (1 byte)	Type (Adv request) (1 byte)	Reserved (1 byte)	Domain name length (1 byte)
Management Domain Name (zero-padded to 32 bytes)			
Starting advertisement to request			

Figure 5-3 *VTP Advertisement Request Format*

Catalyst switches in server mode store VTP information separately from the switch configuration in NVRAM. VLAN and VTP data are saved in the vlan.dat file on the switch's flash memory file system. All VTP information, including the VTP configuration revision number, is retained even when the switch power is off. In this manner, a switch can recover the last known VLAN configuration from its VTP database after it reboots.

VTP Synchronization

Key Topic

Whenever a switch receives a VTP advertisement with a configuration revision number that is greater than the value stored locally, it considers the advertisement to contain newer information. The switch will overwrite its own VLAN data with the newer version—even if the newer version contains irrelevant information. Because of this, it is very important to always force any newly added network switches to have revision number 0 before being attached to the network. Otherwise, a switch might have stored a revision number that is greater than the value currently in use in the domain.

The VTP revision number is stored in NVRAM and is not altered by a power cycle of the switch; therefore, the revision number can be initialized to 0 only by using one of the following methods:

- Change the switch's VTP mode to transparent and then change the mode back to server.

- Change the switch's VTP domain to a bogus name (a nonexistent VTP domain), and then change the VTP domain back to the original name.

If the VTP revision number is not reset to 0, the switch might enter the network as a VTP server and have a preexisting revision number (from a previous life) that is higher than in previous legitimate advertisements. The new switch's VTP information would be seen as more recent, so all other switches in the VTP domain would gladly accept its database of VLANs and overwrite their good VLAN database entries with null or deleted VLAN status information.

Key Topic

In other words, a new server switch might inadvertently cause every other working switch to flush all records of every VLAN in production. The VLANs would be deleted from the VTP database and from the switches, causing any switch port assigned to them to be returned to the default VLAN 1. This is referred to as a *VTP synchronization problem*. For critical portions of your network, you should consider using VTP transparent or off mode to prevent the synchronization problem from ever becoming an issue.

Tip   It might seem intuitive that a switch acting as a VTP server could come online with a higher configuration revision number and wreak havoc on the whole domain. You should also be aware that this same thing can happen if a VTP client comes online with a higher revision, too!

Even though it seems as if a client should strictly listen to advertisements from servers, a client can and does send out its own advertisements. When it first powers up, a client sends a summary advertisement from its own stored database. It realizes that it has a greater revision number if it receives an inferior advertisement from a server. Therefore, it sends out a subset advertisement with the greater revision number, which VTP servers will accept as more up-to-date information. Even in VTP client mode, a switch will store the last known VTP information—including the configuration revision number. Do not assume that a VTP client will start with a clean slate when it powers up.

In the days when networks were flat and VLANs stretched end to end, VTP was a convenient administrative tool. VLANs could be created or deleted on all switches in a VTP domain very easily. In this book, you have learned that end-to-end VLANs are not a good idea. Instead, VLANs should be contained within a single switch block or a single access switch.

In such small areas, VTP is not really necessary at all. In fact, Cisco recommends a best practice of configuring all switches in VTP transparent or off mode. You should understand VTP because you might encounter it in an existing network and you should know how to maintain and disable it.

VTP Configuration

By default, every switch operates in VTP server mode for the management domain NULL (a blank string), with no password or secure mode. If the switch hears a VTP summary advertisement on a trunk port from any other switch, it automatically learns the VTP domain name, VLANs, and the configuration revision number it hears. This makes it easy to bring up a new switch in an existing VTP domain. However, be aware that the new switch stays in VTP server mode, something that might not be desirable.

Tip   You should get into the habit of double-checking the VTP configuration of any switch before you add it into your network. Make sure that the VTP configuration revision number is set to 0. You can do this by isolating the switch from the network, powering it up, and using the **show vtp status** command, as demonstrated in the following output:

```
Switch# show vtp status
VTP Version capable             : 1 to 3
VTP version running             : 1
VTP Domain Name                 :
VTP Pruning Mode                : Disabled
VTP Traps Generation            : Disabled
Device ID                       : aca0.164f.3f80
Configuration last modified by 0.0.0.0 at 0-0-00 00:00:00
Local updater ID is 0.0.0.0 (no valid interface found)
Feature VLAN:
--------------
VTP Operating Mode              : Server
Maximum VLANs supported locally : 1005
Number of existing VLANs        : 5
Configuration Revision          : 0
MD5 digest                      : 0x57 0xCD 0x40 0x65 0x63 0x59 0x47 0xBD
                                  0x56 0x9D 0x4A 0x3E 0xA5 0x69 0x35 0xBC
                                  Switch#
```

Here, the switch has a configuration revision number of 0, and is in the default state of VTP server mode with an undefined VTP domain name. This switch would be safe to add to a network.

The following sections discuss the commands and considerations that you should use to configure a switch for VTP operation.

Configuring the VTP Version

Three versions of VTP are available for use in a management domain. Catalyst switches can run either VTP Version 1, 2, or 3. Within a management domain, the versions are not fully interoperable. Therefore, the same VTP version should be configured on every switch in a domain. Switches use VTP Version 1 by default.

However, a switch can make some adjustments to be more compatible with neighbors using different VTP versions. For example, a switch running VTPv1 will attempt to change to VTPv2 if it hears a switch running Version 2 or 3 in the domain and it is capable of running Version 2. A switch running VTPv3 will begin sending scaled-down advertisements if it hears a VTPv1 switch. One exception is if extended range VLANs (1006 to 4094) are in use; the extended range is supported only on switches capable of VTPv3.

Key Topic

The VTP versions differ in the features they support. VTP Versions 2 and 3 offer additional features over Version 1, as listed in Tables 5-2 and 5-3, respectively.

Table 5-2 *Additional Features Supported by VTP Version 2*

VTP v2 Feature	Description
Version-dependent transparent mode	Relay VTP messages in transparent mode without checking for version mismatches.
Consistency checks	Check VTP and VLAN parameters entered from the command-line interface (CLI) or Simple Network Management Protocol (SNMP) to prevent errors from being propagated to other switches.
Token Ring support	Token Ring switching and VLANs can be advertised.
Unrecognized Type-Length-Value (TLV) support	VTP messages are relayed even if they contain advertisements other than known types. This allows VTP to be extended to include new advertisement types.

Table 5-3 *Additional Features Supported by VTP Version 3*

VTP v3 Feature	Description
Extended VLAN range	VLANs 1 through 4094 can be advertised throughout a VTPv3 domain.
Enhanced authentication	Switches can authenticate with each other through a secret key that can be hidden from the configuration.
Database propagation	Databases other than VTP can be advertised.
Primary and secondary servers	By default, all VTPv3 switches operate as secondary servers and can send updates throughout the domain. A primary server is only needed to take control of a domain.
Per-port VTP	VTPv3 can be enabled on a per-trunk port basis, rather than a switch as a whole.

The VTP version number is configured using the following global configuration command:

```
Switch(config)# vtp version {1 | 2 | 3}
```

By default, a switch uses VTP Version 1.

Configuring a VTP Management Domain

Key Topic

Before a switch is added into a network, the VTP management domain should be identified. If this switch is the first one on the network, the management domain must be created. Otherwise, the switch might have to join an existing management domain with other existing switches.

You can use the following global configuration command to assign a switch to a management domain, where the *domain-name* is a text string up to 32 characters long:

```
Switch(config)# vtp domain domain-name
```

Configuring the VTP Mode

Next, you need to choose the VTP mode for the new switch. The VTP modes of operation and their guidelines for use are as follows:

Key
Topic

- **Server mode:** Server mode can be used on any switch in a management domain, even if other server and client switches are already in use. This mode provides some redundancy in case of a server failure in the domain. Each VTP management domain should have at least one server. The first server defined in a network also defines the management domain that will be used by future VTP servers and clients. Server mode is the default VTP mode and allows VLANs to be created and deleted.

Note Multiple VTP servers can coexist in a domain. This is usually recommended for redundancy. The servers do not elect a primary or secondary server; except in the case of VTPv3, they all simply function as servers. If one server is configured with a new VLAN or VTP parameter, it advertises the changes to the rest of the domain. All other servers synchronize their VTP databases to this advertisement, just as any VTP client would.

- **Client mode:** If other switches are in the management domain, you should configure a new switch for client mode operation. In this way, the switch is forced to learn any existing VTP information from a reliable existing server. After the switch has learned the current VTP information, you can reconfigure it for server mode if it will be used as a redundant server.

- **Transparent mode:** This mode is used if a switch will not share VLAN information with any other switch in the network. VLANs still can be manually created, deleted, and modified on the transparent switch (and on every other transparent switch that the VLANs touch). However, they are not advertised to other neighboring switches. VTP advertisements received by a transparent switch, however, are forwarded to other switches on trunk links.

  Keeping switches in transparent mode can eliminate the chance for duplicate, overlapping VLANs in a large network with many network administrators. For example, two administrators might configure VLANs on switches in their respective areas but use the same VLAN identification or VLAN number. Even though the two VLANs have different meanings and purposes, they could overlap if both administrators advertised them using VTP servers.

- **Off mode:** You can use off mode to disable all VTP activity on a switch. No VTP advertisements are sent, none will be received and processed, and none will be relayed to other neighboring switches.

Key Topic

You can configure the VTP mode with the following sequence of global configuration commands:

```
Switch(config)# vtp mode {server | client | transparent | off}
Switch(config)# vtp password password [hidden | secret]
```

If the domain is operating in secure mode, a password also can be defined. The password can be configured only on VTP servers and clients. The password itself is not sent; instead, a message digest 5 (MD5) authentication or hash code is computed and sent in VTP advertisements (servers) and is used to validate received advertisements (clients). The password is a string of 1 to 32 characters (case sensitive). For VTP Version 3, the password can be hidden (only a hash of the password is saved in the running configuration) or secret (the password is saved in the running configuration).

If secure VTP is implemented using passwords, begin by configuring a password on the VTP servers. The client switches retain the last-known VTP information but cannot process received advertisements until the same password is configured on them, too.

Table 5-4 shows a summary of the VTP modes. You can use this table for quick review as you study VTP operation.

Table 5-4   *Catalyst VTP Modes*

VTP Mode	Characteristics
Server	All VLAN and VTP configuration changes occur here. The server advertises settings and changes to all other servers and clients in a VTP domain. (This is the default mode for Catalyst switches.)
Client	Listens to all VTP advertisements from servers in a VTP domain. Advertisements are relayed out other trunk links. No VLAN or VTP configuration changes can be made on a client.
Transparent	VLAN configuration changes are made locally, independent of any VTP domain. VTP advertisements are not received but merely are relayed out other trunk links, if possible.
Off	VLAN configuration changes are made locally; incoming VTP advertisements are not processed locally, but simply relayed instead.

VTP Configuration Example

As an example, a switch is configured as a VTP Version 1 server in a domain named MyCompany. The domain uses secure VTP with the password bigsecret. You can use the following configuration commands to accomplish this:

```
Switch(config)# vtp version 1
Switch(config)# vtp domain MyCompany
Switch(config)# vtp mode server
Switch(config)# vtp password bigsecret
```

To follow the best practice and put a switch into VTP transparent mode, you can use the following command:

```
Switch(config)# vtp mode transparent
```

VTP Status

The current VTP parameters for a management domain can be displayed using the **show vtp status** command. Example 5-1 demonstrates some sample output of this command from a switch acting as a VTP client in the VTP domain called CampusDomain.

Example 5-1   show vtp status *Reveals VTP Parameters for a Management Domain*

```
Switch# show vtp status
VTP Version capable             : 1 to 3
VTP version running             : 1
VTP Domain Name                 : CampusDomain
VTP Pruning Mode                : Disabled
VTP Traps Generation            : Disabled
Device ID                       : aca0.164f.3f80
Configuration last modified by 0.0.0.0 at 3-30-11 04:42:25


Feature VLAN:
--------------
VTP Operating Mode              : Client
Maximum VLANs supported locally : 1005
Number of existing VLANs        : 17
Configuration Revision          : 25
MD5 digest                      : 0x6E 0x21 0x14 0x12 0x56 0x0E 0x0A 0x21
                                  0x4A 0x32 0x6C 0xB7 0xA8 0xA5 0x28 0x08
Switch#
```

You can also use the **show vtp status** command to verify that a switch is operating in the VTP transparent mode, as shown in Example 5-2.

Example 5-2   show vtp status *Verifies VTP Transparent Mode*

```
Switch# show vtp status
VTP Version capable             : 1 to 3
VTP version running             : 1
VTP Domain Name                 :
VTP Pruning Mode                : Disabled
VTP Traps Generation            : Disabled
```

```
Device ID                     : aca0.164f.3f80
Configuration last modified by 0.0.0.0 at 0-0-00 00:00:00


Feature VLAN:
--------------
VTP Operating Mode            : Transparent
Maximum VLANs supported locally   : 1005
Number of existing VLANs      : 5
Configuration Revision        : 0
MD5 digest                    : 0x5E 0x0E 0xA7 0x4E 0xC7 0x4C 0x6F 0x3B
                                0x9E 0x17 0x1F 0x31 0xE0 0x05 0x91 0xCE
Switch#
```

VTP Pruning

Recall that, by definition, a switch must forward broadcast frames out all available ports in the broadcast domain because broadcasts are destined everywhere there is a listener. Unless forwarded by more intelligent means, multicast frames follow the same pattern.

In addition, frames destined for an address that the switch has not yet learned or has *forgotten* (the MAC address has aged out of the address table) must be forwarded out all ports in an attempt to find the destination. These frames are referred to as *unknown unicast*.

When forwarding frames out all ports in a broadcast domain or VLAN, trunk ports are included if they transport that VLAN. By default, a trunk link transports traffic from all VLANs, unless specific VLANs are removed from the trunk. Generally, in a network with several switches, trunk links are enabled between switches, and VTP might be used to manage the propagation of VLAN information. This scenario causes the trunk links between switches to carry traffic from *all* VLANs, not just from the specific VLANs created. Consider the network shown in Figure 5-4. When end user Host PC in VLAN 3 sends a broadcast, Catalyst switch C forwards the frame out all VLAN 3 ports, including the trunk link to Catalyst A. Catalyst A, in turn, forwards the broadcast on to Catalysts B and D over those trunk links. Catalysts B and D forward the broadcast out only their access links that have been configured for VLAN 3. If Catalysts B and D do not have any active users in VLAN 3, forwarding that broadcast frame to them would consume bandwidth on the trunk links and processor resources in both switches, only to have switches B and D discard the frames.

Key Topic

VTP pruning makes more efficient use of trunk bandwidth by reducing unnecessary flooded traffic. Broadcast, multicast, and unknown unicast frames on a VLAN are forwarded over a trunk link only if the switch on the receiving end of the trunk has ports in that VLAN.

VTP pruning occurs as an extension to VTP version 1, using an additional VTP message type. When a Catalyst switch has a port associated with a VLAN, the switch sends an advertisement to its neighbor switches that it has active ports on that VLAN. The neighbors keep this information, enabling them to decide whether flooded traffic from a VLAN should be allowed on the trunk links.

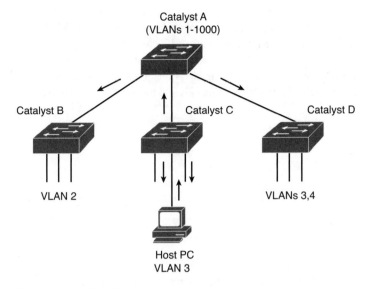

Figure 5-4   *Flooding in a Catalyst Switch Network*

Figure 5-5 shows the network from Figure 5-4 with VTP pruning enabled. Because Catalyst B has not advertised its use of VLAN 3, Catalyst A will prune VLAN 3 from the trunk to B and will choose not to flood VLAN 3 traffic to Catalyst B over the trunk link. Catalyst D has advertised the need for VLAN 3, so traffic will be flooded to it.

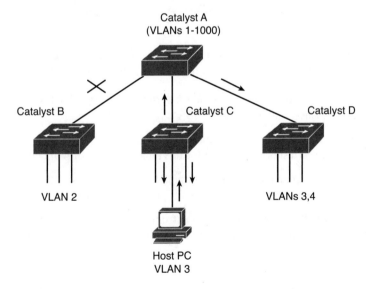

Figure 5-5   *Flooding in a Catalyst Switch Network Using VTP Pruning*

> **Tip**   Even when VTP pruning has determined that a VLAN is not needed on a trunk,
> an instance of the Spanning Tree Protocol (STP) will run for every VLAN that is allowed
> on the trunk link. To reduce the number of STP instances, you should manually "prune"
> unneeded VLANs from the trunk and allow only the needed ones. Use the **switchport
> trunk allowed vlan** command to identify the VLANs that should be added or removed
> from a trunk.

Enabling VTP Pruning

By default, VTP pruning is disabled. To enable pruning, use the following global configuration command:

```
Switch(config)# vtp pruning
```

If you use this command on a VTP server, it also advertises that pruning needs to be
enabled for the entire management domain. All other switches listening to that advertisement will also enable pruning.

When pruning is enabled, all general-purpose VLANs become eligible for pruning on
all trunk links, if needed. However, you can modify the default list of pruning eligibility
with the following interface-configuration command:

```
Switch(config)# interface type member/module/number
Switch(config-if)# switchport trunk pruning vlan {{{add | except |  remove}
vlan-list} | none}
```

By default, VLANs 2 through 1001 are eligible, or "enabled," for potential pruning on
every trunk. Use one of the following keywords with the command to tailor the list:

■   *vlan-list*: An explicit list of eligible VLAN numbers (anything from 2 to 1001), separated by commas or by dashes, but no spaces.

■   **add** *vlan-list*: A list of VLAN numbers (anything from 2 to 1001) is added to the
already configured list; this is a shortcut to keep from typing a long list of numbers.

■   **except** *vlan-list*: All VLANs are eligible except for the VLAN numbers listed (anything from 2 to 1001); this is a shortcut to keep from typing a long list of numbers.

■   **remove** *vlan-list*: A list of VLAN numbers (anything from 2 to 1001) is removed
from the already configured list; this is a shortcut to keep from typing a long list of
numbers.

■   **None:** No VLAN will be eligible for pruning.

Tip Be aware that VTP pruning has no effect on switches in the VTP transparent mode. Instead, those switches must be configured manually to "prune" VLANs from trunk links. By default, VLANs 2 to 1001 are eligible for pruning. VLAN 1 has a special meaning because it is sometimes used for control traffic and is the default access VLAN on switch ports. Because of these historical reasons, VLAN 1 is never eligible for pruning. In addition, VLANs 1002 through 1005 are reserved for Token Ring and FDDI VLANs and are never eligible for pruning.

Troubleshooting VTP

If a switch does not seem to be receiving updated information from a VTP server, consider these possible causes:

- The switch is configured for VTP transparent mode. In this mode, incoming VTP advertisements are not processed; they are relayed only to other switches in the domain.

- If the switch is configured as a VTP client, there might not be another switch functioning as a VTP server. In this case, configure the local switch to become a VTP server itself.

- The link toward the VTP server is not in trunking mode. VTP advertisements are sent only over trunks. Use the **show interface type** *member/module/number* **switchport** to verify the operational mode as a trunk.

- Make sure that the VTP domain name is configured correctly to match that of the VTP server.

- Make sure that the VTP version is compatible with other switches in the VTP domain.

- Make sure that the VTP password matches others in the VTP domain. If the server does not use a password, make sure the password is disabled or cleared on the local switch.

Tip Above all else, verify a switch's VTP configuration before connecting it to a production network. If the switch has been configured previously or used elsewhere, it might already be in VTP server mode and have a VTP configuration revision number that is higher than that of other switches in the production VTP domain. In that case, other switches will listen and learn from the new switch because it has a higher revision number and must know more recent information. This could cause the new switch to introduce bogus VLANs into the domain or, worse yet, to cause all other switches in the domain to delete all their active VLANs.

To prevent this from happening, reset the configuration revision number of every new switch before it is added to a production network. Even better, avoid using VTP completely!

Table 5-5 lists and describes the commands that are useful for verifying or troubleshooting VTP configuration.

Table 5-5   *VTP Configuration Troubleshooting Commands*

Function	Command Syntax
Displays current VTP parameters, including the last advertising server	**show vtp status**
Displays defined VLANs	**show vlan brief**
Displays trunk status, including pruning eligibility	**show interface** *type member/module/number* **switchport**
Displays VTP pruning state	**show interface** *type member/module/number* **pruning**

Exam Preparation Tasks

Review All Key Topics

Review the most important topics in the chapter, noted with the Key Topic icon in the outer margin of the page. Table 5-6 lists a reference of these key topics and the page numbers on which each is found.

Table 5-6 *Key Topics for Chapter 5*

Key Topic Element	Description	Page Number
Paragraph	Describes VTP modes	127
Paragraph	Explains the VPN configuration revision number	128
Paragraph	Discusses the VTP synchronization problem and how to prevent it from occurring	131
Paragraph	Describes VTP version operation	134
List	Explains how to configure the VTP mode	135
Example 5-1	Discusses how to verify VTP operation	137
Paragraph	Explains VTP pruning	138

Complete Tables and Lists from Memory

Print a copy of Appendix C, "Memory Tables," (found on the CD), or at least the section for this chapter, and complete the tables and lists from memory. Appendix D, "Memory Table Answer Key," also on the CD, includes completed tables and lists to check your work.

Define Key Terms

Define the following key terms from this chapter, and check your answers in the glossary:

VTP, VTP domain, VTP configuration revision number, VTP synchronization problem, VTP pruning

Use Command Reference to Check Your Memory

This section includes the most important configuration and EXEC commands covered in this chapter. It might not be necessary to memorize the complete syntax of every command, but you should remember the basic keywords that are needed.

To test your memory of the VTP-related commands, cover the right side of Table 5-7 with a piece of paper, read the description on the left side, and then see how much of the command you can remember.

Remember that the CCNP exam focuses on practical or hands-on skills that are used by a networking professional. For the skills covered in this chapter, remember that the commands always involve the **vtp** keyword.

Table 5-7 *VTP Configuration Commands*

Task	Command Syntax
Define the VTP domain.	Switch(config)# **vtp domain** *domain-name*
Set the VTP mode.	Switch(config)# **vtp mode** {**server** | **client** | **transparent** | **off**}
Define an optional VTP password.	Switch(config)# **vtp password** *password* [**hidden** | **secret**]
Configure VTP version.	Switch(config)# **vtp version** {1 | 2 | 3}
Enable VTP pruning.	Switch(config)# **vtp pruning**
Select VLANs eligible for pruning on a trunk interface.	Switch(config)# **interface** *type member/ module/number*
	Switch(config-if)# **switchport trunk pruning vlan** {**add** | **except** | **none** | **remove**} *vlan-list*

This chapter covers the following topics that you need to master for the CCNP SWITCH exam:

■ **IEEE 802.1D Overview:** This section discusses the original, or more traditional, Spanning Tree Protocol (STP). This protocol is the foundation for the default Catalyst STP and for all the enhancements that are described in Chapters 7, "Spanning-Tree Configuration," through 9, "Advanced Spanning Tree Protocol."

■ **Types of STP:** This section discusses other types of STP that might be running on a Catalyst switch— specifically, the Common Spanning Tree, Per-VLAN Spanning Tree (PVST), and PVST+.

CHAPTER 6

Traditional Spanning Tree Protocol

Previous chapters covered ways to connect two switches together with a VLAN trunk link. What if something happens to the trunk link? The two switches would be isolated from each other. A more robust network design would add redundant links between switches. Although this increases the network availability, it also opens up the possibility for conditions that would impair the network. In a Layer 2 switched network, preventing bridging loops from forming over redundant paths is important. Spanning Tree Protocol (STP) was designed to monitor and control the Layer 2 network so that a loop-free topology is maintained.

This chapter discusses the theory and operation of the STP. More specifically, the original, or traditional, STP is covered, as defined in IEEE 802.1D. Several chapters explain STP topics in this book. Here is a brief roadmap so that you can chart a course:

- **Chapter 6, "Traditional Spanning Tree Protocol"**: Covers the theory of IEEE 802.1D

- **Chapter 7, "Spanning-Tree Configuration"**: Covers the configuration commands needed for IEEE 802.1D

- **Chapter 8, "Protecting the Spanning Tree Protocol Topology"**: Covers the features and commands to filter and protect a converged STP topology from conditions that could destabilize it

- **Chapter 9, "Advanced Spanning Tree Protocol"**: Covers the newer 802.1w and 802.1s enhancements to STP, allowing more scalability and faster convergence

"Do I Know This Already?" Quiz

The "Do I Know This Already?" quiz allows you to assess whether you should read this entire chapter thoroughly or jump to the "Exam Preparation Tasks" section. If you are in doubt based on your answers to these questions or your own assessment of your knowledge of the topics, read the entire chapter. Table 6-1 outlines the major headings in this chapter and the "Do I Know This Already?" quiz questions that go with them. You can find the answers in Appendix A, "Answers to the 'Do I Know This Already?' Quizzes."

Table 6-1   *"Do I Know This Already?" Foundation Topics Section-to-Question Mapping*

Foundation Topics Section	Questions Covered in This Section
IEEE 802.1D Overview	1–9
Types of STP	10–11

1. How is a bridging loop best described?

    a. A loop formed between switches for redundancy

    b. A loop formed by the Spanning Tree Protocol

    c. A loop formed between switches where frames circulate endlessly

    d. The round-trip path a frame takes from source to destination

2. Which of these is one of the parameters used to elect a root bridge?

    a. Root path cost

    b. Path cost

    c. Bridge priority

    d. BPDU revision number

3. If all switches in a network are left at their default STP values, which one of the following is not true?

    a. The root bridge will be the switch with the lowest MAC address.

    b. The root bridge will be the switch with the highest MAC address.

    c. One or more switches will have a bridge priority of 32,768.

    d. A secondary root bridge will be present on the network.

4. Configuration BPDUs are originated by which of the following?

    a. All switches in the STP domain

    b. Only the root bridge switch

    c. Only the switch that detects a topology change

    d. Only the secondary root bridge when it takes over

5. What happens to a port that is neither a root port nor a designated port?

    a. It is available for normal use.

    b. It can be used for load balancing.

    c. It is put into the Blocking state.

    d. It is disabled.

6. What is the maximum number of root ports that a Catalyst switch can have?

   a. 1

   b. 2

   c. Unlimited

   d. None

7. What mechanism is used to set STP timer values for all switches in a network?

   a. Configuring the timers on every switch in the network.

   b. Configuring the timers on the root bridge switch.

   c. Configuring the timers on both primary and secondary root bridge switches.

   d. The timers cannot be adjusted.

8. MAC addresses can be placed into the CAM table, but no data can be sent or received if a switch port is in which of the following STP states?

   a. Blocking

   b. Forwarding

   c. Listening

   d. Learning

9. What is the default "hello" time for IEEE 802.1D?

   a. 1 second

   b. 2 seconds

   c. 30 seconds

   d. 60 seconds

10. Which of the following is the Spanning Tree Protocol that is defined in the IEEE 802.1Q standard?

   a. PVST

   b. CST

   c. EST

   d. MST

11. If a switch has ten VLANs defined and active, how many instances of STP will run using PVST+ versus CST?

    a. 1 for PVST+, 1 for CST

    b. 1 for PVST+, 10 for CST

    c. 10 for PVST+, 1 for CST

    d. 10 for PVST+, 10 for CST

Foundation Topics

IEEE 802.1D Overview

A robust network design not only includes efficient transfer of packets or frames, but also considers how to recover quickly from faults in the network. In a Layer 3 environment, the routing protocols in use keep track of redundant paths to a destination network so that a secondary path can be used quickly if the primary path fails. Layer 3 routing allows many paths to a destination to remain up and active, and allows load sharing across multiple paths.

In a Layer 2 environment (switching or bridging), however, no routing protocols are used, and active redundant paths are neither allowed nor desirable. Instead, some form of bridging provides data transport between networks or switch ports. The Spanning Tree Protocol (STP) provides network link redundancy so that a Layer 2 switched network can recover from failures without intervention in a timely manner. The STP is defined in the IEEE 802.1D standard.

STP is discussed in relation to the problems it solves in the sections that follow.

Bridging Loops

Recall that a Layer 2 switch mimics the function of a transparent bridge. A transparent bridge must offer segmentation between two networks while remaining transparent to all the end devices connected to it. For the purpose of this discussion, consider a two-port Ethernet switch and its similarities to a two-port transparent bridge.

A transparent bridge (and the Ethernet switch) must operate as follows:

■ The bridge has no initial knowledge of any end device's location; therefore, the bridge must "listen" to frames coming into each of its ports to figure out on which network each device resides. The bridge assumes that a device using the source MAC address is located behind the port that the frame arrives on. As the listening process continues, the bridge builds a table that correlates source MAC addresses with the bridge port numbers where they were detected.

■ The bridge can constantly update its bridging table on detecting the presence of a new MAC address or on detecting a MAC address that has changed location from one bridge port to another. The bridge then can forward frames by looking at the destination MAC address, looking up that address in the bridge table, and sending the frame out the port where the destination device is known to be located.

■ If a frame arrives with the broadcast address as the destination address, the bridge must forward, or flood, the frame out all available ports. However, the frame is not forwarded out the port that initially received the frame. In this way, broadcasts can reach all available Layer 2 networks. A bridge segments only collision domains; it does not segment broadcast domains.

- If a frame arrives with a destination address that is not found in the bridge table, the bridge cannot determine which port to forward the frame to for transmission. This type of frame is known as an *unknown unicast*. In this case, the bridge treats the frame as if it were a broadcast and floods it out all remaining ports. When a reply to that frame is overheard, the bridge can learn the location of the unknown station and can add it to the bridge table for future use.

- Frames forwarded across the bridge cannot be modified by the bridge itself. Therefore, the bridging process is effectively *transparent*.

Bridging or switching in this fashion works well. Any frame forwarded, whether to a known or unknown destination, is forwarded out the appropriate port or ports so that it is likely to be received successfully at the intended destination. Figure 6-1 shows a simple two-port switch functioning as a bridge, forwarding frames between two end devices. However, this network design offers no additional links or paths for redundancy if the switch or one of its links fails. In that case, the networks on either side of the bridge would become isolated from each other.

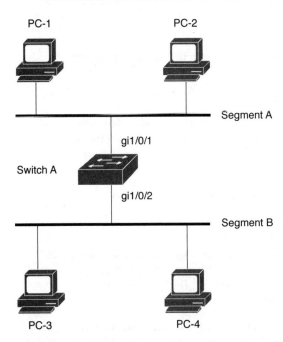

Figure 6-1 *Transparent Bridging with a Switch*

To add some redundancy, you can add a second switch between the two original network segments, as shown in Figure 6-2. Now, two switches offer the transparent bridging function in parallel. In theory, a single switch or a single link can fail without causing end-to-end connectivity to fail.

Consider what happens when PC 1 sends a frame to PC 4. For now, assume that both PC 1 and PC 4 are known to the switches and are in their address tables. PC 1 sends the frame onto network Segment A. Switch A and switch B both receive the frame on their gi1/0/1 ports. Because PC 4 already is known to the switches, the frame is forwarded out ports gi1/0/2 on each switch onto Segment B. The end result is that PC 4 receives two copies of the frame from PC 1. This is not ideal, but it is not disastrous, either.

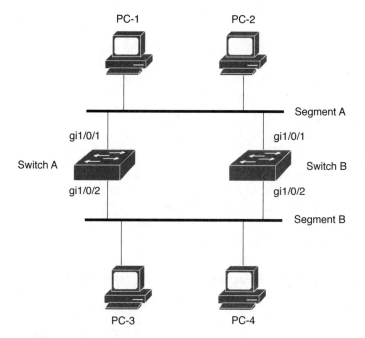

Figure 6-2   *Redundant Bridging with Two Switches*

Key Topic

Now, consider the same process of sending a frame from PC 1 to PC 4. This time, however, neither switch knows anything about the location of PC 1 or PC 4. PC 1 sends the frame to PC 4 by placing it on Segment A. The sequence of events is as follows:

Step 1.   Both Switch A and Switch B receive the frame on their gi1/0/1 ports. Because the MAC address of PC 1 has not yet been seen or recorded, each switch records PC 1's MAC address in its address table along with the receiving port number, gi1/0/1. From this information, both switches infer that PC 1 must reside on Segment A.

Step 2.   Because the location of PC 4 is unknown, both switches correctly decide that they must flood the frame out all available ports. This is an unknown unicast condition and is their best effort to make sure that the frame eventually reaches its destination.

Step 3.   Each switch floods or copies the frame to its gi1/0/2 port on Segment B. PC 4, located on Segment B, receives the two frames destined for it. However, on Segment B, Switch A now hears the new frame forwarded by Switch B, and Switch B hears the new frame forwarded by Switch A.

Step 4.   Switch A sees that the "new" frame is from PC 1 to PC 4. From the address table, the switch previously learned that PC 1 was on port gi1/0/1, or Segment

A. However, the source address of PC 1 has just been heard on port gi1/0/2, or Segment B. By definition, the switch must relearn the location of PC 1 with the most recent information, which it now incorrectly assumes to be Segment B. (Switch B follows the same procedure, based on the "new" frame from Switch A.)

Step 5. At this point, neither Switch A nor Switch B has learned the location of PC 4 because no frames have been received with PC 4 as the source address. Therefore, the new frame must be flooded out all available ports in an attempt to find PC 4. This frame then is sent out Switch A's gi1/0/1 port and on to Segment A, as well as Switch B's gi1/0/1 port and on to Segment A.

Step 6. Now both switches relearn the location of PC 1 as Segment A and forward the "new" frames back onto Segment B; then the entire process repeats.

This process of forwarding a single frame around and around between two switches is known as a *bridging loop*. Neither switch is aware of the other, so each happily forwards the same frame back and forth between its segments. Also note that because two switches are involved in the loop, the original frame has been duplicated and now is sent around in two counter-rotating loops. What stops the frame from being forwarded in this fashion forever? Nothing! PC 4 begins receiving frames addressed to it as fast as the switches can forward them.

Notice how the learned location of PC 1 keeps changing as frames get looped. Even a simple unicast frame has caused a bridging loop to form, and each switch's bridge table is repeatedly corrupted with incorrect data.

What would happen if PC 1 sent a broadcast frame instead? The bridging loops (remember that two of them are produced by the two parallel switches) form exactly as before. The broadcast frames continue to circulate forever. Now, however, every end-user device located on both Segments A and B receives and processes every broadcast frame. This type of broadcast storm can easily saturate the network segments and bring every host on the segments to a halt.

The only way to end the bridging loop condition is to physically break the loop by disconnecting switch ports or shutting down a switch. Obviously, it would be better to *prevent* bridging loops than to be faced with finding and breaking them after they form.

Preventing Loops with Spanning Tree Protocol

Bridging loops form because parallel switches (or bridges) are unaware of each other. STP was developed to overcome the possibility of bridging loops so that redundant switches and switch paths could be used for their benefits. Basically, the protocol enables switches to become aware of each other so they can negotiate a loop-free path through the network.

Note Because STP is involved in loop detection, many people refer to the catastrophic loops as *spanning-tree loops*. This is technically incorrect because the Spanning Tree Protocol's entire function is to prevent bridging loops. The correct terminology for this condition is a *bridging loop*.

Loops are discovered before they are made available for use, and redundant links are effectively shut down to prevent the loops from forming. In the case of redundant links, switches can be made aware that a link shut down for loop prevention should be brought up quickly in case of a link failure. The section "Redundant Link Convergence" in Chapter 7 provides more information.

STP is communicated among all connected switches on a network. Each switch executes the spanning-tree algorithm based on information received from other neighboring switches. The algorithm chooses a reference point in the network and calculates all the redundant paths to that reference point. When redundant paths are found, the spanning-tree algorithm picks one path by which to forward frames and disables, or blocks, forwarding on the other redundant paths.

As its name implies, STP computes a tree structure that spans all switches in a subnet or network. Redundant paths are placed in a Blocking or Standby state to prevent frame forwarding. The switched network is then in a loop-free condition. However, if a forwarding port fails or becomes disconnected, the spanning-tree algorithm recomputes the spanning-tree topology so that the appropriate blocked links can be reactivated.

Spanning-Tree Communication: Bridge Protocol Data Units

Key Topic

STP operates as switches communicate with one another. Data messages are exchanged in the form of bridge protocol data units (BPDUs). A switch sends a BPDU frame out a port, using the unique MAC address of the port itself as a source address. The switch is unaware of the other switches around it, so BPDU frames are sent with a destination address of the well-known STP multicast address 01-80-c2-00-00-00.

Two types of BPDU exist:

■ **Configuration BPDU**, used for spanning-tree computation

■ **Topology Change Notification (TCN) BPDU**, used to announce changes in the network topology

The Configuration BPDU message contains the fields shown in Table 6-2. The TCN BPDU is discussed in the "Topology Changes" section later in this chapter.

Table 6-2 *Configuration BPDU Message Content*

Field Description	Number of Bytes
Protocol ID (always 0)	2
Version	1
Message Type (Configuration or TCN BPDU)	1
Flags	1
Root Bridge ID	8
Root Path Cost	4

Field Description	Number of Bytes
Sender Bridge ID	8
Port ID	2
Message age (in 256ths of a second)	2
Maximum age (in 256ths of a second)	2
Hello time (in 256ths of a second)	2
Forward delay (in 256ths of a second)	2

The exchange of BPDU messages works toward the goal of electing reference points as a foundation for a stable spanning-tree topology. Also, loops can be identified and removed by placing specific redundant ports in a Blocking or Standby state. Notice that several key fields in the BPDU are related to bridge (or switch) identification, path costs, and timer values. These all work together so that the network of switches can converge on a common spanning-tree topology and select the same reference points within the network. These reference points are defined in the sections that follow.

By default, BPDUs are sent out all switch ports every 2 seconds so that current topology information is exchanged and loops are identified quickly.

Electing a Root Bridge

For all switches in a network to agree on a loop-free topology, a common frame of reference must exist to use as a guide. This reference point is called the *root bridge*. (The term *bridge* continues to be used even in a switched environment because STP was developed for use in bridges. Therefore, when you see *bridge*, think *switch*.)

An election process among all connected switches chooses the root bridge. Each switch has a unique *bridge* ID that identifies it to other switches. The bridge ID is an 8-byte value consisting of the following fields:

- **Bridge Priority (2 bytes):** The priority or weight of a switch in relation to all other switches. The Priority field can have a value of 0 to 65,535 and defaults to 32,768 (or 0x8000) on every Catalyst switch.

- **MAC Address (6 bytes):** The MAC address used by a switch can come from the Supervisor module, the backplane, or a pool of 1024 addresses that are assigned to every supervisor or backplane, depending on the switch model. In any event, this address is hard-coded and unique, and the user cannot change it.

When a switch first powers up, it has a narrow view of its surroundings and assumes that it is the root bridge itself. (This notion probably will change as other switches check in and enter the election process.) The election process then proceeds as follows: Every switch begins by sending out BPDUs with a root bridge ID equal to its own bridge ID and a sender bridge ID that is its own bridge ID. The sender bridge ID simply tells other switches who is the actual sender of the BPDU message. (After a root bridge is decided on, configuration BPDUs are sent only by the root bridge. All other bridges must forward or relay the BPDUs, adding their own sender bridge IDs to the message.)

Received BPDU messages are analyzed to see if a "better" root bridge is being announced. A root bridge is considered better if the root bridge ID value is *lower* than another. Again, think of the root bridge ID as being broken into Bridge Priority and MAC Address fields. If two bridge priority values are equal, the lower MAC address makes the bridge ID better. When a switch hears of a better root bridge, it replaces its own root bridge ID with the root bridge ID announced in the BPDU. The switch then is required to recommend or advertise the new root bridge ID in its own BPDU messages, although it still identifies itself as the sender bridge ID.

Sooner or later, the election converges and all switches agree on the notion that one of them is the root bridge. As might be expected, if a new switch with a lower bridge priority powers up, it begins advertising itself as the root bridge. Because the new switch does indeed have a lower bridge ID, all the switches soon reconsider and record it as the new root bridge. This can also happen if the new switch has a bridge priority equal to that of the existing root bridge but has a lower MAC address. Root bridge election is an ongoing process, triggered by root bridge ID changes in the BPDUs every 2 seconds.

As an example, consider the small network shown in Figure 6-3. For simplicity, assume that each switch has a MAC address of all 0s, with the last hex digit equal to the switch label.

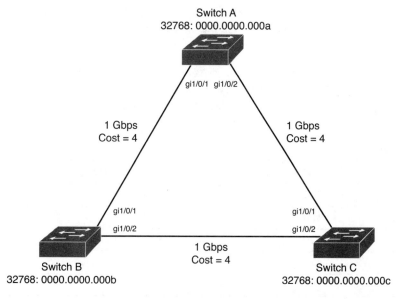

Figure 6-3 *Example of Root Bridge Election*

In this network, each switch has the default bridge priority of 32,768. The switches are interconnected with Gigabit Ethernet links. All three switches try to elect themselves as the root, but all of them have equal bridge priority values. The election outcome produces the root bridge, determined by the lowest MAC address—that of Switch A.

Electing Root Ports

Now that a reference point has been nominated and elected for the entire switched network, each nonroot switch must figure out where it is in relation to the root bridge. This action can be performed by selecting only one *root port* on each nonroot switch. The root port always points toward the current root bridge.

STP uses the concept of cost to determine many things. Selecting a root port involves evaluating the *root path cost*. This value is the cumulative cost of all the links leading to the root bridge. A particular switch link also has a cost associated with it, called the *path cost*. To understand the difference between these values, remember that only the root path cost is carried inside the BPDU. (Refer to Table 6-2.) As the root path cost travels along, other switches can modify its value to make it cumulative. The path cost, however, is not contained in the BPDU. It is known only to the local switch where the port (or "path" to a neighboring switch) resides.

Path costs are defined as a 1-byte value, with the default values shown in Table 6-3. Generally, the higher the bandwidth of a link, the lower the cost of transporting data across it. The original IEEE 802.1D standard defined path cost as 1000 Mbps divided by the link bandwidth in megabits per second. These values are shown in the center column of the table. Modern networks commonly use Gigabit and 10-Gigabit Ethernet, which are both either too close to or greater than the maximum scale of 1000 Mbps. The IEEE now uses a nonlinear scale for path cost, as shown in the right column of the table.

Tip   Be aware that there are two STP path cost scales, one that is little used with a linear scale and one commonly used that is nonlinear. If you decide to memorize some common path cost values, learn only the ones in the New STP Cost column of the table.

Table 6-3   *STP Path Cost*

Link Bandwidth	Old STP Cost	New STP Cost
4 Mbps	250	250
10 Mbps	100	100
16 Mbps	63	62
45 Mbps	22	39
100 Mbps	10	19
155 Mbps	6	14
622 Mbps	2	6
1 Gbps	1	4
10 Gbps	0	2

The root path cost value is determined in the following manner:

1. The root bridge sends out a BPDU with a root path cost value of 0 because its ports sit directly on the root bridge.

2. When the next-closest neighbor receives the BPDU, it adds the path cost of its own port where the BPDU arrived. (This is done as the BPDU is *received*.)

3. The neighbor sends out BPDUs with this new cumulative value as the root path cost.

4. The root path cost is incremented by the ingress port path cost as the BPDU is received at each switch down the line.

5. Notice the emphasis on incrementing the root path cost as BPDUs are *received*. When computing the spanning-tree algorithm manually, remember to compute a new root path cost as BPDUs *come in* to a switch port, not as they go out.

After incrementing the root path cost, a switch also records the value in its memory. When a BPDU is received on another port and the new root path cost is lower than the previously recorded value, this lower value becomes the new root path cost. In addition, the lower cost tells the switch that the path to the root bridge must be better using this port than it was on other ports. The switch has now determined which of its ports has the best path to the root: the root port.

Figure 6-4 shows the same network from Figure 6-3 in the process of root port selection.

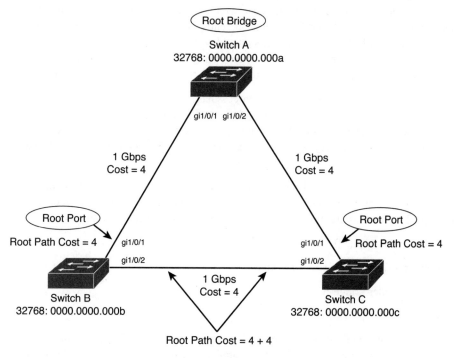

Figure 6-4 *Example of Root Port Selection*

The root bridge, Switch A, already has been elected. Therefore, every other switch in the network must choose one port that has the best path to the root bridge. Switch B selects its port gi1/0/1, with a root path cost of 0 plus 4. Port gi1/0/2 is not chosen because its root path cost is 0 (BPDU from Switch A) plus 4 (path ost of A-C link), plus 4 (path cost of C-B link), or a total of 8. Switch C makes an identical choice of port gi1/0/1.

Electing Designated Ports

By now, you should begin to see the process unfolding: A starting or reference point has been identified, and each switch "connects" itself toward the reference point with the single link that has the best path. A tree structure is beginning to emerge, but links have only been identified at this point. All links still are connected and could be active, leaving bridging loops.

To remove the possibility of bridging loops, STP makes a final computation to identify one *designated port* on each network segment. Suppose that two or more switches have ports connected to a single common network segment. If a frame appears on that segment, all the bridges attempt to forward it to its destination. Recall that this behavior was the basis of a bridging loop and should be avoided.

Instead, only one of the links on a segment should forward traffic to and from that segment—the one that is selected as the designated port. Switches choose a designated port based on the lowest cumulative root path cost to the root bridge. For example, a switch always has an idea of its own root path cost, which it announces in its own BPDUs. If a neighboring switch on a shared LAN segment sends a BPDU announcing a lower root path cost, the neighbor must have the designated port. If a switch learns only of higher root path costs from other BPDUs received on a port, however, it then correctly assumes that its own receiving port is the designated port for the segment.

Notice that the entire STP determination process has served only to identify bridges and ports. All ports are still active, and bridging loops still might lurk in the network. STP has a set of progressive states that each port must go through, regardless of the type or identification. These states actively prevent loops from forming and are described in the next section.

In each determination process discussed so far, two or more links might have identical root path costs. This results in a tie condition, unless other factors are considered. All tie-breaking STP decisions are based on the following sequence of four conditions:

1. Lowest root bridge ID

2. Lowest root path cost to root bridge

3. Lowest sender bridge ID

4. Lowest sender port ID

Figure 6-5 demonstrates an example of designated port selection. This figure is identical to Figure 6-3 and Figure 6-4, with further spanning-tree development shown. The only changes are the choices of designated ports, although seeing all STP decisions shown on one network diagram is handy.

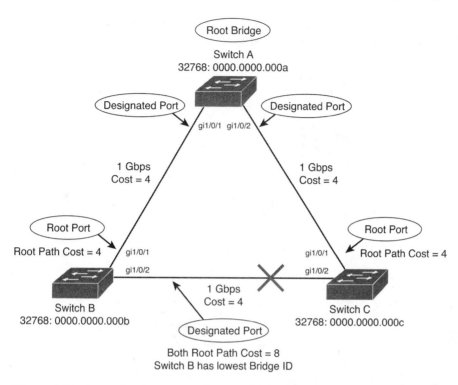

Figure 6-5   *Example of Designated Port Selection*

The three switches have chosen their designated ports (DPs) for the following reasons:

- **Catalyst A:** Because this switch is the root bridge, all its active ports are designated ports, by definition. At the root bridge, the root path cost of each port is 0.

- **Catalyst B:** Switch A port gi1/0/1 is the DP for the Segment A–B because it has the lowest root path cost (0). Switch B port gi1/0/2 is the DP for segment B–C. The root path cost for each end of this segment is 4, determined from the incoming BPDU on port gi1/0/1. Because the root path cost is equal on both ports of the segment, the DP must be chosen by the next criteria—the lowest sender bridge ID. When Switch B sends a BPDU to Switch C, it has the lowest MAC address in the bridge ID. Switch C also sends a BPDU to Switch B, but its sender bridge ID is higher. Therefore, Switch B port gi1/0/2 is selected as the segment's DP.

- **Catalyst C:** Switch A port gi1/0/2 is the DP for Segment A–C because it has the lowest root path cost (0). Switch B port gi1/0/2 is the DP for Segment B–C. Therefore, Switch C port gi1/0/2 will be neither a root port nor a designated port. As discussed in the next section, any port that is not elected to either position enters the Blocking state. Where blocking occurs, bridging loops are broken.

As a final step, it is often helpful to see the resulting network topology after STP has made its decisions. Figure 6-6 shows the topology without all of the STP notation and clutter. Even though the three switches are physically connected in a closed loop, STP has detected that possibility and has blocked the link between Switches B and C, effectively preventing a loop from forming. Both B and C can still pass traffic through Switch A, so the network is still fully functional.

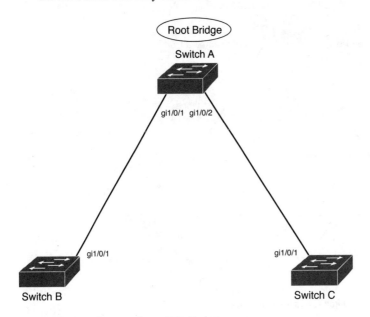

Figure 6-6 *The Resulting STP Topology*

Think about how this topology might apply to a real network, where Switch A is in the distribution layer and Switches B and C are in the access layer. The root bridge is located higher in the network hierarchy, feeding lower-level switches with active links. The loop will be broken farthest away from the root, where traffic might have traveled between switches inefficiently.

STP States

To participate in STP, each port of a switch must progress through several states. A port begins its life in a Disabled state, moving through several passive states and, finally, into an active state if allowed to forward traffic. The STP port states are as follows:

- **Disabled:** Ports that are administratively shut down by the network administrator, or by the system because of a fault condition, are in the Disabled state. This state is special and is not part of the normal STP progression for a port.

- **Blocking:** After a port initializes, it begins in the Blocking state so that no bridging loops can form. In the Blocking state, a port cannot receive or transmit data and cannot add MAC addresses to its address table. Instead, a port is allowed to receive only BPDUs so that the switch can hear from other neighboring switches. In addition, ports that are put into standby mode to remove a bridging loop enter the Blocking state.

- **Listening:** A port is moved from Blocking to Listening if the switch thinks that the port can be selected as a root port or designated port. In other words, the port is on its way to begin forwarding traffic.

  In the Listening state, the port still cannot send or receive data frames. However, the port is allowed to receive and send BPDUs so that it can actively participate in the Spanning Tree topology process. Here, the port finally is allowed to become a root port or designated port because the switch can advertise the port by sending BPDUs to other switches. If the port loses its root port or designated port status, it returns to the Blocking state.

- **Learning:** After a period of time called the *forward delay* in the Listening state, the port is allowed to move into the Learning state. The port still sends and receives BPDUs as before. In addition, the switch now can learn new MAC addresses to add to its address table. This gives the port an extra period of silent participation and allows the switch to assemble at least some address information. The port cannot yet send any data frames, however.

- **Forwarding:** After another forward delay period of time in the Learning state, the port is allowed to move into the Forwarding state. The port now can send and receive data frames, collect MAC addresses in its address table, and send and receive BPDUs. The port is now a fully functioning switch port within the spanning-tree topology.

Remember that a switch port is allowed into the Forwarding state only if no redundant links (or loops) are detected and if the port has the best path to the root bridge as the root port or designated port.

Table 6-4 summarizes the STP port states and what can and cannot be done in those states.

Table 6-4   *STP States and Port Activity*

STP State	The Port Can...	The Port Cannot...	Duration
Disabled	N/A	Send or receive data	N/A
Blocking	Receive BPDUs	Send or receive data or learn MAC addresses	Indefinite if loop has been detected
Listening	Send and receive BPDUs	Send or receive data or learn MAC addresses	Forward Delay timer (15 seconds)
Learning	Send and receive BPDUs and learn MAC addresses	Send or receive data	Forward Delay timer (15 seconds)
Forwarding	Send and receive BPDUs, learn MAC addresses, and send and receive data		Indefinite as long as port is up and loop is not detected

Example 6-1 shows the output from a switch as one of its ports progresses through the STP port states.

Example 6-1 *Switch Port Progressing Through the STP Port States*

```
Switch(config)# interface gigabitethernet1/0/1
Switch(config-if)# no shutdown
Switch(config-if)# ^Z
Switch#
Mar 30 08:12:11.199: STP SW: Gi1/0/1 new blocking req for 1 vlans

Mar 30 08:12:13.196: %LINK-3-UPDOWN: Interface GigabitEthernet1/0/1, changed state
to up
Mar 30 08:12:14.203: %LINEPROTO-5-UPDOWN: Line protocol on Interface GigabitEther-
net1/0/1, changed state to up

Switch# show spanning interface gigabitethernet1/0/1
Vlan               Role Sts Cost      Prio.Nbr Type
------------------ ---- --- --------- -------- --------------------------------
VLAN0001           Desg LIS 4         128.1    P2p

Mar 30 08:12:26.207: STP SW: Gi1/0/1 new learning req for 1 vlans

Switch# show spanning interface gigabitethernet1/0/1
Vlan               Role Sts Cost      Prio.Nbr Type
------------------ ---- --- --------- -------- --------------------------------
VLAN0001           Desg LRN 4         128.1    P2p

Mar 30 08:12:41.214: STP SW: Gi1/0/1 new forwarding req for 1 vlans

Switch# show spanning interface gigabitethernet1/0/1

Vlan               Role Sts Cost      Prio.Nbr Type
------------------ ---- --- --------- -------- --------------------------------
VLAN0001           Desg FWD 4         128.1    P2p
Switch#
```

The example begins as the port is administratively disabled from the command line. When the port is enabled, successive **show spanning-tree interface type** member/*module*/*number* commands display the port state as Listening, Learning, and then Forwarding. These are shown in the shaded text of the example. Notice also the time stamps and port states provided by the **debug spanning-tree switch state** command, which give a sense of the timing between port states. Because this port was eligible as a root port, the **show** command never could execute fast enough to show the port in the Blocking state.

You can manually work out a spanning-tree topology using a network diagram. Follow the basic steps listed in Table 6-5 to add information to the network diagram. By the time you reach step 5, your STP will have converged, just like the switches in a live network would do.

Table 6-5   *Manual STP Computation*

Task	Description
1. Identify path costs on links.	For each link between switches, write the path cost that each switch uses for the link.
2. Identify the root bridge.	Find the switch with the lowest bridge ID; mark it on the drawing.
3. Select root ports (1 per switch).	For each switch, find the one port that has the best path to the root bridge. This is the one with the lowest root path cost. Mark the port with an RP label.
4. Select designated ports (1 per segment).	For each link between switches, identify which end of the link will be the designated port. This is the one with the lowest root path cost; if equal on both ends, use STP tie-breakers. Mark the port with a DP label.
5. Identify the blocking ports.	Every switch port that is neither a root nor a designated port will be put into the Blocking state. Mark these with an *X*.

STP Timers

STP operates as switches send BPDUs to each other in an effort to form a loop-free topology. The BPDUs take a finite amount of time to travel from switch to switch. In addition, news of a topology change (such as a link or root bridge failure) can suffer from propagation delays as the announcement travels from one side of a network to the other. Because of the possibility of these delays, keeping the spanning-tree topology from settling out or converging until all switches have had time to receive accurate information is important.

STP uses three timers to make sure that a network converges properly before a bridging loop can form. The timers and their default values are as follows:

- **Hello timer:** The time interval between Configuration BPDUs sent by the root bridge. The hello time value configured in the root bridge switch determines the hello time for all nonroot switches because they just relay the Configuration BPDUs as they are received from the root. However, all switches have a locally configured hello time that is used to time TCN BPDUs when they are retransmitted. The IEEE 802.1D standard specifies a default hello time value of 2 seconds.

- **Forward Delay timer:** The time interval that a switch port spends in both the Listening and Learning states. The default value is 15 seconds.

■ **Max (Maximum) Age timer:** The time interval that a switch stores a BPDU before discarding it. While executing the STP, each switch port keeps a copy of the "best" BPDU that it has heard. If the switch port loses contact with the BPDU's source (no more BPDUs are received from it), the switch assumes that a topology change must have occurred after the max age time elapsed and so the BPDU is aged out. The default Max Age timer value is 20 seconds.

The STP timers can be configured or adjusted from the switch command line. However, the timer values never should be changed from the defaults without careful consideration. Then the values should be changed only on the root bridge switch. Recall that the timer values are advertised in fields within the BPDU. The root bridge ensures that the timer values propagate to all other switches.

Tip The default STP timer values are based on some assumptions about the size of the network and the length of the hello time. A reference model of a network having a diameter of seven switches derives these values. The diameter is measured from the root bridge switch outward, including the root bridge.

In other words, if you draw the STP topology, the diameter is the number of switches connected in series from the root bridge out to the end of any branch in the tree. The hello time is based on the time it takes for a BPDU to travel from the root bridge to a point seven switches away. This computation uses a hello time of 2 seconds.

The network diameter can be configured on the root bridge switch to more accurately reflect the true size of the physical network. Making that value more accurate reduces the total STP convergence time during a topology change. Cisco also recommends that if changes need to be made, only the network diameter value should be modified on the root bridge switch. When the diameter is changed, the switch calculates new values for all three timers automatically.

Table 6-6 summarizes the STP timers, their functions, and their default values.

Table 6-6 *STP Timers*

Timer	Function	Default Value
Hello	Interval between configuration BPDUs.	2 seconds
Forward delay	Time spent in Listening and Learning states before transitioning toward Forwarding state.	15 seconds
Max age	Maximum length of time a BPDU can be stored without receiving an update. Timer expiration signals an indirect failure with designated or root bridge.	20 seconds

Topology Changes

To announce a change in the active network topology, switches send a TCN BPDU. Table 6-7 shows the format of these messages.

Table 6-7 *Topology Change Notification BPDU Message Content*

Field Description	Number of Bytes
Protocol ID (always 0)	2
Version (always 0)	1
Message Type (Configuration or TCN BPDU)	1

Key Topic

A topology change occurs when a switch either moves a port into the Forwarding state or moves a port from the Forwarding or Learning states into the Blocking state. In other words, a port on an active switch comes up or goes down. The switch sends a TCN BPDU out its root port so that, ultimately, the root bridge receives news of the topology change. Notice that the TCN BPDU carries no data about the change but informs recipients only that a change has occurred. Also notice that the switch will not send TCN BPDUs if the port has been configured with PortFast enabled.

The switch continues sending TCN BPDUs every hello time interval until it gets an acknowledgment from its upstream neighbor. As the upstream neighbors receive the TCN BPDU, they propagate it on toward the root bridge and send their own acknowledgments. When the root bridge receives the TCN BPDU, it also sends out an acknowledgment. However, the root bridge sets the Topology Change flag in its Configuration BPDU, which is relayed to every other bridge in the network. This is done to signal the topology change and cause all other bridges to shorten their bridge table aging times from the default (300 seconds) to the forward delay value (default 15 seconds).

This condition causes the learned locations of MAC addresses to be flushed out much sooner than they normally would, easing the bridge table corruption that might occur because of the change in topology. However, any stations that are actively communicating during this time are kept in the bridge table. This condition lasts for the sum of the forward delay and the max age (default 15 + 20 seconds).

The theory behind topology changes is fairly straightforward, but it is often difficult to grasp how a working network behaves during a change. For example, suppose that you have a Layer 2 network (think of a single VLAN or a single instance of STP) that is stable and loop free. If a switch uplink suddenly failed or a new uplink was added, how would the various switches in the network react? Would users all over the network lose connectivity while the STP "recomputes" or reconverges?

Examples of different types of topology changes are presented in the following sections, along with the sequence of STP events. Each type has a different cause and a different effect. To provide continuity as the STP concepts are presented, the same network previously shown in Figures 6-3 through 6-5 is used in each of these examples.

Direct Topology Changes

A direct topology change is one that can be detected on a switch interface. For example, if a trunk link suddenly goes down, the switch on each end of the link can immediately detect a link failure. The absence of that link changes the bridging topology, so other switches should be notified.

Figure 6-7 shows a network that has converged into a stable STP topology. The VLAN is forwarding on all trunk links except port gi1/0/2 on Switch C, where it is in the Blocking state.

This network has just suffered a link failure between Switch A and Switch C. The sequence of events unfolds as follows:

1. Switch C detects a link down on its port gi1/0/1; Switch A detects a link down on its port gi1/0/2.

2. Switch C removes the previous "best" BPDU it had received from the root over port gi1/0/1. Port gi1/0/1 is now down so that BPDU is no longer valid.

   Normally, Switch C would try to send a TCN message out its root port, to reach the root bridge. Here, the root port is broken, so that is not possible. Without an advanced feature such as STP UplinkFast, Switch C is not yet aware that another path exists to the root.

   Also, Switch A is aware of the link down condition on its own port gi1/0/2. It normally would try to send a TCN message out its root port to reach the root bridge. Here, Switch A is the root, so that is not really necessary.

3. The root bridge, Switch A, sends a Configuration BPDU with the TCN bit set out its port gi1/0/1. This is received and relayed by each switch along the way, informing each one of the topology change.

4. Switches B and C receive the TCN message. The only reaction these switches take is to shorten their bridging table aging times to the forward delay time. At this point, they do not know how the topology has changed; they only know to force fairly recent bridging table entries to age out.

5. Switch C basically just sits and waits to hear from the root bridge again. The Configuration BPDU TCN message is received on port gi1/0/2, which was previously in the Blocking state. This BPDU becomes the "best" one received from the root, so port gi1/0/2 becomes the new root port.

   Switch C now can progress port gi1/0/2 from Blocking through the Listening, Learning, and Forwarding states.

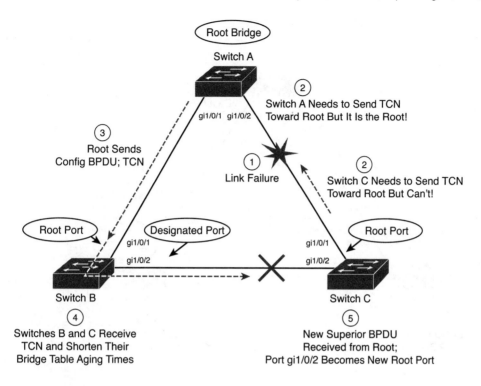

Figure 6-7   *Effects of a Direct Topology Change*

As a result of a direct link failure, the topology has changed and STP has converged again. Notice that only Switch C has undergone any real effects from the failure. Switches A and B heard the news of the topology change but did not have to move any links through the STP states. In other words, the whole network did not go through a massive STP reconvergence.

The total time that users on Switch C lost connectivity was roughly the time that port gi1/0/2 spent in the Listening and Learning states. With the default STP timers, this amounts to about two times the forward delay period (15 seconds), or 30 seconds total.

Indirect Topology Changes

Figure 6-8 shows the same network as Figure 6-7, but this time the link failure indirectly involves Switches A and C. The link status at each switch stays up, but something between them has failed or is filtering traffic. This could be another device, such as a service provider's switch, a firewall, and so on. As a result, no data (including BPDUs) can pass between those switches.

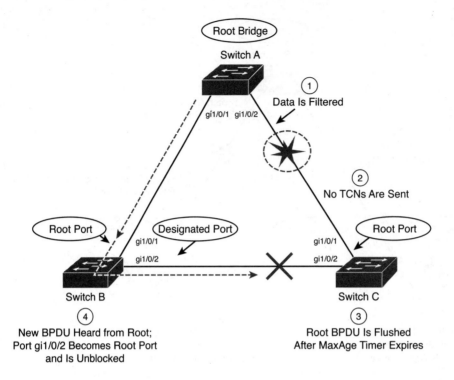

Figure 6-8 *Effects of an Indirect Topology Change*

STP can detect and recover from indirect failures, thanks to timer mechanisms. The sequence of events unfolds as follows:

1. Switches A and C both show a link up condition; data begins to be filtered elsewhere on the link.

2. No link failure is detected, so no TCN messages are sent.

3. Switch C already has stored the "best" BPDU it had received from the root over port gi1/0/1. No further BPDUs are received from the root over that port. After the Max Age timer expires, no other BPDU is available to refresh the "best" entry, so it is flushed. Switch C now must wait to hear from the Root again on any of its ports.

4. The next Configuration BPDU from the root is heard on Switch C port gi1/0/2. This BPDU becomes the new "best" entry, and port gi1/0/2 becomes the root port. Now the port is progressed from Blocking through the Listening, Learning, and finally Forwarding states.

As a result of the indirect link failure, the topology does not change immediately. The absence of BPDUs from the root causes Switch C to take some action. Because this type of failure relies on STP timer activity, it generally takes longer to detect and mitigate.

In this example, the total time that users on Switch C lost connectivity was roughly the time until the max age timer expired (20 seconds), plus the time until the next

Configuration BPDU was received (2 seconds) on port gi1/0/2, plus the time that port gi1/0/2 spent in the Listening (15 seconds) and Learning (15 seconds) states. In other words, 52 seconds elapse if the default timer values are used.

Insignificant Topology Changes

Figure 6-9 shows the same network topology as Figure 6-7 and Figure 6-8, with the addition of a user PC on access layer switch Switch C. The user's switch port, gi1/0/33/, is just another link as far as the switch is concerned. If the link status goes up or down, the switch must view that as a topology change and inform the root bridge.

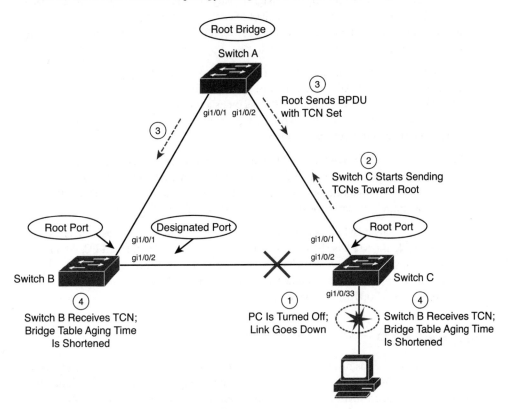

Figure 6-9 *Effects of an Insignificant Topology Change*

Obviously, user ports are expected to go up and down as the users reboot their machines, turn them on and off as they go to and from work, and so on. Regardless, TCN messages are sent by the switch, just as if a trunk link between switches had changed state.

To see what effect this has on the STP topology and the network, consider the following sequence of events:

1. The PC on switch port gi1/0/33 is turned off. The switch detects the link status going down.

2.   Switch C begins sending TCN BPDUs toward the root, over its root port (gi1/0/1).

3.   The root sends a TCN acknowledgment back to Switch C and then sends a Configuration BPDU with the TCN bit set to all downstream switches. This is done to inform every switch of a topology change somewhere in the network.

4.   The TCN flag is received from the root, and both Switches B and C shorten their bridge table aging times. This causes recently idle entries to be flushed, leaving only the actively transmitting stations in the table. The aging time stays short for the duration of the Forward Delay and Max Age timers.

Notice that this type of topology change is mostly cosmetic. No actual topology change occurred because none of the switches had to change port states to reach the root bridge. Instead, powering off the PC caused all the switches to age out entries from their bridge or CAM tables much sooner than normal.

At first, this does not seem like a major problem because the PC link state affects only the "newness" of the CAM table contents. If CAM table entries are flushed as a result, they probably will be learned again. This becomes a problem when every user PC is considered. Now every time *any* PC in the network powers up or down, *every* switch in the network must age out CAM table entries.

Given enough PCs, the switches could be in a constant state of flushing bridge tables. Also remember that when a switch does not have a CAM entry for a destination, the packet must be flooded out all its ports. Flushed tables mean more unknown unicasts, which mean more broadcasts or flooded packets throughout the network.

Fortunately, Catalyst switches have a feature that can designate a port as a special case. You can enable the STP PortFast feature on a port with a single attached PC. As a result, TCNs are not sent when the port changes state, and the port is brought right into the Forwarding state when the link comes up. The section "Redundant Link Convergence," in Chapter 7, covers PortFast in more detail.

Types of STP

So far, this chapter has discussed STP in terms of its operation to prevent loops and to recover from topology changes in a timely manner. STP was originally developed to operate in a bridged environment, basically supporting a single LAN (or one VLAN). Implementing STP into a switched environment has required additional consideration and modification to support multiple VLANs. Because of this, the IEEE and Cisco have approached STP differently. This section reviews the three traditional types of STP that are encountered in switched networks and how they relate to one another. No specific configuration commands are associated with the various types of STP here. Instead, you need a basic understanding of how they interoperate in a network.

> **Note** The IEEE 802.1D standard also includes spanning-tree enhancements that greatly improve on its scalability and convergence aspects. These are covered in Chapter 9. When you have a firm understanding of the more traditional forms of STP presented in this chapter, you can grasp the enhanced versions much easier.

Common Spanning Tree

The IEEE 802.1Q standard specifies how VLANs are to be trunked between switches. It also specifies only a single instance of STP that encompasses all VLANs. This instance is referred to as the *Common Spanning Tree* (CST). All CST BPDUs are transmitted over trunk links using the native VLAN with untagged frames.

Having a single STP for many VLANs simplifies switch configuration and reduces switch CPU load during STP calculations. However, having only one STP instance can cause limitations, too. Redundant links between switches will be blocked with no capability for load balancing. Conditions also can occur that would cause CST to mistakenly enable forwarding on a link that does not carry a specific VLAN, whereas other links would be blocked.

Per-VLAN Spanning Tree

Cisco has a proprietary version of STP that offers more flexibility than the CST version. Per-VLAN Spanning Tree (PVST) operates a separate instance of STP for each individual VLAN. This allows the STP on each VLAN to be configured independently, offering better performance and tuning for specific conditions. Multiple spanning trees also make load balancing possible over redundant links when the links are assigned to different VLANs. One link might forward one set of VLANs, while another redundant link might forward a different set.

Because of its proprietary nature, PVST requires the use of Cisco Inter-Switch Link (ISL) trunking encapsulation between switches. In networks where PVST and CST coexist, interoperability problems occur. Each requires a different trunking method, so BPDUs are never exchanged between STP types.

Per-VLAN Spanning Tree Plus

Cisco has a second proprietary version of STP that allows devices to interoperate with both PVST and CST. Per-VLAN Spanning Tree Plus (PVST+) effectively supports three groups of STP operating in the same campus network:

- Catalyst switches running PVST
- Catalyst switches running PVST+
- Switches running CST over 802.1Q

Table 6-8 summarizes the three STP types and their basic functions.

Table 6-8 *Types of STP*

Type of STP	Function
CST	1 instance of STP, over the native VLAN; 802.1Q based
PVST	1 instance of STP per VLAN; Cisco ISL based
PVST+	Provides interoperability between CST and PVST; operates over both 802.1Q and ISL

To do this, PVST+ acts as a translator between groups of CST switches and groups of PVST switches. PVST+ can communicate directly with PVST by using ISL trunks. To communicate with CST, however, PVST+ exchanges BPDUs with CST as untagged frames over the native VLAN. BPDUs from other instances of STP (other VLANs) are propagated across the CST portions of the network by tunneling. PVST+ sends these BPDUs by using a unique multicast address so that the CST switches forward them on to downstream neighbors without interpreting them first. Eventually, the tunneled BPDUs reach other PVST+ switches where they are understood.

Exam Preparation Tasks

Review All Key Topics

Review the most important topics in the chapter, noted with the Key Topic icon in the outer margin of the page. Table 6-9 lists a reference of these key topics and the page numbers on which each is found.

Key Topic

Table 6-9   *Key Topics for Chapter 6*

Key Topic Element	Description	Page Number
List	Describes transparent bridge operation	151
List	Explains a bridging loop	153
Paragraph	Discusses BPDUs	155
Paragraph	Discusses root bridge election	156
Paragraph	Explains root port selection and root path cost	158
Paragraph	Discusses designated port selection	160
List	Explains tie-breaking decision process	160
List	Discusses the sequence of STP port states	162
List	Explains the three STP timers and their uses	165
Paragraph	Explains STP topology changes	167
Paragraph	Describes the Common Spanning Tree	173
Paragraph	Describes Per-VLAN Spanning Tree+	173

Complete Tables and Lists from Memory

Print a copy of Appendix C, "Memory Tables," (found on the CD), or at least the section for this chapter, and complete the tables and lists from memory. Appendix D, "Memory Table Answer Key," also on the CD, includes completed tables and lists to check your work.

Define Key Terms

Define the following key terms from this chapter, and check your answers in the glossary:

transparent bridge, bridging loop, Spanning Tree Protocol (STP), BPDU, root bridge, root port, root path cost, designated port, hello time, forward delay, max age time, TCN, Common Spanning Tree (CST), PVST, PVST+

This chapter covers the following topics that you need to master for the CCNP SWITCH exam:

- **STP Root Bridge:** This section discusses the importance of identifying a root bridge and suggestions for its placement in the network. This section also presents the root bridge configuration commands.

- **Spanning-Tree Customization:** This section covers the configuration commands that enable you to alter the spanning-tree topology.

- **Tuning Spanning-Tree Convergence:** This section discusses how to alter, or tune, the STP timers to achieve optimum convergence times in a network.

- **Redundant Link Convergence:** This section describes the methods that cause a network to converge more quickly after a topology change.

- **Monitoring STP:** This section offers a brief summary of the commands that you can use to verify that an STP instance is working properly.

CHAPTER 7

Spanning-Tree Configuration

This chapter presents the design and configuration considerations necessary to implement the IEEE 802.1D Spanning Tree Protocol (STP) in a campus network. This chapter also discusses the commands needed to configure the STP features, previously described in Chapter 6, "Traditional Spanning Tree Protocol."

You can also tune STP or make it converge more efficiently in a given network. This chapter presents the theory and commands needed to accomplish this.

"Do I Know This Already?" Quiz

The "Do I Know This Already?" quiz allows you to assess whether you should read this entire chapter thoroughly or jump to the "Exam Preparation Tasks" section. If you are in doubt based on your answers to these questions or your own assessment of your knowledge of the topics, read the entire chapter. Table 7-1 outlines the major headings in this chapter and the "Do I Know This Already?" quiz questions that go with them. You can find the answers in Appendix A, "Answers to the 'Do I Know This Already?' Quizzes."

Table 7-1 *"Do I Know This Already?" Foundation Topics Section-to-Question Mapping*

Foundation Topics Section	Questions Covered in This Section
STP Root Bridge	1-6
Spanning-Tree Customization	7-8
Tuning Spanning-Tree Convergence	9-10
Redundant Link Convergence	11-13
Monitoring STP	14

1. Which of these is the single most important design decision to be made in a network running STP?

    a. Removing any redundant links

    b. Making sure all switches run the same version of IEEE 802.1D

    c. Root bridge placement

    d. Making sure all switches have redundant links

2. Where should the root bridge be placed on a network?

   a. On the fastest switch

   b. Closest to the most users

   c. Closest to the center of the network

   d. On the least-used switch

3. Which of the following is a result of a poorly placed root bridge in a network?

   a. Bridging loops form.

   b. STP topology cannot be resolved.

   c. STP topology can take unexpected paths.

   d. Root bridge election flapping occurs.

4. Which of these parameters should you change to make a switch become a root bridge?

   a. Switch MAC address

   b. Path cost

   c. Port priority

   d. Bridge priority

5. What is the default base 802.1D STP bridge priority on a Catalyst switch?

   a. 0

   b. 1

   c. 32,768

   d. 65,535

6. Which of the following commands is most likely to make a switch become the root bridge for VLAN 5, assuming that all switches have the default STP parameters?

   a. spanning-tree root

   b. spanning-tree root vlan 5

   c. spanning-tree vlan 5 priority 100

   d. spanning-tree vlan 5 root

7. What is the default path cost of a Gigabit Ethernet switch port?

   a. 1

   b. 2

   c. 4

   d. 19

   e. 1000

8. What command can change the path cost of interface Gigabit Ethernet 1/0/3 to a value of 8?

    a. spanning-tree path-cost 8

    b. spanning-tree cost 8

    c. spanning-tree port-cost 8

    d. spanning-tree gig 1/0/3 cost 8

9. What happens if the root bridge switch and another switch are configured with different STP Hello timer values?

    a. Nothing; each sends hellos at different times.

    b. A bridging loop could form because the two switches are out of sync.

    c. The switch with the lower Hello timer becomes the root bridge.

    d. The other switch changes its Hello timer to match the root bridge

10. What network diameter value is the basis for the default STP timer calculations?

    a. 1

    b. 3

    c. 7

    d. 9

    e. 15

11. Where should the STP PortFast feature be used?

    a. An access layer switch port connected to a PC

    b. An access layer switch port connected to a hub

    c. A distribution layer switch port connected to an access layer switch

    d. A core layer switch port

12. Where should the STP UplinkFast feature be enabled?

    a. An access layer switch.

    b. A distribution layer switch.

    c. A core layer switch.

    d. All these answers are correct.

13. If used, the STP BackboneFast feature should be enabled on which of these?

   a. All backbone or core layer switches

   b. All backbone and distribution layer switches

   c. All access layer switches

   d. All switches in the network

14. Which one of the following commands enables you to verify the current root bridge in VLAN 10?

   a. show root vlan 10

   b. show root-bridge vlan 10

   c. show spanning-tree vlan 10 root

   d. show running-config

Foundation Topics

STP Root Bridge

Spanning Tree Protocol (STP) and its computations are predictable; however, other factors might subtly influence STP decisions, making the resulting tree structure neither expected nor ideal.

As the network administrator, you can make adjustments to the spanning-tree operation to control its behavior. The location of the root bridge should be determined as part of the design process. You can use redundant links for load balancing in parallel, if configured correctly. You can also configure STP to converge quickly and predictably if a major topology change occurs.

Tip   By default, STP is enabled for all active VLANs and on all ports of a switch. STP should remain enabled in a network to prevent bridging loops from forming. However, you might find that STP has been disabled in some way.

If an entire instance of STP has been disabled, you can reenable it with the following global configuration command:

```
Switch(config)# spanning-tree vlan vlan-id
```

If STP has been disabled for a specific VLAN on a specific port, you can reenable it with the following interface configuration command:

```
Switch (config-if)# spanning-tree vlan vlan-id
```

Root Bridge Placement

Although STP is wonderfully automatic with its default values and election processes, the resulting tree structure might perform quite differently than expected. The root bridge election is based on the idea that one switch is chosen as a common reference point, and all other switches choose ports that have the best-cost path to the root. The root bridge election is also based on the idea that the root bridge can become a central hub that interconnects other legs of the network. Therefore, the root bridge can be faced with heavy switching loads in its central location.

If the root bridge election is left to its default state, several things can occur to result in a poor choice. For example, the *slowest* switch (or bridge) could be elected as the root bridge. If heavy traffic loads are expected to pass through the root bridge, the slowest switch is not the ideal candidate. Recall that the only criteria for root bridge election is that the switch must have the lowest bridge ID (bridge priority and MAC address), which is not necessarily the best choice to ensure optimal performance. If the slowest switch has the same bridge priority as the others and has the lowest MAC address, the slowest switch will be chosen as the root.

A second factor to consider relates to redundancy. If all switches are left at their default states, only one root bridge is elected, with no clear choice for a backup. What happens if that switch fails? Another root bridge election occurs, but again, the choice might not be the ideal switch or the ideal location.

The final consideration is the location of the root bridge switch. As before, an election with default switch values could place the root bridge in an unexpected location in the network. More important, an inefficient spanning-tree structure could result, causing traffic from a large portion of the network to take a long and winding path just to pass through the root bridge.

Figure 7-1 shows a portion of a hierarchical campus network that is staged for just such an inefficient topology. A single VLAN extends end to end, from the core to the access layer. End-to-end VLANs are considered a bad practice, but will serve nicely for an STP scenario.

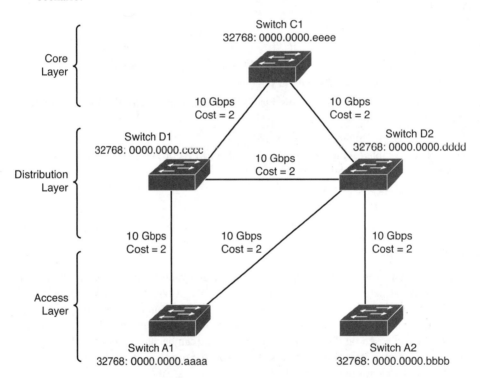

Figure 7-1   *Campus Network with an Inefficient Root Bridge Election*

Catalyst switches A1 and A2 are two access layer devices; Catalysts D1 and D2 form the distribution layer, and Catalyst C1 makes up the network core. Notice that most of the switches use redundant links to other layers of the hierarchy. At the time of this example, however, Switch A2 still has only a single uplink. This switch is slated for an "upgrade," in which a redundant link will be added to the other half of the distribution layer.

As you will see, Catalyst A1 will become the root bridge because of its low MAC address. All switches have been left to their default STP states—the bridge priority of each is 32,768 (or 32,768 plus the VLAN ID, if the extended system ID is enabled).

Figure 7-2 shows the converged state of STP. For the purposes of this discussion, the root ports and designated ports are simply shown on the network diagram. As an exercise, work through the spanning-tree process yourself; begin with the information shown in Figure 7-1 and see whether you arrive at the results shown in Figure 7-2. The more examples you can work out by hand, the better you will understand the entire spanning-tree process.

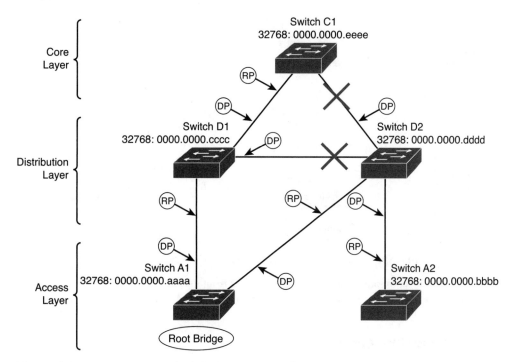

Figure 7-2   *Campus Network with STP Converged*

Notice that Switch A1, one of the access layer switches, has been elected the root bridge. Note the location of the X symbols over the ports that are neither root ports nor designated ports. These ports will enter the Blocking state, and no data packets will pass through them.

Finally, Figure 7-3 shows the same network with the blocking links and other clutter removed. Now you can see the true structure of the final spanning tree.

Switch A1, an access layer switch, is the root bridge. Workstations connected to Switch A1 can reach resources elsewhere on the network by crossing through the distribution (Switch D1) and core layer (Switch C1), as expected. However, notice what has happened to the other access layer switch, Switch A2. Data frames from workstations on this switch must cross into the distribution layer (Switch D2), back into the access layer (Switch A1), back through the distribution (Switch D1), and finally into the core (Switch C1).

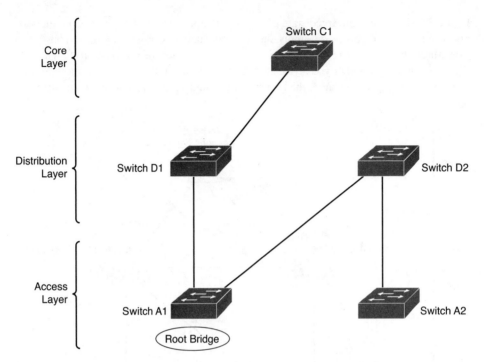

Figure 7-3 *Final Spanning-Tree Structure for the Campus Network*

This action is obviously inefficient. Data frames from users connected to Switch A2 are forced to thread through the winding path that will likely become a major bottleneck.

Root Bridge Configuration

To prevent the surprises outlined in the previous section, you should always do two things:

■ Configure one switch as a root bridge in a determined fashion.

■ Configure another switch as a secondary root bridge, in case of a primary root bridge failure.

As the common reference point, the root bridge (and the secondary) should be placed near the center of the Layer 2 network. For example, a switch in the distribution layer would make a better root bridge choice than one in the access layer because more traffic is expected to pass through the distribution layer devices.

Tip A Catalyst switch can be configured to use one of the following formats for its STP bridge ID:

- Traditional 802.1D bridge priority value (16 bits), followed by the unique switch MAC address for the VLAN

- The 802.1t extended system ID (4-bit priority multiplier, plus a 12-bit VLAN ID), followed by a nonunique switch MAC address for the VLAN

If the switch cannot support 1024 unique MAC addresses for its own use, the extended system ID is always enabled by default. Otherwise, the traditional method is enabled by default.

To begin using the extended system ID method, you can use the following global configuration command:

```
Switch(config)# spanning-tree extend system-id
```

Otherwise, you can use the traditional method by beginning the command with the **no** keyword.

You can configure a Catalyst switch to become the root bridge using one of two methods, which are configured as follows:

- Manually setting the bridge priority value so that a switch is given a lower-than-default bridge ID value to win a root bridge election. You must know the bridge priorities of every other switch in a VLAN so that you can choose a value that is less than all the others. The command to accomplish this is as follows:

```
Switch(config)# spanning-tree vlan vlan-list priority bridge-priority
```

The bridge-priority value defaults to 32,768, but you can also assign a value of 0 to 65,535. If STP extended system ID is enabled, the default bridge-priority is 32,768 plus the VLAN number. In that case, the value can range from 0 to 61,440, but only as multiples of 4096. A lower bridge priority is preferable.

Remember that Catalyst switches run one instance of STP for each VLAN (PVST+), so the VLAN ID must always be given. You should designate an appropriate root bridge for each VLAN. For example, you could use the following command to set the bridge priority for VLAN 5 and VLANs 100 through 200 to 4096:

```
Switch(config)# spanning-tree vlan 5,100-200 priority 4096
```

If you are not sure that your priority value will be accepted, enter it anyway. The switch will respond with a list of accepted values that are multiples of 4096:

```
Switch(config)#spanning vlan 5,100-200 priority 4000
% Bridge Priority must be in increments of 4096.
% Allowed values are:
  0     4096  8192  12288 16384 20480 24576 28672
  32768 36864 40960 45056 49152 53248 57344 61440
Switch(config)#
```

Key Topic

- Causing the would-be root bridge switch to choose its own priority, based on some assumptions about other switches in the network. You can accomplish this with the following command:

```
Switch(config)# spanning-tree vlan vlan-id root {primary |
secondary} [diameter diameter]
```

This command is actually a macro on the switch that executes several other commands. The result is a more direct and automatic way to force one switch to become the root bridge. Notice that the actual bridge priorities are not given in the command. Instead, the switch modifies its STP values according to the current values in use within the active network. *These values are modified only once, when the macro command is issued.* Use the **primary** keyword to make the switch attempt to become the primary root bridge. This command modifies the switch's bridge priority value to become less than the bridge priority of the current root bridge. If the current root priority is more than 24,576, the local switch sets its priority to 24,576. If the current root priority is less than that, the local switch sets its priority to 4096 less than the current root.

For the **secondary** root bridge, the root priority is set to an artificially low value of 28,672. There is no way to query or listen to the network to find another potential secondary root simply because there are no advertisements or elections of secondary root bridges. Instead, the fixed secondary priority is used under the assumption that it will be less than the default priorities (32,768) that might be used on switches elsewhere.

You can also modify the network diameter by adding the **diameter** keyword to this command. This modification is discussed further in the "Tuning Spanning-Tree Convergence" section, later in the chapter.

As a final example, consider a switch that is currently using its default bridge priority for VLAN 100. In the extended system-id mode, the default priority is 32,768 plus 100 (the VLAN number). The output in Example 7-1 demonstrates this under the bridge ID information. The default priority is greater than the current root bridge priority of 4200, so the local switch cannot become the root.

Example 7-1 *Displaying the STP Bridge Priority Values*

```
Switch# show spanning-tree vlan 100
VLAN0100
  Spanning tree enabled protocol ieee
  Root  ID  Priority  4196
            Address     000b.5f65.1f80
            Cost        4
            Port        1 (GigabitEthernet1/0/1)
            Hello Time   2 sec  Max Age 20 sec  Forward Delay 15 sec

  Bridge  ID  Priority  32868  (priority  32768  sys-id-ext  100)
            Address     000c.8554.9a80
            Hello Time   2 sec  Max Age 20 sec  Forward Delay 15 sec
            Aging Time 300
[output omitted]
```

As an alternative, the automatic method is used to attempt to make the switch become root for VLAN 100, using the command demonstrated in Example 7-2.

Example 7-2 *Using a Macro Command to Configure a Root Bridge*

```
Switch(config)# spanning-tree vlan 100 root primary
% Failed to make the bridge root for vlan 100
% It may be possible to make the bridge root by setting the priority
% for some (or all) of these instances to zero.
Switch(config)#
```

Why did this method fail? The current root bridge has a bridge priority of 4196. Because that priority is less than 24,576, the local switch will try to set its priority to 4096 less than the current root. Although the resulting priority would be 100, the local switch is using an extended system ID, which requires bridge priority values that are multiples of 4096. The only value that would work is 0, but the automatic method will not use it. Instead, the only other option is to manually configure the bridge priority to 0 with the following command:

```
Switch(config)# spanning-tree vlan 100 priority 0
```

Remember that on switches that use an extended system ID, the bridge priority is the configured priority (multiple of 4096) plus the VLAN number. Even though the priority was set to 0 with the previous command, the switch is actually using a value of 100—priority 0 plus VLAN number 100, as the output in Example 7-3 reveals.

Example 7-3 *Displaying Bridge Priorities with Extended System IDs*

```
Switch# show spanning-tree vlan 100
VLAN0100
  Spanning tree enabled protocol ieee
  Root  ID  Priority  100
            Address      000c.8554.9a80
            This bridge is the root
            Hello Time   2 sec  Max Age 20 sec  Forward Delay 15 sec

  Bridge  ID  Priority  100  (priority  0  sys-id-ext  100)
            Address      000c.8554.9a80
            Hello Time   2 sec  Max Age 20 sec  Forward Delay 15 sec
            Aging Time 300
[output omitted]
```

Note   The **spanning-tree vlan** *vlan-id* **root** command will not be shown in a Catalyst switch configuration because the command is actually a macro executing other switch commands. The actual commands and values produced by the macro will be shown, however. For example, the macro can potentially adjust the four STP values, as follows:

```
Switch(config)# spanning-tree vlan 1 root primary
vlan 1 bridge priority set to 24576
vlan 1 bridge max aging time unchanged at 20
vlan 1 bridge hello time unchanged at 2
vlan 1 bridge forward delay unchanged at 15
```

Be aware that this macro does not guarantee that the switch will become the root and maintain that status. After the macro is used, it is entirely possible for another switch in the network to have its bridge priority configured to a lower value. The other switch would become the new root, displacing the switch that ran the macro.

On the root, it is usually good practice to directly modify the bridge priority to an artificially low value (even priority 1 or 0) with the **spanning-tree vlan** *vlan-id* **priority** *bridge-priority* command. This makes it more difficult for another switch in the network to win the root bridge election, unless it is manually configured with a priority that is even lower.

Spanning-Tree Customization

The most important decision you can make when designing your spanning-tree topology is the placement of the root bridge. Other decisions, such as the exact loop-free path structure, will occur automatically as a result of the spanning-tree algorithm (STA). Occasionally, the path might need additional tuning, but only under special circumstances and after careful consideration.

Recall the sequence of four criteria that STP uses to choose a path:

1. Lowest bridge ID
2. Lowest root path cost
3. Lowest sender bridge ID
4. Lowest sender port ID

The previous section discussed how to tune a switch's bridge ID to force it to become the root bridge in a network. You can also change the bridge priority on a switch to influence the value it uses in the sender bridge ID that it announced as it relays bridge protocol data units (BPDUs) to other neighboring switches.

Only the automatic STP computation has been discussed, using the default switch port costs to make specific path decisions. The following sections discuss ways you can influence the exact topology that results.

Tuning the Root Path Cost

The root path cost for each active port of a switch is determined by the cumulative cost as a BPDU travels along. As a switch *receives* a BPDU, the port cost of the receiving port is added to the root path cost in the BPDU. The port or port path cost is inversely proportional to the port's bandwidth. If desired, a port's cost can be modified from the default value.

> **Note**   Before modifying a switch port's path cost, you should always calculate the root path costs of other alternative paths through the network. Changing one port's cost might influence STP to choose that port as a root port, but other paths still could be preferred. You also should calculate a port's existing path cost to determine what the new cost value should be. Careful calculation will ensure that the desired path indeed will be chosen.

Key Topic

Use the following interface configuration command to set a switch port's path cost:

```
Switch (config-if)# spanning-tree [vlan vlan-id] cost cost
```

If the **vlan** parameter is given, the port cost is modified only for the specified VLAN. Otherwise, the cost is modified for the port as a whole (all active VLANs). The **cost** value can range from 1 to 200,000,000. There are standard or default values that correspond to port bandwidth, as shown in Table 7-2.

Table 7-2 *STP Port Cost*

Link Bandwidth	STP Cost
4 Mbps	250
10 Mbps	100
16 Mbps	62
45 Mbps	39
100 Mbps	19
155 Mbps	14
622 Mbps	6
1 Gbps	4
10 Gbps	2

For example, a Gigabit Ethernet interface has a default port cost of 4. You can use the following command to change the cost to 2, but only for VLAN 10:

```
Switch(config-if)# spanning-tree vlan 10 cost 2
```

You can see the port cost of an interface by using the following command:

```
Switch# show spanning-tree interface type member/module/number [cost]
```

As an example, Gigabit Ethernet 1/0/1 is configured as a trunk port, carrying VLANs 1, 10, and 20. Example 7-4 shows the port cost for each of the VLANs.

Example 7-4 *Displaying STP Port Cost Values on an Interface*

```
Switch# show spanning-tree interface gigabitEthernet1/0/1
Vlan              Role Sts Cost      Prio.Nbr Type
----------------- ---- --- ---------- -------- ----------------------------
VLAN0001          Root FWD 4         128.1    P2p
VLAN0010          Desg FWD 2         128.1    P2p
VLAN0020          Root FWD 4         128.1    P2p
```

Tuning the Port ID

The fourth criteria of an STP decision is the port ID. The port ID value that a switch uses is actually a 16-bit quantity: 8 bits for the port priority, and 8 bits for the port number. The port priority is a value from 0 to 255 and defaults to 128 for all ports. The port number can range from 0 to 255 and represents the port's actual physical mapping. Port numbers generally begin with 1 at port 1/0/1 and increment across each module, then across each stack member or slot. However, the numbers might not be completely intuitive or consecutive because each member or module is assigned a particular range of numbers. In addition, ports that are bundled into an EtherChannel or port channel interface always have a higher port ID than they would if they were not bundled.

> **Tip**   Port numbers are usually intuitive on a single fixed configuration switch. For example, the STP port number can simply be the interface number, from 1 to 48. However, it is not easy to find the STP port number in a switch with many modules and many ports. Notice how Gigabit Ethernet 1/0/1 is known as port number 1 (shown as Prio.Nbr 128.1), whereas 2/0/44 is known as port number 102 in the following example:
>
> ```
> Switch# show spanning-tree interface gi1/0/1
> Vlan              Role Sts Cost      Prio.Nbr Type
> ----------------- ---- --- ---------- -------- ----------------
> VLAN0100          Desg FWD 4         128.1    P2p Edge
> Switch# show spanning-tree interface gi2/0/44
> Vlan              Role Sts Cost      Prio.Nbr Type
> ----------------- ---- --- ---------- -------- ----------------
> VLAN0100          Desg FWD 4         128.102  P2p Edge
> Switch#
> ```

Obviously, a switch port's port number is fixed because it is based only on its hardware location or index. The port ID, however, can be modified to influence an STP decision by using the port priority. You can configure the port priority with this interface-configuration command:

```
Switch(config-if)# spanning-tree [vlan vlan-list] port-priority port-priority
```

You can modify the port priority for one or more VLANs by using the **vlan** parameter. The VLAN numbers are given as *vlan-list*, a list of single values or ranges of values separated by commas. Otherwise, the port priority is set for the port as a whole (all active

VLANs). The value of *port-priority* can range from 0 to 255 and defaults to 128. A lower port priority value indicates a more preferred path toward the root bridge.

As an example, you can use the following command sequence to change the port priority of Gigabit Ethernet 2/0/44 from 128 (the default) to 64 for VLANs 10 and 100:

```
Switch(config)# interface gigabitethernet 2/0/44
Switch(config-if)# spanning-tree vlan 10,100 port-priority 64
```

You can confirm the changes with the **show spanning-tree interface** command, as demonstrated in Example 7-5.

Example 7-5 *Confirming STP Port Priority Values After Configuration*

```
Switch# show spanning-tree interface gigabitEthernet 2/0/44
Vlan            Role Sts Cost      Prio.Nbr Type
---------------- ---- --- --------- -------- ----------------------------
VLAN0010         Desg FWD 4         64.102   Edge P2p
VLAN0100         Desg FWD 4         64.102   Edge P2p
VLAN0200         Desg FWD 4         128.102  Edge P2p
Switch#
```

Tuning Spanning-Tree Convergence

STP uses several timers, a sequence of states that ports must move through, and specific topology change conditions to prevent bridging loops from forming in a complex network. Each of these parameters or requirements is based on certain default values for a typical network size and function. For the majority of cases, the default STP operation is sufficient to keep the network loop free and enable users to communicate.

However, in certain situations, the default STP can cause network access to be delayed while timers expire and while preventing loops on links where loops are not possible. For example, when a single PC is connected to a switch port, a bridging loop is simply not possible. Another situation relates to the size of a Layer 2 switched network: The default STP timers are based on a benchmark network size.

In a network that is smaller, waiting until the default timer values expire might not make sense when they could be safely set to shorter values. In situations like this, you can safely make adjustments to the STP convergence process for more efficiency.

Modifying STP Timers

Recall that STP uses three timers to keep track of various port operation states and communication between bridges. The three STP timers can be adjusted by using the commands documented in the sections that follow. Remember that the timers need to be modified only on the root bridge because the root bridge propagates all three timer values throughout the network as fields in the configuration BPDU.

Manually Configuring STP Timers

Use one or more of the following global configuration commands to modify STP timers:

```
Switch(config)# spanning-tree [vlan vlan-id] hello-time seconds
Switch(config)# spanning-tree [vlan vlan-id] forward-time seconds
Switch(config)# spanning-tree [vlan vlan-id] max-age seconds
```

Notice that the timers can be changed for a single instance (VLAN) of STP on the switch by using the **vlan** *vlan-id* parameters. If you omit the **vlan** keyword, the timer values are configured for *all* instances (all VLANs) of STP on the switch.

The *Hello timer* triggers periodic "hello" (actually, the configuration BPDU) messages that are sent from the root to other bridges in the network. This timer also sets the interval in which a bridge expects to hear a hello relayed from its neighboring bridges. Configuration BPDUs are sent every 2 seconds, by default. You can modify the Hello timer with the **hello-time** keyword, along with a value of 1 to 10 seconds, as in the following command:

```
Switch(config)# spanning-tree hello-time 1
```

The *Forward Delay timer* determines the amount of time a port stays in the Listening state before moving into the Learning state, and how long it stays in the Learning state before moving to the Forwarding state. You can modify the Forward Delay timer with the **forward-time** keyword. The default value is 15 seconds, but this can be set to a value of 4 to 30 seconds. This timer should be modified only under careful consideration because the value depends on the diameter of the network and the propagation of BPDUs across all switches. A value that is too low allows loops to form, possibly crippling a network.

The Max Age timer specifies a stored BPDU's lifetime that has been received from a neighboring switch with a designated port. Suppose that BPDUs are being received on a nondesignated switch port every 2 seconds, as expected. Then an indirect failure, or one that does not involve a physical link going down, occurs that prevents BPDUs from being sent. The receiving switch waits until the Max Age timer expires to listen for further BPDUs. If none is received, the nondesignated port moves into the Listening state, and the receiving switch generates configuration BPDUs. This port then becomes the designated port to restore connectivity on the segment.

To modify the Max Age timer, use the **max-age** keyword. The timer value defaults to 20 seconds but can be set from 6 to 40 seconds.

Automatically Configuring STP Timers

Modifying STP timers can be tricky, given the conservative nature of the default values and the calculations needed to derive proper STP operation. Timer values are basically dependent on the Hello Time and the switched network's diameter, in terms of switch hops. Catalyst switches offer a single command that can change the timer values in a more controlled fashion. As described earlier, the **spanning-tree vlan** *vlan-list* **root** macro command is a better tool to use than setting the timers with the individual commands. This global configuration command has the following syntax:

```
Switch(config)# spanning-tree vlan vlan-list root {primary | secondary} [diameter
diameter [hello-time hello-time]]
```

Here, STP timers will be adjusted according to the formulas specified in the 802.1D standard by giving only the network's diameter (the maximum number of switches that traffic will traverse across a Layer 2 network) and an optional *hello-time*. If you do not specify a hello time, the default value of 2 seconds is assumed.

This command can be used only on a per-VLAN basis to modify the timers for a particular VLAN's spanning tree instance. The network diameter can be a value from 1 to 7 switch hops; the default STP timers are based on a diameter of 7. Because this command makes a switch become the root bridge, all the modified timer values resulting from this command will be propagated to other switches through the configuration BPDU.

Suppose, for example, that a small network consists of three switches connected in a triangle fashion. The command output in Example 7-6 shows the current (default) STP timer values that are in use for VLAN 100.

Example 7-6   *Displaying the STP Timer Values in Use*

```
Switch# show spanning-tree vlan 100
VLAN0100
  Spanning tree enabled protocol ieee
  Root ID    Priority    100
             Address     000c.8554.9a80
             This bridge is the root
             Hello Time  2  sec  Max  Age  20  sec  Forward  Delay  15   sec

  Bridge ID  Priority    100    (priority 0 sys-id-ext 100)
             Address     000c.8554.9a80
             Hello Time   2 sec  Max Age 20 sec  Forward Delay 15 sec
             Aging Time 300
[output omitted]
```

The longest path that a packet can take through the sample network is three switches. This is considerably less than the reference diameter of seven that is used to calculate the default timer values. Therefore, you can safely assume that this network diameter is three, provided that no additional switches will be added to lengthen the longest path. Suppose that a hello time of 1 second is also desired, to shorten the time needed to detect a dead neighbor. The following command attempts to make the local switch become the root bridge and automatically adjusts the STP timers:

```
Switch(config)# spanning-tree vlan 100 root primary diameter 3 hello-time 1
```

You can confirm the new timer values with the **show spanning-tree vlan** *vlan-id* command, as demonstrated in Example 7-7.

Example 7-7   *Confirming STP Timer Configuration Changes*

```
Switch# show spanning-tree vlan 100
VLAN0100
  Spanning tree enabled protocol ieee
  Root ID    Priority    100
             Address      000c.8554.9a80
             This bridge is the root
             Hello  Time  1  sec  Max  Age  7  sec  Forward  Delay  5  sec

  Bridge ID  Priority    100      (priority 0 sys-id-ext 100)
             Address      000c.8554.9a80
             Hello Time   1 sec  Max Age  7 sec  Forward Delay  5 sec
             Aging Time 300
```

Redundant Link Convergence

Some additional methods allow faster STP convergence if a link failure occurs:

■ **PortFast:** Enables fast connectivity to be established on access layer switch ports to workstations that are booting

■ **UplinkFast:** Enables fast-uplink failover on an access layer switch when dual uplinks are connected into the distribution layer

■ **BackboneFast:** Enables fast convergence in the network backbone or core layer switches after a spanning-tree topology change occurs

Instead of modifying timer values, these methods work by controlling convergence on specifically located ports within the network hierarchy.

Tip   The STP has been enhanced to allow almost instantaneous topology changes instead of having to rely on these Cisco-proprietary extensions. This enhancement is known as the *Rapid Spanning Tree Protocol*, or *IEEE 802.1w*, and is covered in Chapter 9, "Advanced Spanning Tree Protocol." You should become familiar with the topics in this chapter first because they provide the basis for the concepts in Chapter 9.

PortFast: Access Layer Nodes

An end-user workstation is usually connected to a switch port in the access layer. If the workstation is powered off and then turned on, the switch will sense that the port link status has gone down and back up. The port will not be in a usable state until STP cycles from the Blocking state to the Forwarding state. With the default STP timers, this transition takes at least 30 seconds (15 seconds for Listening to Learning, and 15 seconds for Learning to Forwarding). Therefore, the workstation cannot transmit or receive any useful data until the Forwarding state finally is reached on the port.

Tip Port initialization delays of up to 50 seconds can be observed. As discussed, 30 of these seconds are due to the STP state transitions. If a switch port is running Port Aggregation Protocol (PAgP) to negotiate EtherChannel configuration, an additional 20-second delay can occur.

On switch ports that connect only to single workstations or specific devices, bridging loops never should be possible. The potential for a loop exists only if the workstation had additional connections back into the network and if it were bridging traffic itself. For example, this can happen on PCs that are running Windows when network bridging has been enabled. In most situations, this is not very likely to happen.

Catalyst switches offer the PortFast feature, which shortens the Listening and Learning states to a negligible amount of time. When a workstation link comes up, the switch immediately moves the PortFast port into the Forwarding state. Spanning-tree loop detection is still in operation, however, and the port moves into the Blocking state if a loop is ever detected on the port.

By default, PortFast is disabled on all switch ports. You can configure PortFast as a global default, affecting all switch ports with a single command. All ports that are configured for access mode (nontrunking) will have PortFast automatically enabled. You can use the following global configuration command to enable PortFast as the default:

```
Switch(config)# spanning-tree portfast default
```

You can also enable or disable the PortFast feature on specific switch ports by using the following interface configuration command:

```
Switch(config-if)# [no] spanning-tree portfast
```

Obviously, you should not enable PortFast on a switch port that is connected to another switch because bridging loops could form. One other benefit of PortFast is that Topology Change Notification (TCN) BPDUs are not sent when a switch port in PortFast mode goes up or down. This simplifies the TCN transmission on a large network when end-user workstations are coming up or shutting down.

Tip You can also use a macro configuration command to force a switch port to support a single host. The following command enables STP PortFast, sets the port to access (nontrunking) mode, and disables PAgP to prevent the port from participating in an EtherChannel:

```
Switch(config)# interface type member/module/number
Switch(config-if)# switchport host
switchport mode will be set to access
spanning-tree portfast will be enabled
channel group will be disabled
```

You can display the current PortFast status with the following command:

```
Switch# show spanning-tree interface type member/module/number portfast
```

For example, the following output shows that port Gigabit Ethernet 1/0/10 supports only access VLAN 10 and has PortFast enabled:

```
Switch# show spanning-tree interface gigabitethernet 1/0/10 portfast
VLAN0010        enabled
Switch#
```

UplinkFast: Access Layer Uplinks

Consider an access layer switch that has redundant uplink connections to two distribution layer switches. Normally, one uplink would be in the Forwarding state and the other would be in the Blocking state. If the primary uplink went down, up to 50 seconds could elapse before the redundant uplink could be used.

Key Topic

The UplinkFast feature on Catalyst switches enables leaf-node switches or switches at the ends of the spanning-tree branches to have a functioning root port while keeping *one or more* redundant or potential root ports in Blocking mode. When the primary root port uplink fails, another blocked uplink immediately can be brought up for use.

Tip   Many Catalyst switches have two built-in, high-speed uplink ports (Gigabit Ethernet, for example). You might get the idea that UplinkFast can only toggle between two leaf-node uplink ports. This is entirely untrue. UplinkFast keeps a record of all parallel paths to the root bridge. All uplink ports but one are kept in the Blocking state. If the root port fails, the uplink with the next-lowest root path cost is unblocked and used without delay.

To enable the UplinkFast feature, use the following global configuration command:

```
Switch(config)# spanning-tree uplinkfast [max-update-rate pkts-per-second]
```

When UplinkFast is enabled, it is enabled for the entire switch and all VLANs. UplinkFast works by keeping track of possible paths to the root bridge. Therefore, the command *is not allowed on the root bridge switch*. UplinkFast also makes some modifications to the local switch to ensure that it does not become the root bridge and that the switch is not used as a transit switch to get to the root bridge. In other words, the goal is to keep UplinkFast limited to leaf-node switches that are farthest from the root.

First, the switch's bridge priority is raised to 49,152, making it unlikely that the switch will be elected to root bridge status. The port cost of all local switch ports is incremented by 3000, making the ports undesirable as paths to the root for any downstream switches.

The command also includes a **max-update-rate** parameter. When an uplink on a switch goes down, UplinkFast makes it easy for the local switch to update its bridging table of MAC addresses to point to the new uplink. However, UplinkFast also provides a mechanism for the local switch to notify other upstream switches that stations downstream (or within the access layer) can be reached over the newly activated uplink.

The switch accomplishes this by sending dummy multicast frames to destination 0100.0ccd.cdcd on behalf of the stations contained in its CAM table. The MAC addresses are used as the source addresses in the dummy frames, as if the stations actually had sent them. The idea is to quickly send the multicast frames over the new uplink, giving upstream hosts a chance to receive the frames and learn of the new path to those source addresses.

These multicast frames are sent out at a rate specified by the **max-update-rate** parameter in packets per second. This limits the amount of bandwidth used for the dummy multicasts if the CAM table is quite large. The default is 150 packets per second (pps), but the rate can range from 0 to 65,535 pps. If the value is 0, no dummy multicasts are sent.

Tip   You can use the following command to display the current status of STP UplinkFast:

```
Switch# show spanning-tree uplinkfast
UplinkFast is enabled
Station update rate set to 150 packets/sec.
UplinkFast statistics
Number of transitions via UplinkFast (all VLANs)            : 2
Number of proxy multicast addresses transmitted (all VLANs)  : 52
Name                   Interface List
--------------------   --------------------------------
VLAN0001               Gi1/0/1(fwd)
VLAN0010               Gi1/0/1(fwd)
VLAN0100               Gi1/0/1(fwd)
Switch#
```

BackboneFast: Redundant Backbone Paths

In the network backbone, or core layer, a different method is used to shorten STP convergence. BackboneFast works by having a switch actively determine whether alternative paths exist to the root bridge, in case the switch detects an *indirect link failure*. Indirect link failures occur when a link that is not directly connected to a switch fails.

A switch detects an indirect link failure when it receives inferior BPDUs from its designated bridge on either its root port or a blocked port. (Inferior BPDUs are sent from a designated bridge that has lost its connection to the root bridge, making it announce itself as the new root.)

Normally, a switch must wait for the Max Age timer to expire before responding to the inferior BPDUs. However, BackboneFast begins to determine whether other alternative paths to the root bridge exist according to the following port types that received the inferior BPDU:

■   If the inferior BPDU arrives on a port in the Blocking state, the switch considers the root port and all other blocked ports to be alternative paths to the root bridge.

■   If the inferior BPDU arrives on the root port itself, the switch considers all blocked ports to be alternative paths to the root bridge.

■   If the inferior BPDU arrives on the root port and no ports are blocked, however, the switch assumes that it has lost connectivity with the root bridge. In this case, the switch assumes that it has become the root bridge, and BackboneFast allows it to do so before the Max Age timer expires.

Detecting alternative paths to the root bridge also involves an interactive process with other bridges. If the local switch has blocked ports, BackboneFast begins to use the *Root Link Query* (RLQ) protocol to see whether upstream switches have stable connections to the root bridge.

First, RLQ Requests are sent out. If a switch receives an RLQ Request and either is the root bridge or has lost connection to the root, it sends an RLQ Reply. Otherwise, the RLQ Request is propagated on to other switches until an RLQ Reply can be generated. On the local switch, if an RLQ Reply is received on its current root port, the path to the root bridge is intact and stable. If it is received on a nonroot port, an alternative root path must be chosen. The Max Age timer immediately is expired so that a new root port can be found.

Key Topic

BackboneFast is simple to configure and operates by short-circuiting the Max Age timer when needed. Although this function shortens the time a switch waits to detect a root path failure, ports still must go through full-length Forward Delay timer intervals during the Listening and Learning states. Where PortFast and UplinkFast enable immediate transitions, BackboneFast can reduce the maximum convergence delay only from 50 to 30 seconds.

To configure BackboneFast, use the following global configuration command:

```
Switch(config)# spanning-tree backbonefast
```

When used, BackboneFast should be enabled on *all* switches in the network because BackboneFast requires the use of the RLQ Request and Reply mechanism to inform switches of Root Path stability. The RLQ protocol is active only when BackboneFast is enabled on a switch. By default, BackboneFast is disabled.

Tip   You can verify the current BackboneFast state with the following command:

```
Switch# show spanning-tree backbonefast
BackboneFast is enabled
Switch#
```

Monitoring STP

Because the STP running in a network uses several timers, costs, and dynamic calculations, predicting the current state is difficult. You can use a network diagram and work out the STP topology by hand, but any change on the network could produce an entirely different outcome. Then, figure in something like PVST+, in which you have one instance of STP running for each VLAN present. Obviously, simply viewing the STP status on the active network devices would be better.

You can display information about many aspects of the STP from a Catalyst switch command-line interface (CLI). Specifically, you need to find out the current root bridge and its location in the network. You also might want to see the bridge ID of the switch where you are connected, to see how it participates in STP. Use the information in Table 7-3 to determine what command is useful for what situation.

Table 7-3   *Commands for Displaying Spanning-Tree Information*

Task	Command Syntax
View all possible STP parameters for all VLANs. Port information is summarized.	Switch# **show spanning tree**
View all possible STP information for all VLANs. Port information is very detailed.	Switch# **show spanning-tree detail**
View the total number of switch ports currently in each of the STP states.	Switch# **show spanning-tree** [vlan *vlan-id*] **summary**
Find the root bridge ID, the root port, and the root path cost.	Switch# **show spanning-tree** [vlan *vlan-id*] **root**
Show the bridge ID and STP timers for the local switch.	Switch# **show spanning-tree** [vlan *vlan-id*] **bridge**
Show the STP activity on a specific interface.	Switch# **show spanning-tree interface** *type port*
Show the STP UplinkFast status.	Switch# **show spanning-tree uplinkfast**
Show the STP BackboneFast status.	Switch# **show spanning-tree backbonefast**

Exam Preparation Tasks

Review All Key Topics

Review the most important topics in the chapter, noted with the Key Topic icon in the outer margin of the page. Table 7-4 lists a reference of these key topics and the page numbers on which each is found.

Key Topic

Table 7-4   *Key Topics for Chapter 7*

Key Topic Element	Description	Page Number
Paragraph	Explains the pitfalls of a default root bridge election	181
Paragraph	Covers best practices for root bridge placement	184
Bullet	Discusses manual root bridge configuration	185
Bullet	Discusses automatic root bridge configuration	186
Paragraph	Explains how to configure the root path cost on an interface	189
Paragraph	Explains how STP timers can be adjusted on the root bridge	191
Paragraph	Explains the PortFast feature	195
Paragraph	Explains the UplinkFast feature	196
Paragraph	Explains the BackboneFast feature	198

Complete Tables and Lists from Memory

There are no memory tables in this chapter.

Define Key Terms

Define the following key terms from this chapter, and check your answers in the glossary:

PortFast, UplinkFast, BackboneFast

Use Command Reference to Check Your Memory

This section includes the most important configuration and EXEC commands covered in this chapter. It might not be necessary to memorize the complete syntax of every command, but you should remember the basic keywords that are needed.

To test your memory of the STP configuration commands, cover the right side of Table 7-5 with a piece of paper, read the description on the left side, and then see how much of the command you can remember.

Remember that the CCNP exam focuses on practical or hands-on skills that are used by a networking professional. For the skills covered in this chapter, notice that the commands always begin with the keyword **spanning-tree**.

Table 7-5 *STP Configuration Commands*

Task	Command Syntax
Enable STP.	Switch(config)# **spanning-tree** *vlan-id*
Set bridge priority.	Switch(config)# **spanning-tree vlan** *vlan-id* **priority** *bridge-priority*
Set root bridge (macro).	Switch(config)# **spanning-tree vlan** *vlan-id* **root** {primary | **secondary**} [**diameter** *diameter*]
Set port cost.	Switch(config-if)# **spanning-tree** [**vlan** *vlan-id*] **cost** *cost*
Set port priority.	Switch(config-if)# **spanning-tree** [**vlan** *vlan-id*] **port-priority** *port-priority*
Set STP timers.	Switch(config)# **spanning-tree** [**vlan** *vlan-id*] **hello-time** *seconds*
	Switch(config)# **spanning-tree** [**vlan** *vlan-id*] **forward-time** *seconds*
	Switch(config)# **spanning-tree** [**vlan** *vlan-id*] **max-age** *seconds*
Set PortFast on an interface.	Switch(config-if)# **spanning-tree portfast**
Set UplinkFast on a switch.	Switch(config)# **spanning-tree uplinkfast** [**max-update-rate** *pkts-per-second*]
Set BackboneFast on a switch.	Switch(config)# **spanning-tree backbonefast**

This chapter covers the following topics that you need to master for the CCNP SWITCH exam:

■ **Protecting Against Unexpected BPDUs:** This section covers the Root Guard and BPDU Guard features, which protect against unexpected root candidates and unexpected BPDUs, respectively.

■ **Protecting Against Sudden Loss of BPDUs:** This section discusses the Loop Guard and Unidirectional Link Detection (UDLD) features, which detect and protect against the loss of root bridge BPDUs and conditions causing unidirectional links, respectively.

■ **Using BPDU Filtering to Disable STP on a Port:** This section explains how to filter BPDUs on a switch port to prevent the port from participating in STP altogether. Bridging loops are neither detected nor prevented.

■ **Troubleshooting STP Protection:** This section summarizes the commands that diagnose or verify actions to protect the topology.

CHAPTER 8

Protecting the Spanning Tree Protocol Topology

Achieving and maintaining a loop-free Spanning Tree Protocol (STP) topology revolves around the simple process of sending and receiving bridge protocol data units (BPDUs). Under normal conditions, with all switches playing fairly and according to the rules, a loop-free topology is determined dynamically.

This chapter discusses two basic conditions that can occur to disrupt the loop-free topology (even while STP is running):

- On a port that has not been receiving BPDUs, BPDUs are not expected. When BPDUs suddenly appear for some reason, the STP topology can reconverge to give unexpected results.

- On a port that normally receives BPDUs, BPDUs always are expected. When BPDUs suddenly disappear for some reason, a switch can make incorrect assumptions about the topology and unintentionally create loops.

"Do I Know This Already?" Quiz

The "Do I Know This Already?" quiz allows you to assess whether you should read this entire chapter thoroughly or jump to the "Exam Preparation Tasks" section. If you are in doubt based on your answers to these questions or your own assessment of your knowledge of the topics, read the entire chapter. Table 8-1 outlines the major headings in this chapter and the "Do I Know This Already?" quiz questions that go with them. You can find the answers in Appendix A, "Answers to the 'Do I Know This Already?' Quizzes."

Table 8-1 *"Do I Know This Already?" Foundation Topics Section-to-Question Mapping*

Foundation Topics Section	Questions Covered in This Section
Protecting Against Unexpected BPDUs	1–5
Protecting Against Sudden Loss of BPDUs	6–11
Using BPDU Filtering to Disable STP on a Port	12
Troubleshooting STP Protection	13

1. Why is it important to protect the placement of the root bridge?

    a. To keep two root bridges from becoming active

    b. To keep the STP topology stable

    c. So all hosts have the correct gateway

    d. So the root bridge can have complete knowledge of the STP topology

2. Which of the following features protects a switch port from accepting superior BPDUs?

    a. STP Loop Guard

    b. STP BPDU Guard

    c. STP Root Guard

    d. UDLD

3. Which of the following commands can you use to enable STP Root Guard on a switch port?

    a. spanning-tree root guard

    b. spanning-tree root-guard

    c. spanning-tree guard root

    d. spanning-tree rootguard enable

4. Where should the STP Root Guard feature be enabled on a switch?

    a. All ports

    b. Only ports where the root bridge should never appear

    c. Only ports where the root bridge should be located

    d. Only ports with PortFast enabled

5. Which of the following features protects a switch port from accepting BPDUs when PortFast is enabled?

    a. STP Loop Guard

    b. STP BPDU Guard

    c. STP Root Guard

    d. UDLD

6. To maintain a loop-free STP topology, which one of the following should a switch uplink be protected against?

    a. A sudden loss of BPDUs

    b. Too many BPDUs

    c. The wrong version of BPDUs

    d. BPDUs relayed from the root bridge

7. Which of the following commands can enable STP Loop Guard on a switch port?

    a. spanning-tree loop guard

    b. spanning-tree guard loop

    c. spanning-tree loop-guard

    d. spanning-tree loopguard enable

8. STP Loop Guard detects which of the following conditions?

    a. The sudden appearance of superior BPDUs

    b. The sudden lack of BPDUs

    c. The appearance of duplicate BPDUs

    d. The appearance of two root bridges

9. Which of the following features can actively test for the loss of the receive side of a link between switches?

    a. POST

    b. BPDU

    c. UDLD

    d. STP

10. UDLD must detect a unidirectional link before which of the following?

    a. The Max Age timer expires.

    b. STP moves the link to the Blocking state.

    c. STP moves the link to the Forwarding state.

    d. STP moves the link to the Listening state.

11. What must a switch do when it receives a UDLD message on a link?

    a. Relay the message on to other switches

    b. Send a UDLD acknowledgment

    c. Echo the message back across the link

    d. Drop the message

12. Which of the following features effectively disables spanning-tree operation on a switch port?

    a. STP PortFast

    b. STP BPDU filtering

    c. STP BPDU Guard

    d. STP Root Guard

13. To reset switch ports that have been put into the errdisable mode by UDLD, which one of the following commands should you use?

    a. clear errdisable udld

    b. udld reset

    c. no udld

    d. show udld errdisable

Foundation Topics

Protecting Against Unexpected BPDUs

A network running STP uses BPDUs to communicate between switches (bridges). Switches become aware of each other and of the topology that interconnects them. After a root bridge is elected, BPDUs are generated by the root and are relayed down through the spanning-tree topology. Eventually, all switches in the STP domain receive the root's BPDUs so that the network converges and a stable loop-free topology forms.

To maintain an efficient topology, the placement of the root bridge must be predictable. Hopefully, you configured one switch to become the root bridge and a second one to be the secondary root. What happens when a "foreign" or rogue switch is connected to the network, and that switch suddenly is capable of becoming the root bridge? Cisco added two STP features that help prevent the unexpected: Root Guard and BPDU Guard.

Root Guard

After an STP topology has converged and becomes loop free, switch ports are assigned the following roles:

- **Root port:** The one port on a switch that is closest (with the lowest root path cost) to the root bridge.

- **Designated port:** The port on a LAN segment that is closest to the root. This port relays, or transmits, BPDUs down the tree.

- **Blocking port:** Ports that are neither root nor designated ports.

- **Alternate port:** Ports that are candidate root ports (they are also close to the root bridge) but are in the Blocking state. These ports are identified for quick use by the STP UplinkFast feature.

- **Forwarding port:** Ports where no other STP activity is detected or expected. These are ports with normal end-user connections.

The root bridge always is expected to be seen on the root port and the alternative ports because these are "closest" (have the best-cost path) to it.

Suppose that another switch is introduced into the network with a bridge priority that is more desirable (lower) than that of the current root bridge. The new switch then would become the root bridge, and the STP topology might reconverge to a new shape. This is entirely permissible by the STP because the switch with the lowest bridge ID always wins the root election.

However, this is not always desirable for you, the network administrator, because the new STP topology might be something totally unacceptable. In addition, while the topology is reconverging, your production network might become unavailable.

Key Topic

The Root Guard feature was developed as a means to control where candidate root bridges can be connected and found on a network. Basically, a switch learns the current root bridge's bridge ID. If another switch advertises a superior BPDU, or one with a better bridge ID, on a port where Root Guard is enabled, the local switch will not allow the new switch to become the root. As long as the superior BPDUs are being received on the port, the port will be kept in the *root-inconsistent* STP state. No data can be sent or received in that state, but the switch can listen to BPDUs received on the port to detect a new root advertising itself.

In essence, Root Guard designates that a port can only forward or relay BPDUs; the port cannot be used to receive BPDUs. Root Guard prevents the port from ever becoming a root port where BPDUs normally would be received from the root bridge.

You can enable Root Guard only on a per-port basis. By default, it is disabled on all switch ports. To enable it, use the following interface configuration command:

```
Switch(config-if)# spanning-tree guard root
```

When the superior BPDUs no longer are received, the port is cycled through the normal STP states to return to normal use.

Use Root Guard on switch ports where you never expect to find the root bridge for a VLAN. In fact, Root Guard affects the entire port so that a root bridge never can be allowed on *any* VLAN on the port. When a superior BPDU is heard on the port, the entire port, in effect, becomes blocked.

Tip You can display switch ports that Root Guard has put into the root-inconsistent state with the following command:

```
Switch# show spanning-tree inconsistentports
```

BPDU Guard

Recall that the traditional STP offers the PortFast feature, in which switch ports are allowed to immediately enter the Forwarding state as soon as the link comes up. Normally, PortFast provides quick network access to end-user devices, where bridging loops never are expected to form. Even while PortFast is enabled on a port, STP still is running and can detect a bridging loop. However, a loop can be detected only in a finite amount of time—the length of time required to move the port through the normal STP states.

Note Remember that enabling PortFast on a port is not the same as disabling the STP on it.

By definition, if you enable PortFast, you do not expect to find anything that can cause a bridging loop—especially another switch or device that produces BPDUs. Suppose that a switch is connected by mistake to a port where PortFast is enabled. Now there is a potential for a bridging loop to form. An even greater consequence is that the potential now exists for the newly connected device to advertise itself and become the new root bridge.

Key Topic

The BPDU Guard feature was developed to further protect the integrity of switch ports that have PortFast enabled. If any BPDU (whether superior to the current root or not) is received on a port where BPDU Guard is enabled, that port immediately is put into the errdisable state. The port is shut down in an error condition and must be either manually reenabled or automatically recovered through the errdisable timeout function.

By default, BPDU Guard is disabled on all switch ports. You can configure BPDU Guard as a global default, affecting all switch ports with a single command. All ports that have PortFast enabled also have BPDU Guard automatically enabled. You can use the following global configuration command to enable BPDU Guard as the default:

```
Switch(config)# spanning-tree portfast bpduguard default
```

You also can enable or disable BPDU Guard on a per-port basis, using the following interface configuration command:

```
Switch(config-if)# [no] spanning-tree bpduguard enable
```

When the BPDUs no longer are received, the port still remains in the errdisable state. See Chapter 3, "Switch Port Configuration," for more information about recovering from the errdisable state.

You should use BPDU Guard on all switch ports where STP PortFast is enabled. This prevents any possibility that a switch will be added to the port, either intentionally or by mistake. An obvious application for BPDU Guard is on access layer switch ports where users and end devices connect. BPDUs normally would not be expected there and would be detected if a switch or hub inadvertently were connected.

Naturally, BPDU Guard does not prevent a bridging loop from forming if an Ethernet hub is connected to the PortFast port. This is because a hub does not transmit BPDUs itself; it merely repeats Ethernet frames from its other ports. A loop could form if the hub became connected to two locations in the network, providing a path for frames to be looped without any STP activity.

You never should enable BPDU Guard on any switch uplink where the root bridge is located. If a switch has multiple uplinks, any of those ports could receive legitimate BPDUs from the root—even if they are in the Blocking state as a result of the UplinkFast feature. If BPDU Guard is enabled on an uplink port, BPDUs will be detected, and the uplink will be put into the errdisable state. This will preclude that uplink port from being used as an uplink into the network.

Protecting Against Sudden Loss of BPDUs

STP BPDUs are used as probes to learn about a network topology. When the switches participating in STP converge on a common and consistent loop-free topology, BPDUs still must be sent by the root bridge and must be relayed by every other switch in the STP domain. The STP topology's integrity then depends on a continuous and regular flow of BPDUs from the root.

What happens if a switch does not receive BPDUs in a timely manner or when it does not receive any? The switch can view that condition as acceptable—perhaps an upstream switch or an upstream link is dead. In that case, the topology must have changed, so blocked ports eventually can be unblocked again.

However, if the absence of BPDUs is actually a mistake and BPDUs are not being received even though there is no topology change, bridging loops easily can form.

Cisco has added two STP features that help detect or prevent the unexpected loss of BPDUs:

- Loop Guard
- Unidirectional Link Detection (UDLD)

Loop Guard

Suppose that a switch port is receiving BPDUs and the switch port is in the Blocking state. The port makes up a redundant path; it is blocking because it is neither a root port nor a designated port. It will remain in the Blocking state as long as a steady flow of BPDUs is received.

If BPDUs are being sent over a link but the flow of BPDUs stops for some reason, the last-known BPDU is kept until the Max Age timer expires. Then that BPDU is flushed, and the switch thinks there is no longer a need to block the port. After all, if no BPDUs are received, there must not be another STP device connected there.

The switch then moves the port through the STP states until it begins to forward traffic—and forms a bridging loop. In its final state, the port becomes a designated port where it begins to relay or send BPDUs downstream, when it actually should be receiving BPDUs from upstream.

Key Topic

To prevent this situation, you can use the Loop Guard STP feature. When enabled, Loop Guard keeps track of the BPDU activity on nondesignated ports. While BPDUs are received, the port is allowed to behave normally. When BPDUs go missing, Loop Guard moves the port into the loop-inconsistent state. The port is effectively blocking at this point to prevent a loop from forming and to keep it in the nondesignated role.

When BPDUs are received on the port again, Loop Guard allows the port to move through the normal STP states and become active. In this fashion, Loop Guard automatically governs ports without the need for manual intervention.

By default, Loop Guard is disabled on all switch ports. You can enable Loop Guard as a global default, affecting all switch ports, with the following global configuration command:

```
Switch(config)# spanning-tree loopguard default
```

You also can enable or disable Loop Guard on a specific switch port by using the following interface-configuration command:

```
Switch(config-if)# [no] spanning-tree guard loop
```

Although Loop Guard is configured on a switch port, its corrective blocking action is taken on a per-VLAN basis. In other words, Loop Guard does not block the entire port; only the offending VLANs are blocked.

You can enable Loop Guard on all switch ports, regardless of their functions. The switch figures out which ports are nondesignated and monitors the BPDU activity to keep them nondesignated. Nondesignated ports are generally the alternative root ports and ports that normally are blocking.

UDLD

In a campus network, switches are connected by bidirectional links, where traffic can flow in two directions. Clearly, if a link has a physical layer problem, the two switches it connects detect a problem, and the link is shown as not connected.

What would happen if just one side of the link (receive or transmit) had an odd failure, such as malfunctioning transmit circuitry in a gigabit interface converter (GBIC) or small form factor pluggable (SFP) modules? In some cases, the two switches still might see a functional bidirectional link, although traffic actually would be delivered in only one direction. This is known as a *unidirectional link*.

A unidirectional link poses a potential danger to STP topologies because BPDUs will not be received on one end of the link. If that end of the link normally would be in the Blocking state, it will not be that way for long. A switch interprets the absence of BPDUs to mean that the port can be moved safely through the STP states so that traffic can be forwarded. However, if that is done on a unidirectional link, a bridging loop forms and the switch never realizes the mistake.

To prevent this situation, you can use the Cisco proprietary UDLD STP feature. When enabled, UDLD interactively monitors a port to see whether the link is truly bidirectional. A switch sends special Layer 2 UDLD frames identifying its switch port at regular intervals. UDLD expects the far-end switch to echo those frames back across the same link, with the far-end switch port's identification added.

If a UDLD frame is received in return and both neighboring ports are identified in the frame, the link must be bidirectional. However, if the echoed frames are not seen, the link must be unidirectional for some reason.

Naturally, an echo process such as this requires both ends of the link to be configured for UDLD. Otherwise, one end of the link will not echo the frames back to the originator. In addition, each switch at the end of a link sends its own UDLD messages independently, expecting echoes from the far end. This means that two echo processes are occurring on any given link.

UDLD messages are sent at regular intervals, as long as the link is active. You can configure the message interval UDLD uses. (The default is 15 seconds.) The objective behind UDLD is to detect a unidirectional link condition before STP has time to move a blocked port into the Forwarding state. To do this, the target time must be less than the Max Age timer plus two intervals of the Forward Delay timer, or 50 seconds. UDLD can detect a unidirectional link after about three times the UDLD message interval (45 seconds total, using the default).

UDLD has two modes of operation:

- **Normal mode:** When a unidirectional link condition is detected, the port is allowed to continue its operation. UDLD merely marks the port as having an undetermined state and generates a syslog message.

- **Aggressive mode:** When a unidirectional link condition is detected, the switch takes action to reestablish the link. UDLD messages are sent out once a second for 8 seconds. If none of those messages is echoed back, the port is placed in the errdisable state so that it cannot be used.

You configure UDLD on a per-port basis, although you can enable it globally for all fiber-optic switch ports (either native fiber or fiber-based GBIC or SFP modules). By default, UDLD is disabled on all switch ports. To enable it globally, use the following global configuration command:

```
Switch(config)# udld {enable | aggressive | message time seconds}
```

For normal mode, use the **enable** keyword; for aggressive mode, use the **aggressive** keyword. You can use **the message time** keywords to set the message interval to *seconds*, ranging from 1 to 90 seconds. The default interval is 7 seconds.

You also can enable or disable UDLD on individual switch ports, if needed, using the following interface configuration command:

```
Switch(config-if)# udld {enable | aggressive | disable}
```

Here, you can use the **disable** keyword to completely disable UDLD on a fiber-optic interface.

Note   The default UDLD message interval times differ among Catalyst switch platforms. Although two neighbors might have mismatched message time values, UDLD still works correctly. This is because each of the two neighbors simply echoes UDLD messages back as they are received, without knowledge of their neighbor's own time interval. The time interval is used only to decide when to send UDLD messages and as a basis for detecting a unidirectional link from the absence of echoed messages.If you decide to change the default message time, make sure that UDLD still can detect a fault *before* STP decides to move a link to the Forwarding state.

You safely can enable UDLD on all switch ports. The switch globally enables UDLD only on ports that use fiber-optic media. Twisted-pair or copper media does not suffer from the physical layer conditions that allow a unidirectional link to form. However, you can enable UDLD on nonfiber links individually, if you want.

At this point, you might be wondering how UDLD can be enabled gracefully on the two end switches. Recall that in aggressive mode, UDLD disables the link if the neighbor does not reflect the messages back within a certain time period. If you are enabling UDLD on a production network, is there a chance that UDLD will disable working links before you can get the far end configured?

The answer is no. UDLD makes some intelligent assumptions when it is enabled on a link for the first time. First, UDLD has no record of any neighbor on the link. It starts sending out messages, hoping that a neighboring switch will hear them and echo them back. Obviously, the device at the far end also must support UDLD so that the messages will be echoed back.

If the neighboring switch does not yet have UDLD enabled, no messages will be echoed. UDLD will keep trying (indefinitely) to detect a neighbor and will not disable the link. After the neighbor has UDLD configured also, both switches become aware of each other and the bidirectional state of the link through their UDLD message exchanges. From then on, if messages are not echoed, the link can accurately be labeled as unidirectional.

Finally, be aware that if UDLD detects a unidirectional condition on a link, it takes action on only that link. This becomes important in an EtherChannel: If one link within the channel becomes unidirectional, UDLD flags or disables only the offending link in the bundle, not the entire EtherChannel. UDLD sends and echoes its messages on each link within an EtherChannel channel independently.

Once UDLD aggressive mode has put a switch port into the errdisable state, you must use the following command to reenable it:

```
Switch# udld reset
```

Actually, all ports errdisabled because of UDLD will be reset and reenabled simultaneously, allowing traffic to begin passing through them again. This behavior differs somewhat from other errdisable conditions, where you would use the **shutdown** and **no shutdown** commands to reenable a port.

Using BPDU Filtering to Disable STP on a Port

Ordinarily, STP operates on all switch ports in an effort to eliminate bridging loops before they can form. BPDUs are sent on all switch ports—even ports where PortFast has been enabled. BPDUs also can be received and processed if any are sent by neighboring switches.

You always should allow STP to run on a switch to prevent loops. However, in special cases when you need to prevent BPDUs from being sent or processed on one or more switch ports, you can use BPDU filtering to effectively disable STP on those ports.

By default, BPDU filtering is disabled on all switch ports. You can configure BPDU filtering as a global default, affecting all switch ports with the following global configuration command:

```
Switch(config)# spanning-tree portfast bpdufilter default
```

The **default** keyword indicates that BPDU filtering will be enabled automatically on all ports that have PortFast enabled. If PortFast is disabled on a port, then BPDU filtering will not be enabled there.

You also can enable or disable BPDU filtering on specific switch ports by using the following interface configuration command:

```
Switch(config-if)# spanning-tree bpdufilter {enable | disable}
```

Be very careful to enable BPDU filtering only under controlled circumstances in which you are absolutely sure that a switch port will have a single host connected and that a loop will be impossible. Enable BPDU filtering only if the connected device cannot allow BPDUs to be accepted or sent. Otherwise, you should permit STP to operate on the switch ports as a precaution.

Tip   Do not confuse BPDU filtering with the BPDU Guard feature. BPDU Guard is used to detect inbound BPDUs on ports where BPDUs are not expected to be seen, then protect the STP stability by preventing those BPDUs from being processed. In contrast, BPDU filtering stops all BPDUs from being received or sent on a switch port, effectively disabling STP.

Troubleshooting STP Protection

With several different types of STP protection features available, you might need to know which (if any) has been configured on a switch port. Table 8-2 lists and describes the EXEC commands useful for verifying the features presented in this chapter.

Table 8-2   *Commands for Verifying and Troubleshooting STP Protection Features*

Display Function	Command Syntax
List the ports that have been labeled in an inconsistent state.	Switch# **show spanning-tree inconsistentports**
Look for detailed reasons for inconsistencies.	Switch# **show spanning-tree interface** *type mod/num* [detail]
Display the global BPDU Guard, BPDU filter, and Loop Guard states.	Switch# **show spanning-tree summary**
Display the UDLD status on one or all ports.	Switch# **show udld** [*type mod/num*]
Reenable ports that UDLD aggressive mode has errdisabled.	Switch# **udld reset**

Exam Preparation Tasks

Review All Key Topics

Review the most important topics in the chapter, noted with the Key Topic icon in the outer margin of the page. Table 8-3 lists a reference of these key topics and the page numbers on which each is found.

Table 8-3 *Key Topics for Chapter 8*

Key Topic Element	Description	Page Number
Paragraph	Discusses the Root Guard feature	208
Paragraph	Discusses the BPDU Guard feature	209
Paragraph	Discusses the Loop Guard feature	210
Paragraph	Discusses the UDLD feature	211
Paragraph	Explains BPDU filtering	213

Complete Tables and Lists from Memory

There are no memory tables in this chapter.

Define Key Terms

Define the following key terms from this chapter, and check your answers in the glossary:

Root Guard, superior BPDU, BPDU Guard, Loop Guard, UDLD, BPDU filtering

Use Command Reference to Check Your Memory

This section includes the most important configuration and EXEC commands covered in this chapter. It might not be necessary to memorize the complete syntax of every command, but you should remember the basic keywords that are needed.

With so many similar and mutually exclusive STP protection features available, you might have a hard time remembering which ones to use where. Use Figure 8-1 as a quick reference.

Figure 8-1 shows two backbone switches (Switch A and B), along with an access layer switch (Switch C), with redundant uplinks. Users are connected to the access switch, where PortFast is in use. An additional access switch (Switch D) has an uplink to access layer switch C. All switch-to-switch links are fiber-based Gigabit Ethernet. Obviously, a root bridge never should appear out of Switch D.

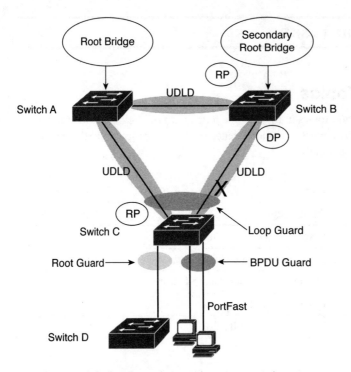

Root guard: Apply to ports where root is never expected.

BPDU guard: Apply to all user ports where PortFast is enabled.

Loop guard: Apply to nondesignated ports but okay to apply to all ports.

UDLD: Apply to all fiber-optic links between switches (must be enabled on both ends).

Permissible combinations on a switch port:
    Loop guard and UDLD
    Root guard and UDLD

Not permissible on a switch port:

    Root guard and Loop guard
    Root guard and BPDU guard

Figure 8-1 *Guidelines for Applying STP Protection Features in a Network*

To test your memory of the STP protection feature commands, cover the rightmost columns of Tables 8-4 and 8-5 with a piece of paper, read the description on the left side, then see how much of the command you can remember.

Remember that the CCNP exam focuses on practical or hands-on skills that are used by a networking professional.

Table 8-4   *STP Protection Configuration Commands*

Task	Global Command Syntax	Interface Command Syntax
Enable Root Guard.	—	Switch(config-if)# **spanning-tree guard root**
Enable BPDU Guard.	Switch(config)# **spanning-tree portfast bpduguard default**	Switch(config-if)# **spanning-tree bpduguard enable**
Enable Loop Guard.	Switch(config)# **spanning-tree loopguard default**	Switch(config-if)# **spanning-tree guard loop**
Enable UDLD.	Switch(config)# **udld {enable | aggressive | message time seconds}**	Switch(config-if)# **udld {enable | aggressive | disable}**
Enable BPDU filtering.	Switch(config)# **spanning-tree bpdufilter default**	Switch(config-if)# **spanning-tree bpdufilter enable**

Table 8-5   *STP Protection Activity Commands*

Task	Command Syntax
Look for ports that have been put in an inconsistent state.	Switch# **show spanning-tree inconsistentports**
Display the global BPDU Guard, BPDU filter, and Loop Guard states.	Switch# **show spanning-tree summary**
Show UDLD status.	Switch# **show udld** [*type mod/num*]
Reenable all ports that UDLD has errdisabled.	Switch# **udld reset**

This chapter covers the following topics that you need to master for the CCNP SWITCH exam:

- **Rapid Spanning Tree Protocol:** This section discusses the enhancements that allow switches to run STP efficiently, offering fast convergence.

- **Multiple Spanning Tree Protocol:** This section discusses the latest IEEE standard that supports a reduced number of STP instances for a campus network while using RSTP for efficient operation.

CHAPTER 9

Advanced Spanning Tree Protocol

Familiarity with the IEEE 802.1D STP standard is essential because that protocol is used universally to maintain loop-free bridged and switched networks. However, it now is considered a legacy protocol, offering topology change and convergence times that are not as acceptable as they once were.

This chapter discusses the many STP enhancements that are available in new standards. Rapid STP (RSTP) is presented first because it provides the foundation for efficient STP activity. RSTP can be coupled with either per-VLAN STP (PVST+) or Multiple STP modes. This allows a Layer 2 campus network to undergo change quickly and efficiently, with little downtime for today's applications.

This chapter also covers Multiple STP (MST or MSTP). MST allows VLANs to be individually mapped into arbitrary STP instances while RSTP operates in the background. You can use MST to greatly simplify the Layer 2 topologies and STP operations when many VLANs (and many instances of STP) are present in a network.

"Do I Know This Already?" Quiz

The "Do I Know This Already?" quiz allows you to assess whether you should read this entire chapter thoroughly or jump to the "Exam Preparation Tasks" section. If you are in doubt based on your answers to these questions or your own assessment of your knowledge of the topics, read the entire chapter. Table 9-1 outlines the major headings in this chapter and the "Do I Know This Already?" quiz questions that go with them. You can find the answers in Appendix A, "Answers to the 'Do I Know This Already?' Quizzes."

Table 9-1   *"Do I Know This Already?" Foundation Topics Section-to-Question Mapping*

Foundation Topics Section	Questions Covered in This Section
Rapid Spanning Tree Protocol	1–8
Multiple Spanning Tree Protocol	9–12

1. Which one of the following commands enables the use of RSTP?

   a. **spanning-tree mode rapid-pvst**

   b. **no spanning-tree mode pvst**

   c. **spanning-tree rstp**

   d. **spanning-tree mode rstp**

   e. None. RSTP is enabled by default.

2. On which standard is RSTP based?

   a. 802.1Q

   b. 802.1D

   c. 802.1w

   d. 802.1s

3. Which of the following is not a port state in RSTP?

   a. Listening

   b. Learning

   c. Discarding

   d. Forwarding

4. When a switch running RSTP receives an 802.1D BPDU, what happens?

   a. The BPDU is discarded or dropped.

   b. An ICMP message is returned.

   c. The switch begins to use 802.1D rules on that port.

   d. The switch disables RSTP.

5. When does an RSTP switch consider a neighbor to be down?

   a. After three BPDUs are missed

   b. After six BPDUs are missed

   c. After the Max Age timer expires

   d. After the Forward timer expires

6. Which process is used during RSTP convergence?

   a. BPDU propagation

   b. Synchronization

   c. Forward timer expiration

   d. BPDU

7. What causes RSTP to view a port as a point-to-point port?

   a. Port speed

   b. Port media

   c. Port duplex

   d. Port priority

8. Which of the following events triggers a topology change with RSTP on a nonedge port?

   a. A port comes up or goes down.

   b. A port comes up.

   c. A port goes down.

   d. A port moves to the Forwarding state.

9. Which of the following is *not* a characteristic of MST?

   a. A reduced number of STP instances

   b. Fast STP convergence

   c. Eliminated need for CST

   d. Interoperability with PVST+

10. Which of the following standards defines the MST protocol?

   a. 802.1Q

   b. 802.1D

   c. 802.1w

   d. 802.1s

11. How many instances of STP are supported in the Cisco implementation of MST?

    a. 1

    b. 16

    c. 256

    d. 4096

12. What switch command can be used to change from PVST+ to MST?

    a. spanning-tree mst enable

    b. no spanning-tree pvst+

    c. spanning-tree mode mst

    d. spanning-tree mst

Foundation Topics

Rapid Spanning Tree Protocol

The IEEE 802.1D Spanning Tree Protocol was designed to keep a switched or bridged network loop free, with adjustments made to the network topology dynamically. A topology change typically takes 30 seconds, with a port moving from the Blocking state to the Forwarding state after two intervals of the Forward Delay timer. As technology has improved, 30 seconds has become an unbearable length of time to wait for a production network to fail over or "heal" itself during a problem.

The IEEE 802.1w standard was developed to use 802.1D's principal concepts and make the resulting convergence much faster. This is also known as the *Rapid Spanning Tree Protocol* (RSTP), which defines how switches must interact with each other to keep the network topology loop free in a very efficient manner.

As with 802.1D, RSTP's basic functionality can be applied as a single instance or multiple instances. This can be done by using RSTP as the underlying mechanism for the Cisco-proprietary Per-VLAN Spanning Tree Protocol (PVST+). The resulting combination is called *Rapid PVST+* (RPVST+). RSTP also is used as part of the IEEE 802.1s Multiple Spanning Tree (MST) operation. RSTP operates consistently in each, but replicating RSTP as multiple instances requires different approaches.

RSTP Port Behavior

In 802.1D, each switch port is assigned a role and a state at any given time. Depending on the port's proximity to the root bridge, it takes on one of the following roles:

- Root port
- Designated port
- Blocking port (neither root nor designated)

The Cisco proprietary UplinkFast feature also reserved a hidden alternate port role for ports that offered parallel paths to the root but were in the Blocking state.

Recall that each switch port also is assigned one of five possible states:

- Disabled
- Blocking
- Listening
- Learning
- Forwarding

Only the Forwarding state allows data to be sent and received. A port's state is somewhat tied to its role. For example, a blocking port cannot be a root port or a designated port.

RSTP achieves its rapid nature by letting each switch interact with its neighbors through each port. This interaction is performed based on a port's role, not strictly on the bridge protocol data units (BPDUs) that are relayed from the root bridge. After the role is determined, each port can be given a state that determines what it does with incoming data.

The root bridge in a network using RSTP is elected just as with 802.1D—by the lowest bridge ID. After all switches agree on the identity of the root, the following port roles are determined:

- **Root port:** The one switch port on each switch that has the best root path cost to the root. This is identical to 802.1D. (By definition, the root bridge has no root ports.)

- **Designated port:** The switch port on a network segment that has the best root path cost to the root.

- **Alternate port:** A port that has an alternative path to the root, different from the path the root port takes. This path is less desirable than that of the root port. (An example of this is an access layer switch with two uplink ports; one becomes the root port, and the other is an alternate port.)

- **Backup port:** A port that provides a redundant (but less desirable) connection to a segment where another switch port already connects. If that common segment is lost, the switch might or might not have a path back to the root.

RSTP defines port states only according to what the port does with incoming frames. (Naturally, if incoming frames are ignored or dropped, so are outgoing frames.) Any port role can have any of these port states:

- **Discarding:** Incoming frames simply are dropped; no MAC addresses are learned. (This state combines the 802.1D Disabled, Blocking, and Listening states because all three did not effectively forward anything. The Listening state is not needed because RSTP quickly can negotiate a state change without listening for BPDUs first.)

- **Learning:** Incoming frames are dropped, but MAC addresses are learned.

- **Forwarding:** Incoming frames are forwarded according to MAC addresses that have been (and are being) learned.

BPDUs in RSTP

In 802.1D, BPDUs basically originate from the root bridge and are relayed by all switches down through the tree. Because of this propagation of BPDUs, 802.1D convergence must wait for steady-state conditions before proceeding.

RSTP uses the 802.1D BPDU format for backward compatibility. However, some previously unused bits in the Message Type field are used. The sending switch port identifies itself by its RSTP role and state. The BPDU version also is set to 2 to distinguish RSTP BPDUs from 802.1D BPDUs. In addition, RSTP uses an interactive process so that two neighboring switches can negotiate state changes. Some BPDU bits are used to flag messages during this negotiation.

BPDUs are sent out every switch port at hello time intervals, regardless of whether BPDUs are received from the root. In this way, any switch anywhere in the network can play an active role in maintaining the topology. Switches also can expect to receive regular BPDUs from their neighbors. When three BPDUs are missed in a row, that neighbor is presumed to be down, and all information related to the port leading to the neighbor immediately is aged out. This means that a switch can detect a neighbor failure in three Hello intervals (default 6 seconds), versus the Max Age timer interval (default 20 seconds) for 802.1D.

Because RSTP distinguishes its BPDUs from 802.1D BPDUs, it can coexist with switches still using 802.1D. Each port attempts to operate according to the STP BPDU that is received. For example, when an 802.1D BPDU (Version 0) is received on a port, that port begins to operate according to the 802.1D rules.

However, each port has a measure that locks the protocol in use, in case BPDUs from both 802.1D and RSTP are received within a short time frame. This can occur if the switches in a network are being migrated from one STP type to another. Instead of flapping or toggling the STP type during a migration, the switch holds the protocol type for the duration of a migration delay timer. After this timer expires, the port is free to change protocols if needed.

RSTP Convergence

The convergence of STP in a network is the process that takes all switches from a state of independence (each thinks it must be the STP root) to one of uniformity, in which each switch has a place in a loop-free tree topology. You can think of convergence as a two-stage process:

1. One common root bridge must be "elected," and all switches must know about it.

2. The state of every switch port in the STP domain must be brought from a Blocking state to the appropriate state to prevent loops.

Convergence generally takes time because messages are propagated from switch to switch. The traditional 802.1D STP also requires the expiration of several timers before switch ports can safely be allowed to forward data.

RSTP takes a different approach when a switch needs to decide how to participate in the tree topology. When a switch first joins the topology (perhaps it was just powered up) or has detected a failure in the existing topology, RSTP requires it to base its forwarding decisions on the type of port.

Port Types

Every switch port can be considered one of the following types:

- **Edge port:** A port at the "edge" of the network, where only a single host connects. Traditionally, this has been identified by enabling the STP PortFast feature. RSTP keeps the PortFast concept for familiarity. By definition, the port cannot form a loop as it connects to one host, so it can be placed immediately in the Forwarding state. However, if a BPDU ever is received on an edge port, the port immediately loses its edge port status.

- **Root port:** The port that has the best cost to the root of the STP instance. Only one root port can be selected and active at any time, although alternative paths to the root can exist through other ports. If alternative paths are detected, those ports are identified as alternative root ports and immediately can be placed in the Forwarding state when the existing root port fails.

- **Point-to-point port:** Any port that connects to another switch and becomes a designated port. A quick handshake with the neighboring switch, rather than a timer expiration, decides the port state. BPDUs are exchanged back and forth in the form of a proposal and an agreement. One switch proposes that its port becomes a designated port; if the other switch agrees, it replies with an agreement message.

Point-to-point ports automatically are determined by the duplex mode in use. Full-duplex ports are considered point to point because only two switches can be present on the link. STP convergence can occur quickly over a point-to-point link through RSTP handshake messages.

Half-duplex ports, on the other hand, are considered to be on a shared medium with possibly more than two switches present. They are not point-to-point ports. STP convergence on a half-duplex port must occur between several directly connected switches. Therefore, the traditional 802.1D style convergence must be used. This results in a slower response because the shared-medium ports must go through the fixed Listening and Learning state time periods.

It is easy to see how two switches quickly can converge to a common idea of which one is the root and which one will have the designated port after just a single exchange of BPDUs. What about a larger network, where 802.1D BPDUs normally would have to be relayed from switch to switch?

RSTP handles the complete STP convergence of the network as a propagation of handshakes over point-to-point links. When a switch needs to make an STP decision, a handshake is made with the nearest neighbor. When that is successful, the handshake sequence is moved to the next switch and the next, as an ever-expanding wave moving toward the network's edges.

During each handshake sequence, a switch must take measures to completely ensure that it will not introduce a bridging loop before moving the handshake outward. This is done through a synchronization process.

Synchronization

To participate in RSTP convergence, a switch must decide the state of each of its ports. Nonedge ports begin in the Discarding state. After BPDUs are exchanged between the switch and its neighbor, the Root Bridge can be identified. If a port receives a superior BPDU from a neighbor, that port becomes the root port.

For each nonedge port, the switch exchanges a proposal-agreement handshake to decide the state of each end of the link. Each switch assumes that its port should become the designated port for the segment, and a proposal message (a configuration BPDU) is sent to the neighbor suggesting this.

When a switch receives a proposal message on a port, the following sequence of events occurs. Figure 9-1 shows the sequence, based on the center Catalyst switch:

1. If the proposal's sender has a superior BPDU, the local switch realizes that the sender should be the designated switch (having the designated port) and that its own port must become the new root port.

2. Before the switch agrees to anything, it must synchronize itself with the topology.

3. All nonedge ports immediately are moved into the Discarding (blocking) state so that no bridging loops can form.

4. An agreement message (a configuration BPDU) is sent back to the sender, indicating that the switch is in agreement with the new designated port choice. This also tells the sender that the switch is in the process of synchronizing itself.

5. The root port immediately is moved to the Forwarding state. The sender's port also immediately can begin forwarding.

6. For each nonedge port that is currently in the Discarding state, a proposal message is sent to the respective neighbor.

7. An agreement message is expected and received from a neighbor on a nonedge port.

8. The nonedge port immediately is moved to the Forwarding state.

Notice that the RSTP convergence begins with a switch sending a proposal message. The recipient of the proposal must synchronize itself by effectively isolating itself from the rest of the topology. All nonedge ports are blocked until a proposal message can be sent, causing the nearest neighbors to synchronize themselves. This creates a moving "wave" of synchronizing switches, which quickly can decide to start forwarding on their links only if their neighbors agree. Figure 9-2 shows how the synchronization wave travels through a network at three successive time intervals. Isolating the switches along the traveling wave inherently prevents bridging loops.

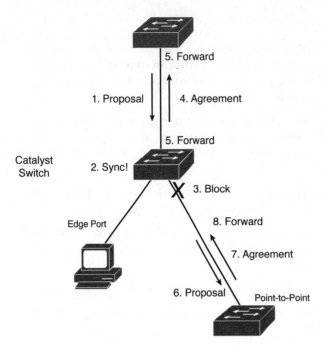

Figure 9-1   *Sequence of Events During RSTP Convergence*

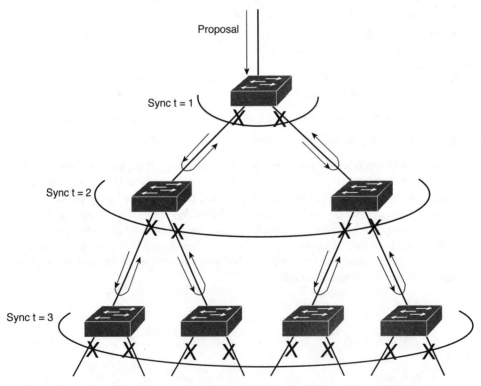

Figure 9-2   *RSTP Synchronization Traveling Through a Network*

The entire convergence process happens quickly, at the speed of BPDU transmission, without the use of any timers. However, a designated port that sends a proposal message might not receive an agreement message reply. Suppose that the neighboring switch does not understand RSTP or has a problem replying. The sending switch then must become overly cautious and must begin playing by the 802.1D rules: The port must be moved through the legacy Listening and Learning states (using the Forward Delay timer) before moving to the Forwarding state.

Topology Changes and RSTP

Recall that when an 802.1D switch detects a port state change (either up or down), it signals the root bridge by sending Topology Change Notification (TCN) BPDUs. The root bridge, in turn, must signal the topology change by sending out a TCN message that is relayed to all switches in the STP domain.

RSTP detects a topology change only when a nonedge port transitions to the Forwarding state. This might seem odd because a link failure is not used as a trigger. RSTP uses all its rapid convergence mechanisms to prevent bridging loops from forming. Therefore, topology changes are detected only so that bridging tables can be updated and corrected as hosts appear first on a failed port and then on a different functioning port.

When a topology change is detected, a switch must propagate news of the change to other switches in the network so that they can correct their bridging tables, too. This process is similar to the convergence and synchronization mechanism; topology change (TC) messages propagate through the network in an ever-expanding wave.

BPDUs, with their TC bit set, are sent out all the nonedge designated ports. This is done until the TC timer expires, after two intervals of the Hello time. This notifies neighboring switches of the new link and the topology change. In addition, all MAC addresses associated with the nonedge designated ports are flushed from the content-addressable memory (CAM) table. This forces the addresses to be relearned after the change, in case hosts now appear on a different link.

All neighboring switches that receive the TC messages also must flush the MAC addresses learned on all ports except the one that received the TC message. Those switches then must send TC messages out their nonedge designated ports, and so on.

RSTP Configuration

By default, a switch operates in Per-VLAN Spanning Tree Plus (PVST+) mode using traditional 802.1D STP. Therefore, RSTP cannot be used until a different spanning-tree mode (MST or RPVST+) is enabled. Remember that RSTP is just the underlying mechanism that a spanning-tree mode can use to detect topology changes and converge a network into a loop-free topology.

The only configuration changes related to RSTP affect the port or link type. The link type is used to determine how a switch negotiates topology information with its neighbors.

To configure a port as an RSTP edge port, use the following interface configuration command:

```
Switch(config-if)# spanning-tree portfast
```

You already should be familiar with this command from the 802.1D STP configuration. After PortFast is enabled, the port is considered to have only one host and is positioned at the edge of the network.

By default, RSTP automatically decides that a port is a point-to-point link if it is operating in full-duplex mode. Ports connecting to other switches are usually full duplex because there are only two switches on the link. However, you can override the automatic determination, if needed. For example, a port connecting to one other switch might be operating at half duplex, for some reason. To force the port to act as a point-to-point link, use the following interface configuration command:

```
Switch(config-if)# spanning-tree link-type point-to-point
```

Rapid Per-VLAN Spanning Tree Protocol

Chapter 6, "Traditional Spanning Tree Protocol," describes PVST+ as the default STP mode on Catalyst switches. In PVST+, one spanning tree instance is created and used for each active VLAN that is defined on the switch. Each STP instance behaves according to the traditional 802.1D STP rules.

You can improve the efficiency of each STP instance by configuring a switch to begin using RSTP instead. This means that each VLAN will have its own independent instance of RSTP running on the switch. This mode is known as Rapid PVST+ (RPVST+).

You need only one configuration step to change the STP mode and begin using RPVST+. You can use the following global configuration command to accomplish this:

```
Switch(config)# spanning-tree mode rapid-pvst
```

Be careful when you use this command on a production network because any STP process that is currently running must be restarted. This can cause functioning links to move through the traditional STP states, preventing data from flowing for a short time.

> **Tip**　To revert back to the default PVST+ mode, using traditional 802.1D STP, you can use the following command:
> ```
> Switch(config)# spanning-tree mode pvst
> ```

After you enable the RPVST+ mode, the switch must begin supporting both RSTP and 802.1D STP neighbors. The switch can detect the neighbor's STP type by the BPDU version that is received. You can see the neighbor type in the output of the **show spanning-tree vlan** *vlan-id* command, as demonstrated in Example 9-1.

Example 9-1   *Detecting a Neighboring Switch's STP Type*

```
Switch# show spanning-tree vlan 171
VLAN0171
Spanning tree enabled protocol rstp
  Root ID    Priority    4267
             Address     00d0.0457.38aa
             Cost        3
             Port        833 (Port-channel1)
             Hello Time   2 sec  Max Age 20 sec  Forward Delay 15 sec

  Bridge ID  Priority    32939  (priority 32768 sys-id-ext 171)
             Address     0007.0d55.a800
             Hello Time   2 sec  Max Age 20 sec  Forward Delay 15 sec
             Aging Time 300


Interface        Role Sts Cost      Prio.Nbr Type
---------------- ---- ---- --------- -------- --------------------------------
Gi1/0/7          Desg FWD 4          128.7    P2p
Gi1/0/9/6        Altn BLK 4          128.9    P2p Peer(STP)
Po1              Root FWD 3          128.104  P2p
Po2              Desg FWD 3          128.834  P2p
Po3              Desg FWD 3          128.835  P2p
Switch#
```

The output in Example 9-1 shows information about the RSTP instance for VLAN 171. The first shaded line confirms that the local switch indeed is running RSTP. (The only other way to confirm the STP mode is to locate the **spanning-tree mode** command in the running configuration.)

In addition, this output displays all the active ports participating in the VLAN 171 instance of RSTP, along with their port types. The string **P2p** denotes a point-to-point RSTP port type in which a full-duplex link connects two neighboring switches that both are running RSTP. If you see *P2p Peer(STP)*, the port is a point-to-point type but the neighboring device is running traditional 802.1D STP.

Multiple Spanning Tree Protocol

Chapter 6 covered two "flavors" of spanning-tree implementations, IEEE 802.1Q and PVST+, both based on the 802.1D STP. These also represent the two extremes of STP operation in a network:

- **802.1Q:** Only a single instance of STP is used for all VLANs. If there are 500 VLANs, only 1 instance of STP will be running. This is called the *Common Spanning Tree* (CST) and operates over the trunk's native VLAN.

- **PVST+:** One instance of STP is used for each active VLAN in the network. If there are 500 VLANs, 500 independent instances of STP will be running.

In most networks, each switch has a redundant path to another switch. For example, an access layer switch usually has two uplinks, each connecting to a different distribution or core layer switch. If 802.1Q's CST is used, only one STP instance will run. This means that there is only one loop-free topology at any given time and that only one of the two uplinks in the access layer switch will be forwarding. The other uplink always will be blocking.

Obviously, arranging the network so that both uplinks can be used simultaneously would be best. One uplink should carry one set of VLANs, whereas the other should carry a different set as a type of load balancing.

PVST+ seems more attractive to meet that goal because it allows different VLANs to have different topologies so that each uplink can be forwarding. But think of the consequences: As the number of VLANs increases, so does the number of independent STP instances. Each instance uses some amount of the switch CPU and memory resources. The more instances that are in use, the fewer CPU resources will be available for switching.

Beyond that, what is the real benefit of having 500 STP topologies for 500 VLANs, when only a small number of possible topologies exist for a switch with two uplinks? Figure 9-3 shows a typical network with an access layer switch connecting to a pair of core switches. Two VLANs are in use, with the root bridges configured to support load balancing across the two uplinks. The right portion of the figure shows every possible topology for VLANs A and B. Notice that because the access layer switch has only two uplinks, only two topologies actually matter—one in which the left uplink forwards, and one in which the right uplink forwards.

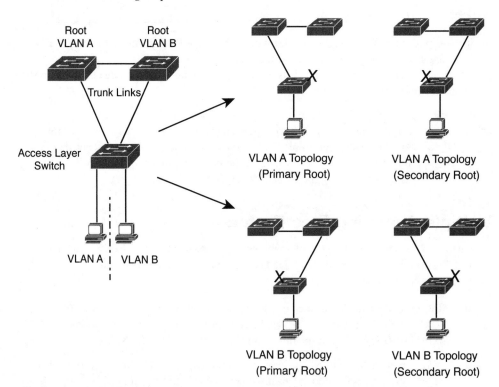

Figure 9-3 *Possible STP Topologies for Two VLANs*

Notice also that the number of useful topologies is independent of the number of VLANs. If 10 or 100 VLANs were used in the figure, there would still be only two possible outcomes at the access layer switch. Therefore, running 10 or 100 instances of STP when only a couple would suffice is rather wasteful.

The Multiple Spanning Tree Protocol was developed to address the lack of and surplus of STP instances. As a result, the network administrator can configure exactly the number of STP instances that makes sense for the enterprise network, no matter how many VLANs are in use. MST is defined in the IEEE 802.1s standard.

MST Overview

MST is built on the concept of mapping one or more VLANs to a single STP instance. Multiple instances of STP can be used (hence the name MST), with each instance supporting a different group of VLANs.

For the network shown in Figure 9-3, only two MST instances would be needed. Each could be tuned to result in a different topology so that Instance 1 would forward on the left uplink, whereas Instance 2 would forward on the right uplink. Therefore, VLAN A would be mapped to Instance 1, and VLAN B would be mapped to Instance 2.

To implement MST in a network, you need to determine the following:

- The number of STP instances needed to support the desired topologies

- Whether to map a set of VLANs to each instance

MST Regions

MST is different from 802.1Q and PVST+, although it can interoperate with them. If a switch is configured to use MST, it somehow must figure out which of its neighbors are using which type of STP. This is done by configuring switches into common MST regions, where every switch in a region runs MST with compatible parameters.

In most networks, a single MST region is sufficient, although you can configure more than one region. Within the region, all switches must run the instance of MST that is defined by the following attributes:

- MST configuration name (32 characters)

- MST configuration revision number (0 to 65535)

- MST instance-to-VLAN mapping table (4096 entries)

If two switches have the same set of attributes, they belong to the same MST region. If not, they belong to two independent regions.

MST BPDUs contain configuration attributes so that switches receiving BPDUs can compare them against their local MST configurations. If the attributes match, the STP instances within MST can be shared as part of the same region. If not, a switch is seen to be at the MST region boundary, where one region meets another or one region meets traditional 802.1D STP.

> **Note** The entire MST instance-to-VLAN mapping table is not sent in the BPDUs because the instance mappings must be configured on each switch. Instead, a digest, or a hash code computed from the table contents, is sent. As the contents of the table change, the digest value will be different. Therefore, a switch quickly can compare a received digest to its own to see if the advertised table is the same.

Spanning-Tree Instances Within MST

MST was designed to interoperate with all other forms of STP. Therefore, it also must support STP instances from each STP type. This is where MST can get confusing. Think of the entire enterprise network as having a single CST topology so that one instance of STP represents any and all VLANs and MST regions present. The CST maintains a common loop-free topology while integrating all forms of STP that might be in use.

To do this, CST must regard each MST region as a single "black box" bridge because it has no idea what is inside the region, nor does it care. CST maintains a loop-free topology only with the links that connect the regions to each other and to standalone switches running 802.1Q CST.

IST Instances

Something other than CST must work out a loop-free topology inside each MST region. Within a single MST region, an Internal Spanning Tree (IST) instance runs to work out a loop-free topology between the links where CST meets the region boundary and all switches inside the region. Think of the IST instance as a locally significant CST, bounded by the edges of the region.

The IST presents the entire region as a single virtual bridge to the CST outside. BPDUs are exchanged at the region boundary only over the native VLAN of trunks, as if a single CST were in operation. And, indeed, it is.

Figure 9-4 shows the basic concept behind the IST instance. The network at the left has an MST region, where several switches are running compatible MST configurations. Another switch is outside the region because it is running only the CST from 802.1Q.

The same network is shown at the right, where the IST has produced a loop-free topology for the network inside the region. The IST makes the internal network look like a single bridge (the "big switch" in the cloud) that can interface with the CST running outside the region.

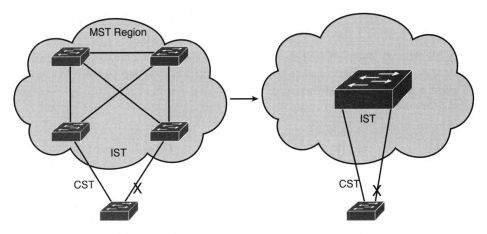

Figure 9-4 *Concepts Behind the IST Instance*

MST Instances

**Key
Topic**

Recall that the whole idea behind MST is the capability to map multiple VLANs to a smaller number of STP instances. Inside a region, the actual MST instances (MSTI) exist alongside the IST. Cisco supports a maximum of 16 MSTIs in each region. The IST always exists as MSTI number 0, leaving MSTIs 1 through 15 available for use.

Figure 9-5 shows how different MSTIs can exist within a single MST region. The left portion of the figure is identical to that of Figure 9-4. In this network, two MST instances, MSTI 1 and MSTI 2, are configured with different VLANs mapped to each. Their topologies follow the same structure as the network on the left side of the figure, but each has converged differently.

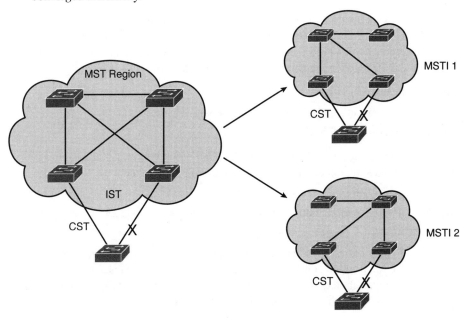

Figure 9-5 *Concepts Behind MST Instances*

Notice that within the MST cloud, there are now three independent STP instances coexisting: MSTI1, MSTI 2, and the IST.

Only the IST (MSTI 0) is allowed to send and receive MST BPDUs. Information about each of the other MSTIs is appended to the MST BPDU as an M-record. Therefore, even if a region has all 16 instances active, only 1 BPDU is needed to convey STP information about them all.

Each of the MSTIs is significant only within a region, even if an adjacent region has the same MSTIs in use. In other words, the MSTIs combine with the IST only at the region boundary to form a subtree of the CST. That means only IST BPDUs are sent into and out of a region.

What if an MST region connects with a switch running traditional PVST+? MST can detect this situation by listening to the received BPDUs. If BPDUs are heard from more than one VLAN (the CST), PVST+ must be in use. When the MST region sends a BPDU toward the PVST+ switch, the IST BPDUs are replicated into all the VLANs on the PVST+ switch trunk.

> **Tip**   Keep in mind that the IST instance is active on every port on a switch. Even if a port does not carry VLANs that have been mapped to the IST, IST must be running on the port.
>
> Also, by default, all VLANs are mapped to the IST instance. You must explicitly map them to other instances, if needed.

MST Configuration

Key
Topic

You must manually configure the MST configuration attributes on each switch in a region. There is currently no method to propagate this information from one switch to another, as is done with a protocol such as VLAN Trunking Protocol (VTP). To define the MST region, use the following configuration commands in the order shown:

Step 1.   Enable MST on the switch:

```
Switch(config)# spanning-tree mode mst
```

Step 2.   Enter the MST configuration mode:

```
Switch(config)# spanning-tree mst configuration
```

Step 3.   Assign a region configuration name (up to 32 characters):

```
Switch(config-mst)# name name
```

Step 4.   Assign a region configuration revision number (0 to 65,535):

```
Switch(config-mst)# revision version
```

The configuration revision number gives you a means of tracking changes to the MST region configuration. Each time you make changes to the configuration, you should increase the number by one. Remember that the region configuration (including the revision number) must match on all switches in the region. Therefore, you also need to update the revision numbers on the other switches to match.

Step 5.   Map VLANs to an MST instance:

```
Switch(config-mst)# instance instance-id vlan vlan-list
```

The *instance-id* (0 to 15) carries topology information for the VLANs listed in *vlan-list*. The list can contain one or more VLANs separated by commas. You also can add a range of VLANs to the list by separating numbers with a hyphen. VLAN numbers can range from 1 to 4094. (Remember that, by default, all VLANs are mapped to instance 0, the IST.)

Step 6.   Show the pending changes you have made:

```
Switch(config-mst)# show pending
```

Step 7.   Exit the MST configuration mode; commit the changes to the active MST region configuration:

```
Switch(config-mst)# exit
```

After MST is enabled and configured, PVST+ operation stops and the switch changes to RSTP operation. A switch cannot run both MST and PVST+ at the same time.

You also can tune the parameters that MST uses when it interacts with CST or traditional 802.1D. The parameters and timers are identical to those discussed in Chapter 7, "Spanning-Tree Configuration." In fact, the commands are very similar except for the addition of the **mst** keyword and the *instance-id*. Instead of tuning STP for a VLAN instance, you use an MST instance.

Table 9-2 summarizes the commands as a quick reference. Notice that the timer configurations are applied to MST as a whole, not to a specific MST instance. This is because all instance timers are defined through the IST instance and BPDUs.

Table 9-2   *MST Configuration Commands*

Task	Command Syntax
Set root bridge (macro).	Switch(config)# **spanning-tree mst** *instance-id* **root** {**primary** | **secondary**} [**diameter** *diameter*]
Set bridge priority.	Switch(config)# **spanning-tree mst** *instance-id* **priority** *bridge-priority*
Set port cost.	Switch(config)# **spanning-tree mst** *instance-id* **cost** *cost*
Set port priority.	Switch(config)# **spanning-tree mst** *instance-id* **port-priority** *port-priority*
Set STP timers.	Switch(config)# **spanning-tree mst hello-time** *seconds*
	Switch(config)# **spanning-tree mst forward-time** *seconds*
	Switch(config)# **spanning-tree mst max-age** *seconds*

Exam Preparation Tasks

Review All Key Topics

Review the most important topics in the chapter, noted with the Key Topic icon in the outer margin of the page. Table 9-3 lists a reference of these key topics and the page numbers on which each is found.

Table 9-3 *Key Topics for Chapter 9*

Key Topic Element	Description	Page Number
Paragraph	Describes RSTP root bridge election and port states	224
Paragraph	Describes RSTP port states	224
Paragraph	Discusses RSTP compatibility with 802.1D STP	225
Bullet	Describes RSTP port types	226
Paragraph	Explains the RSTP synchronization process	227
Paragraph	Discusses how RSTP detects topology changes	229
Paragraph	Explains how to configure an RSTP edge port	230
Paragraph	Explains how to enable the RPVST+ mode, using RSTP	230
Paragraph	Discusses how MST is organized into regions	233
Paragraph	Describes the IST instance	234
Paragraph	Describes MST instances	235
List	Explains how to configure MST	236

Complete Tables and Lists from Memory

Print a copy of Appendix C, "Memory Tables," (found on the CD), or at least the section for this chapter, and complete the tables and lists from memory. Appendix D, "Memory Table Answer Key," also on the CD, includes completed tables and lists to check your work.

Define Key Terms

Define the following key terms from this chapter, and check your answers in the glossary:

RSTP, RPVST+, alternate port, backup port, discarding state, edge port, point-to-point port, synchronization, MST, MST region, IST instance, MST instance (MSTI)

Use Command Reference to Check Your Memory

This section includes the most important configuration and EXEC commands covered in this chapter. It might not be necessary to memorize the complete syntax of every command, but you should remember the basic keywords that are needed.

To test your memory of the Rapid STP and MST commands, cover the right side of Tables 9-4 and 9-5 with a piece of paper, read the description on the left side, and then see how much of the command you can remember.

Table 9-4 *RSTP Configuration Commands*

Task	Command Syntax
Define an edge port.	Switch(config-if)# **spanning-tree portfast**
Override a port type.	Switch(config-if)# **spanning-tree link-type point-to-point**

Table 9-5 *MST Region Configuration Commands*

Task	Command Syntax
Enable MST on a switch.	Switch(config)# **spanning-tree mode mst**
Enter MST configuration mode.	Switch(config)# **spanning-tree mst configuration**
Name the MST region.	Switch(config-mst)# **name** *name*
Set the configuration revision number.	Switch(config-mst)# **revision** *version*

This chapter covers the following topics that you need to master for the CCNP SWITCH exam:

■ **Switch Port Aggregation with EtherChannel:** This section discusses the concept of aggregating, or "bundling," physical ports into a single logical link. Methods for load balancing traffic across the physical links also are covered.

■ **EtherChannel Negotiation Protocols:** This section covers two protocols that dynamically negotiate and control EtherChannels: Port Aggregation Protocol (PAgP), a Cisco proprietary protocol, and Link Aggregation Control Protocol (LACP), a standards-based protocol.

■ **EtherChannel Configuration:** This section explains the Catalyst switch commands needed to configure EtherChannel.

■ **Troubleshooting an EtherChannel:** This section gives a brief summary of things to consider and commands to use when an aggregated link is not operating properly.

CHAPTER 10

Aggregating Switch Links

In previous chapters, you learned about connecting switches and organizing users and devices into common workgroups. Using these principles, end users can be given effective access to resources both on and off the campus network. However, today's mission-critical applications and services demand networks that provide high availability and reliability.

This chapter presents technologies that you can use in a campus network to provide higher bandwidth and reliability between switches.

"Do I Know This Already?" Quiz

The "Do I Know This Already?" quiz allows you to assess whether you should read this entire chapter thoroughly or jump to the "Exam Preparation Tasks" section. If you are in doubt based on your answers to these questions or your own assessment of your knowledge of the topics, read the entire chapter. Table 10-1 outlines the major headings in this chapter and the "Do I Know This Already?" quiz questions that go with them. You can find the answers in Appendix A, "Answers to the 'Do I Know This Already?' Quizzes."

Table 10-1 *"Do I Know This Already?" Foundation Topics Section-to-Question Mapping*

Foundation Topics Section	Questions Covered in This Section
Switch Port Aggregation with EtherChannel	1–7
EtherChannel Negotiation Protocols	8–10
EtherChannel Configuration	11–12
Troubleshooting an EtherChannel	13

1. If Gigabit Ethernet ports are bundled into an EtherChannel, what is the maximum throughput supported on a Catalyst switch?

    a. 1 Gbps

    b. 2 Gbps

    c. 4 Gbps

    d. 8 Gbps

    e. 16 Gbps

2. Which of these methods distributes traffic over an EtherChannel?

   a. Round robin

   b. Least-used link

   c. A function of address

   d. A function of packet size

3. What type of interface represents an EtherChannel as a whole?

   a. Channel

   b. Port

   c. Port channel

   d. Channel port

4. Which of the following is not a valid method for EtherChannel load balancing?

   a. Source MAC address

   b. Source and destination MAC addresses

   c. Source IP address

   d. IP precedence

   e. UDP/TCP port

5. How can the EtherChannel load-balancing method be set?

   a. Per switch port

   b. Per EtherChannel

   c. Globally per switch

   d. Cannot be configured

6. What logical operation is performed to calculate EtherChannel load balancing as a function of two addresses?

   a. OR

   b. AND

   c. XOR

   d. NOR

7. Which one of the following is a valid combination of ports for an EtherChannel?

   a. Two access links (one VLAN 5, one VLAN 5)

   b. Two access links (one VLAN 1, one VLAN 10)

   c. Two trunk links (one VLANs 1 to 10, one VLANs 1, 11 to 20)

   d. Two 10/100/1000 Ethernet links (both full duplex, one 100 Mbps)

8. Which of these is a method for negotiating an EtherChannel?

   a. PAP

   b. CHAP

   c. LAPD

   d. LACP

9. Which of the following is a valid EtherChannel negotiation mode combination between two switches?

   a. PAgP auto, PAgP auto

   b. PAgP auto, PAgP desirable

   c. on, PAgP auto

   d. LACP passive, LACP passive

10. When is PAgP's "desirable silent" mode useful?

   a. When the switch should not send PAgP frames

   b. When the switch should not form an EtherChannel

   c. When the switch should not expect to receive PAgP frames

   d. When the switch is using LACP mode

11. Which of the following EtherChannel modes does not send or receive any negotiation frames?

   a. channel-group 1 mode passive

   b. channel-group 1 mode active

   c. channel-group 1 mode on

   d. channel-group 1 mode desirable

   e. channel-group 1 mode auto

12. Two computers are the only hosts sending IP data across an EtherChannel between two switches. Several different applications are being used between them. Which of these load-balancing methods would be more likely to use the most links in the EtherChannel?

   a. Source and destination MAC addresses.

   b. Source and destination IP addresses.

   c. Source and destination TCP/UDP ports.

   d. None of the other answers is correct.

13. Which command enables you to see the status of an EtherChannel's links?

    a. show channel link

    b. show etherchannel status

    c. show etherchannel summary

    d. show ether channel status

Foundation Topics

Switch Port Aggregation with EtherChannel

As discussed in Chapter 3, "Switch Port Configuration," switches can use Ethernet, Fast Ethernet, Gigabit, or 10-Gigabit Ethernet ports to scale link speeds by a factor of 10. It might seem logical to simply add more links between two switches to scale the bandwidth incrementally. Suppose two switches have a single Gigabit Ethernet link between them. If you add a second link, will the available bandwidth double? No, because each link acts independently, a bridging loop could easily form through them. As the left portion of Figure 10-1 shows, STP will detect the loop potential and will place one of the links in the blocking state. The end result is still a single active link between switches. Even if you add several more links, STP will keep all but one in the blocking state, as shown on the right portion of Figure 10-1.

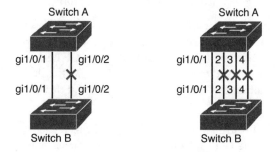

Figure 10-1 *The Effects of Trying to Scale Bandwidth with Individual Links*

Cisco offers another method of scaling link bandwidth by aggregating, or *bundling*, parallel links, termed the *EtherChannel* technology. Two to eight links of either Fast Ethernet (FE), Gigabit Ethernet (GE), or 10-Gigabit Ethernet (10GE) can be bundled as one logical link of Fast EtherChannel (FEC), Gigabit EtherChannel (GEC), or 10-Gigabit Etherchannel (10GEC), respectively. This bundle provides a full-duplex bandwidth of up to 1600 Mbps (eight links of Fast Ethernet), 16 Gbps (eight links of GE), or 160 Gbps (eight links of 10GE).

This also provides an easy means to "grow," or expand, a link's capacity between two switches, without having to continually purchase hardware for the next magnitude of throughput. For example, a single Fast Ethernet link (200 Mbps throughput) can be incrementally expanded up to eight Fast Ethernet links (1600 Mbps) as a single Fast EtherChannel. If the traffic load grows beyond that, the growth process can begin again with a single GE link (2 Gbps throughput), which can be expanded up to eight GE links as a Gigabit EtherChannel (16 Gbps). The process repeats again by moving to a single 10GE link, and so on.

Ordinarily, having multiple or parallel links between switches creates the possibility of bridging loops, an undesirable condition. EtherChannel avoids this situation by bundling parallel links into a single, logical link, which can act as either an access or a trunk link.

Switches or devices on each end of the EtherChannel link must understand and use the EtherChannel technology for proper operation. Figure 10-2 demonstrates how the links added in Figure 10-1 can be configured as an EtherChannel bundle. All the bundled physical links are collectively known by the logical EtherChannel interface, port channel 1. Notice that none of the physical links are in the Blocking state; STP is aware of the single port channel interface, which is kept in the Forwarding state.

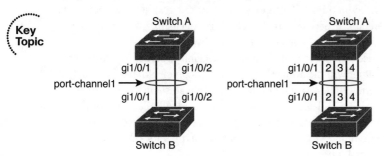

Figure 10-2 *Scaling Bandwidth by Bundling Physical Links into an EtherChannel*

Although an EtherChannel link is seen as a single logical link, the link does not necessarily have an inherent total bandwidth equal to the sum of its component physical links. For example, suppose that a GEC link is made up of four full-duplex 1-Gbps GE links. Although it is possible for the GEC link to carry a total throughput of 8 Gbps (if each link becomes fully loaded), the single resulting GEC bundle does not operate at this speed.

Instead, traffic is distributed across the individual links within the EtherChannel. Each of these links operates at its inherent speed (2 Gbps full duplex for GE) but carries only the frames placed on it by the EtherChannel hardware. If the load-distribution algorithm favors one link within the bundle, that link will carry a disproportionate amount of traffic. In other words, the load is not always distributed equally among the individual links. The load-balancing process is explained further in the next section.

EtherChannel also provides redundancy with several bundled physical links. If one of the links within the bundle fails, traffic sent through that link is automatically moved to an adjacent link. Failover occurs in less than a few milliseconds and is transparent to the end user. As more links fail, more traffic is moved to further adjacent links. Likewise, as links are restored, the load automatically is redistributed among the active links.

As you plan on configuring an EtherChannel, you should give some thought to several different failure scenarios. For example, the failure of a single physical link within an EtherChannel is not catastrophic because the switches compensate by moving traffic to the other, still functioning, links. However, what if all of the physical links are connected to the same switch, as shown in Figure 10-2? The switch itself might fail someday, taking all of the physical links of the EtherChannel down with it.

A more robust solution involves distributing the physical links across multiple switches at each end of the EtherChannel. This is possible when the switches are configured as one logical or virtual switch, such as the Cisco stackable Catalyst switches or chassis-based Virtual Switching System (VSS) switch families. In Figure 10-3, a four-port GEC is made up of two links connected to the first switch in a stack and two links connected to the second switch in a stack. This is known as a *multichassis EtherChannel* (MEC). Even if one switch fails within a stack, the MEC will keep functioning thanks to the other stacked switch.

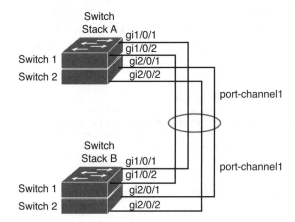

Figure 10-3   *Increasing Availability with a Multichassis EtherChannel*

Bundling Ports with EtherChannel

EtherChannel bundles can consist of up to eight physical ports of the same Ethernet media type and speed. Some configuration restrictions exist to ensure that only similarly configured links are bundled.

Generally, all bundled ports first must belong to the same VLAN. If used as a trunk, bundled ports must be in trunking mode, have the same native VLAN, and pass the same set of VLANs. Each of the ports should have the same speed and duplex settings before being bundled. Bundled ports also must be configured with identical spanning-tree settings.

Distributing Traffic in EtherChannel

Traffic in an EtherChannel is distributed across the individual bundled links in a deterministic fashion; however, the load is not necessarily balanced equally across all the links. Instead, frames are forwarded on a specific link as a result of a hashing algorithm. The algorithm can use source IP address, destination IP address, or a combination of source and destination IP addresses, source and destination MAC addresses, or TCP/UDP port numbers. The hash algorithm computes a binary pattern that selects a link number in the bundle to carry each frame.

If only one address or port number is hashed, a switch forwards each frame by using one or more low-order bits of the hash value as an index into the bundled links. If two addresses or port numbers are hashed, a switch performs an exclusive-OR (XOR) operation on one or more low-order bits of the addresses or TCP/UDP port numbers as an index into the bundled links.

For example, an EtherChannel consisting of two links bundled together requires a 1-bit index. If the index is 0, link 0 is selected; if the index is 1, link 1 is used. Either the lowest-order address bit or the XOR of the last bit of the addresses in the frame is used as the index. A four-link bundle uses a hash of the last 2 bits. Likewise, an eight-link bundle uses a hash of the last 3 bits. The hashing operation's outcome selects the EtherChannel's outbound link. Table 10-2 shows the results of an XOR on a two-link bundle, using the source and destination addresses.

Table 10-2 *Frame Distribution on a Two-Link EtherChannel*

Binary Address	Two-Link EtherChannel XOR and Link Number
Addr1: ... xxxxxxx0 Addr2: ... xxxxxxx0	... xxxxxxx0: Use link 0
Addr1: ... xxxxxxx0 Addr2: ... xxxxxxx1	... xxxxxxx1: Use link 1
Addr1: ... xxxxxxx1 Addr2: ... xxxxxxx0	... xxxxxxx1: Use link 1
Addr1: ... xxxxxxx1 Addr2: ... xxxxxxx1	... xxxxxxx0: Use link 0

The XOR operation is performed independently on each bit position in the address value. If the two address values have the same bit value, the XOR result is always 0. If the two address bits differ, the XOR result is always 1. In this way, frames can be distributed statistically among the links with the assumption that MAC or IP addresses themselves are distributed statistically throughout the network. In a four-link EtherChannel, the XOR is performed on the lower 2 bits of the address values, resulting in a 2-bit XOR value (each bit is computed separately) or a link number from 0 to 3.

As an example, consider a packet being sent from IP address 192.168.1.1 to 172.31.67.46. Because EtherChannels can be built from two to eight individual links, only the rightmost (least-significant) 3 bits are needed as a link index. From the source and destination addresses, these bits are 001 (1) and 110 (6), respectively. For a two-link EtherChannel, a 1-bit XOR is performed on the rightmost address bit: 1 XOR 0 = 1, causing Link 1 in the bundle to be used. A four-link EtherChannel produces a 2-bit XOR: 01 XOR 10 = 11, causing Link 3 in the bundle to be used. Finally, an eight-link EtherChannel requires a 3-bit XOR: 001 XOR 110 = 111, where Link 7 in the bundle is selected.

A conversation between two devices always is sent through the same EtherChannel link because the two endpoint addresses stay the same. However, when a device talks to several other devices, chances are that the destination addresses are distributed equally with 0s and 1s in the last bit (even and odd address values). This causes the frames to be distributed across the EtherChannel links.

Note that the load distribution is still proportional to the volume of traffic passing between pairs of hosts or link indexes. For example, suppose that there are two pairs of hosts talking across a two-link channel, and each pair of addresses results in a unique link index. Frames from one pair of hosts always travel over one link in the channel, whereas frames from the other pair travel over the other link. The links are both being used as a result of the hash algorithm, so the load is being distributed across every link in the channel.

However, if one pair of hosts has a much greater volume of traffic than the other pair, one link in the channel will be used much more than the other. This still can create a load imbalance. To remedy this condition, you should consider other methods of hashing algorithms for the channel. For example, a method that combines the source and destination addresses along with UDP or TCP port numbers in a single XOR operation can distribute traffic much differently. Then, packets are placed on links within the bundle based on the applications (port numbers) used within conversations between two hosts. The possible hashing methods are discussed in the following section.

Configuring EtherChannel Load Balancing

The hashing operation can be performed on either MAC or IP addresses and can be based solely on source or destination addresses, or both. Use the following command to configure frame distribution for all EtherChannel switch links:

```
Switch(config)# port-channel load-balance method
```

Notice that the load-balancing method is set with a global configuration command. You must set the method globally for the switch, not on a per-port basis. Table 10-3 lists the possible values for the method variable, along with the hashing operation and some sample supporting switch models.

Table 10-3 *Types of EtherChannel Load-Balancing Methods*

Method Value	Hash Input	Hash Operation	Switch Model
src-ip	Source IP address	Bits	All models
dst-ip	Destination IP address	Bits	All models
src-dst-ip	Source and destination IP address	XOR	All models
src-mac	Source MAC address	Bits	All models
dst-mac	Destination MAC address	Bits	All models
src-dst-mac	Source and destination MAC	XOR	All models
src-port	Source port number	Bits	4500, 6500

Method Value	Hash Input	Hash Operation	Switch Model
dst-port	Destination port number	Bits	4500, 6500
src-dst-port	Source and destination port	XOR	4500, 6500

The default configuration depends on the switch model and hardware capabilities. In common access layer switch models such as the Catalyst 3750-X, the default is **src-mac**. You can verify the load-balancing method currently in use with the **show etherchannel load-balance** command, as shown in Example 10-1.

Example 10-1   *Displaying the Current EtherChannel Load-Balancing Method*

```
Switch# show etherchannel load-balance
EtherChannel Load-Balancing Configuration:
        src-mac


EtherChannel Load-Balancing Addresses Used Per-Protocol:
Non-IP: Source MAC address
  IPv4: Source MAC address
  IPv6: Source MAC address
Switch#
```

Normally, the default action should result in a statistical distribution of frames; however, you should determine whether the EtherChannel is imbalanced according to the traffic patterns present. For example, if a single server is receiving most of the traffic on an EtherChannel, the server's address (the destination IP address) always will remain constant in the many conversations. This can cause one link to be overused if the destination IP address is used as a component of a load-balancing method. In the case of a four-link EtherChannel, perhaps two of the four links are overused. Configuring the use of MAC addresses, or only the source IP addresses, might cause the distribution to be more balanced across all the bundled links.

Tip   To verify how effectively a configured load-balancing method is performing, you can use the **show etherchannel port-channel** command. Each link in the channel is displayed, along with a hex "Load" value. Although this information is not intuitive, you can use the hex values to get an idea of each link's traffic loads relative to the others.

In some applications, EtherChannel traffic might consist of protocols other than IP. For example, IPX or SNA frames might be switched along with IP. Non-IP protocols need to be distributed according to MAC addresses because IP addresses are not applicable. Here, the switch should be configured to use MAC addresses instead of the IP default.

> **Tip**   A special case results when a router is connected to an EtherChannel. Recall that a router always uses its burned-in MAC address in Ethernet frames, even though it is forwarding packets to and from many different IP addresses. In other words, all the traffic sent by the router will use the router's MAC address as the source. As well, many end stations send frames to their local router address with the router's MAC address as the destination. This means that the destination MAC address is the same for all frames destined through the router.
>
> Usually, this will not present a problem because the source MAC addresses are all different. When two routers are forwarding frames to each other, however, both source and destination MAC addresses remain constant, and only one link of the EtherChannel is used. If the MAC addresses remain constant, choose IP addresses instead. Beyond that, if most of the traffic is between the same two IP addresses, as in the case of two servers talking, choose IP port numbers to disperse the frames across different links.

You should choose the load-balancing method that provides the greatest distribution or variety when the channel links are indexed. Also consider the type of addressing that is being used on the network. If most of the traffic is IP, it might make sense to load balance according to IP addresses or TCP/UDP port numbers.

But if IP load balancing is being used, what happens to non-IP frames? If a frame cannot meet the load-balancing criteria, the switch automatically falls back to the "next lowest" method. With Ethernet, MAC addresses must always be present, so the switch distributes those frames according to their MAC addresses.

A switch also provides some inherent protection against bridging loops with EtherChannels. When ports are bundled into an EtherChannel, no inbound (received) broadcasts and multicasts are sent back out over any of the remaining ports in the channel. Outbound broadcast and multicast frames are load-balanced like any other: The broadcast or multicast address becomes part of the hashing calculation to choose an outbound channel link.

EtherChannel Negotiation Protocols

EtherChannels can be negotiated between two switches to provide some dynamic link configuration. Two protocols are available to negotiate bundled links in Catalyst switches. The Port Aggregation Protocol (PAgP) is a Cisco proprietary solution, and the Link Aggregation Control Protocol (LACP) is standards based. Table 10-4 summarizes the negotiation protocols and their operation.

Table 10-4   *EtherChannel Negotiation Protocols*

Negotiation	Mode	Negotiation Packets Sent?	Characteristics
PAgP	LACP		
On	On	No	All ports channeling
Auto	Passive	Yes	Waits to channel until asked
Desirable	Active	Yes	Actively asks to form a channel

Port Aggregation Protocol

To provide automatic EtherChannel configuration and negotiation between switches, Cisco developed the Port Aggregation Protocol. PAgP packets are exchanged between switches over EtherChannel-capable ports. Neighbors are identified and port group capabilities are learned and compared with local switch capabilities. Ports that have the same neighbor device ID and port group capability are bundled together as a bidirectional, point-to-point EtherChannel link.

PAgP forms an EtherChannel only on ports that are configured for either identical static VLANs or trunking. PAgP also dynamically modifies parameters of the EtherChannel if one of the bundled ports is modified. For example, if the configured VLAN, speed, or duplex mode of a port in an established bundle is changed, PAgP reconfigures that parameter for all ports in the bundle.

PAgP can be configured in active mode (desirable), in which a switch actively asks a far-end switch to negotiate an EtherChannel, or in passive mode (auto, the default), in which a switch negotiates an EtherChannel only if the far end initiates it.

Link Aggregation Control Protocol

LACP is a standards-based alternative to PAgP, defined in IEEE 802.3ad (also known as *IEEE 802.3 Clause 43, "Link Aggregation"*). LACP packets are exchanged between switches over EtherChannel-capable ports. As with PAgP, neighbors are identified and port group capabilities are learned and compared with local switch capabilities. However, LACP also assigns roles to the EtherChannel's endpoints.

The switch with the lowest *system priority* (a 2-byte priority value followed by a 6-byte switch MAC address) is allowed to make decisions about what ports actively are participating in the EtherChannel at a given time.

Ports are selected and become active according to their *port priority* value (a 2-byte priority followed by a 2-byte port number), where a low value indicates a higher priority. A set of up to 16 potential links can be defined for each EtherChannel. Through LACP, a switch selects up to eight of these having the lowest port priorities as active EtherChannel links at any given time. The other links are placed in a standby state and will be enabled in the EtherChannel if one of the active links goes down.

Like PAgP, LACP can be configured in active mode (active), in which a switch actively asks a far-end switch to negotiate an EtherChannel, or in passive mode (passive), in which a switch negotiates an EtherChannel only if the far end initiates it.

EtherChannel Configuration

For each EtherChannel on a switch, you must choose the EtherChannel negotiation protocol and assign individual switch ports to the EtherChannel. Both PAgP- and LACP-negotiated EtherChannels are described in the following sections. You also can configure an EtherChannel to use the on mode, which unconditionally bundles the links. In this case, neither PAgP nor LACP packets are sent or received.

As ports are configured to be members of an EtherChannel, the switch automatically creates a logical port-channel interface. This interface represents the channel as a whole.

Configuring a PAgP EtherChannel

To configure switch ports for PAgP negotiation (the default), use the following commands:

Key Topic

```
Switch(config)# interface type member/module/number
Switch(config-if)# channel-protocol pagp
Switch(config-if)# channel-group number mode {on | {{auto | desirable}
[non-silent]}}
```

Each interface that will be included in a single EtherChannel bundle must be configured and assigned to the same unique channel group *number* (1 to 64). Channel negotiation must be set to **on** (unconditionally channel, no PAgP negotiation), **auto** (passively listen and wait to be asked), or **desirable** (actively ask).

By default, PAgP operates in silent submode with the **desirable** and **auto** modes, and allows ports to be added to an EtherChannel even if the other end of the link is silent and never transmits PAgP packets. This might seem to go against the idea of PAgP, in which two endpoints are supposed to negotiate a channel. After all, how can two switches negotiate anything if no PAgP packets are received?

The key is in the phrase "*if* the other end is silent." The silent submode listens for any PAgP packets from the far end, looking to negotiate a channel. If none is received, silent submode assumes that a channel should be built anyway, so no more PAgP packets are expected from the far end.

This allows a switch to form an EtherChannel with a device such as a file server or a network analyzer that does not participate in PAgP. In the case of a network analyzer connected to the far end, you also might want to see the PAgP packets generated by the switch, as if you were using a normal PAgP EtherChannel.

If you expect a PAgP-capable switch to be on the far end, you should add the **non-silent** keyword to the desirable or auto mode. This requires each port to receive PAgP packets before adding them to a channel. If PAgP is not heard on an active port, the port remains in the up state, but PAgP reports to the Spanning Tree Protocol (STP) that the port is down.

> **Tip**   In practice, you might notice a delay from the time the links in a channel group are connected until the time the channel is formed and data can pass over it. You will encounter this if both switches are using the default PAgP auto mode and silent submode. Each interface waits to be asked to form a channel, and each interface waits and listens before accepting silent channel partners. The silent submode amounts to approximately a 15-second delay.
>
> Even if the two interfaces are using PAgP auto mode, the link will still eventually come up, although not as a channel. You might notice that the total delay before data can pass over the link is actually approximately 45 or 50 seconds. The first 15 seconds are the result of PAgP silent mode waiting to hear inbound PAgP messages, and the final 30 seconds are the result of the STP moving through the listening and learning stages.

As an example of PAgP configuration, suppose that you want a switch to use an EtherChannel load-balancing hash of both source and destination port numbers. A Gigabit EtherChannel will be built from interfaces Gigabit Ethernet 1/0/1 through 1/0/4, with the switch actively negotiating a channel. The switch should not wait to listen for silent partners. You can use the following configuration commands to accomplish this:

```
Switch(config)# port-channel load-balance src-dst-port
Switch(config)# interface range gig 1/0/1 - 4
Switch(config-if)# channel-protocol pagp
Switch(config-if)# channel-group 1 mode desirable non-silent
```

Configuring a LACP EtherChannel

To configure switch ports for LACP negotiation, use the following commands:

```
Switch(config)# lacp system-priority priority
Switch(config)# interface type member/module/number
Switch(config-if)# channel-protocol lacp
Switch(config-if)# channel-group number mode {on | passive | active}
Switch(config-if)# lacp port-priority priority
```

First, the switch should have its LACP system priority defined (1 to 65,535; default 32,768). If desired, one switch should be assigned a lower system priority than the other so that it can make decisions about the EtherChannel's makeup. Otherwise, both switches will have the same system priority (32,768), and the one with the lower MAC address will become the decision maker.

Each interface included in a single EtherChannel bundle must be assigned to the same unique channel group *number* (1 to 64). Channel negotiation must be set to **on** (unconditionally channel, no LACP negotiation), **passive** (passively listen and wait to be asked), or **active** (actively ask).

You can configure more interfaces in the channel group number than are allowed to be active in the channel. This prepares extra standby interfaces to replace failed active ones. Use the **lacp port-priority** command to configure a lower port priority (1 to 65,535; default 32,768) for any interfaces that must be active, and a higher priority for interfaces that might be held in the standby state. Otherwise, just use the default scenario, in which all ports default to 32,768 and the lower port numbers (in interface number order) are used to select the active ports.

As an example of LACP configuration, suppose that you want to configure a switch to negotiate a Gigabit EtherChannel using interfaces Gigabit Ethernet 1/0/1 through 1/0/4 and 2/0/1 through 2/0/4. Interfaces Gigabit Ethernet 1/0/5 through 1/0/8 and 2/0/5 through 2/0/8 are also available, so these can be used as standby links to replace failed links in the channel. This switch should actively negotiate the channel and should be the decision maker about the channel operation.

You can use the following configuration commands to accomplish this:

```
Switch(config)# lacp system-priority 100
Switch(config)# interface range gig 1/0/1 - 4 , gig 2/0/1 - 4
Switch(config-if)# channel-protocol lacp
Switch(config-if)# channel-group 1 mode active
Switch(config-if)# lacp port-priority 100
Switch(config-if)# exit
Switch(config)# interface range gig 1/0/5 - 8 , gig 2/0/5 - 8
Switch(config-if)# channel-protocol lacp
Switch(config-if)# channel-group 1 mode active
```

Notice that interfaces Gigabit Ethernet 1/0/5-8 and 2/0/5-8 have been left to their default port priorities of 32,768. This is higher than the others, which were configured for 100, so they will be held as standby interfaces.

Avoiding Misconfiguration with EtherChannel Guard

Once you configure a set of physical interfaces on one switch to participate in an EtherChannel, you should configure the corresponding interfaces on the neighboring switch. Your goal should be to keep the EtherChannel configurations as predictable as possible, so that nothing unexpected can happen,

What might happen anyway? Suppose that you configure two interfaces on Switch A to form an unconditional EtherChannel that carries all active VLANs. Your associate configures Switch B for the same set of two interfaces, but manages to plug the cables into the wrong two interfaces. It is entirely possible that a bridging loop might form over the dual links because an EtherChannel has not formed on both ends. STP will not operate consistently on all interfaces because Switch A is expecting a working EtherChannel.

If you decide to use PAgP or LACP to negotiate an EtherChannel, the chances of a misconfiguration are slim. An EtherChannel will not be built if it cannot be negotiated on all member links on the switches at both ends.

To reduce the chances of a misconfigured EtherChannel, Cisco Catalyst switches run the EtherChannel Guard feature by default. You can control the feature with the following global configuration command:

```
Switch(config)# [no] spanning-tree etherchannel guard misconfig
```

Notice that the command is directly related to STP operation over an EtherChannel. If a misconfiguration is detected once the interfaces are enabled, the switch will log the problem and will automatically shut the interfaces down and place them in the errdisable state.

In Example 10-2, two interfaces should have formed an EtherChannel, but a misconfiguration has been detected. Notice that both member interfaces, as well as the port channel 1 EtherChannel interface, have been errdisabled. To see the reason behind this action, you can use the **show interfaces status err-disabled** command.

Example 10-2 *Detecting EtherChannel Misconfiguration with EtherChannel Guard*

```
Mar 30 05:02:16.073: %PM-4-ERR_DISABLE: channel-misconfig (STP) error detected on
Gi1/0/25, putting Gi1/0/25 in err-disable state
Mar 30 05:02:16.081: %PM-4-ERR_DISABLE: channel-misconfig (STP) error detected on
Gi1/0/26, putting Gi1/0/26 in err-disable state
Mar 30 05:02:16.115: %PM-4-ERR_DISABLE: channel-misconfig (STP) error detected on
Po1, putting Gi1/0/25 in err-disable state
Mar 30 05:02:16.115: %PM-4-ERR_DISABLE: channel-misconfig (STP) error detected on
Po1, putting Gi1/0/26 in err-disable stning-ate
Mar 30 05:02:16.115: %PM-4-ERR_DISABLE: channel-misconfig (STP) error detected on
Po1, putting Po1 in err-disable state
Mar 30 05:02:17.079: %LINEPROTO-5-UPDOWN: Line protocol on Interface GigabitEther-
net1/0/25, changed state to down
Mar 30 05:02:17.096: %LINEPROTO-5-UPDOWN: Line protocol on Interface GigabitEther-
net1/0/26, changed state to down
Mar 30 05:02:17.104: %LINEPROTO-5-UPDOWN: Line protocol on Interface Port-channel1,
changed state to down
Switch# show interface status err-disabled
Port      Name         Status       Reason            Err-disabled Vlans
Gi1/0/25               err-disabled channel-misconfig (STP)
Gi1/0/26               err-disabled channel-misconfig (STP)
Po1                    err-disabled channel-misconfig (STP)
Switch#
```

To recover from a misconfigured EtherChannel, first review the interface configuration on both switches. After you have corrected the problem, you must shut down the port channel interface and reenable it. The member interfaces will follow suit automatically, as shown in Example 10-3.

Example 10-3 *Reenabling a Misconfigured EtherChannel*

```
Switch(config)# interface port-channel1
Switch(config-if)# shutdown
Switch(config-if)# no shutdown
Switch(config-if)# ^Z
Switch#
Mar 30 05:09:21.518: %SYS-5-CONFIG_I: Configured from console by console
Mar 30 05:09:21.719: %LINK-3-UPDOWN: Interface GigabitEthernet1/0/25, changed state
to up
Mar 30 05:09:21.736: %LINK-3-UPDOWN: Interface GigabitEthernet1/0/26, changed state
to up
```

```
Mar 30 05:09:25.536: %LINEPROTO-5-UPDOWN: Line protocol on Interface GigabitEther-
net1/0/25, changed state to up

Mar 30 05:09:25.544: %LINEPROTO-5-UPDOWN: Line protocol on Interface GigabitEther-
net1/0/26, changed state to up

Mar 30 05:09:26.509: %LINK-3-UPDOWN: Interface Port-channel1, changed state to up

Mar 30 05:09:27.516: %LINEPROTO-5-UPDOWN: Line protocol on Interface Port-channel1,
changed state to up

Switch#
```

Troubleshooting an EtherChannel

If you find that an EtherChannel is having problems, remember that the whole concept is based on consistent configurations on both ends of the channel. Here are some reminders about EtherChannel operation and interaction:

- EtherChannel **on** mode does not send or receive PAgP or LACP packets. Therefore, both ends should be set to **on** mode before the channel can form.

- EtherChannel **desirable** (PAgP) or **active** (LACP) mode attempts to ask the far end to bring up a channel. Therefore, the other end must be set to either **desirable** or **auto** mode.

- EtherChannel **auto** (PAgP) or **passive** (LACP) mode participates in the channel protocol, but only if the far end asks for participation. Therefore, two switches in the **auto** or **passive** mode will not form an EtherChannel.

- PAgP **desirable** and **auto** modes default to the silent submode, in which no PAgP packets are expected from the far end. If ports are set to **non-silent** submode, PAgP packets must be received before a channel will form.

First, verify the EtherChannel state with the **show etherchannel summary** command. Each port in the channel is shown, along with flags indicating the port's state, as shown in Example 10-4.

Example 10-4   show etherchannel summary *Command Output*

```
Switch# show etherchannel summary
Flags:  D - down        P - in port-channel
        I - stand-alone s - suspended
        H - Hot-standby (LACP only)
        R - Layer3       S - Layer2
        u - unsuitable for bundling
        U - in use      f - failed to allocate aggregator
        d - default port
Number of channel-groups in use: 1
Number of aggregators:           1
```

```
Group  Port-channel  Protocol   Ports
------+--------------+----------+------------------------------------------------

1      Po1(SU)        LACP       Gi1/0/1(P)  Gi1/0/2(P)  Gi1/0/3(D)  Gi1/0/4(P)
                                 Gi2/0/1(P)  Gi2/0/2(P)  Gi2/0/3(P)  Gi2/0/4(P)
```

The status of the port channel shows the EtherChannel logical interface as a whole. This should show SU (Layer 2 channel, in use) if the channel is operational. You also can examine the status of each port within the channel. Notice that most of the channel ports have flags (P), indicating that they are active in the port-channel. One port shows (D) because it is physically not connected or down. If a port is connected but not bundled in the channel, it will have an independent, or (I), flag. You can verify the channel negotiation mode with the **show etherchannel port** command, as shown in Example 10-5. The local switch interface Gigabit Ethernet 1/0/25 is shown using LACP active mode. Notice that you also verify each end's negotiation mode under the Flags heading—the local switch as A (active mode) and the partner, or far end switch, as P (passive mode).

Example 10-5 show etherchannel port *Command Output*

```
Switch# show etherchannel port
                Channel-group listing:
                ----------------------


Group: 1
----------
                Ports in the group:
                -------------------
Port: Gi1/0/25
-----------


Port state    = Up Mstr Assoc In-Bndl
Channel group = 1                Mode = Active          Gcchange = -
Port-channel  = Po1        GC   =  -             Pseudo port-channel = Po1
Port index    = 0          Load = 0x00          Protocol =   LACP


Flags:  S - Device is sending Slow LACPDUs   F - Device is sending fast LACPDUs.
        A - Device is in active mode.        P - Device is in passive mode.


Local information:
                       LACP port   Admin   Oper   Port     Port
Port      Flags  State   Priority    Key     Key    Number   State
Gi1/0/25  SA     bndl    32768       0x1     0x1    0x11A    0x3D


Partner's information:

                  LACP port                  Admin  Oper  Port    Port
Port     Flags  Priority  Dev ID       Age    key    Key   Number  State
```

```
Gi1/0/25  SP 32768    aca0.164e.8280  21s    0x0    0x1    0x21A   0x3C

Age of the port in the current state: 0d:00h:02m:37s
[output truncated for clarity]
```

Within a switch, an EtherChannel cannot form unless each of the component or member ports is configured consistently. Each must have the same switch mode (access or trunk), native VLAN, trunked VLANs, port speed, port duplex mode, and so on.

You can display a port's configuration by looking at the **show running-config interface** *type mod/ num* output. Also, the **show interface** *type member/module/number* **etherchannel** shows all active EtherChannel parameters for a single port. If you configure a port inconsistently with others for an EtherChannel, you see error messages from the switch.

Some messages from the switch might look like errors but are part of the normal EtherChannel process. For example, as a new port is configured as a member of an existing EtherChannel, you might see this message:

```
4d00h: %EC-5-L3DONTBNDL2: GigabitEthernet1/0/11 suspended:
incompatible partner port with GigabitEthernet1/0/10
```

When the port is first added to the EtherChannel, it is incompatible because the STP runs on the channel and the new port. After STP takes the new port through its progression of states, the port is automatically added into the EtherChannel.

Other messages do indicate a port-compatibility error. In these cases, the cause of the error is shown. For example, the following message announces that Gigabit Ethernet1/0/3 has a different duplex mode than the other ports in the EtherChannel:

```
4d00h: %EC-5-CANNOT_BUNDLE2: GigabitEthernet1/0/3 is not compatible
with GigabitEthernet1/0/1 and will be suspended (duplex of Gi1/0/3
is full, Gi1/0/1 is half)
```

Finally, you can verify the EtherChannel load-balancing or hashing algorithm with the **show etherchannel load-balance** command. Remember that the switches on either end of an EtherChannel can have different load-balancing methods. The only drawback to this is that the load balancing will be asymmetric in the two directions across the channel.

Table 10-5 lists the commands useful for verifying or troubleshooting EtherChannel operation.

Table 10-5 *EtherChannel Troubleshooting Commands*

Display Function	Command Syntax
Current EtherChannel status of each member port	show etherchannel summary
	show etherchannel port
Time stamps of EtherChannel changes	show etherchannel port-channel

Display Function	Command Syntax
Detailed status about each EtherChannel component	show etherchannel detail
Load-balancing hashing algorithm	show etherchannel load-balance
Load-balancing port index used by hashing algorithm	show etherchannel port-channel
EtherChannel neighbors on each port	show {pagp | lacp} neighbor
LACP system ID	show lacp sys-id

Exam Preparation Tasks

Review All Key Topics

Review the most important topics in the chapter, noted with the Key Topic icon in the outer margin of the page. Table 10-6 lists a reference of these key topics and the page numbers on which each is found.

Table 10-6 *Key Topics for Chapter 10*

Key Topic Element	Description	Page Number
Figure 10-2	Illustrates aggregating links into EtherChannels	246
Paragraph	Explains how traffic is distributed in an EtherChannel	247
Table 10-3	Lists EtherChannel load-balancing methods	249
Paragraph	Describes the PAgP negotiation protocol	252
Paragraph	Describes the LACP negotiation protocol	252
Paragraph	Explains PAgP configuration	253
Paragraph	Explains LACP configuration	254
Paragraph	Discusses rules of thumb for proper EtherChannel operation	257

Complete Tables and Lists from Memory

Print a copy of Appendix C, "Memory Tables," (found on the CD), or at least the section for this chapter, and complete the tables and lists from memory. Appendix D, "Memory Table Answer Key," also on the CD, includes completed tables and lists to check your work.

Define Key Terms

Define the following key terms from this chapter, and check your answers in the glossary:

EtherChannel, PAgP, LACP, multichassis EtherChannel, EtherChannel Guard

Command Reference to Check Your Memory

This section includes the most important configuration and EXEC commands covered in this chapter. It might not be necessary to memorize the complete syntax of every command, but you should be able to remember the basic keywords that are needed.

To test your memory of the commands related to EtherChannels, cover the right side of Table 10-7 with a piece of paper, read the description on the left side, and then see how much of the command you can remember.

Remember that the CCNP exam focuses on practical or hands-on skills that are used by a networking professional. For the skills covered in this chapter, remember that an EtherChannel is called a port channel interface when you are configuring it. When you are displaying information about an EtherChannel, begin the commands with the **show etherchannel** keywords.

Table 10-7   *EtherChannel Configuration Commands*

Task	Command Syntax
Select a load-balancing method for the switch.	**port-channel load-balance** *method*
Use a PAgP mode on an interface.	**channel-protocol pagp**
	channel-group *number* **mode {on	{{auto	desirable} [non-silent]}}**
Assign the LACP system priority.	**lacp system-priority** *priority*
Use an LACP mode on an interface.	**channel-protocol lacp**
	channel-group *number* **mode {on	passive	active}**
	lacp port-priority *priority*
Configure EtherChannel Guard	**[no] spanning-tree etherchannel guard misconfig**

This chapter covers the following topics that you need to master for the CCNP SWITCH exam:

■ **Inter-VLAN Routing:** This section discusses how you can use a routing function with a switch to forward packets between VLANs.

■ **Multilayer Switching with CEF:** This section discusses Cisco Express Forwarding (CEF) and how it is implemented on Catalyst switches. CEF forwards or routes packets in hardware at a high throughput.

■ **Verifying Multilayer Switching:** This section provides a brief summary of the commands that can verify the configuration and operation of inter-VLAN routing, CEF, and fallback bridging.

CHAPTER 11

Multilayer Switching

Chapter 2, "Switch Operation," presents a functional overview of how multilayer switching (MLS) is performed at Layers 3 and 4. The actual MLS process can take two forms: inter-VLAN routing and Cisco Express Forwarding (CEF). This chapter expands on multilayer switch operation by discussing both of these topics in greater detail.

"Do I Know This Already?" Quiz

The "Do I Know This Already?" quiz allows you to assess whether you should read this entire chapter thoroughly or jump to the "Exam Preparation Tasks" section. If you are in doubt based on your answers to these questions or your own assessment of your knowledge of the topics, read the entire chapter. Table 11-1 outlines the major headings in this chapter and the "Do I Know This Already?" quiz questions that go with them. You can find the answers in Appendix A, "Answers to the 'Do I Know This Already?' Quizzes."

Table 11-1 *"Do I Know This Already?" Section-to-Question Mapping*

Foundation Topics Section	Questions Covered in This Section
Inter-VLAN Routing	1–5
Multilayer Switching with CEF	6–10
Verifying Multilayer Switching	11

1. Which of the following arrangements can be considered inter-VLAN routing?

   a. One switch, two VLANs, one connection to a router.

   b. One switch, two VLANs, two connections to a router.

   c. Two switches, two VLANs, two connections to a router.

   d. All of these answers are correct.

2. How many interfaces are needed in a "router-on-a-stick" implementation for inter-VLAN routing among four VLANs?

   a. 1

   b. 2

   c. 4

   d. Cannot be determined

3. Which of the following commands configures a switch port for Layer 2 operation?

   a. switchport

   b. no switchport

   c. ip address 192.168.199.1 255.255.255.0

   d. no ip address

4. Which of the following commands configures a switch port for Layer 3 operation?

   a. switchport

   b. no switchport

   c. ip address 192.168.199.1 255.255.255.0

   d. no ip address

5. Which one of the following interfaces is an SVI?

   a. interface fastethernet 0/1

   b. interface gigabit 0/1

   c. interface vlan 1

   d. interface svi 1

6. What information must be learned before CEF can forward packets?

   a. The source and destination of the first packet in a traffic flow

   b. The MAC addresses of both the source and destination

   c. The contents of the routing table

   d. The outbound port of the first packet in a flow

7. Which of the following best defines an adjacency?

   a. Two switches connected by a common link.

   b. Two contiguous routes in the FIB.

   c. Two multilayer switches connected by a common link.

   d. The MAC address of a host is known.

8. Assume that CEF is active on a switch. What happens to a packet that arrives, but an ICMP redirect must be sent in return?

    a. The packet is switched by CEF and kept intact.

    b. The packet is fragmented by CEF.

    c. The packet is dropped.

    d. The packet is sent to the Layer 3 engine.

9. Suppose that a host sends a packet to a destination IP address and that the CEF-based switch does not yet have a valid MAC address for the destination. How is the ARP entry (MAC address) of the next-hop destination in the FIB obtained?

    a. The sending host must send an ARP request for it.

    b. The Layer 3 forwarding engine (CEF hardware) must send an ARP request for it.

    c. CEF must wait until the Layer 3 engine sends an ARP request for it.

    d. All packets to the destination are dropped.

10. During a packet rewrite, what happens to the source MAC address?

    a. There is no change.

    b. It is changed to the destination MAC address.

    c. It is changed to the MAC address of the outbound Layer 3 switch interface.

    d. It is changed to the MAC address of the next-hop destination.

11. What command can you use to view the CEF FIB table contents?

    a. show fib

    b. show ip cef fib

    c. show ip cef

    d. show fib-table

Foundation Topics

Inter-VLAN Routing

Recall that a Layer 2 network is defined as a broadcast domain. A Layer 2 network can also exist as a VLAN inside one or more switches. VLANs essentially are isolated from each other so that packets in one VLAN cannot cross into another VLAN.

To transport packets between VLANs, you must use a Layer 3 device. Traditionally, this has been a router's function. The router must have a physical or logical connection to each VLAN so that it can forward packets between them. This is known as *inter-VLAN routing*.

Inter-VLAN routing can be performed by an external router that connects to each of the VLANs on a switch. Separate physical connections can be used, or the router can access each of the VLANs through a single trunk link. Part A of Figure 11-1 illustrates this concept. The external router also can connect to the switch through a single trunk link, carrying all the necessary VLANs, as illustrated in Part B of Figure 11-1. Part B illustrates what commonly is referred to as a "router-on-a-stick" or a "one-armed router" because the router needs only a single interface to do its job.

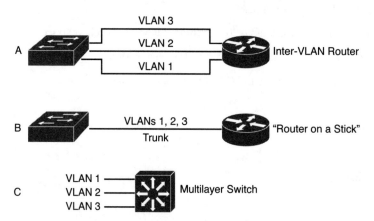

Figure 11-1 *Examples of Inter-VLAN Routing Connections*

Finally, Part C of Figure 11-1 shows how the routing and switching functions can be combined into one device: a multilayer switch. No external router is needed.

Types of Interfaces

Multilayer switches can perform both Layer 2 switching and inter-VLAN routing, as appropriate. Layer 2 switching occurs between interfaces that are assigned to Layer 2 VLANs or Layer 2 trunks. Layer 3 switching can occur between any type of interface, as long as the interface can have a Layer 3 address assigned to it.

As with a router, a multilayer switch can assign a Layer 3 address to a physical interface. It also can assign a Layer 3 address to a logical interface that represents an entire VLAN. This is known as a *switched virtual interface* (SVI), sometimes called a *switch virtual interface* (SVI). Keep in mind that the Layer 3 address you configure becomes the default gateway for any hosts that are connected to the interface or VLAN. The hosts will use the Layer 3 interface to communicate outside of their local broadcast domains.

Configuring Inter-VLAN Routing

Inter-VLAN routing first requires that routing be enabled for the Layer 3 protocol. In the case of IP, you would enable IP routing. In addition, you must configure static routes or a dynamic routing protocol. These topics are covered fully in the CCNP ROUTE course. By default, every switch port on most Catalyst switch platforms is a Layer 2 interface, whereas every switch port on a Catalyst 6500 is a Layer 3 interface. If an interface needs to operate in a different mode, you must explicitly configure it.

An interface is either in Layer 2 or Layer 3 mode, depending on the use of the **switchport** interface configuration command. You can display a port's current mode with the following command:

```
Switch# show interface type member/module/number switchport
```

If the **switchport:** line in the command output is shown as enabled, the port is in Layer 2 mode. If this line is shown as disabled, as in the following example, the port is in Layer 3 mode:

```
Switch# show interface gigabitethernet 1/0/1 switchport
Name: Gi1/0/1
Switchport: Disabled
Switch#
```

Tip   Whenever you see the term *switch port*, think Layer 2. So if the switch port is disabled, it must be Layer 3.

Figure 11-2 shows how the different types of interface modes can be used within a single switch.

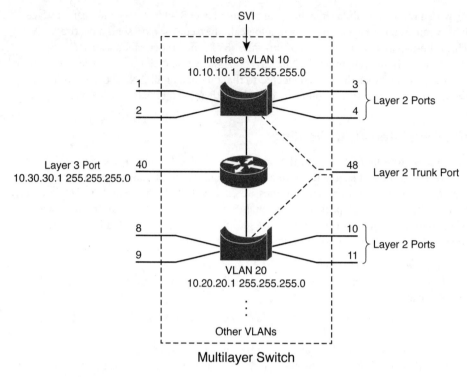

Figure 11-2 *Catalyst Switch with Various Types of Ports*

Layer 2 Port Configuration

If an interface is in Layer 3 mode and you need to reconfigure it for Layer 2 functionality instead, use the following command sequence:

```
Switch(config)# interface type member/module/number
Switch(config-if)# switchport
```

The **switchport** command puts the port in Layer 2 mode. Then you can use other **switchport** command keywords to configure trunking, access VLANs, and so on. As displayed in Figure 11-2, several Layer 2 ports exist, each assigned to a specific VLAN. A Layer 2 port also can act as a trunk, transporting multiple Layer 2 VLANs.

Layer 3 Port Configuration

Physical switch ports also can operate as Layer 3 interfaces, where a Layer 3 network address is assigned and routing can occur, as shown previously in Figure 11-2. For Layer 3 functionality, you must explicitly configure switch ports with the following command sequence:

```
Switch(config)# interface type member/module/number
Switch(config-if)# no switchport
Switch(config-if)# ip address ip-address mask [secondary]
```

The **no switchport** command takes the port out of Layer 2 operation. You then can assign a network address to the port, as you would to a router interface.

Tip By default, a Catalyst switch sets aside the appropriate amounts of TCAM space to perform Layer 3 operation for IPv4. If you intend to use IPv6 also, be sure to reconfigure the SDM template with the **sdm prefer dual-ipv4-and-ipv6** command.

Note Keep in mind that a Layer 3 port assigns a network address to one specific physical interface. If several interfaces are bundled as an EtherChannel, the EtherChannel can also become a Layer 3 port. In that case, the network address is assigned to the port-channel interface—not to the individual physical links within the channel.

SVI Port Configuration

On a multilayer switch, you also can enable Layer 3 functionality for an entire VLAN on the switch. This allows a network address to be assigned to a logical interface—that of the VLAN itself. This is useful when the switch has many ports assigned to a common VLAN, and routing is needed in and out of that VLAN.

In Figure 11-2, you can see how an IP address is applied to the SVI called VLAN 10. Notice that the SVI itself has no physical connection to the outside world; to reach the outside, VLAN 10 must extend through a Layer 2 port or trunk to the outside.

The logical Layer 3 interface is known as an *SVI*. However, when it is configured, it uses the much more intuitive interface name **vlan** *vlan-id*, as if the VLAN itself is a physical interface. First, define or identify the VLAN interface; then assign any Layer 3 functionality to it with the following configuration commands:

```
Switch(config)# interface vlan vlan-id
Switch(config-if)# ip address ip-address mask [secondary]
```

The VLAN must be defined and active on the switch before the SVI can be used. Make sure that the new VLAN interface also is enabled with the **no shutdown** interface configuration command.

Note The VLAN and the SVI are configured separately, even though they interoperate. Creating or configuring the SVI does not create or configure the VLAN; you still must define each one independently.

As an example, the following commands show how VLAN 100 is created and then defined as a Layer 3 SVI:

```
Switch(config)# vlan 100
Switch(config-vlan)# name Example_VLAN
Switch(config-vlan)# exit
Switch(config)# interface vlan 100
Switch(config-if)# ip address 192.168.100.1 255.255.255.0
Switch(config-if)# no shutdown
```

Be aware that an SVI cannot become active until at least one Layer 2 port assigned to the VLAN has also become active and STP has converged. By automatically keeping the SVI down until the VLAN is ready, no other switching or routing functions can attempt to use the SVI prematurely. This function is called SVI autostate.

You might sometimes want the SVI to stay up even when no Layer 2 ports are active on the VLAN. For example, you might have a Layer 2 port configured for port mirroring to capture traffic. In that case, the port would not be up and functioning normally, so it should be excluded from affecting the state of the SVI. You can exclude a switch port with the following interface configuration command:

```
Switch(config-if)# switchport autostate exclude
```

Multilayer Switching with CEF

Catalyst switches can use several methods to forward packets based on Layer 3 and Layer 4 information. The current generation of Catalyst multilayer switches uses the efficient Cisco Express Forwarding (CEF) method. This section describes the evolution of multilayer switching and discusses CEF in detail. Although CEF is easy to configure and use, the underlying switching mechanisms are more involved and should be understood.

Traditional MLS Overview

Multilayer switching began as a dual effort between a route processor (RP) and a switching engine (SE). The basic idea is to "route once and switch many." The RP receives the first packet of a new traffic flow between two hosts, as usual. A routing decision is made, and the packet is forwarded toward the destination.

To participate in multilayer switching, the SE must know the identity of each RP. The SE then can listen in to the first packet going to the router and also going away from the router. If the SE can switch the packet in both directions, it can learn a "shortcut path" so that subsequent packets of the same flow can be switched directly to the destination port without passing through the RP.

This technique also is known as *NetFlow switching* or *route cache switching*. Traditionally, NetFlow switching was performed on legacy Cisco hardware, such as the Catalyst 6000 Supervisor 1/1a and Multilayer Switch Feature Card (MSFC), Catalyst 5500 with a Route Switch Module (RSM), Route Switch Feature Card (RSFC), or external router. Basically, the hardware consisted of an independent RP component and a NetFlow-capable SE component.

CEF Overview

NetFlow switching has given way to a more efficient form of multilayer switching: Cisco Express Forwarding. Cisco developed CEF for its line of routers, offering high-performance packet forwarding through the use of dynamic lookup tables. CEF also has been carried over to the Catalyst switching platforms. CEF runs by default, taking advantage of the specialized hardware.

A CEF-based multilayer switch consists of two basic functional blocks, as shown in Figure 11-3: The Layer 3 engine is involved in building routing information that the Layer 3 forwarding engine can use to switch packets in hardware.

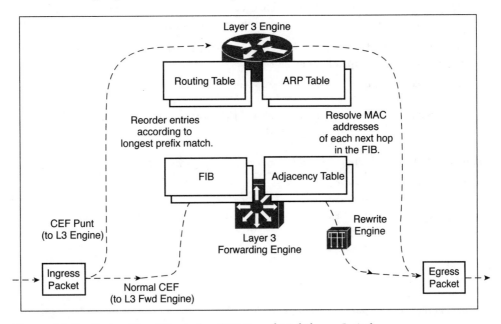

Figure 11-3 *Packet Flow Through a CEF-Based Multilayer Switch*

Forwarding Information Base

The Layer 3 engine (essentially a router) maintains routing information, whether from static routes or dynamic routing protocols. Basically, the routing table is reformatted into an ordered list with the most specific route first, for each IP destination subnet in the table. The new format is called a Forwarding Information Base (FIB) and contains routing or forwarding information that the network prefix can reference.

In other words, a route to 10.1.0.0/16 might be contained in the FIB along with routes to 10.1.1.0/24 and 10.1.1.128/25, if those exist. Notice that these examples are increasingly more specific subnets, as designated by the longer subnet masks. In the FIB, these would be ordered with the most specific, or longest match, first, followed by less specific subnets. When the switch receives a packet, it easily can examine the destination address and find the longest-match destination route entry in the FIB.

The FIB also contains the next-hop address for each entry. When a longest-match entry is found in the FIB, the Layer 3 next-hop address is found, too.

You might be surprised to know that the FIB also contains host route (subnet mask 255.255.255.255) entries. These normally are not found in the routing table unless they are advertised or manually configured. Host routes are maintained in the FIB for the most efficient routing lookup to directly connected or adjacent hosts.

As with a routing table, the FIB is dynamic in nature. When the Layer 3 engine sees a change in the routing topology, it sends an update to the FIB. Anytime the routing table receives a change to a route prefix or the next-hop address, the FIB receives the same change. Also, if a next-hop address is changed or aged out of the Address Resolution Protocol (ARP) table, the FIB must reflect the same change.

You can display FIB table entries related to a specific interface or VLAN with the following form of the **show ip cef** command:

```
Switch# show ip cef [type member/module/number | vlan vlan-id] [detail]
```

The FIB entries corresponding to the VLAN 101 switched virtual interface might be shown as demonstrated in Example 11-1.

Example 11-1 *Displaying FIB Table Entries for a Specified VLAN*

```
Switch# show ip cef vlan 101
Prefix              Next Hop            Interface
10.1.1.0/24         attached            Vlan101
10.1.1.2/32         10.1.1.2            Vlan101
10.1.1.3/32         10.1.1.3            Vlan101
Switch#
```

You also can view FIB entries by specifying an IP prefix address and mask, using the following form of the **show ip cef** command:

```
Switch# show ip cef [prefix-ip prefix-mask] [longer-prefixes] [detail]
```

The output in Example 11-2 displays any subnet within 10.1.0.0/16 that is known by the switch, regardless of the prefix or mask length. Normally, only an exact match of the IP prefix and mask will be displayed if it exists in the CEF table. To see other longer match entries, you can add the **longer-prefixes** keyword.

Example 11-2 *Displaying FIB Table Entries for a Specified IP Prefix Address/Mask*

```
Switch# show ip cef 10.1.0.0 255.255.0.0 longer-prefixes
Prefix              Next Hop            Interface
10.1.1.0/24         attached            Vlan101
10.1.1.2/32         10.1.1.2            Vlan101
10.1.1.3/32         10.1.1.3            Vlan101
10.1.2.0/24         attached            Vlan102
10.1.3.0/26         192.168.1.2         Vlan99
                    192.168.1.3         Vlan99
10.1.3.64/26        192.168.1.2         Vlan99
                    192.168.1.3         Vlan99
10.1.3.128/26       192.168.1.4         Vlan99
                    192.168.1.3         Vlan99
[output omitted]
Switch#
```

Notice that the first three entries are the same ones listed in Example 11-1. Other subnets also are displayed, along with their next-hop router addresses and switch interfaces.

You can add the **detail** keyword to see more information about each FIB table entry for CEF, as demonstrated in Example 11-3.

Example 11-3 *Displaying Detailed CEF Entry Information*

```
Switch# show ip cef 10.1.3.0 255.255.255.192 detail
10.1.3.0/26, version 270, epoch 0, per-destination sharing
0 packets, 0 bytes
  via 192.168.1.2, Vlan99, 0 dependencies
    traffic share 1
    next hop 192.168.1.2, Vlan99
    valid adjacency
  via 192.168.1.3, Vlan99, 0 dependencies
    traffic share 1
    next hop 192.168.1.3, Vlan99
    valid adjacency
  0 packets, 0 bytes switched through the prefix
  tmstats: external 0 packets, 0 bytes
           internal 0 packets, 0 bytes
Switch#
```

The version number describes the number of times the CEF entry has been updated since the table was generated. The epoch number denotes the number of times the CEF table has been flushed and regenerated as a whole. The 10.1.3.0/26 subnet has two next-hop router addresses, so the local switch is using per-destination load sharing between the two routers.

After the FIB is built, packets can be forwarded along the bottom dashed path in Figure 11-3. This follows the hardware switching process, in which no "expensive" or time-consuming operations are needed. At times, however, a packet cannot be switched in hardware, according to the FIB. Packets then are marked as "CEF punt" and immediately are sent to the Layer 3 engine for further processing, as shown in the top dashed path in Figure 11-3. Some of the conditions that can cause this are as follows:

- An entry cannot be located in the FIB.

- The FIB table is full.

- The IP Time-To-Live (TTL) has expired.

- The maximum transmission unit (MTU) is exceeded, and the packet must be fragmented.

- An Internet Control Message Protocol (ICMP) redirect is involved.

- The encapsulation type is not supported.

- Packets are tunneled, requiring a compression or encryption operation.

- An access list with the **log** option is triggered.

- A Network Address Translation (NAT) operation must be performed.

CEF operations can be handled on a single, fixed hardware platform. The FIB is generated and contained centrally in the switch. CEF also can be optimized through the use of specialized forwarding hardware, using the following techniques:

- **Accelerated CEF (aCEF):** CEF is distributed across multiple Layer 3 forwarding engines, typically located on individual line cards in chassis-based Catalyst switches. These engines do not have the capability to store and use the entire FIB, so only a portion of the FIB is downloaded to them at any time. This functions as an FIB "cache," containing entries that are likely to be used again. If FIB entries are not found in the cache, requests are sent to the Layer 3 engine for more FIB information. The net result is that CEF is accelerated on the line cards, but not necessarily at a sustained wire-speed rate.

- **Distributed CEF (dCEF):** CEF can be distributed completely among multiple Layer 3 forwarding engines for even greater performance. Because the FIB is self-contained for complete Layer 3 forwarding, it can be replicated across any number of independent Layer 3 forwarding engines. For example, the Catalyst 6500 has line cards that support dCEF, each with its own FIB table and forwarding engine. A central Layer 3 engine maintains the routing table and generates the FIB, which is then dynamically downloaded in full to each of the line cards.

Adjacency Table

A router normally maintains a routing table containing Layer 3 network and next-hop information, and an ARP table containing Layer 3 to Layer 2 address mapping. These tables are kept independently.

Recall that the FIB keeps the Layer 3 next-hop address for each entry. To streamline packet forwarding even more, the FIB has corresponding Layer 2 information for every next-hop entry. This portion of the FIB is called the *adjacency table*, consisting of the MAC addresses of nodes that can be reached in a single Layer 2 hop.

You can display the adjacency table's contents with the following command:

```
Switch# show adjacency [type member/module/number | vlan vlan-id] [summary |
detail]
```

As an example, the total number of adjacencies known on each physical or VLAN interface can be displayed with the **show adjacency summary** command, as demonstrated in Example 11-4.

Example 11-4 *Displaying the Total Number of Known Adjacencies*

```
Switch# show adjacency summary
Adjacency Table has 106 adjacencies
  Table epoch: 0 (106 entries at this epoch)
  Interface            Adjacency Count
  Vlan99               21
  Vlan101              3
  Vlan102              1
  Vlan103              47
  Vlan104              7
  Vlan105              27
Switch#
```

Adjacencies are kept for each next-hop router and each host that is connected directly to the local switch. You can see more detailed information about the adjacencies by using the **detail** keyword, as demonstrated in Example 11-5.

Example 11-5 *Displaying Detailed Information About Adjacencies*

```
Switch# show adjacency vlan 99 detail
Protocol Interface             Address
IP      Vlan99                192.168.1.2(5)
                              0 packets, 0 bytes
                              epoch 0
                              sourced in sev-epoch 0
                              Encap length 14
                              000A5E45B145000E387D51000800
                              L2 destination address byte offset 0
                              L2 destination address byte length 6
                              Link-type after encap: ip
                              ARP
IP      Vlan99                192.168.1.3(5)
                              1 packets, 104 bytes
                              L2 destination address byte offset 0
                              L2 destination address byte length 6
                              Link-type after encap: ip
                              ARP
                              000CF1C909A0000E387D51000800
                              L2 destination address byte offset 0
                              L2 destination address byte length 6
                              Link-type after encap: ip
                              ARP
```

Notice that the adjacency entries include both the IP address (Layer 3) and the MAC address (Layer 2) of the directly attached host. The MAC address could be shown as the first six octets of the long string of hex digits (as shaded in the previous output) or on a line by itself. The remainder of the string of hex digits contains the MAC address of the Layer 3 engine's interface (six octets, corresponding to the Vlan99 interface in the example) and the EtherType value (two octets, where 0800 denotes IP).

The adjacency table information is built from the ARP table. Example 11-5 shows adjacency with the age of its ARP entry. As a next-hop address receives a valid ARP entry, the adjacency table is updated. If an ARP entry does not exist, the FIB entry is marked as "CEF glean." This means that the Layer 3 forwarding engine cannot forward the packet in hardware because of the missing Layer 2 next-hop address. The packet is sent to the Layer 3 engine so that it can generate an ARP request and receive an ARP reply. This is known as the *CEF glean state*, in which the Layer 3 engine must glean the next-hop destination's MAC address.

The glean state can be demonstrated in several ways, as demonstrated in Example 11-6.

Example 11-6   *Displaying Adjacencies in the CEF Glean State*

```
Switch# show ip cef adjacency glean
Prefix              Next Hop            Interface
10.1.1.2/32         attached            Vlan101
127.0.0.0/8         attached            EOBC0/0
[output omitted]
Switch# show ip arp 10.1.1.2
Switch# show ip cef 10.1.1.2 255.255.255.255 detail
10.1.1.2/32, version 688, epoch 0, attached, connected
0 packets, 0 bytes
  via Vlan101, 0 dependencies
    valid glean adjacency
Switch#
```

Notice that the FIB entry for directly connected host 10.1.1.2/32 is present but listed in the glean state. The **show ip arp** command shows that there is no valid ARP entry for the IP address.

During the time that an FIB entry is in the CEF glean state waiting for the ARP resolution, subsequent packets to that host are immediately dropped so that the input queues do not fill and the Layer 3 engine does not become too busy worrying about the need for duplicate ARP requests. This is called *ARP throttling* or *throttling adjacency*. If an ARP reply is not received in 2 seconds, the throttling is released so that another ARP request can be triggered. Otherwise, after an ARP reply is received, the throttling is released, the FIB entry can be completed, and packets can be forwarded completely in hardware.

The adjacency table also can contain other types of entries so that packets can be handled efficiently. For example, you might see the following adjacency types listed:

■ **Null adjacency:** Used to switch packets destined for the null interface. The null interface always is defined on a router or switch; it represents a logical interface that silently absorbs packets without actually forwarding them.

- **Drop adjacency:** Used to switch packets that cannot be forwarded normally. In effect, these packets are dropped without being forwarded. Packets can be dropped because of an encapsulation failure, an unresolved address, an unsupported protocol, no valid route present, no valid adjacency, or a checksum error. You can gauge drop adjacency activity with the following command:

```
Switch# show cef drop
CEF Drop Statistics
Slot   Encap_fail  Unresolved Unsupported   No_route    No_adj  ChkSum_Err
RP       8799327            1       45827    5089667         32           0
Switch#
```

- **Discard adjacency:** Used when packets must be discarded because of an access list or other policy action.

- **Punt adjacency:** Used when packets must be sent to the Layer 3 engine for further processing. You can gauge the CEF punt activity by looking at the various punt adjacency reasons listed by the **show cef not-cef-switched** command:

```
Switch# show cef not-cef-switched
CEF Packets passed on to next switching layer
Slot  No_adj  No_encap  Unsupp'ted  Redirect  Receive  Options  Access  Frag
RP   3579706         0           0         0  41258564        0       0     0
Switch#
```

The reasons shown are as follows:

- **No_adj:** An incomplete adjacency

- **No_encap:** An incomplete ARP resolution

- **Unsupp'ted:** Unsupported packet features

- **Redirect:** ICMP redirect

- **Receive:** Layer 3 engine interfaces; includes packets destined for IP addresses that are assigned to interfaces on the Layer 3 engine, IP network addresses, and IP broadcast addresses

- **Options:** IP options present

- **Access:** Access list evaluation failure

- **Frag:** Fragmentation failure

Packet Rewrite

When a multilayer switch finds valid entries in the FIB and adjacency tables, a packet is almost ready to be forwarded. One step remains: The packet header information must be rewritten. Keep in mind that multilayer switching occurs as quick table lookups to find the next-hop address and the outbound switch port. The packet is untouched and still has the original destination MAC address of the switch itself. The IP header also must be adjusted, as if a traditional router had done the forwarding.

The switch has an additional functional block that performs a packet rewrite in real time. The packet rewrite engine (shown in Figure 11-3) makes the following changes to the packet just before forwarding:

- **Layer 2 destination address:** Changed to the next-hop device's MAC address

- **Layer 2 source address:** Changed to the outbound Layer 3 switch interface's MAC address

- **Layer 3 IP TTL:** Decremented by one because one router hop has just occurred

- **Layer 3 IP checksum:** Recalculated to include changes to the IP header

- **Layer 2 frame checksum:** Recalculated to include changes to the Layer 2 and Layer 3 headers

A traditional router normally would make the same changes to each packet. The multilayer switch must act as if a traditional router were being used, making identical changes. However, the multilayer switch can do this very efficiently with dedicated packet-rewrite hardware and address information obtained from table lookups.

Configuring CEF

CEF is enabled on all CEF-capable Catalyst switches by default. In fact, many switches run CEF inherently, so CEF never can be disabled.

Tip Switches such as the Catalyst 3750 and 4500 run CEF by default, but you can disable CEF on a per-interface basis. You can use the **no ip route-cache cef** and **no ip cef** interface configuration commands to disable CEF on the Catalyst 3750 and 4500, respectively.

You should always keep CEF enabled whenever possible, except when you need to disable it for debugging purposes.

Verifying Multilayer Switching

The multilayer switching topics presented in this chapter are not difficult to configure; however, you might need to verify how a switch is forwarding packets. In particular, the following sections discuss the commands that you can use to verify the operation of inter-VLAN routing and CEF.

Verifying Inter-VLAN Routing

To verify the configuration of a Layer 2 port, you can use the following EXEC command:

```
Switch# show interface type member/module/number switchport
```

The output from this command displays the access VLAN or the trunking mode and native VLAN. The administrative modes reflect what has been configured for the port, whereas the operational modes show the port's active status.

You can use this same command to verify the configuration of a Layer 3 or routed port. In this case, you should see the switchport (Layer 2) mode disabled, as in Example 11-7.

Example 11-7   *Verifying Configuration of a Layer 3 Switch Port*

```
Switch# show interface gigabitethernet 1/0/1 switchport
Name: Gi1/0/1
Switchport: Disabled
Switch#
```

To verify the configuration of an SVI, you can use the following EXEC command:

```
Switch# show interface vlan vlan-id
```

The VLAN interface should be up, with the line protocol also up. If this is not true, either the interface is disabled with the **shutdown** command, the VLAN itself has not been defined on the switch, or there are no active Layer 2 switch interfaces configured to use the VLAN. Use the **show vlan** command to see a list of configured VLANs.

Example 11-8 shows the output produced from the **show vlan** command. Notice that each defined VLAN is shown, along with the switch ports that are assigned to it.

Example 11-8   *Displaying a List of Configured VLANs*

```
Switch# show vlan

VLAN Name                             Status     Ports
---- -------------------------------- ---------- -------------------------------
1    default                          active     Gi1/0/1, Gi1/0/2, Gi1/0/3
                                                 Gi1/0/4, Gi1/0/5, Gi1/0/6
                                                 Gi1/0/7, Gi1/0/8, Gi1/0/9
                                                 Gi1/0/10, Gi1/0/11, Gi1/0/12
                                                 Gi1/0/13, Gi1/0/14, Gi1/0/15
                                                 Gi1/0/16, Gi1/0/17, Gi1/0/18
                                                 Gi1/0/19, Gi1/0/20, Gi1/0/21
                                                 Gi1/0/25, Gi1/0/26, Te1/0/1
                                                 Te1/0/2
2    VLAN0002                         active     Gi1/0/22
5    VLAN0005                         active
10   VLAN0010                         active
11   VLAN0011                         active     Gi1/0/23
12   VLAN0012                         active
99   VLAN0099                         active     Gi1/0/24
Switch#
```

You also can display the IP-related information about a switch interface with the **show ip interface** command, as demonstrated in Example 11-9.

Example 11-9 *Displaying IP-Related Information About a Switch Interface*

```
Switch# show ip interface vlan 101
Vlan101 is up, line protocol is up
  Internet address is 10.1.1.1/24
  Broadcast address is 255.255.255.255
  Address determined by setup command
  MTU is 1500 bytes
  Helper address is not set
  Directed broadcast forwarding is disabled
  Outgoing access list is not set
  Inbound  access list is not set
  Proxy ARP is enabled
  Local Proxy ARP is disabled
  Security level is default
  Split horizon is enabled
  ICMP redirects are always sent
  ICMP unreachables are always sent
  ICMP mask replies are never sent
  IP fast switching is enabled
  IP fast switching on the same interface is disabled
  IP Flow switching is disabled
  IP CEF switching is enabled
  IP Feature Fast switching turbo vector
  IP Feature CEF switching turbo vector
  IP multicast fast switching is enabled
  IP multicast distributed fast switching is disabled
  IP route-cache flags are Fast, Distributed, CEF
  Router Discovery is disabled
  IP output packet accounting is disabled
  IP access violation accounting is disabled
  TCP/IP header compression is disabled
  RTP/IP header compression is disabled
  Probe proxy name replies are disabled
  Policy routing is disabled
  Network address translation is disabled
  WCCP Redirect outbound is disabled
  WCCP Redirect inbound is disabled
  WCCP Redirect exclude is disabled
  BGP Policy Mapping is disabled
  Sampled Netflow is disabled
  IP multicast multilayer switching is disabled
Switch#
```

You can use the **show ip interface brief** command to see a summary listing of the Layer 3 interfaces involved in routing IP traffic, as demonstrated in Example 11-10.

Example 11-10 *Displaying a Summary Listing of Interfaces Routing IP Traffic*

```
Switch# show ip interface brief
Interface               IP-Address      OK? Method Status                Protocol
Vlan1                   unassigned      YES NVRAM  administratively down down
Vlan54                  10.3.1.6        YES manual up                    up
Vlan101                 10.1.1.1        YES manual up                    up
GigabitEthernet1/0/10   10.1.5.1        YES manual up                    up
[output omitted]
Switch#
```

Verifying CEF

CEF operation depends on the correct routing information being generated and down-loaded to the Layer 3 forwarding engine hardware. This information is contained in the FIB and is maintained dynamically. To view the entire FIB, use the following EXEC command:

```
Switch# show ip cef
```

Example 11-11 shows sample output from this command.

Example 11-11 *Displaying the FIB Contents for a Switch*

```
Switch# show ip cef
Prefix              Next Hop            Interface
0.0.0.0/32          receive
192.168.199.0/24    attached            Vlan1
192.168.199.0/32    receive
192.168.199.1/32    receive
192.168.199.2/32    192.168.199.2       Vlan1
192.168.199.255/32  receive
Switch#
```

On this switch, only VLAN 1 has been configured with the IP address 192.168.199.1 255.255.255.0. Notice several things about the FIB for such a small configuration:

- **0.0.0.0/32:** An FIB entry has been reserved for the default route. No next hop is defined, so the entry is marked "receive" so that packets will be sent to the Layer 3 engine for further processing.

- **192.168.199.0/24:** The subnet assigned to the VLAN 1 interface is given its own entry. This is marked "attached" because it is connected directly to an SVI, VLAN 1.

- **192.168.199.0/32:** An FIB entry has been reserved for the exact network address. This is used to contain an adjacency for packets sent to the network address, if the network is not directly connected. In this case, there is no adjacency, and the entry is marked "receive."

- **192.168.199.1/32:** An entry has been reserved for the VLAN 1 SVI's IP address. Notice that this is a host route (/32). Packets destined for the VLAN 1 interface must be dealt with internally, so the entry is marked "receive."

- **192.168.199.2/32:** This is an entry for a neighboring multilayer switch, found on the VLAN 1 interface. The Next Hop field has been filled in with the same IP address, denoting that an adjacency is available.

- **192.168.199.255/32:** An FIB entry has been reserved for the 192.168.199.0 subnet's broadcast address. The route processor (Layer 3 engine) handles all directed broadcasts, so the entry is marked "receive."

To see complete FIB table information for a specific interface, use the following EXEC command:

```
Switch# show ip cef type member/module/number [detail]
```

Exam Preparation Tasks

Review All Key Topics

Review the most important topics in the chapter, noted with the Key Topic icon in the outer margin of the page. Table 11-2 lists a reference of these key topics and the page numbers on which each is found.

Table 11-2   *Key Topics for Chapter 11*

Key Topic Element	Description	Page Number
Paragraph	Describes inter-VLAN routing	268
Paragraph	Describes SVIs	269
Paragraph	Explains Layer 2 interface mode configuration	270
Paragraph	Explains Layer 3 interface mode configuration	270
Paragraph	Explains how to configure an SVI	271
Paragraph	Discusses the FIB and its contents	273
Paragraph	Explains the CEF adjacency table	276
List	Explains which IP packet fields are changed during the packet rewrite process	280

Complete Tables and Lists from Memory

There are no memory tables in this chapter.

Define Key Terms

Define the following key terms from this chapter, and check your answers in the glossary:

inter-VLAN routing, SVI, FIB, adjacency table, packet rewrite

Use Command Reference to Check Your Memory

This section includes the most important configuration and EXEC commands covered in this chapter. It might not be necessary to memorize the complete syntax of every command, but you should be able to remember the basic keywords that are needed.

To test your memory of the inter-VLAN routing and CEF configuration and verification commands, use a piece of paper to cover the right side of Tables 11-3 and 11-4, respectively. Read the description on the left side, and then see how much of the command you can remember. Remember that the CCNP exam focuses on practical or hands-on skills that are used by a networking professional.

Table 11-3   *Inter-VLAN Routing Configuration Commands*

Task	Command Syntax
Put a port into Layer 2 mode.	Switch(config-if)# **switchport**
Put a port into Layer 3 mode.	Switch(config-if)# **no switchport**
Define an SVI.	Switch(config)# **interface vlan** *vlan-id*

Table 11-4   *Multilayer Switching Verification Commands*

Task	Command Syntax
Show a Layer 2 port status.	Switch# **show interface** *type member/ module/number* **switchport**
Show a Layer 3 port status.	Switch# **show interface** *type member/ module/number*
Show an SVI status.	Switch# **show interface vlan** *vlan-id*
View the FIB contents.	Switch# **show ip cef**
View FIB information for an interface.	Switch# **show ip cef** [*type member/ module/number* | **vlan** *vlan-id*] [**detail**]
View FIB information for an IP prefix.	Switch# **show ip cef** [*prefix-ip prefix-mask*] [**longer-prefixes**] [**detail**]
View FIB adjacency information.	Switch# **show adjacency** [*type member/ module/number* | **vlan** *vlan-id*] [**summary** | **detail**]
View counters for packets not switched by CEF.	Switch# **show cef not-cef-switched**

This chapter covers the following topics that you need to master for the CCNP SWITCH exam:

■ **Configuring an IPv4 DHCP Server:** This section covers the basic configuration needed to make a switch act as a DHCP server or as a DHCP relay so that IPv4 hosts can request addresses and learn their local default gateway addresses and other necessary information.

■ **Configuring DHCP to Support IPv6:** This section discusses several mechanisms that hosts can use to obtain IPv6 addresses and other network information.

CHAPTER 12

Configuring DHCP

This chapter explains how a multilayer switch can be configured as a Dynamic Host Configuration Protocol (DHCP) server or relay to supply IP addressing information to client devices. Both IPv4 and IPv6 addressing services are discussed.

"Do I Know This Already?" Quiz

The "Do I Know This Already?" quiz allows you to assess whether you should read this entire chapter thoroughly or jump to the "Exam Preparation Tasks" section. If you are in doubt based on your answers to these questions or your own assessment of your knowledge of the topics, read the entire chapter. Table 12-1 outlines the major headings in this chapter and the "Do I Know This Already?" quiz questions that go with them. You can find the answers in Appendix A, "Answers to the 'Do I Know This Already?' Quizzes."

Table 12-1 *"Do I Know This Already?" Section-to-Question Mapping*

Foundation Topics Section	Questions Covered in This Section
Configuring an IPv4 DHCP Server	1-5
Configuring DHCP to Support IPv6	6-8

1. If a DHCP scope is configured on a Catalyst switch, which one of the following must also be configured so that the switch becomes a DHCP server for client machines connected to VLAN 3?

   a. A corresponding **ip dhcp server** command configured on interface VLAN 3

   b. A corresponding IP address configured on interface VLAN 3

   c. An **ip helper-address** command configured on interface VLAN 3

   d. A switch cannot operate as a DHCP server

2. Which one of the following commands can be used to prevent IP addresses 192.168.16.10 through 192.168.16.30 from being assigned by the DHCP server running on a switch?

   a. ip dhcp reserve-address 192.168.16.10 – 192.168.16.30

   b. ip dhcp pool users

   no network 192.168.16.10 192.168.16.30

   c. ip dhcp excluded-address 192.168.16.10 192.168.16.30

   d. ip dhcp pool users

   no lease 192.168.16.10 192.168.16.30

3. To configure a manual DHCP binding for two different IP addresses, which one of the following approaches should you take?

   a. Define two DHCP pools that contain a single host address each.

   b. Define a DHCP pool that contains the network of the host addresses.

   c. Enter two **ip dhcp excluded-address** commands to configure the host addresses.

   d. Define one DHCP pool that contains a **host** command for each host address binding.

4. Which one of the following answers represents configuration commands needed to implement a DHCP relay function?

   a. interface vlan 5

   ip address 10.1.1.1 255.255.255.0

   ip helper-address 10.1.1.10

   b. interface vlan 5

   ip address 10.1.1.1 255.255.255.0

   ip dhcp-relay

   c. ip dhcp pool staff

   network 10.1.1.0 255.255.255.0

   default-router 10.1.1.1

   exit

   d. hostname Switch

   ip helper-address 10.1.1.10

5. Which one of the following commands can be used to display IPv4 addresses that have been assigned through the DHCP server on a switch?

   a. show ip dhcp pool

   b. show ip dhcp clients

   c. show ip dhcp binding

   d. show ip dhcp leases

6. Which one of the following forms of IPv6 address does a host use to discover its local router?

   a. CDPv6

   b. ICMPv6

   c. Stateless address

   d. Link-local address

7. Without a DHCP server available, which one of the following represents a valid method for a host to obtain a unique IPv6 address?

   a. The local switch interface will assign one, provided it has an IPv6 address configured

   b. Stateless autoconfiguration

   c. DHCP relay

   d. Link-local address proxy

8. To exclude specific IPv6 addresses from being handed out by a DHCPv6 server configured on a Catalyst switch, which one of the following describes the correct strategy?

   a. Enter the **ip dhcp excluded-address** command along with the IPv6 addresses to exclude.

   b. Enter the **no address prefix** *ipv6-address* command as part of the DHCPv6 pool configuration.

   c. Define a separate DHCPv6 pool for each excluded address.

   d. None of these answers; you cannot exclude addresses with DHCPv6.

Foundation Topics

Using DHCP with a Multilayer Switch

When a switch is configured with a Layer 3 address on an interface, it becomes the router or default gateway that connected hosts will use to send traffic to and from their local VLAN or subnet. How do those hosts know to use the Layer 3 interface as their default gateway? As well, how do those hosts know what IP address to use for their own identities?

Hosts can be manually configured to use a static IP address, subnet mask, default gateway address, and so on. That might be appropriate for some devices, such as servers, which would need stable and reserved addresses. For the majority of end user devices, static address assignment can become a huge administrative chore.

Instead, the Dynamic Host Configuration Protocol (DHCP) is usually leveraged to provide a means for dynamic address assignment to any host that can use the protocol. DHCP is defined in RFC 2131 and is built around a client/server model: Hosts requesting IP addresses use a DHCP client, and address assignment is handled by a DHCP server.

Suppose a host connects to the network, but does not yet have an IP address. It needs to request an address via DHCP. How can it send a packet to a DHCP server without having a valid IP address to use as a source address? The answer lies in the DHCP negotiation, which plays out in the following four steps:

Key Topic

1. **The client sends a "DHCP Discover" message as a broadcast:** Even without a valid source address, the client can send to the broadcast address to find any DHCP server that might be listening. The client's MAC address is included in the broadcast message.

2. **A DHCP server replies with a "DHCP Offer" message:** The offer contains an offer for the use of an IP address, subnet mask, default gateway, and some parameters for using the IP address.

    The server also includes its own IP address to identify who is making the offer. (There could be multiple addresses offered, if more than one DHCP server received the broadcast DHCP Discover message.) Because the client does not yet have a valid IP address, the server must broadcast the offer so the client can receive it.

3. **The client sends a "DHCP Request" message:** When it is satisfied with a DHCP offer, the client formally requests use of the offered address. A record of the offer is included so that only the server that sent the offer will set aside the requested IP address. Again, the request is sent as a broadcast as a public announcement to any other servers that may have responded, and because the client hasn't officially started using a valid address.

4. **The DHCP server replies with a "DHCP ACK" message:** The IP address and all parameters for its use are returned to the client as formal approval to begin using the address. The ACK message is sent as a unicast, but may be broadcast instead.

Because DHCP is a dynamic mechanism, IP addresses are offered on a leased basis. Before the offered lease time expires, the client must try to renew its address; otherwise, that address may be offered up to a different client.

Notice that DHCP is designed to work within a broadcast domain. Most of the messages in a DHCP exchange are sent as broadcasts. On this basis, the DHCP server would need to be located in the same broadcast domain as the client. In this scenario, you might have a dedicated DHCP server connected to the network and located in the same VLAN as the client. You can also configure a multilayer switch to operate as a DHCP server if you have configured a Layer 3 address on the switch interface or SVI where the client is located.

This design would require one DHCP server for each broadcast domain or VLAN on the network—something that is not always practical at all! You can get around this requirement by configuring a multilayer switch to relay the DHCP negotiation across VLAN boundaries.

The following sections explain how to configure a DHCP server on a multilayer switch within a VLAN and how to configure DHCP relay between VLANs.

Configuring an IPv4 DHCP Server

First, configure a Layer 3 address on a switch interface so that the switch can participate in IP-related activities. Then you can configure a DHCP server that runs natively on the switch itself. You can configure a pool of addresses that are offered by the DHCP server, as well as addresses that are reserved or manually assigned. In all of those cases, the DHCP server address scope must correlate with a Layer 3 IP subnet that is configured on a switch interface. The switch will then intercept DHCP broadcast packets from client machines within a VLAN. Use the following command sequence to configure a DHCP server:

Key Topic

```
Switch(config)# ip dhcp excluded-address start-ip end-ip
Switch(config)# ip dhcp pool pool-name
Switch(config-dhcp)# network ip-address subnet-mask
Switch(config-dhcp)# default-router ip-address [ip-address2] [ip-address3] ...
Switch(config-dhcp)# lease {infinite | {days [hours [minutes]]}}
Switch(config-dhcp)# exit
```

If some addresses within the IP subnet should be reserved and not offered to clients, use the **ip dhcp excluded-address** command. You can define a range of addresses or a single address to be excluded. You do not have to worry about excluding the addresses used by a switch interface or a broadcast address; the switch automatically excludes those.

The **ip dhcp pool** command uses a text string *pool-name* to define the pool or scope of addresses that will be offered. The **network** command identifies the IP subnet and subnet mask of the address range. The subnet should be identical to the one configured on the Layer 3 interface. In fact, the switch uses the **network** command to bind its DHCP server to the matching Layer 3 interface. By definition, the network and broadcast addresses for the subnet won't be offered to any client. The **default-router** command identifies the default router address that will be offered to clients. Generally, the default router should be the IP address of the corresponding Layer 3 interface on the switch.

Finally, you can set the IP address lease duration with the **lease** command. By default, leases are offered with a 1 day limit.

In Example 12-1, a DHCP scope for the 192.168.1.0/24 subnet has been configured. Addresses 192.168.1.2 through 192.168.1.5 are excluded to preserve them for future use.

Example 12-1 *Configuring a DHCP Server with a Pool of Addresses*

```
Switch(config)# interface vlan10
Switch(config-if)# ip address 192.168.1.1 255.255.255.0
Switch(config-if)# no shutdown
Switch(config-if)# exit
Switch(config)# ip dhcp excluded-address 192.168.1.2 192.168.1.5
Switch(config)# ip dhcp pool Users
Switch(dhcp-config)# network 192.168.1.0 255.255.255.0
Switch(dhcp-config)# default-router 192.168.1.1
Switch(dhcp-config)# exit
```

You can monitor the DHCP server address leases with the **show ip dhcp binding** command. Example 12-2 lists three IP addresses that have been assigned by the DHCP server configured in Example 12-1.

Example 12-2 *Displaying Current DHCP Server Address Assignments*

```
Switch# show ip dhcp binding
Bindings from all pools not associated with VRF:
IP address          Client-ID/             Lease expiration      Type
                    Hardware address/
                    User name
192.168.1.2         0100.50b6.5bc0.b5      Aug 31 2014 01:57 AM  Automatic
192.168.1.3         010c.8bfd.752e.c4      Aug 30 2014 12:03 AM  Automatic
192.168.1.4         010e.8bfd.752e.c0      Aug 30 2011 08:03 PM  Automatic
Switch#
```

An address lease is normally released or cleared by the client that is using it. In some cases, you may need to clear an address binding manually with the following command. You can enter a specific IP address to be cleared or an asterisk to clear all address bindings.

```
Switch# clear ip dhcp binding {* | ip-address}
```

Configuring a Manual Address Binding

Not all clients and applications can operate with an IP address that might change over time because of the dynamic nature of DHCP address assignments. If a device requires an IP address that will always be assigned to it, you can configure a manual address binding on the DHCP server.

Define a manual binding just as you would a regular DHCP pool. The difference is that the manual binding "pool" consists of one IP address that you configure with the **host** *ip-address subnet-mask* command. When a client requests an address, it can be identified by its client identifier (DHCP requests) or its hardware MAC address (BOOTP requests), configured with the **client-identifier** or **hardware-address** commands, respectively.

Sometimes it can be difficult to know how to enter the appropriate client information in a manual binding. For example, you should use the **client-identifier** command for clients that request an address through DHCP. The client identifier is a string of hex digits arranged in groups of four, separated by dots. Typical identifier strings are shown in the list of address bindings in Example 12-2. Notice how they appear to be MAC addresses, but end with an extra pair of hex digits.

Client identifiers commonly consist of the digits 01 followed by the client's MAC address. The 01 prefix, indicating that the client uses Ethernet, causes the dotted hex notation to appear shifted from the familiar form. In some cases, the client might send a different identifier string in its DHCP requests. If you find that the client does not pick up the address you are expecting (or none at all), you can use the **debug ip dhcp server** command to display detailed information about the client's request.

In Example 12-3, a manual address binding is configured for the client, so that it always receives IP address 192.168.1.99. The debug output displays the client MAC address (0050.b65b.c0b5) and its client identifier (0100.50b6.5bc0.b5).

Example 12-3 *Finding a Client Identifier and Configuring a Manual Binding*

```
Switch(config)# ip dhcp pool my-pc
Switch(dhcp-config)# host 192.168.1.99 255.255.255.0
Switch(dhcp-config)# client-identifier 0100.50b6.5bc0.b5
Switch(dhcp-config)# exit
Switch(config)# exit


Switch# debug ip dhcp server
Mar 31 02:40:35.528: DHCPD: Sending notification of DISCOVER:
Mar 31 02:40:35.528:   DHCPD: htype 1 chaddr 0050.b65b.c0b5
Mar 31 02:40:35.528:   DHCPD: interface = Vlan1
Mar 31 02:40:35.528:   DHCPD: class id 4d53465420352e30
Mar 31 02:40:35.528:   DHCPD: out_vlan_id 0
Mar 31 02:40:37.541: DHCPD: assigned IP address 192.168.1.99 to client
0100.50b6.5bc0.b5. (2069 0)
Mar 31 02:40:37.541: DHCPD: DHCPOFFER notify setup address 192.168.1.99 mask
255.255.255.0
Mar 31 02:40:37.541: DHCPD: Sending notification of ASSIGNMENT:
Mar 31 02:40:37.541:   DHCPD: address 192.168.1.99 mask 255.255.255.0
Mar 31 02:40:37.541:   DHCPD: htype 1 chaddr 0050.b65b.c0b5
Mar 31 02:40:37.541:   DHCPD: lease time remaining (secs) = 86400
Mar 31 02:40:37.541:   DHCPD: interface = Vlan1
Mar 31 02:40:37.541:   DHCPD: out_vlan_id 0
```

Configuring DHCP Options

Client devices sometimes need more information beyond the basic set of IP address, subnet mask, gateway address, and lease time. Depending on the nature of the device, it might also need some bootstrap information so that it can find the address of a machine offering a needed service. You can accomplish this by specifying DHCP options as part of the DHCP server configuration.

You can configure a DHCP option in a DHCP pool with the following command:

```
Switch(dhcp-config)# option option-num value
```

The *option-num* parameter is the decimal number of a predefined DHCP option. Table 12-2 lists some common options and their functions. The option *value* can be one or more IP addresses, a string of hex digits, or other value.

Table 12-2   *Common DHCP Options*

Option Number	Function
43	Location of a wireless LAN controller for lightweight wireless access points
69	Location of an SMTP server
70	Location of a POP3 mail server
150	Location of a TFTP server for Cisco IP phones

Tip   Many more commands are available for configuring the DHCP server. For the CCNP SWITCH exam, try to keep things simple and know the basic structure of DHCP pool configuration, as previously shown.

Configuring a DHCP Relay

In a large network, you may encounter a DHCP server that is centrally located, rather than distributed on individual switches. In that case, you can configure the multilayer switch to relay DHCP messages between clients and the server, even if they are located on different VLANs or subnets.

First, configure a Layer 3 interface that is bound to the same VLAN as the client machines. This interface can be the default gateway for the clients and can act as a DHCP relay. Next, use the **ip helper-address** interface configuration command to identify the IP address of the actual DHCP server, as in the following example:

```
Switch(config)# interface vlan5
Switch(config-if)# ip address 192.168.1.1 255.255.255.0
Switch(config-if)# ip helper-address 192.168.199.4
Switch(config-if)# exit
```

As a DHCP relay, the switch will intercept the broadcast DHCP messages from the client and will forward them on to the server address as unicast messages. The switch keeps track of the subnet where the client messages arrived so that it can relay the DHCP server responses back appropriately.

You can configure more than one helper address by repeating the **ip helper-address** command with different addresses. In this case, the switch will relay each DHCP request from a client to each of the helper addresses simultaneously. If more than one server replies, each reply will be relayed back to the client and the client will have to choose one acceptable response.

Configuring DHCP to Support IPv6

In addition to traditional IPv4, Cisco Catalyst switches can support IPv6 addressing and routing, as well as DHCP services. IPv6 topics are normally covered in the Cisco CCNP ROUTE course and exam, but you might find DHCP support in the SWITCH course and exam.

As a quick review, recall that IPv4 addresses use 32 bits while IPv6 uses 128 bits. IPv6 leverages a vastly increased address space, removing the need for address translation within enterprise networks. In fact, IPv6 addresses are inherently globally unique.

IPv6 offers some very efficient and convenient mechanisms for devices to use when they join a network. By discovering a local IPv6 router, a device can learn about which address prefix to use and can generate its own globally unique address. To discover a neighboring router, the device can use a special *link-local address*.

Link-local addresses always begin with the IPv6 prefix FE80::/10. A device then appends its own interface identifier, which includes the MAC address. Even though the link-local address might seem unique, devices must always go through a duplicate address detection process to see if any other device might be using the same address. If the address proves to be unique, then a device can begin to discover any local routers that are connected to the local network segment. The link-local address provides a means to come online and learn about the Layer 3 surroundings—with very little intervention.

The ultimate goal for any IPv6 device joining a network is to find a globally unique address that it can use to communicate outside of the local link. In the IPv4 world, this can be done through static IP address configuration or dynamically through DHCP. IPv6 is somewhat different; a device can be configured with a static IPv6 address or it can obtain an address dynamically, but not normally through DHCP. The following sections describe the mechanisms that can be used to provide IPv6 addresses and parameters.

Tip   Remember that IPv6 addresses are always 128 bits long, represented by eight groups of four hex digits that are separated by colons. Leading 0s do not have to be shown. To shorten the address notation, you can replace one long string of consecutive 0s with a double colon. For example, the full address 3000:A120:000B:0000:0000:0000:0000:0021 can be rewritten as 3000:A120:B::21.

Stateless Autoconfiguration

A client can create a globally unique address by combining information advertised from a router with information from the client's own network adapter. The router provides 64 bits from the Layer 3 subnet prefix, while the client appends a 64-bit EUI-64 interface ID. The interface ID consists of the upper half of the interface's MAC address (24 bits), followed by the hex string FFFE (16 bits), followed by the lower half of the MAC address (24 bits).

As a result, a client can quickly join a network with a unique unicast IPv6 address with little intervention. The client can also pick up other necessary information from the router, like the default router address and the maximum transmission unit (MTU). Router advertisements are sent periodically or the client can request one on-demand to reduce the wait time.

This process is called *stateless autoconfiguration or serverless client configuration*. IPv6 addresses are determined on the fly, with no dependence upon a DHCP server at all, which greatly simplifies the client configuration. All of the necessary addressing information is found on the local IPv6 router, which is also very easy to configure. After you have identified a Layer 3 interface on a switch, configure an IPv6 address prefix on it with the **ipv6 address** interface configuration command. In Example 12-4, the VLAN 5 switch virtual interface (SVI) has been configured with IPv6 prefix 2001:db8:00 0a:0000:0000:0000:0001.

Example 12-4 *Configuring a Layer 3 Interface for IPv6 Stateless Autoconfiguration*

```
Switch(config)# interface vlan 5
Switch(config-if)# ipv6 address 2001:db8:a::1/64
Switch(config-if)# no shutdown
```

DHCPv6

Notice that stateless autoconfiguration provides only the most basic information a client needs to communicate: an IPv6 address, the IPv6 prefix, and the default router address. To get anything more, such as a domain name, DNS server address, and so on, a client must depend on a DHCP server.

Catalyst switches can function as a DHCPv6 server, which is compatible with IPv6. In order to use DHCPv6, clients must determine whether the service is available. Routers can indicate that DHCPv6 is offered in their router advertisements or a client can send a request asking for the service.

To configure DHCPv6, begin by defining an IPv6 address pool with the following global configuration command:

```
Switch(config)# ipv6 dhcp pool pool-name
```

If you intend for the DHCPv6 server to assign IPv6 addresses to client machines, specify the IPv6 address prefix for the scope with the following command:

```
Switch(config-dhcpv6)# address prefix ipv6-prefix
```

> **Tip** DHCPv6 does not allow you to exclude addresses as you can with DHCPv4. As well, you cannot configure manual address bindings with DHCPv6.

Within the DHCPv6 pool, you can assign any necessary options with the following commands:

```
Switch(config-dhcpv6)# dns-server dns-address
Switch(config-dhcpv6)# domain-name name
```

Finally, configure a Layer 3 interface with both an IPv6 address and the DHCPv6 pool with the following commands:

```
Switch(config)# interface type member/module/number
Switch(config-if)# ipv6 address ipv6-address
Switch(config-if)# ipv6 dhcp server pool-name
Switch(config-if)# no shutdown
```

In Example 12-5, a DHCPv6 pool named v6-users has been configured. The DHCPv6 pool has been bound to interface VLAN 5.

Example 12-5 *Configuring a DHCPv6 Pool*

```
Switch(config)# ipv6 dhcp pool v6-users
Switch(config-dhcpv6)# address prefix 2001:db8:a::/64
Switch(config-dhcpv6)# dns-server 2001:db8:c12::10
Switch(config-dhcpv6)# domain-name mydomain.com
Switch(config-dhcpv6)# exit
Switch(config)# interface vlan 5
Switch(config-if)# ipv6 address 2001:db8:a::1/64
Switch(config-if)# ipv6 dhcp server v6-users
Switch(config-if)# no shutdown
```

DHCPv6 Lite

Cisco also offers DHCPv6 Lite, which combines the simplicity of stateless autoconfiguration for address management with the DHCP option management function of DHCPv6.

You can configure DHCPv6 Lite by defining a DHCPv6 pool. However, you should omit the **address prefix** command from the pool so that clients cannot use DHCPv6 to obtain their addresses. The clients will rely on the normal stateless autoconfiguration using the IPv6 prefix that you have configured on the Layer 3 interface. The DHCPv6 pool should contain any options you would like to push out to the clients.

After you configure an IPv6 address prefix on the Layer 3 interface, you should reference the DHCPv6 pool and also enter the following interface configuration command. This will inform the clients that options are available via the DHCPv6 Lite server after stateless autoconfig yields a usable IPv6 address. The complete configuration is listed in Example 12-6.

```
Switch(config-if)# ipv6 nd other-config-flag
```

Example 12-6 *Configuring DHCPv6 Lite*

```
Switch(config)# ipv6 dhcp pool v6-users
Switch(config-dhcpv6)# dns-server 2001:db8:c12::10
Switch(config-dhcpv6)# domain-name mydomain.com
Switch(config-dhcpv6)# exit

Switch(config)# interface vlan 5
Switch(config-if)# ipv6 address 2001:db8:a::1/64
Switch(config-if)# ipv6 dhcp server v6-users
Switch(config-if)# ipv6 nd other-config-flag
Switch(config-if)# no shutdown
```

Configuring a DHCPv6 Relay Agent

Sometimes you might have a DHCPv6 server operating on an external machine that is located elsewhere in the network. Like DHCPv4, you can enable a DHCP relay agent on the Layer 3 interface. Use the following command to relay DHCPv6 requests between clients and the DHCPv6 server located at the IPv6 address.

```
Switch(config-if)# ipv6 dhcp relay destination ipv6-address
```

Verifying IPv6 DHCP Operation

Like DHCP for IPv4, you can monitor DHCPv6 address bindings with the **show ipv6 dhcp pool** and **show ipv6 dhcp binding** EXEC commands. Example 12-7 demonstrates these commands to show that there is one IPv6 client with an address binding.

Example 12-7 *Displaying DHCPv6 Address Bindings*

```
Switch# show ipv6 dhcp pool
DHCPv6 pool: v6-users
  Domain name: myV6domain.net
  Active clients: 1
Switch#
Switch# show ipv6 dhcp binding
Client: FE80::DA5:D707:B5F2:8E81 (Vlan1)
  DUID: 00010001194C482DC48508B164FD
  IA NA: IA ID 0x220050B6, T1 0, T2 0
Switch#
```

You can also manually clear an address binding with the following EXEC command:

```
Switch# clear ipv6 dhcp binding {* | ipv6-address}
```

Exam Preparation Tasks

Review All Key Topics

Review the most important topics in the chapter, noted with the Key Topic icon in the outer margin of the page. Table 12-3 lists a reference of these key topics and the page numbers on which each is found.

Table 12-3 *Key Topics for Chapter 12*

Key Topic Element	Description	Page Number
List	Explains DHCP address negotiation	292
Paragraph	Covers how to configure a DHCP pool	293
Table 12-2	Common DHCP options	296
Paragraph	Discusses how to configure a DHCP relay	296
Paragraph	Explains IPv6 stateless autoconfiguration	298
Paragraph	Discusses how to configure DHCPv6	298

Complete Tables and Lists from Memory

There are no memory tables in this chapter.

Define Key Terms

Define the following key terms from this chapter, and check your answers in the glossary:

DHCP, DHCP relay, link-local address, DHCPv6, stateless autoconfiguration, DHCPv6 Lite

Use Command Reference to Check Your Memory

This section includes the most important configuration and EXEC commands covered in this chapter. It might not be necessary to memorize the complete syntax of every command, but you should be able to remember the basic keywords that are needed.

To test your memory of the DHCP configuration and verification commands related to IPv4 and IPv6, use a piece of paper to cover the right side of Tables 12-4 and 12-5, respectively. Read the description on the left side, and then see how much of the command you can remember. Remember that the CCNP exam focuses on practical or hands-on skills that are used by a networking professional.

Table 12-4 *DHCP Commands Related to IPv4*

Task	Command Syntax
Exclude addresses from a DHCP server scope.	Switch(config-if)# **ip dhcp excluded-address** *start-ip end-ip*
Define a DHCP server scope.	Switch(config-if)# **ip dhcp pool** *pool-name*
Identify the IP subnet for the server scope.	Switch(config-dhcp)# **network** *ip-address subnet-mask*
Identify the default router used in the server scope.	Switch(config-dhcp)# **default-router** *ip-address* [*ip-address2*] [*ip-address3*] ...
Define the DHCP server lease time.	Switch(config-dhcp)# **lease** {infinite	{*days* [*hours* [*minutes*]]}}
Define a DHCP option.	Switch(dhcp-config)# **option** *option-num value*
Configure a manual DHCP binding.	Switch(config)# **ip dhcp pool** *pool-name*
	Switch(dhcp-config)# **host** *ip-address mask*
	Switch(dhcp-config)# **client-identifier** *identifier*
	Switch(dhcp-config)# **exit**
Enable DHCP relay on a Layer 3 interface.	Switch(config-if)# **ip helper-address** *ip-address*
Display current DHCP bindings.	Switch# **show ip dhcp binding**
Manually clear a DHCP binding.	Switch# **clear ip dhcp binding** {*	*ip-address*}

Table 12-5 *DHCP Commands Related to IPv6*

Task	Command Syntax
Define an IPv6 address prefix on a Layer 3 interface.	Switch(config)# **interface** *type member/module/number*
	Switch(config-if)# **ipv6 address** *ipv6-prefix*
Define a DHCPv6 pool.	Switch(config)# **ipv6 dhcp pool** *pool-name*
	Switch(config-dhcpv6)# **address prefix** *ipv6-prefix*
	Switch(config-dhcpv6)# **dns-server** *dns-address*
	Switch(config-dhcpv6)# **domain-name** *name*
Bind a DHCPv6 pool to a Layer 3 interface.	Switch(config)# **interface** *type member/module/number*
	Switch(config-if)# **ipv6 address** *ipv6-address*
	Switch(config-if)# **ipv6 dhcp server** *pool-name*
Enable DHCPv6 Lite options.	Switch(config-if)# **ipv6 nd other-config-flag**

Task	Command Syntax
Enable DHCPv6 relay on a Layer 3 interface.	Switch(config-if)# **ipv6 dhcp relay destination** *ipv6-address*
Manually clear a DHCPv6 binding.	Switch# **clear ipv6 dhcp binding** {*	*ipv6-address*}
Display a summary of DHCPv6 pool activity.	Switch# **show ipv6 dhcp pool**
Display current DHCPv6 bindings.	Switch# **show ipv6 dhcp binding** [*ipv6-address*]

This chapter covers the following topics that you need to master for the CCNP SWITCH exam:

- **Syslog Messages:** This section explains how a switch can maintain a log of important events and send the logging messages to various destinations.

- **Adding Time Stamps to Syslog Messages:** This section discusses ways you can set the internal switch clock and synchronize to an accurate source. The switch can then add time stamps to its logging messages as a record of event history.

CHAPTER 13

Logging Switch Activity

This chapter discusses the logging methods you can use to monitor Catalyst switches and collect their event logs. Switch messages should be generated with an accurate time stamp so that you can correlate events across devices. The chapter also covers several methods to set the switch clock and keep it accurate.

"Do I Know This Already?" Quiz

The "Do I Know This Already?" quiz allows you to assess whether you should read this entire chapter thoroughly or jump to the "Exam Preparation Tasks" section. If you are in doubt based on your answers to these questions or your own assessment of your knowledge of the topics, read the entire chapter. Table 13-1 outlines the major headings in this chapter and the "Do I Know This Already?" quiz questions that go with them. You can find the answers in Appendix A, "Answers to the 'Do I Know This Already?' Quizzes."

Table 13-1 *"Do I Know This Already?" Foundation Topics Section-to-Question Mapping*

Foundation Topics Section	Questions Covered in This Section
Syslog Messages	1-4
Adding Time Stamps to Syslog Messages	5-8

1. Which one of the following syslog severity levels would generate the most types of logging messages?

   a. Emergencies

   b. Alerts

   c. Critical

   d. Warnings

   e. Informational

2. The **logging trap 0** command sends logging messages to which one of the following destinations?

   a. Switch console

   b. Internal buffer

   c. SNMP server

   d. Syslog server

   e. Nowhere; logging is disabled

3. If you have configured a switch to send logging messages to an internal buffer, which one of the following commands will let you review the buffer contents?

   a. **show logging buffer**

   b. **show buffer logging**

   c. **show logging**

   d. **show event log**

4. Which one of the following syslog severity levels will generate only messages about the most critical or severe events?

   a. 0

   b. 1

   c. 5

   d. 7

   e. 10

5. Which one of the following protocols is used to synchronize time between networked devices?

   a. TSP

   b. NTP

   c. STP

   d. RTP

6. Which one of the following time servers is considered to be the most accurate?

   a. Stratum 0

   b. Stratum 1

   c. Stratum 10

   d. Stratum 100

7. Suppose you configure a switch with the command **ntp server 192.168.100.100**. Which one of the following is a true statement?

   a. The switch will become only an NTP client.

   b. The switch will become only an NTP server.

   c. The switch will become both an NTP server and an NTP client.

   d. The switch will not use NTP until you enter the **ntp enable** command.

8. Which one of the following answers correctly describes SNTP?

   a. Secure Network Time Protocol

   b. Simplified Network Time Protocol

   c. Syslog Network Time Protocol

   d. Switched Network Time Protocol

Foundation Topics

This book presents a variety of features and functions that you can leverage to build a working network and accomplish design goals. How can you stay aware of what is going on inside a switch while it operates? You can use **show** commands to display various information from time to time, but you may not catch an event as it happens in real time. Suppose, for instance, that a link goes down for some reason. If you do not know about it and are not able to fix it right away, you might miss an opportunity to keep the network functioning properly. Likewise, you might get news of a problem within the network and need to start troubleshooting.

You should leverage the logging system available in each switch so that you can collect messages as they are generated. By doing so, you can monitor the network to detect failures and gather information about switch activity.

Syslog Messages

Catalyst switches can be configured to generate an audit trail of messages describing important events that have occurred. These system message logs (syslog) can then be collected and analyzed to determine what has happened, when it happened, and how severe the event was.

When system messages are generated, they always appear in a consistent format, as shown in Figure 13-1. Each message contains the following fields:

- **Timestamp:** The date and time from the internal switch clock. By default, the amount of time that the switch has been up is used.

- **Facility Code:** A system identifier that categorizes the switch function or module that has generated the message; the facility code always begins with a percent sign.

- **Severity:** A number from 0 to 7 that indicates how important or severe the event is; a lower severity means the event is more critical.

- **Mnemonic:** A short text string that categorizes the event within the facility code.

- **Message Text:** A description of the event or condition that triggered the system message.

In Figure 13-1, an event in the System or SYS facility has triggered the system message. The event is considered to be severity level 5. From the mnemonic CONFIG_I, you can infer that something happened with the switch configuration. Indeed, the text description says that the switch was configured by someone connected to the switch console port.

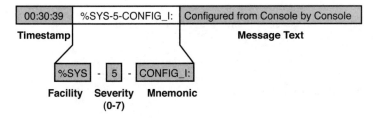

Figure 13-1 *Catalyst Switch Syslog Message Format*

Generally, you should configure a switch to generate syslog messages that are occurring at or above a certain level of importance; otherwise, you might collect too much information from a switch that logs absolutely everything or too little information from a switch that logs almost nothing.

You can use the severity level to define that threshold. Figure 13-2 shows each of the logging severity levels, along with a general list of the types of messages that are generated. Think of the severity levels as concentric circles. When you configure the severity level threshold on a switch, the switch will only generate logging messages that occur at that level or at any other level that is contained within it.

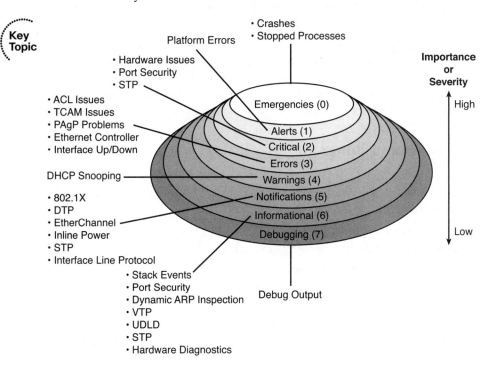

Figure 13-2 *Syslog Severity Levels*

For example, if the syslog severity level is set to critical (severity level 2), the switch will generate messages in the Critical, Alerts, and Emergencies levels, but nothing else. Notice that the severity levels are numbered such that the most urgent events are reported at level 0 and the least urgent at level 7.

> **Tip**   You should try to have a good understanding of the severity level names and numbers, as well as their order, in case you need to identify them on the exam.
>
> Remember that the severity numbers are opposite of what you might perceive as the actual message importance. If the exam asks about an event that has a "high" or "greater" severity, that means the severity level number will be lower.

System messages can be sent to the switch console, collected in an internal memory buffer, and sent over the network to be collected by a syslog server. The following sections cover the configuration commands for each of these destinations.

Logging to the Switch Console

By default, system messages are sent to the switch console port at the Debugging level. You can change the console severity level with the following command:

```
Switch(config)# logging console severity
```

The *severity* parameter can be either a severity level keyword, such as **informational**, or the corresponding numeric value (0 to 7).

Remember that syslog information can be seen on the console only when you are connected to the console port. Even then, the console is not a very efficient way to collect and view system messages because of its low throughput. If you are connected to a switch through a Telnet or Secure Shell (SSH) session, you can redirect the console messages to your remote access session by using the **terminal monitor** command.

Logging to the Internal Buffer

Every Catalyst switch has an internal memory buffer where syslog messages can be collected. The internal buffer is an efficient way to collect messages over time. As long as the switch is powered up, the logging buffer is available.

By default, the internal logging buffer is disabled. To enable it and begin sending system messages into the buffer, you can use the following command:

```
Switch(config)# logging buffered severity
```

The *severity* parameter can be either a severity level keyword, such as **informational**, or the corresponding numeric value (0 to 7).

The logging buffer has a finite size and operates in a circular fashion. If the buffer fills, the oldest messages roll off as new ones arrive. By default, the logging buffer is 4096 bytes or characters long, which is enough space to collect 50 lines of full-length text. If you depend on the logging buffer to keep a running history of logging messages, you might need to increase its size with the following command:

```
Switch(config)# logging buffered size
```

The buffer length is set to *size* (4096 to 2147483647) bytes. Be careful not to set the length too big because the switch reserves the logging buffer space from the memory it might need for other operations.

To review the internal logging buffer at any time, you can use the **show logging** command.

Logging to a Remote Syslog Server

Syslog servers provide the most robust method of logging message collection. Messages are sent from a switch to a syslog server over the network using UDP port 514. This means that a syslog server can be located anywhere, as long as it is reachable by the switch. Keep in mind that UDP is not a reliable means of communication because it is not connection-oriented like TCP. Therefore, logging messages are not acknowledged; they are just sent toward a syslog server on a best effort basis.

A syslog server can collect logs from many different devices simultaneously and can archive the logging information for a long period of time. To identify a syslog server and begin sending logging messages to it, you can use the following commands:

```
Switch(config)# logging host ip-address
Switch(config)# logging trap severity
```

The syslog server is located at the hostname or IP address specified. You can enter the **logging host** command more than once if you have more than one syslog server collecting logging information. The syslog server *severity* level can be either a severity level keyword, such as **informational**, or the corresponding numeric value (0 to 7).

Tip   Notice that each of the logging message destinations can have a unique severity level configured. For example, you might collect messages of severity level Debugging into the internal buffer, while collecting severity level Notifications to a syslog server.

Tip   By default, a switch will generate a system message every time it detects an interface going up or down. That sounds like a good thing, until you realize that the syslog server will be receiving news of every user powering their PC on and off each day. Each link state change will generate a message at the Errors (3) severity level, in addition to a line protocol state change at the Notifications (5) severity level. To prevent this from happening with access layer interfaces where end users are connected, you can use the following interface configuration command:

```
Switch(config-if)# no logging event link-status
```

Adding Time Stamps to Syslog Messages

If you are watching system messages appear in real time, it is obvious what time those events have occurred; however, if you need to review messages that have been collected and archived in the internal logging buffer or on a syslog server, message time stamps become really important.

By default, Catalyst switches add a simple "uptime" time stamp to logging messages. This is a cumulative counter that shows the hours, minutes, and seconds since the switch has been booted. Suppose that you find an important event in the logs and you want to know exactly when it occurred. With the uptime time stamp, you would have to backtrack and compute the time of the event based on how long the switch has been operating.

Even worse, as time goes on, the uptime time stamp becomes more coarse and difficult to interpret. In the following output, an interface went down 20 weeks and 2 days after the switch was booted. Someone made a configuration change 21 weeks and 3 days after the switch booted. At exactly what date and time did that occur? Who knows!

```
20w2d: %LINK-3-UPDOWN: Interface FastEthernet1/0/27, changed state to down
21w3d: %SYS-5-CONFIG_I: Configured from console by vty0 (172.25.15.246)
```

Instead, you can configure the switch to add accurate clock-like time stamps that are easily interpreted. Sometimes you also will need to correlate events in the logs of several network devices. In that case, it is important to synchronize the clocks (and time stamps) across all those devices.

Setting the Internal System Clock

Each Cisco switch has an internal time clock that runs continuously without any intervention. However, do not assume that a switch already has its internal clock set to the correct date and time. You can use the **show clock** command to find out, as in the following example:

```
Switch# show clock
*00:54:09.691 UTC Mon Mar 1 1993
Switch#
```

Here the clock has been set to its default value, and it is March 1, 1993! Clearly, that is not useful at all.

You can use the following commands as a guideline to define the time zone and summer (daylight savings) time and to set the clock:

```
Switch(config)# clock timezone name offset-hours [offset-minutes]
Switch(config)# clock summer-time name date start-month date year hh:mm
  end-month day year hh:mm [offset-minutes]
```

Or

```
Switch(config)# clock summer-time name recurring [start-week day month
  hh:mm end-week day month hh:mm [offset-minutes]
Switch(config)# exit
Switch# clock set hh:mm:ss
```

In the following example, the switch is configured for the eastern time zone in the U.S. and the clock is set for 3:23 p.m. If no other parameters are given with the **clock summer-time recurring** command, U.S. daylight savings time is assumed:

```
Switch(config)# clock timezone EST -5
Switch(config)# clock summer-time EDT recurring
Switch(config)# exit
Switch# clock set 15:23:00
```

Using NTP to Synchronize with an External Time Source

To synchronize the clocks across multiple switches in your network from common, trusted time sources, you should use the Network Time Protocol (NTP). Each switch still maintains its own internal clock, but each periodically synchronizes its clock with one or more external time sources. The goal is to synchronize to a source with some level of implied trust that the time is accurate. NTP can also cope with the delay that occurs from the time a source transmits its current time until a switch receives the message.

With NTP, time sources or servers are arranged in a hierarchical fashion, with each layer of time servers synchronizing with other servers in a higher layer. Ideally, a networked device should synchronize its time clock with an authoritative source, or one that offers the most accuracy. Authoritative time sources can use an atomic clock or a GPS receiver to maintain very accurate time. However, it often is not practical or scalable to point every device in your network toward one authoritative source. Instead, the time synchronization process can be distributed so that one layer of NTP servers synchronizes with the authoritative source, then another layer of devices synchronizes with the next highest layer, and so on.

Each layer of the hierarchy is known as a *stratum*, where the stratum number indicates the number of NTP "hops" needed to reach the top. Authoritative time servers are located in stratum 1. NTP servers that synchronize with stratum 1 servers are designated as stratum 2. The NTP stratums keep incrementing toward the servers that client devices use for their synchronization, as shown in Figure 13-3.

The NTP hierarchy is also flexible. For example, you might have an authoritative time source located somewhere in your network. You can configure all of your switches, routers, firewalls, and clients to synchronize their clocks with your stratum 1 NTP server. For a more scalable solution, you could configure a few centrally located switches as NTP servers and point them toward stratum 1 servers. Your NTP server switches would then become stratum 2 servers. All of your other devices could then synchronize their clocks with the stratum 2 servers.

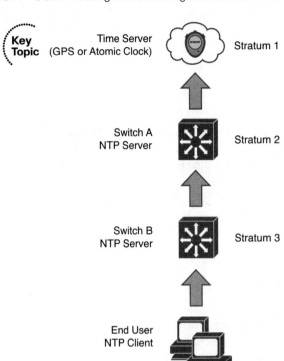

Figure 13-3   *The NTP Hierarchy of Stratums*

The NTP stratum numbers also serve as an indicator of time accuracy. For instance, if a device has a choice of synchronizing with a stratum 4 server or a stratum 3 server, it will prefer the stratum 3 server because it is ultimately better synchronized with an authoritative source.

Table 13-2 lists the possible NTP modes that a device can use.

Table 13-2   *NTP Modes*

NTP Mode	Description
Server	The device synchronizes with a source in a lower stratum and provides time synchronization with servers or clients in a higher stratum.
Client	The device synchronizes its clock with an NTP server.
Peer	The device exchanges time information with another peer device.
Broadcast/multicast	The device operates as an NTP server, but pushes time information out to any listening device. Because the "push" is in only one direction, the time accuracy can suffer somewhat.

To configure NTP on a switch, enter the following command, along with the IP address of an upstream NTP server. You can repeat the **ntp server** command to specify more than one time source to use. In that case, you can add the **prefer** keyword to identify which server to prefer over others. By default, NTP Version 3 is used; NTP Version 4 adds IPv6 capability.

Key Topic

```
Switch(config)# ntp server ip-address [prefer] [version {3 | 4}]
```

Example 13-1 lists the commands used to enable NTP and use the local NTP server at 192.168.2.168 as an authoritative source. A second server at 24.56.178.140 (time.nist.gov) is added as well.

Example 13-1   *Configuring NTP and Identifying Servers*

```
Switch(config)# ntp server 192.168.2.168 prefer
Switch(config)# ntp server 24.56.178.140
```

After NTP is configured and enabled, you can use the **show ntp status** command to verify that the switch clock is synchronized to the NTP server. You can also use the **show ntp associations** command to see a summary of all the NTP relationships a switch has. In Example 13-2, the switch has synchronized its clock with the stratum 1 server at 192.168.2.168. The switch is associated with the server at 192.168.2.168, which uses a GPS receiver as its reference clock, and a server at 24.56.178.140, which uses an atomic clock time source (ACTS).

Example 13-2   *Verifying NTP Operation*

```
Switch# show ntp status
Clock is synchronized, stratum 1, reference is 192.168.2.168
nominal freq is 250.0000 Hz, actual freq is 249.9978 Hz, precision is 2**18
reference time is D74EEAB6.8408DB3D (13:15:34.515 EDT Wed Aug 20 2014)
clock offset is -0.0089 msec, root delay is 0.82 msec
root dispersion is 10.45 msec, peer dispersion is 0.03 msec
Switch#
Switch# show ntp associations
      address         ref clock     st  when  poll reach  delay  offset    disp
*~192.168.2.168     .GPS.            1   335   512  377    3.0   -1.00     0.9
+~24.56.178.140     .ACTS.           1   268   512  377   68.3   -9.90     1.2
 * master (synced), # master (unsynced), + selected, - candidate, ~ configured
Switch#
```

Tip   Be aware that an NTP server can provide accurate time from a global perspective, but it is not able to provide a time zone or seasonal time change information. You should use the **clock timezone** and **clock summer-time** commands to configure a switch to reference the NTP time to its local settings.

Securing NTP

Notice that the NTP configurations in the preceding section reference only the IP addresses of NTP servers, implying that time synchronization is open for any device to use. You can take some additional measures to secure NTP in your network.

First, you can enable NTP authentication. The authentication process does not encrypt the NTP data; it is used to authenticate an NTP server so that the NTP client knows it is a trusted source. Without authentication, a client might mistakenly synchronize its clock with an attacker posing as an NTP server.

Use the following global configuration commands to enable NTP authentication. Define an authentication key, then enable authentication, then specify the authentication key number to use when communicating with an NTP server:

```
Switch(config)# ntp authentication-key key-number md5 key-string
Switch(config)# ntp authenticate
Switch(config)# ntp trusted-key key-number
Switch(config)# ntp server ip-address key key-number
```

NTP authentication only provides a means to validate the server; it does not limit which IP addresses can synchronize time with the server. In fact, any IP address is permitted to synchronize time, even if an authentication key is configured on the server. You should also consider adding an access list to limit which devices can communicate with a switch using NTP.

Use the following global configuration commands to define an access list and to apply it to NTP operation. Only addresses permitted by the access list are allowed to use NTP services:

```
Switch(config)# access-list acl-num permit ip-address mask
Switch(config)# ntp access-group {serve-only | serve | peer | query-only} acl-num
```

For the **ntp access-group** command, you should use one of the following keywords to specify which type of NTP activity should be permitted:

- **serve-only:** Only synchronization requests are permitted.

- **serve:** Synchronization and control requests are permitted; the device is not permitted to synchronize its own time clock.

- **peer:** Synchronization and control requests are permitted; the device can synchronize its own time clock.

- **query-only:** Permit only control queries.

Using SNTP to Synchronize Time

In the preceding section, you learned that the **ntp server** command enables NTP so that a switch can synchronize its clock with a specified server. You might be surprised to learn that the command also enables the NTP service on every configured Layer 3 interface so that the switch becomes an NTP server for any other device that tries to synchronize time with it.

As its name implies, the Simplified Network Time Protocol (SNTP) offers a reduced set of NTP functions. When a switch is configured for SNTP, it operates as an NTP client only. In other words, the switch can synchronize its clock with an NTP server, but it cannot allow other devices to synchronize from its own clock. Time synchronization is also simplified, resulting in a slightly less accurate result.

To configure SNTP, use the typical NTP commands and substitute **sntp** for the **ntp** keyword. For example, the following SNTP configuration commands correspond to their NTP counterparts:

```
Switch(config)# sntp authentication-key key-number md5 key-string
Switch(config)# sntp authenticate
Switch(config)# sntp trusted-key key-number
Switch(config)# sntp server ip-address key key-number
```

Adding Time Stamps to Logging Messages

Finally, you can use the following command to begin using the switch clock as an accurate time stamp for syslog messages:

```
Switch(config)# service timestamps log datetime [localtime] [show-timezone] [msec]
[year]
```

Use the **localtime** keyword to use the local time zone configured on the switch; otherwise, coordinated universal time (UTC) is assumed. Add the **show-timezone** keyword if you want the time zone name added to the time stamps. Use the **msec** keyword to add milliseconds and the **year** keyword to add the year to the time stamps.

In the following example, the local time zone and milliseconds have been added into the time stamps of the logging messages shown:

```
Switch(config)# service timestamps log datetime localtime show-timezone msec
Switch(config)# exit
Switch# show logging
*May  2 02:39:23.871 EDT: %DIAG-SP-6-DIAG_OK: Module 1: Passed Online Diagnostics
*May  2 02:39:27.827 EDT: %HSRP-5-STATECHANGE: Vlan62 Grp 1 state Standby ->
Active
*May  2 02:41:40.431 EDT: %OIR-SP-6-INSCARD: Card inserted in slot 9, interfaces
are now online
*May  3 08:24:13.944 EDT: %IP-4-DUPADDR: Duplicate address 10.1.2.1 on Vlan5,
sourced by 0025.64eb.216f
*May 13 09:55:57.139 EDT: %SYS-5-CONFIG_I: Configured from console by herring on
vty0 (10.1.1.7)
```

Exam Preparation Tasks

Review All Key Topics

Review the most important topics in the chapter, noted with the Key Topic icon in the outer margin of the page. Table 13-3 lists a reference of these key topics and the page numbers on which each is found.

Table 13-3   *Key Topics for Chapter 13*

Key Topic Element	Description	Page Number
Figure 13-2	Syslog security levels	309
Figure 13-3	NTP hierarchy	314
Paragraph	Configuring an NTP server	315
Paragraph	Adding time stamps to logging messages	317

Complete Tables and Lists from Memory

Print a copy of Appendix C, "Memory Tables," (found on the CD), or at least the section for this chapter, and complete the tables and lists from memory. Appendix D, "Memory Table Answer Key," also on the CD, includes completed tables and lists to check your work.

Define Key Terms

Define the following key terms from this chapter, and check your answers in the glossary:

NTP, stratum, syslog, syslog severity level

Use Command Reference to Check Your Memory

This section includes the most important configuration and EXEC commands covered in this chapter. It might not be necessary to memorize the complete syntax of every command, but you should remember the basic keywords that are needed.

To test your memory of the port configuration commands, cover the right side of Tables 13-4 and 13-5 with a piece of paper, read the description on the left side, and then see how much of the command you can remember.

Remember that the CCNP exam focuses on practical or hands-on skills that are used by a networking professional. Therefore, you should remember the commands needed to configure and test a switch interface.

Table 13-4 *Switch Logging Configuration Commands*

Task	Command Syntax
Log to the console port.	Switch(config)# **logging console** *severity*
Log to a buffer.	Switch(config)# **logging buffered** *severity* Switch(config)# **logging buffered** *size*
Display the logging buffer.	Switch# **show logging**
Log to a syslog server.	Switch(config)# **logging host** Switch(config)# **logging trap** *severity*

Table 13-5 *Time Clock Configuration Commands*

Task	Command Syntax
Display the clock.	Switch# **show clock** [detail]
Set the local time zone.	Switch(config)# **clock timezone** *name offset-hours* [*offset-minutes*] Switch(config)# **clock summer-time** *name* **date** *start-month date year hh:mm end-month day year hh:mm* [*offset-minutes*]
Synchronize with an NTP server.	Switch(config)# **ntp server** *ip-address* [prefer] [version {3 | 4}]
Verify NTP synchronization.	Switch# **show ntp status** Switch# **show ntp associations**
Use NTP authentication.	Switch(config)# **ntp authentication-key** *key-number* **md5** *key-string* Switch(config)# **ntp authenticate** Switch(config)# **ntp trusted-key** *key-number* Switch(config)# **ntp server** *ip-address* **key** *key-number*
Limit NTP access.	Switch(config)# **access-list** *acl-num* **permit** *ip-address mask* Switch(config)# **ntp access-group** {serve-only | serve | peer | query-only} *acl-num*
Add time stamps to logging messages.	Switch(config)# **service timestamps log datetime** [localtime] [show-timezone] [msec] [year]

This chapter covers the following topics that you need to master for the CCNP SWITCH exam:

■ **SNMP Overview:** This section discusses SNMP basics such as the system roles, data organization, data operations, and SNMP versions.

■ **Configuring SNMP:** This section explains the steps and commands required to configure each SNMP version on a switch.

CHAPTER 14

Managing Switches with SNMP

The Simple Network Management Protocol (SNMP) can be used to manage switches and other network devices remotely, usually from a central network management platform. This chapter discusses three versions of SNMP that you can leverage to lighten the administrative load when you are monitoring or configuring many switches.

"Do I Know This Already?" Quiz

The "Do I Know This Already?" quiz allows you to assess whether you should read this entire chapter thoroughly or jump to the "Exam Preparation Tasks" section. If you are in doubt based on your answers to these questions or your own assessment of your knowledge of the topics, read the entire chapter. Table 14-1 outlines the major headings in this chapter and the "Do I Know This Already?" quiz questions that go with them. You can find the answers in Appendix A, "Answers to the 'Do I Know This Already?' Quizzes."

Table 14-1 *"Do I Know This Already?" Foundation Topics Section-to-Question Mapping*

Foundation Topics Section	Questions Covered in This Section
SNMP Overview	1–4
Configuring SNMP	5–8

1. SNMP access is configured on a switch. Which one of the following roles does the switch play during SNMP communication?

    a. SNMP agent

    b. SNMP server

    c. SNMP manager

    d. SNMP responder

2. Which one of the following contains information about a switch, its interfaces, and many other counters and statistics?

    a. FIB

    b. RIB

    c. MIB

    d. OID

3. SNMP communication utilizes which one of the following protocols and port numbers?

    a. GRE port 2

    b. UDP port 112

    c. TCP port 21

    d. UDP port 161

    e. TCP port 443

4. Which one of the following event message types is sent via SNMP and must be acknowledged?

    a. SNMP poll

    b. SNMP trap

    c. SNMP inform

    d. SNMP alarm

5. Which one of the following credentials does SNMPv1 use to authenticate management platforms?

    a. Username

    b. Community string

    c. Group name

    d. Certificate

6. Which SNMP version can use MD5 or SHA as a security means to authenticate packets?

    a. SNMPv1

    b. SNMPv2

    c. SNMPv2C

    d. SNMPv3

7. The **snmp-server host** command is used to define which one of the following?

   a. The polling SNMP manager

   b. The SNMP user's machine

   c. The machine that will receive traps and informs

   d. The machines that are allowed to poll

8. SNMPv3 can leverage which of the following attributes to control access to switch information? (Choose all that apply.)

   a. SNMP group

   b. SNMP user

   c. IP address

   d. SNMP view

   e. All of these answers are correct.

Foundation Topics

SNMP Overview

The Simple Network Management Protocol (SNMP) enables a network device to share information about itself and its activities. A complete SNMP system consists of the following parts:

- **SNMP manager:** A network management system that uses SNMP to poll and receive data from any number of network devices. The SNMP manager usually is an application that runs in a central location.

- **SNMP agent:** A process that runs on the network device being monitored. All types of data are gathered by the device itself and stored in a local database. The agent can then respond to SNMP polls and queries with information from the database, and it can send unsolicited alerts or "traps" to an SNMP manager.

In the case of Catalyst switches in the network, each switch automatically collects data about itself, its resources, and each of its interfaces. This data is stored in a Management Information Base (MIB) database in memory and is updated in real time.

The MIB is organized in a structured, hierarchical fashion, forming a tree structure. In fact, the entire MIB is really a collection of variables that are stored in individual, more granular MIBs that form the branches of the tree. Each MIB is based on the Abstract Syntax Notation 1 (ASN.1) language. Each variable in the MIB is referenced by an object identifier (OID), which is a long string of concatenated indexes that follow the path from the root of the tree all the way to the variable's location. For example, a counter for the number of inbound bytes on an interface can be found at OID 1.3.6.1.2.1.2.2.1.10 in the IF (interface) MIB.

Fortunately, only the SNMP manager and agent need to be concerned with interpreting the MIBs. As far as the SWITCH exam and course go, you should just be aware that the MIB structure exists and that it contains everything about a switch that can be monitored.

To see any of the MIB data, an SNMP manager must send an SNMP poll or query to the switch. The query contains the OID of the specific variable being requested so that the agent running on the switch knows what information to return. An SNMP manager can use the following mechanisms to communicate with an SNMP agent, all over UDP port 161:

- **Get request:** The value of one specific MIB variable is needed.

- **Get next request:** The next or subsequent value following an initial get request is needed.

- **Get bulk request:** Whole tables or lists of values in a MIB variable are needed.

- **Set request:** A specific MIB variable needs to be set to a value.

SNMP polls or requests are usually sent by the SNMP manager at periodic intervals. This makes real-time monitoring difficult because changing variables will not be noticed until the next poll cycle. However, SNMP agents can send unsolicited alerts to notify the SNMP manager of real-time events at any time. Alerts can be sent using the following mechanisms over UDP port 162:

- **SNMP trap:** News of an event (interface state change, device failure, and so on) is sent without any acknowledgment that the trap has been received.

- **Inform request:** News of an event is sent to an SNMP manager, and the manager is required to acknowledge receipt by echoing the request back to the agent.

As network management has evolved, SNMP has developed into three distinct versions. The original, SNMP Version 1 (SNMPv1), is defined in RFC 1157. It uses simple one-variable Get and Set requests, along with simple SNMP traps. SNMP managers can gain access to SNMP agents by matching a simple "community" text string. When a manager wants to read or write a MIB variable on a device, it sends the community string in the clear, as part of the request. The request is granted if that community string matches the agent's community string.

In theory, only managers and agents belonging to the same community should be able to communicate. In practice, any device has the potential to read or write variables to an agent's MIB database by sending the right community string, whether it is a legitimate SNMP manager or not. This creates a huge security hole in SNMPv1.

The second version of SNMP, SNMPv2C (RFC 1901), was developed to address some efficiency and security concerns. For example, SNMPv2C adds 64-bit variable counters, extending the useful range of values over the 32-bit counters used in SNMPv1. With 64-bit counters, a switch can keep track of very large numbers, such as byte counters found on high-speed interfaces.

In addition, SNMPv2C offers the bulk request, by which MIB variables can be retrieved in a bulk form with a single request. Event notifications sent from an SNMPv2C agent can be in the form of SNMP traps or inform requests. The latter form requires an acknowledgment from the SNMP manager that the inform message was received. Despite the intentions of its developers, SNMPv2C does not address any security concerns over that of SNMPv1. In addition, there were other implementations of SNMPv2 that were incompatible with SNMPv2C, which acted as a further deterrent to its acceptance.

The third generation of SNMP, SNMPv3, is defined in RFCs 3410 through 3415. It addresses the security features that are lacking in the earlier versions. SNMPv3 can authenticate SNMP managers through usernames. When usernames are configured on the SNMP agent of a switch, they can be organized into SNMPv3 group names. In addition, access to MIB information can be controlled on a per-group basis. You can configure a "view" that defines which MIB variable trees can be read or written.

Each SNMPv3 group is defined with a security level that describes the extent to which the SNMP data will be protected. Data packets can be authenticated to preserve their integrity, encrypted to obscure their contents, or both. The following security levels are available. The naming scheme uses auth to represent packet authentication and priv to represent data privacy or encryption:

- **noAuthNoPriv:** SNMP packets are neither authenticated nor encrypted.

- **authNoPriv:** SNMP packets are authenticated but not encrypted.

- **authPriv:** SNMP packets are authenticated and encrypted.

As a best practice, you should use SNMPv3 to leverage its superior security features whenever possible. If you must use SNMPv1 for a device, you should configure the switch to limit SNMP access to a read-only role. Never permit read-write access because the simple community string authentication can be exploited to make unexpected changes to a switch configuration.

Catalyst switches offer one additional means of limiting SNMP access—an access list can be configured to permit only specific (and known) SNMP manager IP addresses. You should configure and apply an access list to your SNMP configurations whenever possible.

Because SNMP is a universal method for monitoring all sorts of network devices, it is not unique to LAN switches. Therefore, you should understand the basics of how SNMP works, the differences between the different SNMP versions, and how you might apply SNMP to monitor a switched network. You can use Table 14-2 as a memory aid for your exam study.

Key Topic

Table 14-2 *Comparison of SNMP Versions and Features*

Version	Authentication	Data Protection	Unique Features
SNMPv1	Community string	None	32-bit counters
SNMPv2c	Community string	None	Adds bulk request and inform request message types, 64-bit counters
SNMPv3	Username	Hash-based MAC (SHA or MD5)DES, 3DES, AES (128-, 192-, 256-bit) encryption	Adds user authentication, data integrity, and encryptionAdds restricted views

Configuring SNMP

SNMP is normally available in three versions. As a best practice, though, you should use SNMPv3. You can find information about configuring all three versions in the sections that follow.

Configuring SNMPv1

You should be familiar with the basic SNMPv1 configuration. Fortunately, this involves just a few commands, as follows:

```
Switch(config)# access-list access-list-number permit ip-addr
Switch(config)# snmp-server community community-string [ro | rw] [access-list-
number]
!
Switch(config)# snmp-server host host-address community-string [trap-type]
```

First, define a standard IP access list that permits only the IP addresses of your SNMP agent machines. Then apply that access list to the SNMPv1 community string with the **snmp-server community** command. Use the **ro** keyword to allow read-only access by the SNMP manager; otherwise, you can use the **rw** keyword to allow both read and write access.

Finally, use the **snmp-server host** command to identify the IP address of the SNMP manager where SNMP traps will be sent. By default, all types of traps are sent. You can use the **?** key in place of *trap-type* to see a list of the available trap types.

In Example 14-1, the switch is configured to allow SNMP polling from network management stations at 192.168.3.99 and 192.168.100.4 only. The community string **MonitorIt** is used to authenticate the SNMP requests. All possible SNMP traps are sent to 192.168.3.99.

Example 14-1   *Configuring SNMPv1 Access*

```
Switch(config)# access-list 10 permit 192.168.3.99
Switch(config)# access-list 10 permit 192.168.100.4
Switch(config)# snmp-server community MonitorIt ro 10
Switch(config)# snmp-server host 192.168.3.99 MonitorIt
```

Configuring SNMPv2C

Configuring SNMPv2C is similar to configuring SNMPv1. The only difference is with SNMP trap or inform configuration. You can use the following commands to configure basic SNMPv2C operation:

```
Switch(config)# access-list access-list-number permit ip-addr
Switch(config)# snmp-server community string [ro | rw] [access-list-number]
!
Switch(config)# snmp-server host host-address [informs] version 2c community-
string
```

In the **snmp-server host** command, use the **version 2c** keywords to identify SNMPv2C operation. By default, regular SNMP traps are sent. To use inform requests instead, add the **informs** keyword.

Configuring SNMPv3

Key Topic

SNMPv3 configuration is a bit more involved than versions 1 or 2C, due mainly to the additional security features. You can use the following steps to configure SNMPv3 on a switch:

Step 1.   You can limit which hosts can access the switch via SNMP by defining a named or numbered IP access list. Permitted addresses will be given SNMPv3 access.

Step 2.   You can use the **snmp-server view** command to define a specific view for the users. Only the MIB variables located under the OID name given as *oid-tree* will be visible to the user group. For example, ifAdminStatus contains the interface administrative status, ifDescr contains the interface description, and so on. You can repeat the **snmp-server view** command to add additional OID names to the view:

```
Switch(config)# snmp-server view view-name oid-tree
```

If no view is configured, all MIB variables are visible to the users.

Step 3.   Use the **snmp-server group** command to configure a group name that will set the security level policies for SNMPv3 users that are assigned to the group. The security level is defined by the **noauth** (no packet authentication or encryption), **auth** (packets are authenticated but not encrypted), or **priv** (packets are both authenticated and encrypted) keyword. Only the security policy is defined in the group; no passwords or keys are required yet.

Tip   The SNMPv3 **priv** keyword and packet encryption can be used only if the switch is running a cryptographic version of its Cisco IOS Software image. The **auth** keyword and packet authentication can be used regardless.

If you configured a view, you can use the **read**, **write**, and **notify** keywords to limit access to read, write, or notification operations. If you configured an access list, you can apply it to the group with the **access** keyword:

```
Switch(config)# snmp-server group group-name v3 {noauth | auth | priv}
[read read-view] [write write-view] [notify notify-view] [access access-
list]
```

Step 4.   Define a username that an SNMP manager will use to communicate with the switch. Use the **snmp-server user** command to define the *user-name* and associate it with the SNMPv3 *group-name*. The **v3** keyword configures the user to use SNMPv3.

The SNMPv3 user must also have some specifics added to its security policy. Use the **auth** keyword to define either message digest 5 (MD5) authentication or the secure hash algorithm (SHA) as the packet authentication method, along with the *auth-password* text string that will be used in the hash computation. The **priv** keyword defines the encryption method (DES, 3DES, or AES 128/192/256-bit) and the *priv-password* text string that will be used in the encryption algorithm.

```
Switch(config)# snmp-server user user-name group-name v3 auth {md5 |
sha} auth-password priv {des | 3des | aes {128 | 192 | 256} priv-
password [access-list-number]
```

The same SNMPv3 username, authentication method and password, and encryption method and password must also be defined on the SNMP manager so it can successfully talk to the switch.

Step 5. You can use the **snmp-server host** command to identify the SNMP manager that will receive either traps or informs. The switch can use SNMPv3 to send traps and informs, using the security parameters that are defined for the SNMPv3 *username*:

```
Switch(config)# snmp-server host host-address [informs] version 3
{noauth | auth |priv} username [trap-type]
```

In Example 14-2, a switch is configured for SNMPv3 operation. Access list 10 permits only stations at 192.168.3.99 and 192.168.100.4 with SNMP access. SNMPv3 access is defined for a group named NetOps using the **priv** (authentication and encryption) security level. One SNMPv3, a user named mymonitor, is defined; the network management station will use that username when it polls the switch for information. The username will require SHA packet authentication and AES-128 encryption, using the s3cr3tauth and s3cr3tpr1v passwords, respectively.

Finally, SNMPv3 informs will be used to send alerts to station 192.168.3.99 using the **priv** security level and username mymonitor.

Example 14-2 *Configuring SNMPv3 Access*

```
Switch(config)# access-list 10 permit 192.168.3.99
Switch(config)# access-list 10 permit 192.168.100.4
Switch(config)# snmp-server group NetOps v3 priv
Switch(config)# snmp-server user mymonitor NetOps v3 auth sha s3cr3tauth priv aes
  128 s3cr3tpr1v 10
Switch(config)# snmp-server host 192.168.3.99 informs version 3 priv mymonitor
```

Exam Preparation Tasks

Review All Key Topics

Review the most important topics in the chapter, noted with the Key Topic icon in the outer margin of the page. Table 14-3 lists a reference of these key topics and the page numbers on which each is found.

Table 14-3 *Key Topics for Chapter 14*

Key Topic Element	Description	Page Number
List	Describes the SNMP manager and agent roles	324
Table 14-2	Lists the SNMP versions and unique features	326
Step list	Lists the configuration steps necessary to implement SNMPv3	328

Complete Tables and Lists from Memory

Print a copy of Appendix C, "Memory Tables," (found on the CD), or at least the section for this chapter, and complete the tables and lists from memory. Appendix D, "Memory Table Answer Key," also on the CD, includes completed tables and lists to check your work.

Define Key Terms

Define the following key terms from this chapter, and check your answers in the glossary:

MIB, OID, Simple Network Management Protocol (SNMP), SNMP manager, SNMP agent, SNMP inform, SNMP trap

Use Command Reference to Check Your Memory

This section includes the most important configuration and EXEC commands covered in this chapter. It might not be necessary to memorize the complete syntax of every command, but you should remember the basic keywords that are needed.

To test your memory of the SNMP configuration commands, cover the right side of Table 14-4 with a piece of paper, read the description on the left side, and then see how much of the command you can remember.

Table 14-4 *SNMP Configuration Commands*

Task	Command Syntax
Define SNMPv1 or SNMPv2C access.	Switch(config)# **snmp-server community** *community-string* [**ro**	**rw**] [*access-list-number*]
Define an SNMPv1 trap receiver.	Switch(config)# **snmp-server host** *host-address community-string* [*trap-type*]
Define an SNMPv2C trap or inform receiver.	Switch(config)# **snmp-server host** *host-address* [**informs**] **version 2c** *community-string*
Define an SNMPv3 view.	Switch(config)# **snmp-server view** *view-name oid-tree*
Define an SNMPv3 user group.	Switch(config)# **snmp-server group** *group-name* **v3** {**noauth**	**auth**	**priv**} [**read** *read-view*] [**write** *write-view*] [**notify** *notify-view*] [**access** *access-list*]
Define an SNMPv3 user.	Switch(config)# **snmp-server user** *user-name group-name* **v3 auth** {**md5**	**sha** *auth-password* **priv** {**des**	**3des**	**aes** {**128**	**192**	**256**} *priv-password* [*access-list*]
Define an SNMPv3 trap or inform receiver.	Switch(config)# **snmp-server host** *host-address* [**informs**] **version 3** {**noauth**	**auth**	**priv**} *user-name* [*trap-type*]

This chapter covers the following topics that you need to master for the CCNP SWITCH exam:

- **IP SLA Overview:** This section provides a brief overview of the IP SLA feature and how you can use it to measure network performance.

- **Configuring IP SLA:** This section explains how you can configure several types of IP SLA tests on Cisco Catalyst switches.

- **Using IP SLA:** This section discusses ways you can set up IP SLA tests and interpret their results.

CHAPTER 15

Monitoring Performance with IP SLA

Switches routinely transport data throughout a network, based on their configuration and how they are interconnected. A well-designed network might move packets efficiently, but many other factors, such as actual traffic loads and link conditions, can change over time and impact time-critical applications.

Once a network is built, you might have a hard time gauging how well it is performing from an end-user perspective. This chapter explains how you can leverage the switches themselves to actively test end-to-end network performance.

"Do I Know This Already?" Quiz

The "Do I Know This Already?" quiz allows you to assess whether you should read this entire chapter thoroughly or jump to the "Exam Preparation Tasks" section. If you are in doubt based on your answers to these questions or your own assessment of your knowledge of the topics, read the entire chapter. Table 15-1 outlines the major headings in this chapter and the "Do I Know This Already?" quiz questions that go with them. You can find the answers in Appendix A, "Answers to the 'Do I Know This Already?' Quizzes."

Table 15-1 *"Do I Know This Already?" Foundation Topics Section-to-Question Mapping*

Foundation Topics Section	Questions Covered in This Section
IP SLA Overview	1-2
Configuring IP SLA	3-4
Using IP SLA	5-6

1. Is the following statement true or false? To use the IP SLA feature, a third-party network management platform must be used.

    a. True

    b. False

2. Which of the following are valid types of IP SLA tests? (Choose all that apply.)

   a. ICMP echo

   b. ICMP time exceeded

   c. UDP jitter

   d. UDP connect

   e. TCP jitter

   f. TCP connect

3. Which one of the following commands will enable a switch to participate in all types of IP SLA tests?

   a. ip sla enable

   b. ip sla all

   c. ip sla reflector

   d. ip sla responder

   e. ip sla reply all

4. Suppose the following configuration commands have been entered on Switch A, which has IP address 10.1.1.1. Which one of the answers correctly identifies the configuration that is needed on the target switch so it can participate in the UDP jitter tests?

```
ip sla 40132
 udp-jitter 10.9.1.100 17000 source-ip 10.1.1.1  num-packets 100
 request-data-size 100
 frequency 300
ip sla schedule 40132 life forever start-time now ageout 3600
```

   a. Enter the same set of commands on the target switch.

   b. Enter the ip sla responder command on the target switch.

   c. Do nothing; the target switch will automatically participate.

   d. Do nothing; UDP jitter is not a valid IP SLA test.

5. To verify that an IP SLA test operation 123 has been configured and is scheduled to run, which one of the following commands should you use?

   a. show ip sla status 123

   b. show ip sla configuration 123

   c. show ip sla operation 123

   d. show ip sla 123

6. According to the following output, how many IP SLA tests have run and gotten results? (Choose one answer.)

```
Switch# show ip sla statistics aggregated 123
Round Trip Time (RTT) for        Index 123
Start Time Index: 09:53:57.314 EDT Fri Aug 8 2014
Type of operation: jitter
Voice Scores:
MinOfICPIF: 0    MaxOfICPIF: 0    MinOfMOS: 0      MaxOfMOS: 0
RTT Values
        Number Of RTT: 1100
        RTT Min/Avg/Max: 1/3/6 ms
Latency one-way time milliseconds
        Number of Latency one-way Samples: 1046
        Source to Destination Latency one way Min/Avg/Max: 0/0/3 ms
        Destination to Source Latency one way Min/Avg/Max: 1/2/4 ms
Jitter time milliseconds
        Number of SD Jitter Samples: 1089
        Number of DS Jitter Samples: 1089
        Source to Destination Jitter Min/Avg/Max: 0/1/3 ms
        Destination to Source Jitter Min/Avg/Max: 0/1/3 ms
Packet Loss Values
        Loss Source to Destination: 0      Loss Destination to Source: 0
        Out Of Sequence: 0      Tail Drop: 0
        Packet Late Arrival: 0  Packet Skipped: 0
Number of successes: 238
Number of failures: 7
```

a. 123

b. 1100

c. 1046

d. 238

e. 7

Foundation Topics

IP SLA Overview

The Cisco IOS IP Service Level Agreement (IP SLA) feature enables you to gather realistic information about how specific types of traffic are being handled end to end across a network. To do this, an IP SLA device runs a preconfigured test and generates traffic that is destined for a far-end device. As the far end responds with packets that are received back at the source, IP SLA gathers data about what happened along the way.

> **Tip**   As the IP SLA feature has evolved, it has been known by several other names. You might also find references to Cisco Response Time Reporter (RTR) and Service Assurance Agent (SAA).

IP SLA can be configured to perform a variety of tests. The simplest test involves Internet Control Message Protocol (ICMP) echo packets that are sent toward a target address, as shown in Figure 15-1. If the target answers with ICMP echo replies, IP SLA can then assess how well the source and destination were able to communicate. In this case, the echo failures (packet loss) and round-trip transit (RTT) times are calculated, as shown in Example 15-1.

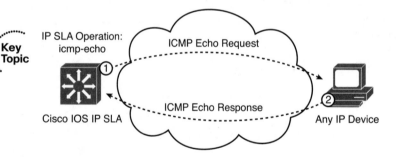

Figure 15-1   *IP SLA ICMP Echo Test Operation*

Example 15-1   *Sample ICMP Echo Test Results*

```
Switch# show ip sla statistics aggregated
Round Trip Time (RTT) for        Index 1
Type of operation: icmp-echo
Start Time Index: 15:10:17.665 EDT Fri Aug 22 2014
RTT Values
        Number Of RTT: 24
        RTT Min/Avg/Max: 1/1/4 ms
Number of successes: 24
Number of failures: 0
```

For the ICMP echo test, IP SLA can use any live device at the far end; after all, most networked devices will reply when they are pinged. IP SLA can also test some network protocols, such as DNS, by sending requests to a server at the far end. Cisco IOS is needed only at the source of the IP SLA test because the far end is simply responding to ordinary request packets.

However, IP SLA is capable of running much more sophisticated tests. Table 15-2 shows some sample test operations that are available with IP SLA.

Table 15-2 *IP SLA Test Operations*

Test Type	Description	IP SLA Required on Target?
icmp-echo	ICMP echo response time	No
path-echo	Hop-by-hop and end-to-end response times over path discovered from ICMP echo	No
path-jitter	Hop-by-hop jitter over ICMP echo path	Yes
dns	DNS query response time	No
dhcp	DHCP IP address request response time	No
ftp	FTP file-retrieval response time	No
http	Web page-retrieval response time	No
udp-echo	End-to-end response time of UDP echo	No
udp-jitter	Round-trip delay, one-way delay, one-way jitter, one-way packet loss, and connectivity using UDP packets	Yes
tcp-connect	Response time to build a TCP connection with a host	No

To leverage its full capabilities, Cisco IOS IP SLA must be available on both the source and the target devices, as shown in Figure 15-2. The source device handles the test scheduling and sets up each test over a special IP SLA control connection with the target device. The source generates the traffic involved in a test operation and analyzes the results as packets return from the target. The target end has a simpler role: respond to the incoming test packets. In fact, the target device is called an *IP SLA responder*.

The responder must also add time stamps to the packets it sends, to flag the time a test packet arrived and the time it left the responder. The idea is to account for any latency incurred while the responder is processing the test packets. For this to work accurately, both the source and responder must synchronize their clocks through NTP.

An IP SLA source device can schedule and keep track of multiple test operations. For example, an ICMP echo operation might run against target 10.1.1.1, while UDP jitter operations are running against targets 10.2.2.2, 10.3.3.3, and 10.4.4.4. Each test runs independently, at a configured frequency and duration.

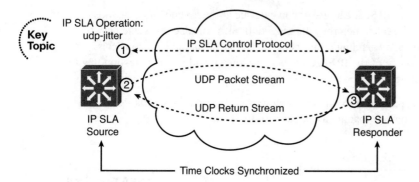

Figure 15-2   *IP SLA UDP Jitter Test Operation*

> **Tip**   To set up an IP SLA operation, the Cisco IP SLA source device begins by opening a control connection to the IP SLA responder over UDP port 1967. The source uses the control connection to inform the responder to begin listening on an additional port where the actual IP SLA test operation will take place.

What in the world does this have to do with LAN switching, and why would you want to run IP SLA on a Catalyst switch anyway? Here's a twofold answer:

- IP SLA will likely appear on your SWITCH exam.

- IP SLA is actually a useful tool in a switched campus network.

To run live tests and take useful measurements without IP SLA, you would need to place some sort of probe devices at various locations in the network—all managed from a central system. With IP SLA, you do not need probes at all! Wherever you have a Catalyst switch, you already have an IP SLA "probe."

By leveraging IP SLA test operations, you can take advantage of some fancy features:

- Generate SNMP traps when certain test thresholds are exceeded

- Schedule further IP SLA tests automatically when test thresholds are crossed

- Track an IP SLA test to trigger a next-hop gateway redundancy protocol, such as Hot Standby Router Protocol (HSRP)

- Gather voice quality measurements from all over a network

Configuring IP SLA

To define an IP SLA operation, you must configure both the source switch and identify the target device. Some test types, such as ICMP echo, can use any target device provided it can reply to the simple test requests. In that case, you do not need to configure anything on the target device.

Other test types, such as UDP jitter, require a target that can negotiate an IP SLA test, keep time stamps during the test, and respond to protocols that do not necessarily require a response. In those cases, the target must be an IP SLA-capable Cisco switch or router. You must enable the IP SLA responder on the target switch so that it can communicate with the source. You should make sure that both switches are configured to use Network Time Protocol (NTP) to synchronize their time clocks with a common, accurate source. Configuring IP SLA on the target switch is easy; just enable the IP SLA responder with the following command. By default, the IP SLA responder is disabled.

```
Switch(config)# ip sla responder
```

Tip   For the most accurate results, you should configure the IP SLA source and target switches to use a trusted NTP server so that the time stamps will be correct and synchronized. NTP configuration is covered in Chapter 13, "Logging Switch Activity."

You can secure IP SLA operations with message digest 5 (MD5) authentication so that only known and trusted devices can participate. Using the following commands, you can define a key chain that consists of keys, each containing an authentication key string. Normally, you will need only one key in the key chain. Assign the key chain to IP SLA with the **ip sla key-chain** command. Be sure to enter the same commands on both the responder and the source switch so that their authentication keys match:

```
Switch(config)# key chain chain-name
Switch(config-keychain)# key key-number
Switch(config-keychain-key)# key-string string
Switch(config-keychain-key)# exit
Switch(config-keychain)# exit
Switch(config)# ip sla key-chain chain-name
```

On the source switch, IP SLA configuration is a bit more involved. You can use the following configuration steps to define and run an IP SLA test operation:

Step 1.   Define a new IP SLA operation on the source switch.

```
Switch(config)# ip sla operation-number
```

The operation-number is an arbitrary index that can range from 1 to a very large number. This number uniquely identifies the test.

Step 2.   Select the type of test operation to perform.

```
Switch(config-ip-sla)# test-type parameters...
```

Some of the possible *test-type* values are the following:

dhcp, dns, ethernet, ftp, http, icmp-echo, mpls, path-echo, path-jitter, slm, tcp-connect, udp-echo, or udp-jitter

The list of parameters following the *test-type* varies according to the test operation. As an example, consider the following **icmp-echo** operation syntax:

```
Switch(config-ip-sla)# icmp-echo destination-ip-addr [source-ip-addr]
```

The parameters are simple: a destination address to ping and an optional source address to use. If a switch has several Layer 3 interfaces, you can specify which one of their IP address to use as the source of the test packets.

As another example, the **udp-jitter** command is useful for testing time-critical traffic paths through a switched network. The command syntax is a little more complex, as follows:

Switch(config-ip-sla)# **udp-jitter** *destination-ip-addr dest-udp-port* [**source-ip** *source-ip-addr*] [**source-port** *source-udp-port*] [**num-packets** *number-of-packets*] [**interval** *packet-interval*]

In addition to the source and destination IP addresses, you can define the UDP port numbers that will be used for the packet stream. By default, 10 packets spaced at 20 milliseconds will be sent. You can override that by specifying the **num-packets** and **interval** keywords.

As an alternative, you can configure the **udp-jitter** operation to test Voice over IP (VoIP) call quality. To do this, the **udp-jitter** command must include the **codec** keyword and a codec definition. The IP SLA operation will then simulate a real-time stream of voice traffic using a specific codec. In this way, you can tailor the test to fit the type of calls that are actually being used in the network.

You can define the UDP jitter codec operation by using the following command syntax:

```
Switch(config-ip-sla)# udp-jitter destination-ip-addr dest-udp-port
codec {g711alaw | g711ulaw | g729a}
```

There are other keywords and parameters you can add to the command, but those are beyond the scope of this book. By default, 1000 packets are sent, 20 milliseconds apart.

Step 3.   Set the frequency of the operation.

By default, IP SLA operations are run at regular 60-second intervals for the lifetime of the test. You can configure the frequency with the following command:

```
Switch(config-ip-sla)# frequency seconds
```

Step 4. Schedule the test operation.

```
Switch(config)# ip sla schedule operation-number [life {forever | sec-
onds}] [start-time {hh:mm[:ss] [month day | day month] | pending | now
| after hh:mm:ss}] [ageout seconds] [recurring]
```

In a nutshell, the **ip sla schedule** command tells the switch when to start the test, how long to let it run, and how long to keep the data that is collected.

Set the lifetime with the **life** keyword: **forever** means the operation will keep running forever, until you manually remove it. Otherwise, specify how many seconds it will run. By default, an IP SLA scheduled operation will run for 3600 seconds (1 hour).

Set the start time with the **start-time** keyword. You can define the start time as a specific time or date, after a delay with the **after** keyword, or right now with the **now** keyword.

By default, the test statistics are collected and held in memory indefinitely. You can use the **ageout** keyword to specify how many seconds elapse before the data is aged out.

The **recurring** keyword can be used to schedule the test operation to run at the same time each day, as long as you have defined the starting time with *hh:mm:ss*, too.

Tip Be aware that the IP SLA operation command syntax has changed along the way. In Cisco IOS Releases 12.2(33) and later, the syntax is as shown in Steps 2 through 4. Before 12.2(33), the commands in Steps 2 through 4 included additional keywords, as follows:

Step 2. **ip sla monitor** *operation-number*

Step 3. **type** *test-type*

Step 4. **ip sla monitor schedule** *operation-number*

Using IP SLA

After you have configured an IP SLA operation, you can verify the configuration with the **show ip sla configuration** [*operation-number*] command. As an example, the following configuration commands are used to define IP SLA operation 100—an ICMP echo test that pings target 172.25.226.1 every 5 seconds:

```
Switch(config)# ip sla 100
Switch(config-ip-sla)# icmp-echo 172.25.226.1
Switch(config-ip-sla)# frequency 5
Switch(config-ip-sla)# exit
Switch(config)# ip sla schedule 100 life forever start-time now
```

Example 15-2 shows the output of the **show ip sla configuration** command.

Example 15-2 *Displaying the Current IP SLA Configuration*

```
Switch# show ip sla configuration
IP SLAs, Infrastructure Engine-II
Entry number: 100
Owner:
Tag:
Type of operation to perform: echo
Target address: 172.25.226.1
Source address: 0.0.0.0
Request size (ARR data portion): 28
Operation timeout (milliseconds): 5000
Type Of Service parameters: 0x0
Verify data: No
Vrf Name:
Schedule:
    Operation frequency (seconds): 5
    Next Scheduled Start Time: Start Time already passed
    Group Scheduled : FALSE
    Randomly Scheduled : FALSE
    Life (seconds): Forever
    Entry Ageout (seconds): never
    Recurring (Starting Everyday): FALSE
    Status of entry (SNMP RowStatus): Active
Threshold (milliseconds): 5000
Distribution Statistics:
    Number of statistic hours kept: 2
    Number of statistic distribution buckets kept: 1
    Statistic distribution interval (milliseconds): 20
History Statistics:
    Number of history Lives kept: 0
    Number of history Buckets kept: 15
    History Filter Type: None
Enhanced History:
```

You can use the **show ip sla statistics [aggregated]** [*operation-number*] command to display the IP SLA test analysis. By default, the most recent test results are shown. You can add the **aggregated** keyword to show a summary of the data gathered over the life of the operation. Example 15-3 shows the statistics gathered for ICMP echo operation 100.

Example 15-3 *Displaying IP SLA Statistics*

```
Switch# show ip sla statistics 100
Round Trip Time (RTT) for       Index 100
        Latest RTT: 1 ms
```

```
Latest operation start time: 15:52:00.834 EDT Fri Aug 29 2014
Latest operation return code: OK
Number of successes: 117
Number of failures: 0
Operation time to live: Forever

Switch# show ip sla statistics aggregated 100
Round Trip Time (RTT) for        Index 100
Type of operation: icmp-echo
Start Time Index: 15:43:55.842 EDT Fri Aug 29 2014
RTT Values
        Number Of RTT: 121
        RTT Min/Avg/Max: 1/1/4 ms
Number of successes: 121
Number of failures: 0
```

It is not too difficult to configure an IP SLA operation manually and check the results every now and then. But does IP SLA have any greater use? Yes, you can also use an IP SLA operation to make some other switch features change behavior automatically, without any other intervention.

For example, HSRP can track the status of an IP SLA operation to automatically decrement the priority value when the target device stops answering ICMP echo packets. To do this, begin by using the **track** command to define a unique track object-number index that will be bound to the IP SLA operation number.

```
Switch(config)# track object-number ip sla operation-number {state | reachability}
```

You can use the **state** keyword to track the return code or state of the IP SLA operation; the state is up if the IP SLA test was successful or down if it was not. The **reachability** keyword differs slightly: The result is up if the IP SLA operation is successful or has risen above a threshold; otherwise, the reachability is down.

Next, configure the HSRP standby group to use the tracked object to control the priority decrement value. As long as the tracked object (the IP SLA operation) is up or successful, the HSRP priority stays unchanged. If the tracked object is down, the HSRP priority is decremented by *decrement-value* (default 10):

```
Switch(config-if)# standby group track object-number decrement decrement-value
```

Tip   HSRP configuration is covered in greater detail in Chapter 18, "Layer 3 High Availability."

In Example 15-4, Switches A and B are configured as an HSRP pair, sharing gateway address 192.168.1.1. Switch A has a higher priority (120) than Switch B (the default 100), so it is normally the active gateway. However, it is configured to ping an upstream router at 192.168.70.1 every 5 seconds; if that router does not respond, Switch A will decrement its HSRP priority by 30, permitting Switch B to take over.

Example 15-4   *Tracking an IP SLA Operation in an HSRP Group*

```
Switch-A(config)# ip sla 10
Switch-A(config-ip-sla)# icmp-echo 192.168.70.1
Switch-A(config-ip-sla)# frequency 5
Switch-A(config-ip-sla)# exit
Switch-A(config)# ip sla schedule 10 life forever start-time now

Switch-A(config)# track 1 ip sla 10 reachability

Switch-A(config)# interface vlan10
Switch-A(config-if)# ip address 192.168.1.3 255.255.255.0
Switch-A(config-if)# standby 1 priority 120
Switch-A(config-if)# standby 1 track 1 decrement 30
Switch-A(config-if)# standby 1 preempt
Switch-A(config-if)# no shutdown
```

In some cases, you might need many IP SLA operations to take many measurements in a network. For example, you could use UDP jitter operations to measure voice call quality across many different parts of the network. Manually configuring and monitoring more than a few IP SLA operations can become overwhelming and impractical. Instead, you can leverage a network management application that can set up and monitor IP SLA tests automatically. To do this, the network management system needs SNMP read and write access to each switch that will use IP SLA. Tests are configured by writing to the IP SLA MIB, and results are gathered by reading the MIB.

Exam Preparation Tasks

Review All Key Topics

Review the most important topics in the chapter, noted with the Key Topic icon in the outer margin of the page. Table 15-3 lists a reference of these key topics and the page numbers on which each is found.

Key Topic

Table 15-3   *Key Topics for Chapter 15*

Key Topic Element	Description	Page Number
Figure 15-1	IP SLA ICMP echo test	336
Table 15-2	IP SLA test types	337
Figure 15-2	IP SLA UDP Jitter test	338

Complete Tables and Lists from Memory

There are no memory tables in this chapter.

Define Key Terms

Define the following key terms from this chapter, and check your answers in the glossary:

IP SLA, IP SLA responder

Use Command Reference to Check Your Memory

This section includes the most important configuration and EXEC commands covered in this chapter. It might not be necessary to memorize the complete syntax of every command, but you should remember the basic keywords that are needed.

To test your memory of the VLAN and trunk-related commands, cover the right side of Table 15-4 with a piece of paper, read the description on the left side, and then see how much of the command you can remember.

Remember that the CCNP exam focuses on practical or hands-on skills that are used by a networking professional.

Table 15-4   *IP SLA Configuration and Monitoring Commands*

Task	Command Syntax
Enable IP SLA responder.	Switch(config)# **ip sla responder**
Authenticate IP SLA operations.	Switch(config)# **key chain** *chain-name* Switch(config-keychain)# **key** *key-number* Switch(config-keychain-key)# **key-string** *string* Switch(config-keychain-key)# **exit** Switch(config-keychain)# **exit** Switch(config)# **ip sla key-chain** *chain-name*
Define a new IP SLA operation.	Switch(config)# **ip sla** *operation-number*
Define an ICMP echo test.	Switch(config-ip-sla)# **icmp-echo** *destination-ip-addr* [*source-ip-addr*]
Define a UDP jitter test.	Switch(config-ip-sla)# **udp-jitter** *destination-ip-addr dest-udp-port* [**source-ip** *source-ip-addr*] [**source-port** *source-udp-port*] [**num-packets** *number-of-packets*] [**interval** *packet-interval*]
Define UDP jitter codec.	Switch(config-ip-sla)# **udp-jitter** *destination-ip-addr dest-udp-port* **codec** {**g711alaw** | **g711ulaw** | **g729a**}
Set the test frequency.	Switch(config-ip-sla)# **frequency** *seconds*
Set the test schedule.	Switch(config)# **ip sla schedule** *operation-number* [**life** {**forever** | *seconds*}] [**start-time** {*hh:mm[:ss]* [*month day* | *day month*] | **pending** | **now** | **after** *hh:mm:ss*}] [**ageout** *seconds*] [**recurring**]
Display the IP SLA test configuration.	Switch# **show ip sla configuration** [*operation-number*]
Display the results of an IP SLA test operation.	Switch# **show ip sla statistics** [*operation-number*] [**aggregated**] [**detail**]

This chapter covers the following topics that you need to master for the CCNP SWITCH exam:

■ **Using Local SPAN:** This section explains how you can use a local SPAN session to mirror traffic from one or more interfaces or VLANs to a different interface, so that the traffic can be captured or monitored.

■ **Using Remote SPAN:** This section expands on the local SPAN idea to include traffic monitoring across two switches that are separated from each other.

■ **Managing SPAN Sessions:** This section explains how you can monitor and delete active SPAN sessions on a switch.

CHAPTER 16

Using Port Mirroring to Monitor Traffic

Sometimes network traffic must be monitored for troubleshooting or analysis purposes. By nature, switches try to forward traffic to a destination as directly as possible. As a result, all traffic is not normally flooded to all switch ports, so you cannot simply connect to a switch and monitor interesting traffic flows.

Catalyst switches can mirror traffic passing through switch ports or VLANs onto other ports so that a network analysis device can capture or "listen in" on interesting traffic within the switch. This chapter explains how you can leverage the Switch Port Analysis (SPAN) feature to mirror traffic between ports on the same switch or across a switched network to a remote switch. In fact, SPAN is also commonly known as *port mirroring*.

"Do I Know This Already?" Quiz

The "Do I Know This Already?" quiz allows you to assess whether you should read this entire chapter thoroughly or jump to the "Exam Preparation Tasks" section. If you are in doubt based on your answers to these questions or your own assessment of your knowledge of the topics, read the entire chapter. Table 16-1 outlines the major headings in this chapter and the "Do I Know This Already?" quiz questions that go with them. You can find the answers in Appendix A, "Answers to the 'Do I Know This Already?' Quizzes."

Table 16-1 *"Do I Know This Already?" Foundation Topics Section-to-Question Mapping*

Foundation Topics Section	Questions Covered in This Section
Using Local SPAN	1-3
Using Remote SPAN	4-6
Managing SPAN Sessions	7-8

1. Which of the following allows traffic on one port to be mirrored to another port on the same switch?

   a. VSPAN

   b. RSPAN

   c. Local SPAN

   d. CSPAN

2. A local SPAN session can use which of the following as a source? (Choose all that apply.)

   a. Physical interface

   b. VLAN

   c. SVI

   d. An interface in an EtherChannel

   e. A port-channel interface

3. Which one of the following answers contains the command(s) to correctly configure a local SPAN session to mirror all traffic from interface Gi1/0/13 to interface Gi1/0/27?

   a. monitor session 1 interface gi1/0/13 interface gi1/0/27

   b. monitor interface gi1/0/13 interface gi1/0/27

   c. monitor session 1 source interface gi1/0/13 both

   monitor session 1 destination interface gi1/0/27

   d. monitor session 1 source interface gi1/0/27 both

   monitor session 1 destination interface gi1/0/13

4. Which one of the following must be configured to connect switches used for RSPAN?

   a. An 802.1Q trunk allowing data VLANs

   b. Access mode switch ports (single VLAN)

   c. A private VLAN over a trunk

   d. An RSPAN VLAN over a trunk

5. Which one of the following correctly describes a difference between an RSPAN VLAN and a regular VLAN?

   a. The RSPAN VLAN disables MAC address learning.

   b. The RSPAN VLAN uses static MAC address definitions.

   c. The RSPAN VLAN has the RSPAN source and destination MAC addresses defined in the CAM table.

   d. The RSPAN VLAN cannot be carried over a trunk link.

6. To configure an RSPAN session's source switch, what is used for the session destination?

   a. The switch port leading to the destination switch

   b. The RSPAN VLAN

   c. The final destination switch port

   d. The next-hop router

7. Which two of the following will correctly display active SPAN sessions on a switch?

  a. show span

  b. show monitor

  c. show running-config

  d. show session

8. Suppose a switch has the following SPAN configuration:

```
monitor session 1 source interface gi1/0/1 both
monitor session 1 destination interface gi1/0/48
monitor session 2 source interface gi1/0/1 both
monitor session 2 destination remote vlan 99
```

Which of the following commands will correctly delete only the local SPAN session?
(Choose all that apply.)

  a. no monitor session all

  b. no monitor session 1

  c. no monitor session 2

  d. no monitor session local

  e. no monitor session remote

Foundation Topics

Suppose that a problem exists on your switched network and you want to use a network analyzer to gather data. Of interest is a conversation between two hosts connected to a switch, one on interface Gigabit Ethernet 1/0/1 and the other on Gigabit Ethernet 1/0/47. Both ports are assigned to VLAN 100. Because other devices are already connected there, you must connect your analyzer to a different switch port. If you connect your analyzer to another port on VLAN 100, what will your packet capture show?

Recall that, by definition, switches learn where MAC addresses are located and forward packets directly to those ports. The only time a packet is flooded to ports other than the specific destination is when the destination MAC address has not already been located or when the packet is destined for a broadcast or multicast address. Therefore, your packet capture will show only the broadcast and multicast packets that are being flooded to the analyzer's switch port. None of the conversation between the two hosts of interest will be overheard.

Catalyst switches can use the Switched Port Analyzer (SPAN) feature to mirror traffic from one source switch port or VLAN to a destination port. This allows a monitoring device, such as a network analyzer or "sniffer," to be attached to the destination port for capturing traffic.

When packets arrive on the source port or VLAN, they are specially marked so that they can be copied to the SPAN destination port as they are delivered to the normal destination port. In this way, the packet capture receives an exact copy of the packets that are being forwarded to and from the SPAN source.

SPAN is available in two different forms:

Key Topic

- **Local SPAN:** Both the SPAN source and destination are located on the local switch. The source is one or more switch ports.

- **Remote SPAN (RSPAN):** The SPAN source and destination are located on different switches. Mirrored traffic is copied over a special-purpose VLAN across trunks between switches from the source to the destination.

The sections that follow describe each of these SPAN forms in more detail.

Using Local SPAN

A local SPAN session exists on only one switch or one logical switch stack. In other words, you must identify one or more source interfaces and a destination interface where monitored traffic will be copied or mirrored. Figure 16-1 illustrates the basic local SPAN operation where the goal is to monitor all traffic coming from PC A. Interface Gi1/0/1, where PC A is connected, is identified as the SPAN source. A network analyzer is connected to interface Gi1/0/48, which is identified as the SPAN destination. As Ethernet frames arrive from PC A on interface Gi1/0/1, the switch makes copies of them and forwards them to the analyzer.

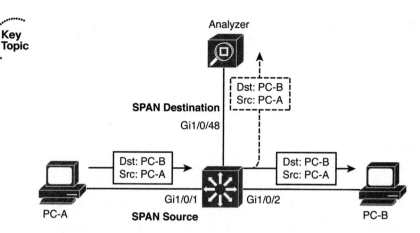

Figure 16-1 *Using Local SPAN to Monitor Received Traffic*

Figure 16-2 shows how SPAN works with traffic in the opposite direction. In this case, the SPAN session is monitoring traffic going toward PC A. As Ethernet frames exit the switch going toward the SPAN source (PC A), they are copied to the SPAN destination (the analyzer). When you configure a SPAN session, you can specify the direction of traffic that will be mirrored, as either received, transmitted, or both.

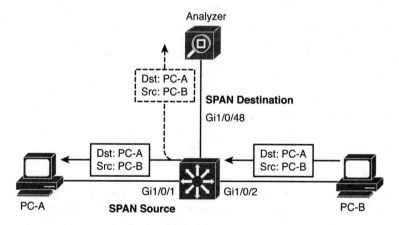

Figure 16-2 *Using Local SPAN to Monitor Transmitted Traffic*

The SPAN source can be identified as one or more physical switch ports on the switch. The ports can belong to the same VLAN or different VLANs. In addition, a trunk port can be used as a SPAN source, causing traffic from all VLANs that are active on the trunk to be copied to the SPAN destination. You can apply a VLAN filter to the SPAN source to limit which VLANs will be monitored on the trunk.

A SPAN source can also be a switch port that is a member of an EtherChannel. In this case, only traffic passing over that physical port in the EtherChannel will be copied to the SPAN destination, allowing you to monitor a single link in the channel. To monitor all traffic passing across an entire EtherChannel, you can identify a port-channel interface as the SPAN source.

To monitor traffic passing within one or more VLANs on the switch, you can identify the VLANs as the SPAN source. This is essentially the same as local SPAN, but is often called *VLAN-based SPAN* or *VSPAN*. All switch ports that are active on a source VLAN become sources themselves.

The destination is identified as a physical interface located on the same switch as the source. Frames that are copied or mirrored from the SPAN source are copied into the SPAN destination port's egress queue. Because the frames are merely copied within the switch, the original data is not affected and is still forwarded normally.

What happens if the SPAN source and destination ports are operating at different speeds? This easily could happen if the source is a VLAN with many hosts, or if the source is a 10-Gigabit Ethernet port and the destination is a Gigabit Ethernet port.

Mirrored frames are copied into the destination port's egress queue, as if normal Layer 2 switching had decided to forward them there. If the destination port becomes congested, the mirrored frames might be dropped from the queue and not transmitted out the destination port. Therefore, if the bandwidth of SPAN source traffic exceeds that of the SPAN destination port, some mirrored traffic might not be seen at the destination port.

Local SPAN Configuration

You can configure one or more simultaneous SPAN sessions on a Catalyst switch. The number of supported SPAN sessions depends on the switch model. For example, a Catalyst 3750-X can support two sessions, whereas a Catalyst 6500 can support up to 64. Each SPAN session is completely independent because there is no interaction between the mirroring processes of each one.

To configure a SPAN session, start by defining the source of the SPAN session data, using the following global configuration command:

```
Switch(config)# monitor session session-number source {interface type
member/mod/num | vlan vlan-id}[rx | tx | both]
```

SPAN sessions must be numbered uniquely using the *session-number* parameter. If multiple SPAN sources are needed, you can repeat this command. The SPAN source must be a physical switch interface or a Layer 2 VLAN, not a logical VLAN interface or SVI. However, you cannot mix both interfaces and VLANs in the same SPAN session. Instead, you can create separate sessions to monitor each type of source.

Traffic can be selected for mirroring based on the direction it is traveling through the SPAN source. For example, you can select only traffic received on the source (**rx**), only traffic transmitted from the source (**tx**), or traffic in both directions (**both**). By default, **both** directions are used.

Next, identify the SPAN destination by using the following global configuration command. Be sure to enter the same session number so that the destination gets bound to the corresponding source:

```
Switch(config)# monitor session session-number destination interface type
member/mod/num [encapsulation replicate]
```

You can define only one destination for each SPAN session. In addition, different SPAN sessions cannot share a common destination. The destination must be a physical interface, not a VLAN SVI interface.

SPAN normally copies packets to the destination without any VLAN trunk tags. As well, SPAN does not normally copy Layer 2 protocols that are sent by the switch itself. Examples include Spanning Tree Protocol (STP) bridge protocol data units (BPDUs), Cisco Discovery Protocol (CDP), Virtual Trunking Protocol (VTP), Dynamic Trunking Protocol (DTP), and Page Aggregation Protocol (PAgP). If you want to capture any VLAN tagging information or the Layer 2 protocol packets, you can add the **encapsulate replicate** keywords.

Be aware that the SPAN destination interface can only transmit mirrored traffic by default. Any frames that are sent into the destination interface are simply dropped. In most cases, the one-way traffic is sufficient because network analyzers only receive frames to be captured and analyzed. If you connect a device that also needs to transmit data back into the network, you can override the default SPAN behavior. Add the following command syntax to the **monitor session destination** command to allow ingress traffic:

```
ingress {dot1q vlan vlan-id | isl | untagged vlan vlan-id}
```

Because the SPAN destination interface is not bound to any specific interface or trunking encapsulation, you must specify how the ingress traffic should be handled. If the ingress traffic uses 802.1Q encapsulation, use the **dot1q** keyword and identify the default VLAN number. If the ingress traffic uses Inter-Switch Link (ISL) encapsulation, enter the **isl** keyword. Otherwise, if the ingress traffic is not encapsulated, use the **untagged** keyword and identify to which VLAN the traffic should be sent.

If the SPAN source is a trunk port, you might want to mirror only traffic from specific VLANs on the trunk. You can specify a list of VLANs with the following global configuration command:

```
Switch(config)# monitor session session-number filter vlan vlan-range
```

Following the scenario from Figure 16-1, suppose you would like to monitor traffic going to and coming from a device connected to interface Gigabit Ethernet 1/0/1. You have connected a network analyzer to interface Gigabit Ethernet1/0/48. Because the source and destination devices are connected to the same logical switch, you can use a local SPAN session to monitor the traffic. Example 16-1 lists the commands that are necessary to set up the SPAN session.

Example 16-1   *Configuring a Local SPAN Session*

```
Switch(config)# monitor session 1 source interface gigabitethernet1/0/1 both
Switch(config)# monitor session 1 destination interface gigabitethernet1/0/48
```

Note   When local SPAN is enabled, STP is disabled on the destination port. This allows STP BPDUs to be captured and monitored but also allows the possibility for a bridging loop to form. Never connect a SPAN session's destination port back into an active network. If the monitored packets need to be sent toward another switch, use RSPAN instead.

Remote SPAN

In a large switched network or one that is geographically separated, it might not always be convenient to take a network analyzer to the switch where a SPAN source is located. To make SPAN more extensible, Cisco developed the Remote SPAN (RSPAN) feature. With RSPAN, the source and destination can be located on different switches in different locations.

The RSPAN source is identified on one switch where the source is connected, just as with local SPAN. The RSPAN destination is identified on another switch where the mirrored traffic will be collected. Then RSPAN will carry only the mirrored data over a special-purpose VLAN across trunk links and intermediate switches between the source and destination. As long as every switch along the way is RSPAN capable, the source can be located at the far-end switch, while the network analyzer might be conveniently located at the switch nearest you.

Figure 16-3 shows an example network that uses RSPAN to mirror traffic from the source on Switch A to the destination on Switch C. The switches are connected by trunk links that carry a VLAN that is set aside for RSPAN traffic. At the source switch, mirrored frames are copied and sent toward the RSPAN destination over the RSPAN VLAN. At the destination switch, packets are pulled off the RSPAN VLAN and copied to the RSPAN destination port.

The RSPAN VLAN has some important differences from a regular VLAN. First, MAC address learning is disabled on the RSPAN VLAN. This is to prevent intermediate switches that transport the RSPAN VLAN from trying to forward the mirrored packets to their real destination MAC addresses. After all, the purpose of SPAN or RSPAN is to simply mirror or copy interesting frames, not forward them normally.

An RSPAN-capable switch also floods the RSPAN packets out all its ports belonging to the RSPAN VLAN, in an effort to send them toward the RSPAN destination. Intermediate switches have no knowledge of the RSPAN source or destination; they know only of the RSPAN VLAN itself. Therefore, the RSPAN VLAN should be limited to the links that participate in RSPAN transport. In other words, the RSPAN VLAN should be allowed on trunks between switches, but should not be assigned to any other switch ports along the path.

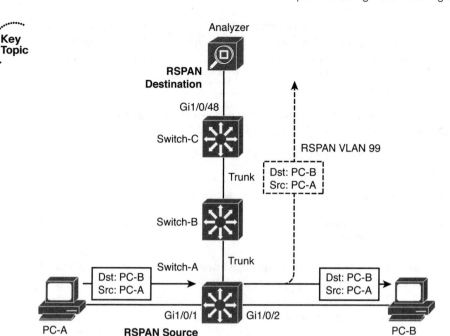

Figure 16-3   *Using RSPAN to Mirror Traffic Across Multiple Switches*

Remote SPAN Configuration

RSPAN configuration begins with the definition of the special-purpose RSPAN VLAN. If you configure the RSPAN VLAN on a VTP server, VTP correctly propagates it to other intermediate switches. If you are not using VTP, be sure to configure this VLAN for RSPAN explicitly on each intermediate switch. Otherwise, the RSPAN packets will not be delivered correctly.

In addition, if VTP pruning is in use, the RSPAN VLAN will be pruned from unnecessary trunks, limiting the traffic impact in unrelated areas of the network.

Create and maintain one or more RSPAN VLANs for the special monitoring purpose only. Set aside one RSPAN VLAN for each RSPAN session that will be used. Do not allow any normal hosts to join an RSPAN VLAN. Define an RSPAN VLAN on each switch between the source and destination with the following configuration commands:

```
Switch(config)# vlan vlan-id
Switch(config-vlan)# remote-span
```

Next, you must identify the RSPAN source *and* destination on the two switches where the source and destination are connected. At the source switch, identify the source and destination with the following global configuration commands:

```
Switch(config)# monitor session session-number source {interface type member/
mod/num | vlan vlan-id}[rx | tx | both]
Switch(config)# monitor session session-number destination remote vlan
rspan-vlan-id
```

Here, the source is either a physical switch interface or a Layer 2 VLAN (not a VLAN SVI interface). Notice that the command syntax is identical to the local SPAN **monitor session source** command. The RSPAN destination is simply the RSPAN VLAN. This allows the mirrored packets to be copied into the special VLAN and sent on their way toward the final RSPAN destination.

As with a local SPAN session, you can also use the **monitor session filter** command to filter VLANs from a trunk interface that is used as a SPAN source.

At the destination switch, you must again identify the RSPAN source and destination by using the following global configuration commands:

```
Switch(config)# monitor session session-number source remote vlan
rspan-vlan-id
Switch(config)# monitor session session-number destination interface
type member/mod/num [encapsulation replicate]
```

Here the roles are reversed. RSPAN packets are pulled from the RSPAN VLAN and placed onto the destination, which is either a physical switch interface or a Layer 2 VLAN. As with local SPAN, you can add the **ingress** keyword and its parameters to allow traffic to be received and forwarded from the destination interface.

Note   Be aware that RSPAN traffic can increase the traffic load on a trunk, even though RSPAN is restricted to one special VLAN within the trunk. If the additional load is significant, the normal production and the monitored traffic contend with each other for available bandwidth. As a result, both types of traffic could suffer.

Also, RSPAN must allow the STP to run on the RSPAN VLAN to prevent bridging loops from forming. As a result, STP BPDUs normally are sent and received on the VLAN. You cannot monitor BPDUs with RSPAN.

Suppose, for instance, that you would like to set up an RSPAN session for the scenario shown in Figure 16-3. The source is connected to Switch A port Gigabit Ethernet 1/0/1. The destination is a network analyzer connected to port Gigabit Ethernet 1/0/48 on Switch C. Switch B simply passes the RSPAN session traffic over VLAN 99, transported by trunk links to switches A and C. The corresponding configuration commands are listed in Examples 16-2, 16-3, and 16-4 for Switches A, B, and C, respectively. For Switch B, only the commands relevant to the RSPAN VLAN are listed. The trunk links are assumed to allow VLAN 99 toward Switches A and C.

Example 16-2   *Configuring RSPAN on Switch A in Figure 16-3*

```
Switch(config)# vlan 99
Switch(config-vlan)# remote-span
Switch(config-vlan)# exit
Switch(config)# monitor session 1 source interface gigabitethernet 1/0/1 both
Switch(config)# monitor session 1 destination remote vlan 99
```

Example 16-3   *Configuring RSPAN on Switch B in Figure 16-3*

```
Switch(config)# vlan 99
Switch(config-vlan)# remote-span
Switch(config-vlan)# exit
```

Example 16-4   *Configuring RSPAN on Switch C in Figure 16-3*

```
Switch(config)# vlan 99
Switch(config-vlan)# remote-span
Switch(config-vlan)# exit
Switch(config)# monitor session 1 source remote vlan 99
Switch(config)# monitor session 1 destination interface gigabitethernet 1/0/48
```

Managing SPAN Sessions

Like any other configuration commands, the **monitor session source** and **monitor session destination** commands are placed into the running configuration of the switch as you enter them. You can display SPAN sessions by searching for the commands in the switch configuration, as Example 16-5 shows.

Example 16-5   *Displaying SPAN Sessions in the Switch Configuration*

```
Switch# show running-config | include monitor
monitor session 1 source interface Gi1/0/1
monitor session 1 destination interface Gi1/0/48
Switch#
```

You can also see information about currently active SPAN sessions by entering the **show monitor** EXEC command. By default, all active sessions are displayed. You can use the **session** keyword to limit the output to specific sessions, all session, only local sessions, or only remote sessions. The command syntax follows:

```
Switch# show monitor [session {session-number | all | local | range range-list |
remote}] [detail]
```

In Example 16-6, two SPAN sessions are in use on a switch.

Example 16-6   *Displaying the Currently Active SPAN Sessions*

```
Switch# show monitor
Session 1
----------
Type                   : Local Session
Source Ports           :
    Both               : Gi1/0/1
Destination Ports      : Gi1/0/48
    Encapsulation      : Native
        Ingress        : Disabled
```

```
Session 2
----------
Type                    : Remote Source Session
Source Ports            :
    Both                : Gi1/0/1
Dest RSPAN VLAN         : 99
Switch#
```

You can delete a SPAN session after the packet analysis is complete. SPAN sessions are numbered, so you can delete them by referencing the session number. Use the following global configuration command to delete one or more sessions:

```
Switch(config)# no monitor session {session | range session-range} | local | all}
```

Session numbers can be given as an individual *session*, a range of sessions, all **local** SPAN sessions, or **all** sessions (local or remote).

When you finish using a SPAN session, you always should disable or delete it; otherwise, someone might try to connect to the port that is configured as the SPAN destination. You could spend a good bit of time troubleshooting that user's connectivity problem only to find that you left a SPAN session active there.

Exam Preparation Tasks

Review All Key Topics

Review the most important topics in the chapter, noted with the Key Topic icon in the outer margin of the page. Table 16-2 lists a reference of these key topics and the page numbers on which each is found.

Table 16-2   *Key Topics for Chapter 16*

Key Topic Element	Description	Page Number
List	Types of SPAN sessions	352
Figure 16-1	Local SPAN session operation	353
Figure 16-3	Remote SPAN session operation	357

Complete Tables and Lists from Memory

There are no memory tables in this chapter.

Define Key Terms

Define the following key terms from this chapter, and check your answers in the glossary:

local SPAN, RSPAN, SPAN, VSPAN

Use Command Reference to Check Your Memory

This section includes the most important configuration and EXEC commands covered in this chapter. It might not be necessary to memorize the complete syntax of every command, but you should remember the basic keywords that are needed.

To test your memory of the VLAN and trunk-related commands, cover the right side of Table 16-3 with a piece of paper, read the description on the left side, and then see how much of the command you can remember.

Remember that the CCNP exam focuses on practical or hands-on skills that are used by a networking professional.

Table 16-3 *IP SLA Configuration and Monitoring Commands*

Task	Command Syntax
Configure a local SPAN session source.	Switch(config)# **monitor session** *session-number* **source** {**interface** *type member/mod/num* | **vlan** *vlan-id*}[**rx** | **tx** | **both**]
Configure a local SPAN session destination.	Switch(config)# **monitor session** *session-number* **destination interface** *type member/mod/num* [**encapsulation replicate**]
Enable ingress traffic from the destination interface.	... **ingress** {**dot1q vlan** *vlan-id* | **isl** | **untagged vlan** *vlan-id*}
Filter VLANs from a trunk link as a SPAN source.	Switch(config)# **monitor session** *session-number* **filter vlan** *vlan-range*
Create an RSPAN VLAN.	Switch(config)# **vlan** *vlan-id* Switch(config-vlan)# **remote-span**
Configure an RSPAN session on the source switch.	Switch(config)# **monitor session** *session-number* **source** {**interface** *type member/mod/num* | **vlan** *vlan-id*}[**rx** | **tx** | **both**] Switch(config)# **monitor session** *session-number* **destination remote vlan** *rspan-vlan-id*
Configure an RSPAN session on the destination switch.	Switch(config)# **monitor session** *session-number* **source remote vlan** *rspan-vlan-id* Switch(config)# **monitor session** *session-number* **destination interface** *type member/mod/num* [**encapsulation replicate**]
Display active SPAN sessions.	Switch# **show monitor** [**session** {*session-number* | **all** | **local** | **range** *range-list* | **remote**}] [**detail**]
Delete SPAN sessions.	Switch(config)# **no monitor session** {*session* | **range** *session-range*} | **local** | **all**}

This chapter covers the following topics that you need to master for the CCNP SWITCH exam:

■ **Leveraging Logical Switches:** This section provides an overview of the StackWise and Virtual Switching System (VSS) techniques that can configure multiple physical switches into a single logical switch. The goals are improved network stability, efficiency, and scalability.

■ **Supervisor and Route Processor Redundancy:** This section covers the methods that can be used on some Catalyst switch platforms to operate an active-standby pair of hardware modules in one chassis. The redundancy modes include route processor redundancy (RPR), RPR+, stateful switchover (SSO), and nonstop forwarding (NSF).

CHAPTER 17

Understanding High Availability

This chapter describes the techniques that can make switching hardware more redundant and available. Multiple switches can be configured to act as a single logical switch. Within a single multilayer switch chassis, two supervisor modules with integrated route processors can be used to provide hardware redundancy. If one supervisor module fails, the other module can pick up the pieces and continue operating the switch.

"Do I Know This Already?" Quiz

The "Do I Know This Already?" quiz allows you to assess whether you should read this entire chapter thoroughly or jump to the "Exam Preparation Tasks" section. If you are in doubt based on your answers to these questions or your own assessment of your knowledge of the topics, read the entire chapter. Table 17-1 outlines the major headings in this chapter and the "Do I Know This Already?" quiz questions that go with them. You can find the answers in Appendix A, "Answers to the 'Do I Know This Already?' Quizzes."

Table 17-1 *"Do I Know This Already?" Foundation Topics Section-to-Question Mapping*

Foundation Topics Section	Questions Covered in This Section
Leveraging Logical Switches	1-5
Supervisor and Route Processor Redundancy	6-7

1. Before a multichassis EtherChannel can be configured and used, which one of the following requirements must be met?

   a. All the MEC links must connect to the same physical switch.

   b. Only chassis-based switches like the Catalyst 4500 or 6500 can be used.

   c. Physical switches must be configured as one logical switch.

   d. Logical switches must be configured as one physical switch.

2. The term *StackWise* refers to which one of the following?

    a. Switches that can be physically mounted or stacked upon each other

    b. Multiple switches can share a common power bus for PoE

    c. Switches that can stack packets and forward them more efficiently

    d. Switches that can be configured as one logical switch

3. When StackWise switches are properly connected, they form which one of the following topologies?

    a. A bidirectional ring

    b. A hub and spoke

    c. A star

    d. An EtherChannel

4. Which one of the following features makes it possible for a switch to be added or removed from a StackWise switch stack without interrupting service?

    a. NSF

    b. SSO

    c. Stacking ring

    d. Multichassis EtherChannel

5. Which one of the following terms refers to two Catalyst 6500 switch chassis that are linked together and configured to act as a single logical switch?

    a. RSS

    b. VSS

    c. ISL

    d. SSO

6. Which one of the following features is used to reduce the amount of time needed to rebuild the routing information after a supervisor module failure?

    a. NFS

    b. NSF

    c. RPR+

    d. SSO

7. Which one of the following features provides the fastest failover for supervisor or route processor redundancy?

   a. SSL

   b. SSO

   c. RPR+

   d. RPR

Foundation Topics

Leveraging Logical Switches

In Chapter 1, "Enterprise Campus Network Design," you learned that networks should be structured in distinct layers, in a modular fashion. Switches at each network layer should be implemented in pairs to provide redundancy in case of a device failure. Likewise, links between switch layers should be arranged in pairs to mitigate the effects of a link failure.

With so much redundancy and high availability, the network should be robust and efficient, right? Consider the network shown in Figure 17-1, which is a single switch block or module. In Chapters 6, "Traditional Spanning Tree Protocol," through 9, "Advanced Spanning Tree Protocol," you learned that the Spanning Tree Protocol (STP) will place some of the redundant links in Blocking mode, preventing bridging loop structures from forming. The end result is a network that still sports redundancy, but not every redundant link can be put to active use forwarding traffic.

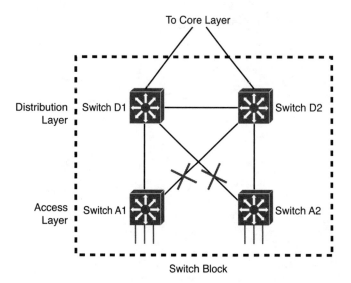

Figure 17-1   *A Typical Redundant Network Design*

Also notice that arranging the switches in pairs does provide switch redundancy, but only in the distribution and core layers. Pairs of access layer switches cannot provide redundancy for each other. In other words, users and their traffic can be spread across two access switches; if the CPU in one of the switches fails, however, the other switch cannot take over because the stranded users are not directly connected to it.

Having independent access switches also restricts some aspects of the access layer. Usually no direct link exists between two access switches, as shown in Figure 17-1. Therefore, each access switch should support a different VLAN for the end users. If there are many users fed out of one access layer room, you might have to use several switches and several different VLANs to maintain.

One way to improve the situation would be to somehow make two redundant physical switches into one logical switch. The single logical switch can group the redundant links into an EtherChannel, removing the dependence on STP to prevent loops and block links. In Figure 17-2, switches A1 and A2 are configured as one logical switch. The pairs of redundant links to the two distribution switches are configured as two EtherChannels. With no blocked links, all the links can actively transport traffic and increase the available bandwidth.

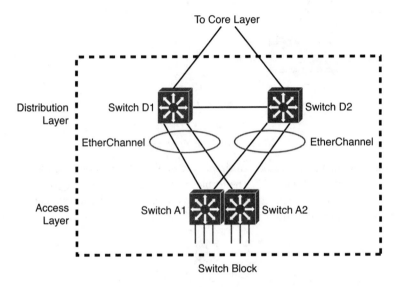

Figure 17-2   *Improving Availability by Creating One Logical Switch from Two*

Having one logical access switch also allows a single VLAN to be used to support the users. As well, you would have to manage and configure only one logical access switch, rather than two physical switches. The logical switch would support one logical control plane for management, while maintaining two separate data planes that are inherent within the physical switches.

Notice that the single logical access switch in Figure 17-2 still has two uplinks—one to each of the two distribution switches, organized as two EtherChannels. It is possible that one of the two EtherChannels might be blocked by STP or that only one of them will lead to the active gateway address upstream. In either case, all the links might not be fully used.

A further improvement would be to leverage the same logical switch scheme upstream in the distribution layer. As Figure 17-3 shows, the network architecture has been reduced to two logical switches (D1/D2 and A1/A2) that are connected by a single EtherChannel. All of the links can be used all the time. Even if one or more links fail, the rest of the EtherChannel will survive. With a single link between switches, STP should always keep it unblocked. The resulting topology becomes more stable because the EtherChannel will stay active even if STP fails or has a problem.

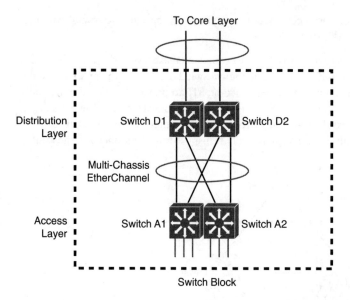

Figure 17-3   *Connecting Two Logical Switches with an EtherChannel*

To see how the logical switch architecture can simplify a whole network, compare the topologies shown in Figures 17-4 and 17-5. The former is full of redundant links to redundant switches, many not in use because STP blocked them. The latter has similar redundancy, but has a simple tree structure that STP will not have to alter.

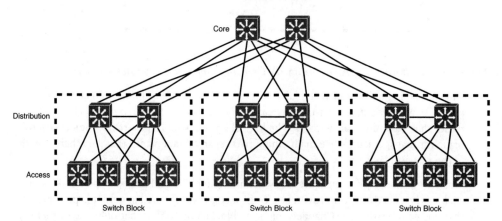

Figure 17-4   *Traditional Redundant Switched Network Architecture*

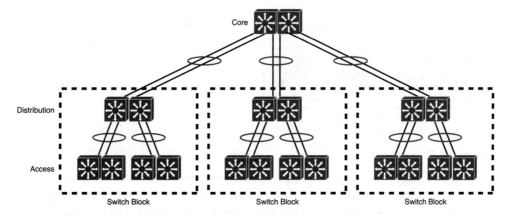

Figure 17-5 *Enhanced Logical Switched Network Architecture*

Cisco offers two approaches to building logical switches, which are discussed in the following sections.

StackWise

Traditionally, access layer switches have been independent physical devices. If you needed multiple switches in one location, you had to configure links between them. Cisco introduced the StackWise and StackWise Plus technologies to enable separate physical switches to act as a single logical switch. StackWise is available on switch models such as the Cisco Catalyst 3750-E, 3750-X, and 3850 platforms.

To create a logical "stacked" switch, individual physical switches must be connected to each other using special-purpose stacking cables. Each switch supports two stack ports; switches are connected in a daisy-chain fashion, one switch to the next, and one final connection connects the chain into a closed loop. You can think of the stacking cables as an extension of the switching fabric. When frames need to be moved from one physical switch to another, they are sent across the bidirectional stacking cable loop to get there. Figure 17-6 illustrates how two physical switches are cabled to become one logical stack. The same daisy-chain scheme can be used to connect up to nine physical switches in a closed ring fashion, as shown in Figure 17-7.

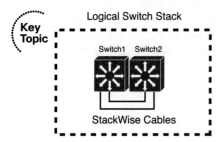

Figure 17-6 *Creating a Logical Switch with StackWise*

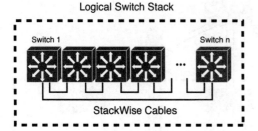

Figure 17-7 *Extending StackWise to Include Multiple Physical Switches*

One advantage of the closed stacking loop is that individual switches can be inserted or removed without breaking the path between switches completely. The ring can be broken to add or remove a switch, but the remaining switches stay connected over the rest of the ring. In other words, you can make changes to the stack without interrupting its operation.

When the physical switches are not part of a stack, each one operates independently and manages its own functions. When switches are connected as a stack, each one still maintains switching functionality, but only one switch becomes the stack master and performs all of the management functions. In fact, the whole stack is managed through a single IP address. If the master switch fails, other member switches can take over the role.

In Chapter 10, "Aggregating Switch Links," you learned about multichassis EtherChannels (MECs). Ports on different physical switches in a stack can be bundled into a MEC. Even if one stack member fails, the MEC links connected to other stack members will stay up and functioning.

Virtual Switching System

Cisco also offers switches that are based on a chassis with slots that can contain multiple switching modules. The chassis must contain a supervisor module that handles all the switch management functions, including things like routing updates and forwarding tables. A chassis can also contain a redundant supervisor module, which can take over in case the current supervisor fails.

With platforms like the Cisco Catalyst 4500R, 6500, and 8500, you can configure two identical chassis to work as one logical switch. This is known as a *Virtual Switching System* (VSS), often called a *VSS pair*. One supervisor in one of the chassis controls the operation of the logical switch. If it fails, a supervisor in the other chassis can take over. To build the logical switch, the two chassis must be linked together by multiple interfaces that have been configured as a virtual switch link (VSL). Figure 17-8 shows two switch chassis operating as a VSS pair.

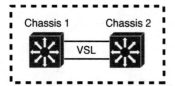

Figure 17-8 *Configuring Two Identical Chassis to Work as One Logical Switch via VSS*

Supervisor and Route Processor Redundancy

The Hot Standby Router Protocol (HSRP), Virtual Router Redundancy Protocol (VRRP), and Gateway Load Balancing Protocol (GLBP) router or gateway redundancy protocols covered in Chapter 18, "Layer 3 High Availability," can provide high availability only for the default gateway addresses. If one of the redundant gateway routers fails, another can pick up the pieces and appear to be the same gateway address.

But what happens to the devices that are connected directly to the router that fails? If the switching or routing engine fails, packets probably will not get routed and interfaces will go down. Some Cisco switches have the capability to provide redundancy for the supervisor engine itself. This is accomplished by having redundant hardware in place within a switch chassis, ready to take over during a failure.

You also should consider switch power as a vital part of achieving high availability. For example, if a switch has a single power supply and a single power cord, the whole switch will fail if the power supply fails or if the power cord is accidentally unplugged. Some switch platforms can have multiple power supplies; if one power supply fails, another immediately takes over the load.

Redundant Switch Supervisors

Modular switch platforms such as the Catalyst 4500R, 6500, and 6800 can accept two supervisor modules installed in a single chassis. The first supervisor module to success-fully boot becomes the active supervisor for the chassis. The other supervisor remains in a standby role, waiting for the active supervisor to fail.

The active supervisor always is allowed to boot and become fully initialized and opera-tional. All switching functions are provided by the active supervisor. The standby super-visor, however, is allowed to boot and initialize only to a certain level. When the active module fails, the standby module can proceed to initialize any remaining functions and take over the active role.

Redundant supervisor modules can be configured in several modes. The redundancy mode affects how the two supervisors handshake and synchronize information. In addi-tion, the mode limits the standby supervisor's state of readiness. The more ready the standby module is allowed to become, the less initialization and failover time will be required.

You can use the following redundancy modes on Catalyst switches:

- **Route processor redundancy (RPR):** The redundant supervisor is only partially booted and initialized. When the active module fails, the standby module must reload every other module in the switch and then initialize all the supervisor func-tions.

- **Route processor redundancy plus (RPR+):** The redundant supervisor is booted, allowing the supervisor and route engine to initialize. No Layer 2 or Layer 3 func-tions are started, however. When the active module fails, the standby module finishes initializing without reloading other switch modules. This allows switch ports to retain their state.

■ **Stateful switchover (SSO):** The redundant supervisor is fully booted and initialized. Both the startup and running configuration contents are synchronized between the supervisor modules. Layer 2 information is maintained on both supervisors so that hardware switching can continue during a failover. The state of the switch interfaces is also maintained on both supervisors so that links do not flap during a failover.

Tip Sometimes the redundancy mode terminology can be confusing. In addition to the RPR, RPR+, and SSO terms, you might see single-router mode (SRM) and dual-router mode (DRM).

SRM simply means that two route processors (integrated into the supervisors) are being used, but only one of them is active at any time. In DRM, two route processors are active at all times. HSRP usually is used to provide redundancy in DRM.

Although RPR and RPR+ have only one active supervisor, the route processor portion is not initialized on the standby unit. Therefore, SRM is not compatible with RPR or RPR+.

SRM is inherent with SSO, which brings up the standby route processor. You usually will find the two redundancy terms together, as "SRM with SSO."

Configuring the Redundancy Mode

Table 17-2 details the redundancy modes you can configure on supported switch platforms.

Table 17-2 *Redundancy Modes and Failover Time*

Redundancy Mode	Failover Time
RPR	Good (> 2 minutes)
RPR+	Better (> 30 seconds)
SSO	Best (> 1 second)

Figure 17-9 shows how the supervisor redundancy modes compare with respect to the functions they perform. The shaded functions are performed as the standby supervisor initializes and then waits for the active supervisor to fail. When a failure is detected, the remaining functions must be performed in sequence before the standby supervisor can become fully active. Notice how the redundancy modes get progressively more initialized and ready to become active.

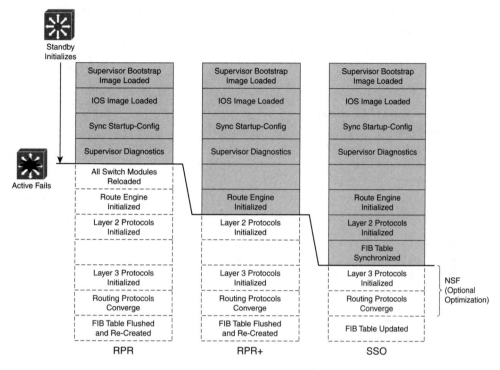

Figure 17-9 *Standby Supervisor Readiness as a Function of Redundancy Mode*

You can configure the supervisor redundancy mode by entering the redundancy configuration mode with the following command:

```
Switch(config)# redundancy
```

Next, select the redundancy mode with one of the following commands:

```
Switch(config-red)# mode {rpr | rpr-plus | sso}
```

If you are configuring redundancy for the first time on the switch, you must enter the previous commands on both supervisor modules. When the redundancy mode is enabled, you will make all configuration changes on the active supervisor only. The running configuration is synchronized automatically from the active to the standby module.

> **Tip**   If you configure RPR+ with the **rpr-plus** keyword, the supervisor attempts to bring up RPR+ with its peer module. The IOS images must be of exactly the same release before RPR+ will work. If the images differ, the supervisor automatically falls back to RPR mode instead.

You can verify the redundancy mode and state of the supervisor modules by using the following command:

```
Switch# show redundancy states
```

The output in Example 17-1 shows that the switch is using RPR+ and that the second supervisor module (denoted by unit ID 2 and "my state") holds the active role. The other supervisor module is in the standby state and is HOT, meaning that it has initialized as far as the redundancy mode will allow.

Example 17-1   *Verifying Supervisor Module Redundancy Mode and State*

```
Switch# show redundancy states
       my state = 13 -ACTIVE
     peer state = 8  -STANDBY HOT
           Mode = Duplex
           Unit = Secondary


       Unit ID = 2


Redundancy Mode (Operational) = Route Processor Redundancy Plus
Redundancy Mode (Configured)  = Route Processor Redundancy Plus
     Split Mode = Disabled
   Manual Swact = Enabled
 Communications = Up


   client count = 11
client_notification_TMR = 30000 milliseconds
        keep_alive TMR = 9000 milliseconds
      keep_alive count = 1
  keep_alive threshold = 18
         RF debug mask = 0x0
Switch#
```

Configuring Supervisor Synchronization

By default, the active supervisor synchronizes its startup configuration and configuration register values with the standby supervisor. You also can specify other information that should be synchronized.

First, use the following commands to enter the main-cpu configuration mode:

```
Switch(config)# redundancy
Switch(config-red)# main-cpu
```

Then use the following command to specify the information that will be synchronized:

```
Switch(config-r-mc)# auto-sync {startup-config | config-register | bootvar}
```

You can repeat the command if you need to use more than one of the keywords. To return to the default, use the **auto-sync standard** command.

Nonstop Forwarding

Key Topic

You can enable another redundancy feature along with SSO. Nonstop forwarding (NSF) is an interactive method that focuses on quickly rebuilding the Routing Information Base (RIB) table after a supervisor switchover. The RIB is used to generate the Forwarding Information Base (FIB) table for CEF, which is downloaded to any switch modules or hardware that can perform Cisco Express Forwarding (CEF).

Instead of waiting on any configured Layer 3 routing protocols to converge and rebuild the FIB, a router can use NSF to get assistance from other NSF-aware neighbors. The neighbors then can provide routing information to the standby supervisor, allowing the routing tables to be assembled quickly. In a nutshell, the Cisco proprietary NSF functions must be built in to the routing protocols on both the router that will need assistance and the router that will provide assistance.

NSF is supported by the Border Gateway Protocol (BGP), Enhanced Interior Gateway Routing Protocol (EIGRP), Open Shortest path First (OSPF), and Intermediate System-to-Intermediate System (IS-IS) routing protocols.

To configure NSF, you must add the commands in Table 17-3 to any routing protocol configuration on the switch.

Table 17-3 *Configuring NSF (by Routing Protocol)*

Routing Protocol	Configuration Commands
BGP	Switch(config)# **router bgp** *as-number*
	Switch(config-router)# **bgp graceful-restart**
EIGRP	Switch(config)# **router eigrp** *as-number*
	Switch(config-router)# **nsf**
OSPF	Switch(config)# **router ospf** *process-id*
	Switch(config-router)# **nsf**
IS-IS	Switch(config)# **router isis** [*tag*]
	Switch(config-router)# **nsf** [**cisco**	**ietf**]
	Switch(config-router)# **nsf interval** [*minutes*]
	Switch(config-router)# **nsf t3** {**manual** [**seconds**]	*adjacency*}
	Switch(config-router)# **nsf interface wait** *seconds*

Exam Preparation Tasks

Review All Key Topics

Review the most important topics in the chapter, noted with the Key Topic icon in the outer margin of the page. Table 17-4 lists a reference of these key topics and the page numbers on which each is found.

Table 17-4   *Key Topics for Chapter 17*

Key Topic Element	Description	Page Number
Figure 17-6	Illustrates StackWise switch topology	371
List	Describes Catalyst supervisor redundancy modes	373
Paragraph	Describes nonstop forwarding	377

Complete Tables and Lists from Memory

Print a copy of Appendix C, "Memory Tables" (found on the CD), or at least the section for this chapter, and complete the tables and lists from memory. Appendix D, "Memory Table Answer Key," also on the CD, includes completed tables and lists to check your work.

Define Key Terms

Define the following key terms from this chapter, and check your answers in the glossary:

StackWise, Virtual Switching System (VSS), route processor redundancy (RPR), route processor redundancy plus (RPR+), stateful switchover (SSO), nonstop forwarding (NSF)

Use Command Reference to Check Your Memory

This section includes the most important configuration and EXEC commands covered in this chapter. It might not be necessary to memorize the complete syntax of every command, but you should remember the basic keywords that are needed.

To test your memory of the configuration commands presented in this chapter, cover the right side of Tables 17-5 and 17-6 with a piece of paper, read the description on the left side, and then see how much of the command you can remember.

Table 17-5 *Supervisor Redundancy Configuration Commands*

Task	Command Syntax
Enable supervisor redundancy.	Switch(config)# **redundancy**
Set the supervisor redundancy mode.	Switch(config-red)# **mode {rpr | rpr-plus | sso}**
Display supervisor redundancy states.	Switch# **show redundancy states**
Enable supervisor redundancy synchronization.	Switch(config-red)# **main-cpu** Switch(config-r-mc)# **auto-sync {startup-config | config-register | bootvar}**

Table 17-6 *Configuring NSF (by Routing Protocol)*

Routing Protocol	Configuration Commands
BGP	Switch(config)# **router bgp** *as-number* Switch(config-router)# **bgp graceful-restart**
EIGRP	Switch(config)# **router eigrp** *as-number* Switch(config-router)# **nsf**
OSPF	Switch(config)# **router ospf** *process-id* Switch(config-router)# **nsf**
IS-IS	Switch(config)# **router isis** [*tag*] Switch(config-router)# **nsf** [**cisco | ietf**] Switch(config-router)# **nsf interval** [*minutes*] Switch(config-router)# **nsf t3 {manual** [**seconds**] **|** *adjacency*} Switch(config-router)# **nsf interface wait** *seconds*

This chapter covers the following first-hop redundancy protocols that you need to master for the CCNP SWITCH exam:

- Hot Standby Routing Protocol (HSRP)

- Virtual Router Redundancy Protocol (VRRP)

- Gateway Load Balancing Protocol (GLBP)

CHAPTER 18

Layer 3 High Availability

A multilayer switch can provide routing functions for devices on a network, as described in Chapter 11, "Multilayer Switching." If that switch happens to fail, clients have no way of having their traffic forwarded; their gateway has gone away.

Other multilayer switches can be added into the network to provide redundancy in the form of redundant router or gateway addresses. This chapter describes the protocols that can be used for redundant router addresses, load balancing across multiple routers, and load balancing into a server farm.

"Do I Know This Already?" Quiz

The "Do I Know This Already?" quiz allows you to assess whether you should read this entire chapter thoroughly or jump to the "Exam Preparation Tasks" section. If you are in doubt based on your answers to these questions or your own assessment of your knowledge of the topics, read the entire chapter. Table 18-1 outlines the major headings in this chapter and the "Do I Know This Already?" quiz questions that go with them. You can find the answers in Appendix A, "Answers to the 'Do I Know This Already?' Quizzes."

Table 18-1 *"Do I Know This Already?" Foundation Topics Section-to-Question Mapping*

Foundation Topics Section	Questions Covered in This Section
Hot Standby Router Protocol	1-5
Virtual Router Redundancy Protocol	6-7
Gateway Load Balancing Protocol	8-10

1. Which one of the following do multilayer switches share when running HSRP?

    a. Routing tables

    b. ARP cache

    c. CAM table

    d. IP address

2. What HSRP group uses the MAC address 0000.0c07.ac11?

   a. Group 0

   b. Group 7

   c. Group 11

   d. Group 17

3. Two routers are configured for an HSRP group. One router uses the default HSRP priority. What priority should be assigned to the other router to make it more likely to be the active router?

   a. 1

   b. 100

   c. 200

   d. 500

4. How many routers are in the Standby state in an HSRP group?

   a. 0

   b. 1

   c. 2

   d. All but the active router

5. A multilayer switch is configured as follows:

   ```
   interface gigabitethernet 1/0/1
   no switchport
   ip address 192.168.199.3 255.255.255.0
   standby 1 ip 192.168.199.2
   ```

   Which IP address should a client PC use as its default gateway?

   a. 192.168.199.1

   b. 192.168.199.2

   c. 192.168.199.3

   d. Any of these

6. Which one of the following is based on an IETF RFC standard?

   a. HSRP

   b. VRRP

   c. GLBP

   d. STP

7. What VRRP group uses the virtual MAC address 0000.5e00.01ff?

   a. Group 0

   b. Group 1

   c. Group 255

   d. Group 94

8. Which one of the following protocols is the best choice for load balancing redundant gateways?

   a. HSRP

   b. VRRP

   c. GLBP

   d. GVRP

9. Which one of the following GLBP functions answers ARP requests?

   a. AVF

   b. VARP

   c. AVG

   d. MVR

10. By default, which of the following virtual MAC addresses will be sent to the next client that looks for the GLBP virtual gateway?

   a. The GLBP interface's MAC address

   b. The next virtual MAC address in the sequence

   c. The virtual MAC address of the least-used router

   d. 0000.0c07.ac00

Foundation Topics

Multilayer switches can act as IP gateways for connected hosts by providing gateway addresses at VLAN switch virtual interfaces (SVIs) and Layer 3 physical interfaces. These switches can also participate in routing protocols, just as traditional routers do.

For high availability, multilayer switches should offer a means of preventing one switch (gateway) failure from isolating an entire VLAN. This chapter discusses several approaches to providing router redundancy, including the following:

- Hot Standby Router Protocol (HSRP)

- Virtual Router Redundancy Protocol (VRRP)

- Gateway Load Balancing Protocol (GLBP)

These are also commonly called first-hop redundancy protocols (FHRP) because the first router hop is given high availability.

Packet-Forwarding Review

When a host must communicate with a device on its local subnet, it can generate an Address Resolution Protocol (ARP) request, wait for the ARP reply, and exchange packets directly. However, if the far end is located on a different subnet, the host must rely on an intermediate system (a router, for example) to relay packets to and from that subnet.

A host identifies its nearest router, also known as the *default gateway* or *next hop*, by its IP address. If the host understands something about routing, it recognizes that all packets destined off-net must be sent to the gateway's MAC address rather than the far end's MAC address. Therefore, the host first sends an ARP request to find the gateway's MAC address. Then packets can be relayed to the gateway directly without having to look for ARP entries for individual destinations.

If the host is not so savvy about routing, it might still generate ARP requests for every off-net destination, hoping that someone will answer. Obviously, the off-net destinations cannot answer because they never receive the ARP request broadcasts; these requests are not forwarded across subnets. Instead, you can configure the gateway to provide a proxy ARP function so that it will reply to ARP requests with its own MAC address, as if the destination itself had responded.

Now the issue of gateway availability becomes important. If the gateway router for a subnet or VLAN goes down, packets have no way of being forwarded off the local subnet. Several protocols are available that allow multiple routing devices to share a common gateway address so that if one goes down, another automatically can pick up the active gateway role. The sections that follow describe these protocols.

Note IPv6 offers some inherent gateway redundancy because every router connected to a subnet advertises its presence. Hosts overhear the advertisements and use the first router received. If that router fails, hosts have to wait up to 40 seconds to discover a replacement router—an inefficient process.

Hot Standby Router Protocol

HSRP is a Cisco proprietary protocol developed to allow several routers (or multilayer switches) to appear as a single gateway IP address. RFC 2281 describes this protocol in more detail.

Basically, each of the routers that provides redundancy for a given gateway address is assigned to a common HSRP group. One router is elected as the primary, or *active*, HSRP router; another is elected as the *standby* HSRP router; and all the others remain in the *listen* HSRP state. The routers exchange HSRP hello messages at regular intervals so that they can remain aware of each other's existence and that of the active router.

Figure 18-1 shows a simple network in which two multilayer switches use HSRP Group 1 to provide the redundant gateway address 192.168.1.1. Switch A is the active router, with priority 200, and answers the ARP request for the gateway address. Because Switch B is in the Standby state, it never is used for traffic sent to 192.168.1.1. Instead, only Switch A performs the gateway routing function, and only its uplink to the access layer is utilized.

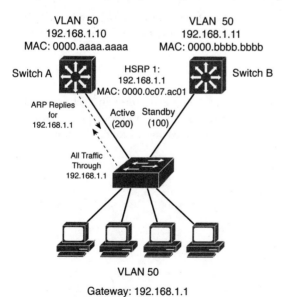

Figure 18-1 *Typical HSRP Scenario with One HSRP Group*

Note   HSRP sends its hello messages to the multicast destination 224.0.0.2 ("all routers") using UDP port 1985.

An HSRP group can be assigned an arbitrary group number, from 0 to 255. If you configure HSRP groups on several VLAN interfaces, it can be handy to make the group number the same as the VLAN number. However, most Catalyst switches support only up to 16 unique HSRP group numbers. If you have more than 16 VLANs, you will quickly run out of group numbers. An alternative is to make the group number the same (that is, 1) for every VLAN interface. This is perfectly valid because the HSRP groups are locally significant only on an interface. In other words, HSRP Group 1 on interface VLAN 10 is unique and independent from HSRP Group 1 on interface VLAN 11.

HSRP Router Election

HSRP election is based on a priority value (0 to 255) that is configured on each router in the group. By default, the priority is 100. The router with the highest priority value (255 is highest) becomes the active router for the group. If all router priorities are equal or set to the default value, the router with the highest IP address on the HSRP interface becomes the active router. To set the priority, use the following interface configuration command:

```
Switch(config-if)# standby group priority priority
```

For example, suppose that one switch is left at its default priority of 100, while the local switch is intended to win the active role election. You can use the following command to set the HSRP priority to 200:

```
Switch(config-if)# standby 1 priority 200
```

When HSRP is configured on an interface, the router progresses through a series of states before becoming active. This forces a router to listen for others in a group and see where it fits into the pecking order. Devices participating in HSRP must progress their interfaces through the following state sequence:

1. Disabled

2. Init

3. Listen

4. Speak

5. Standby

6. Active

Only the standby (the one with the second-highest priority) router monitors the hello messages from the active router. By default, hellos are sent every 3 seconds. If hellos are missed for the duration of the Hold-Time timer (default 10 seconds, or three times the

Hello timer), the active router is presumed to be down. The standby router is then clear to assume the active role.

At that point, if other routers are sitting in the Listen state, the next-highest priority router is allowed to become the new standby router.

If you need to change the timer values, use the following interface configuration command. If you decide to change the timers on a router, you should change them identically on all routers in the HSRP group.

```
Switch(config-if)# standby group timers [msec] hello [msec] holdtime
```

The *hello* and *holdtime* values can be given in seconds or in milliseconds, if the **msec** keyword precedes a value. The *hello* time can range from 1 to 254 seconds or from 15 to 999 milliseconds. The *holdtime* always should be at least three times the Hello timer and can range from 1 to 255 seconds or 50 to 3000 milliseconds.

For example, you can use the following command to set the hello time at 100 milliseconds and the hold time to 300 milliseconds:

```
Switch(config-if)# standby 1 timers msec 100 msec 300
```

Note   Be aware that decreasing the HSRP hello time allows a router failure to be detected more quickly. At the same time, HSRP hellos will be sent more often, increasing the amount of traffic on the interface.

Normally, after the active router fails and the standby becomes active, the original active router cannot immediately become active when it is restored. In other words, if a router is not already active, it cannot become active again until the current active router fails—even if its priority is higher than that of the active router. An interesting case arises when routers are just being powered up or added to a network. The first router to bring up its interface becomes the HSRP active router, even if it has the lowest priority of all.

You can configure a router to preempt or immediately take over the active role if its priority is the highest at any time. Use the following interface configuration command to allow preemption:

```
Switch(config-if)# standby group preempt [delay [minimum seconds] [reload
seconds]]
```

By default, the local router immediately can preempt another router that has the active role. To delay the preemption, use the **delay** keyword followed by one or both of the following parameters:

■   Add the **minimum** keyword to force the router to wait for seconds (0 to 3600 seconds) before attempting to overthrow an active router with a lower priority. This delay time begins as soon as the router is capable of assuming the active role, such as after an interface comes up or after HSRP is configured.

■ Add the **reload** keyword to force the router to wait for seconds (0 to 3600 seconds) after it has been reloaded or restarted. This is handy if there are routing protocols that need time to converge. The local router should not become the active gateway before its routing table is fully populated; otherwise, it might not be capable of routing traffic properly.

■ HSRP also can use an authentication method to prevent unexpected devices from spoofing or participating in HSRP. All routers in the same standby group must have an identical authentication method and key. You can use either plain-text or MD5 authentication, as described in the following sections.

Plain-Text HSRP Authentication

HSRP messages are sent with a plain-text key string (up to eight characters) as a simple method to authenticate HSRP peers. If the key string in a message matches the key configured on an HSRP peer, the message is accepted.

When keys are sent in the clear, they can be easily intercepted and used to impersonate legitimate peers. Plain-text authentication is intended only to prevent peers with a default configuration from participating in HSRP. Cisco devices use cisco as the default key string.

You can configure a plain-text authentication key for an HSRP group with the following interface configuration command:

```
Switch(config-if)# standby group authentication string
```

MD5 Authentication

A message digest 5 (MD5) authentication hash is computed on a portion of each HSRP message and a secret key known only to legitimate HSRP group peers. The MD5 hash value is sent along with HSRP messages. As a message is received, the peer recomputes the hash of the expected message contents and its own secret key; if the hash values are identical, the message is accepted.

MD5 authentication is more secure than plain-text authentication because the hash value contained in the HSRP messages is extremely difficult (if not impossible) to reverse. The hash value itself is not used as a key; instead, the hash is used to validate the message contents.

You can configure MD5 authentication by associating a key string with an interface, using the following interface configuration command:

```
Switch(config-if)# standby group authentication md5 key-string [0 | 7] string
```

By default, the key *string* (up to 64 characters) is given as plain text. This is the same as specifying the 0 keyword. After the key string is entered, it is shown as an encrypted value in the switch configuration. You also can copy and paste an encrypted key string value into this command by preceding the string with the 7 keyword.

Alternatively, you can define an MD5 key string as a key on a key chain. This method is more flexible, enabling you to define more than one key on the switch. Any of the keys then can be associated with HSRP on any interface. If a key needs to be changed, you simply add a new key to the key chain and retire (delete) an old key.

First define the key chain globally with the **key chain** command; then add one key at a time with the **key** and **key-string** commands. The *key-number* index is arbitrary, but keys are tried in sequential order. Finally, associate the key chain with HSRP on an interface by referencing its *chain-name*. You can use the following commands to configure HSRP MD5 authentication:

```
Switch(config)# key chain chain-name
Switch(config-keychain)# key key-number
Switch(config-keychain-key)# key-string [0 | 7] string
Switch(config)# interface type mod/num
Switch(config-if)# standby group authentication md5 key-chain chain-name
```

Conceding the Election

Consider an active router in an HSRP group: A group of clients sends packets to it for forwarding, and it has one or more links to the rest of the world. If one of those links fails, the router remains active. If all of those links fail, the router still remains active. But sooner or later, the path to the rest of the world is either crippled or removed, and packets from the clients no longer can be forwarded.

HSRP has a mechanism for detecting link failures and swaying the election, giving another router an opportunity to take over the active role. When a specific interface is tracked, HSRP reduces the router's priority by a configurable amount as soon as the interface goes down. If more than one interface is tracked, the priority is reduced even more with each failed interface. The priority is incremented by the same amount as interfaces come back up.

This proves particularly useful when a switch has several paths out of a VLAN or subnet; as more interfaces fail and remove the possible paths, other HSRP peers should appear to be more desirable and take over the active role. To configure interface tracking, use the following interface configuration command:

```
Switch(config-if)# standby group track type mod/num [decrementvalue]
```

By default, the *decrementvalue* for an interface is 10. Keep in mind that interface tracking does not involve the state of the HSRP interface itself. Instead, the state of other specific interfaces affects the usefulness of the local router as a gateway. You also should be aware that the only way another router can take over the active role after interface tracking reduces the priority is if the following two conditions are met:

■ Another router now has a higher HSRP priority.

■ That same router is using **preempt** in its HSRP configuration.

Without preemption, the active role cannot be given to any other router.

HSRP Gateway Addressing

Each router in an HSRP group has its own unique IP address assigned to an interface. This address is used for all routing protocol and management traffic initiated by or destined to the router. In addition, each router has a common gateway IP address, the virtual router address, which is kept alive by HSRP. This address also is referred to as the *HSRP address* or the *standby address*. Clients can point to that virtual router address as their default gateway, knowing that a router always keeps that address active. Keep in mind that the actual interface address and the virtual (standby) address must be configured to be in the same IP subnet.

You can assign the HSRP address with the following interface command:

```
Switch(config-if)# standby group ip ip-address [secondary]
```

When HSRP is used on an interface that has secondary IP addresses, you can add the **secondary** keyword so that HSRP can provide a redundant secondary gateway address.

> **Note**   To use HSRP with IPv6, use the following commands to enable HSRP Version 2 and set the HSRP address:
> ```
> Switch(config-if)# standby version 2
> Switch(config-if)# standby ipv6 autoconfig
> ```

Key Topic

Naturally, each router keeps a unique MAC address for its interface. This MAC address is always associated with the unique IP address configured on the interface. For the virtual router address, HSRP defines a special MAC address of the form 0000.0c07.acxx, where xx represents the HSRP group number as a two-digit hex value. For example, HSRP Group 1 appears as 0000.0c07.ac01, HSRP Group 16 appears as 0000.0c07.ac10, and so on.

Example 18-1 shows the configuration commands you can use to configure switches A and B to implement the scenario shown in Figure 18-1.

Example 18-1   *Configuring an HSRP Group on a Switch*

```
Switch-A(config)# interface vlan 50
Switch-A(config-if)# ip address 192.168.1.10 255.255.255.0
Switch-A(config-if)# standby 1 priority 200
Switch-A(config-if)# standby 1 preempt
Switch-A(config-if)# standby 1 ip 192.168.1.1
Switch-A(config-if)# no shutdown


Switch-B(config)# interface vlan 50
Switch-B(config-if)# ip address 192.168.1.11 255.255.255.0
Switch-B(config-if)# standby 1 priority 100
Switch-B(config-if)# standby 1 preempt
Switch-B(config-if)# standby 1 ip 192.168.1.1
Switch-B(config-if)# no shutdown
```

Load Balancing with HSRP

Consider a network in which HSRP is used on two distribution switches to provide a redundant gateway address for access layer users. Only one of the two becomes the active HSRP router; the other remains in standby. All the users send their traffic to the active router over the uplink to the active router. The standby router and its uplink essentially sit idle until a router failure occurs.

Load balancing traffic across two uplinks to two HSRP routers with a single HSRP group is not possible. Then how is it possible to load balance with HSRP? The trick is to use two HSRP groups:

■   One group assigns an active router to one switch.

■   The other group assigns another active router to the other switch.

In this way, two different virtual router or gateway addresses can be used simultaneously. The rest of the trick is to make each switch function as the standby router for its partner's HSRP group. In other words, each router is active for one group and standby for the other group. The clients or end users also must have their default gateway addresses configured as one of the two virtual HSRP group addresses.

Figure 18-2 presents this scenario. Now, Switch A is not only the active router for HSRP Group 1 (192.168.1.1), but it is also the standby router for HSRP Group 2 (192.168.1.2). Switch B is configured similarly, but with its roles reversed. The remaining step is to configure half of the client PCs with the HSRP Group 1 virtual router address and the other half with the Group 2 address. This makes load balancing possible and effective. Each half of the hosts uses one switch as its gateway over one uplink.

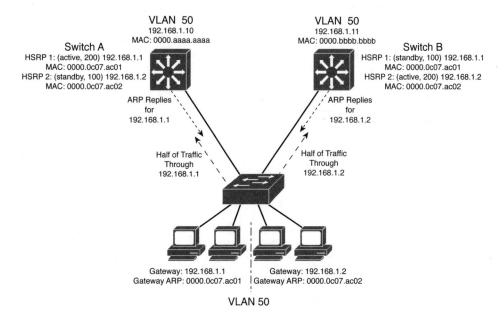

Figure 18-2   *Load Balancing with Two HSRP Groups*

Example 18-2 shows the configuration commands you can use for the scenario shown in Figure 18-2.

Example 18-2 *Configuring Load Balancing Between HSRP Groups*

```
Switch-A(config)# interface vlan 50
Switch-A(config-if)# ip address 192.168.1.10 255.255.255.0
Switch-A(config-if)# standby 1 priority 200
Switch-A(config-if)# standby 1 preempt
Switch-A(config-if)# standby 1 ip 192.168.1.1
Switch-A(config-if)# standby 1 authentication MyKey
Switch-A(config-if)# standby 2 priority 100
Switch-A(config-if)# standby 2 ip 192.168.1.2
Switch-A(config-if)# standby 2 authentication MyKey
Switch-B(config)# interface vlan 50
Switch-B(config-if)# ip address 192.168.1.11 255.255.255.0
Switch-B(config-if)# standby 1 priority 100
Switch-B(config-if)# standby 1 ip 192.168.1.1
Switch-B(config-if)# standby 1 authentication MyKey
Switch-B(config-if)# standby 2 priority 200
Switch-B(config-if)# standby 2 preempt
Switch-B(config-if)# standby 2 ip 192.168.1.2
Switch-B(config-if)# standby 2 authentication MyKey
```

You can use the following command to display information about the status of one or more HSRP groups and interfaces:

```
Router# show standby [brief] [vlan vlan-id | type mod/num]
```

Based on the configuration in Example 18-2, the output in Example 18-3 shows that Switch A is the active router for HSRP Group 1 and the standby router for HSRP Group 2 on interface VLAN 50.

Example 18-3 *Displaying the HSRP Router Role of a Switch: Switch A*

```
Switch-A# show standby vlan 50 brief
                    P indicates configured to preempt.
                    |
Interface   Grp Prio P State   Active addr    Standby addr   Group addr
Vl50         1   200 P Active   local          192.168.1.11   192.168.1.1
Vl50         2   100   Standby  192.168.1.11   local          192.168.1.2
Switch-A#
Switch-A# show standby vlan 50
Vlan50 - Group 1

  Local state is Active, priority 200, may preempt
  Hellotime 3 sec, holdtime 10 sec
  Next hello sent in 2.248
```

```
     Virtual IP address is 192.168.1.1 configured
     Active router is local
     Standby router is 192.168.1.11 expires in 9.860
     Virtual mac address is 0000.0c07.ac01
     Authentication text "MyKey"
     2 state changes, last state change 00:11:58
     IP redundancy name is "hsrp-Vl50-1" (default)
Vlan50 - Group 2
     Local state is Standby, priority 100
     Hellotime 3 sec, holdtime 10 sec
     Next hello sent in 1.302
     Virtual IP address is 192.168.1.2 configured
     Active router is 192.168.1.11, priority 200 expires in 7.812
     Standby router is local
     Authentication text "MyKey"
     4 state changes, last state change 00:10:04
     IP redundancy name is "hsrp-Vl50-2" (default)
Switch-A#
```

The output from Switch B in Example 18-4 shows that it has inverted roles from Switch A for HSRP Groups 1 and 2.

Example 18-4   *Displaying the HSRP Router Role of a Switch: Switch B*

```
Switch-B# show standby vlan 50 brief
                     P indicates configured to preempt.
                   |
Interface   Grp Prio P State   Active addr    Standby addr   Group addr
Vl50        1   100    Standby 192.168.1.10   local          192.168.1.1
Vl50        2   200  P Active  local          192.168.1.10   192.168.1.2
Switch-B#
Switch-B# show standby vlan 50
Vlan50 - Group 1

     Local state is Standby, priority 100
     Hellotime 3 sec, holdtime 10 sec
     Next hello sent in 0.980
     Virtual IP address is 192.168.1.1 configured
     Active router is 192.168.1.10, priority 200 expires in 8.128
     Standby router is local
     Authentication text "MyKey"
     1 state changes, last state change 00:01:12
     IP redundancy name is "hsrp-Vl50-1" (default)
Vlan50 - Group 2
     Local state is Active, priority 200, may preempt
     Hellotime 3 sec, holdtime 10 sec
     Next hello sent in 2.888
```

```
Virtual IP address is 192.168.1.2 configured
Active router is local
Standby router is 192.168.1.10 expires in 8.500
Virtual mac address is 0000.0c07.ac02
Authentication text "MyKey"
1 state changes, last state change 00:01:16
Switch-B#
```

Virtual Router Redundancy Protocol

The Virtual Router Redundancy Protocol (VRRP) is a standards-based alternative to HSRP, defined in IETF standard RFC 2338. VRRP is so similar to HSRP that you need to learn only slightly different terminology and a couple of slight functional differences. When you understand HSRP operation and configuration, you will also understand VRRP. This section is brief, highlighting only the differences between HSRP and VRRP.

Key Topic

VRRP provides one redundant gateway address from a group of routers. The active router is called *the master router*, whereas all others are in the *backup state*. The master router is the one with the highest router priority in the VRRP group.

VRRP group numbers range from 0 to 255; router priorities range from 1 to 254. (254 is the highest, 100 is the default.)

The virtual router MAC address is of the form 0000.5e00.01xx, where xx is a two-digit hex VRRP group number.

VRRP advertisements are sent at 1-second intervals. Backup routers optionally can learn the advertisement interval from the master router.

By default, all VRRP routers are configured to preempt the current master router if their priorities are greater.

Note   VRRP sends its advertisements to the multicast destination address 224.0.0.18 (VRRP), using IP protocol 112. VRRP was introduced in Cisco IOS Software Release 12.0(18)ST for routers, but is not supported consistently across all switching platforms.

To configure VRRP, use the interface configuration commands documented in Table 18-2.

Table 18-2   *VRRP Configuration Commands*

Task	Command Syntax
Assign a VRRP router priority (default 100).	Switch(config-if)# **vrrp** *group* **priority** *level*
Alter the advertisement timer (default 1 second).	Switch(config-if)# **vrrp** *group* **timers advertise** [*msec*] *interval*
Learn the advertisement interval from the master router.	Switch(config-if)# **vrrp** *group* **timers learn**

Task	Command Syntax
Disable preempting (default is to preempt).	Switch(config-if)# **no vrrp** *group* **preempt**
Change the preempt delay (default 0 seconds).	Switch(config-if)# **vrrp** *group* **preempt** [**delay** *seconds*]
Use authentication for advertisements.	Switch(config-if)# **vrrp** *group* **authentication** *string*
Assign a virtual IP address.	Switch(config-if)# **vrrp** *group* **ip** *ip-address* [**secondary**]
Track an object.	Switch(config-if)# **vrrp** *group* **track** *object-number* [**decrement** *priority*]

As an example, the load-balancing scenario shown in Figure 18-2 is implemented using VRRP. You would use the configuration commands in Example 18-5 on the two Catalyst switches.

Example 18-5   *Configuring Load Balancing with VRRP*

```
Switch-A(config)# interface vlan 50
Switch-A(config-if)# ip address 192.168.1.10 255.255.255.0
Switch-A(config-if)# vrrp 1 priority 200
Switch-A(config-if)# vrrp 1 ip 192.168.1.1
Switch-A(config-if)# vrrp 2 priority 100
Switch-A(config-if)# no vrrp 2 preempt
Switch-A(config-if)# vrrp 2 ip 192.168.1.2

Switch-B(config)# interface vlan 50
Switch-B(config-if)# ip address 192.168.1.11 255.255.255.0
Switch-B(config-if)# vrrp 1 priority 100
Switch-B(config-if)# no vrrp 1 preempt
Switch-B(config-if)# vrrp 1 ip 192.168.1.1
Switch-B(config-if)# vrrp 2 priority 200
Switch-B(config-if)# vrrp 2 ip 192.168.1.2
```

You can use the following command to display information about VRRP status on one or more interfaces:

```
Switch# show vrrp [brief]
```

Example 18-6 shows this command executed on both Switch A and Switch B, with the output showing the alternating roles for the two VRRP groups configured in Example 18-5.

Example 18-6   *Displaying Switch Roles for VRRP Load Balancing*

```
Switch-A# show vrrp brief
Interface          Grp Pri Time  Own Pre State   Master addr     Group addr
Vlan50               1   200 3218     Y   Master  192.168.1.10    192.168.1.1
```

```
Vlan50              2   100 3609        Backup  192.168.1.11   192.168.1.2
Switch-A#


Switch-B# show vrrp brief
Interface          Grp Pri Time  Own Pre State   Master addr     Group addr
Vlan50              1   100 3609          Backup  192.168.1.10    192.168.1.1
Vlan50              2   200 3218       Y  Master  192.168.1.11    192.168.1.2
Switch-B#
```

Table 18-3 compares the detailed VRRP status between the Switch A and Switch B switches.

Table 18-3 *Verifying VRRP Status for multiple VRRP Groups*

Switch A	Switch B
Switch-A# **show vrrp**	Switch-B# **show vrrp**
Vlan50 - Group 1	Vlan50 - Group 1
State is Master	State is Backup
Virtual IP address is 192.168.1.1	Virtual IP address is 192.168.1.1
Virtual MAC address is 0000.5e00.0101	Virtual MAC address is 0000.5e00.0101
Advertisement interval is 1.000 sec	Advertisement interval is 1.000 sec
Preemption is enabled	Preemption is disabled
min delay is 0.000 sec	Priority is 100
Priority is 200	Authentication is enabled
Authentication is enabled	Master Router is 192.168.1.10, priority
Master Router is 192.168.1.10 (local),	is 200
priority is 200	Master Advertisement interval is 1.000
Master Advertisement interval is 1.000	sec
sec	Master Down interval is 3.609 sec
Master Down interval is 3.218 sec	(expires in 2.833 sec)
Vlan50 - Group 2	Vlan50 - Group 2
State is Backup	State is Master
Virtual IP address is 192.168.1.2	Virtual IP address is 192.168.1.2
Virtual MAC address is 0000.5e00.0102	Virtual MAC address is 0000.5e00.0102
Advertisement interval is 1.000 sec	Advertisement interval is 1.000 sec
Preemption is disabled	Preemption is enabled
Priority is 100	min delay is 0.000 sec
Authentication is enabled	Priority is 200
Master Router is 192.168.1.11, priority	Authentication is enabled
is 200	Master Router is 192.168.1.11 (local),
Master Advertisement interval is 1.000	priority is 200
sec	Master Advertisement interval is 1.000
Master Down interval is 3.609 sec	sec
(expires in 2.977 sec)	Master Down interval is 3.218 sec
Switch-A#	Switch-B#

Gateway Load Balancing Protocol

You should now know how both HSRP and VRRP can effectively provide a redundant gateway (virtual router) address. You can accomplish load balancing by configuring only multiple HSRP/VRRP groups to have multiple virtual router addresses. More manual configuration is needed so that the client machines are divided among the virtual routers. Each group of clients must point to the appropriate virtual router. This makes load balancing somewhat labor-intensive, having a more or less fixed, or static, behavior.

The Gateway Load Balancing Protocol (GLBP) is a Cisco proprietary protocol designed to overcome the limitations of existing redundant router protocols. Some of the concepts are the same as with HSRP/VRRP, but the terminology is different, and the behavior is much more dynamic and robust.

Note GLBP was introduced in Cisco IOS Software Release 12.2(14)S for routers, but is not consistently supported across all switching platforms.

To provide a virtual router, multiple switches (routers) are assigned to a common GLBP group. Instead of having just one active router performing forwarding for the virtual router address, *all* routers in the group can participate and offer load balancing by forwarding a portion of the overall traffic.

The advantage is that none of the clients has to be pointed toward a specific gateway address; they can all have the same default gateway set to the virtual router IP address. The load balancing is provided completely through the use of virtual router MAC addresses in ARP replies returned to the clients. As a client sends an ARP request looking for the virtual router address, GLBP sends back an ARP reply with the virtual MAC address of a selected router in the group. The result is that all clients use the same gateway address but have differing MAC addresses for it.

Active Virtual Gateway

The trick behind this load balancing lies in the GLBP group. One router is elected the active virtual gateway (AVG). This router has the highest priority value, or the highest IP address in the group, if there is no highest priority. The AVG answers all ARP requests for the virtual router address. Which MAC address it returns depends on which load-balancing algorithm it is configured to use. In any event, the virtual MAC address supported by one of the routers in the group is returned.

The AVG also assigns the necessary virtual MAC addresses to each of the routers participating in the GLBP group. Up to four virtual MAC addresses can be used in any group. Each of these routers is referred to as an *active virtual forwarder* (AVF), forwarding traffic received on its virtual MAC address. Other routers in the group serve as backup or secondary virtual forwarders, in case the AVF fails. The AVG also assigns secondary roles.

Assign the GLBP priority to a router with the following interface configuration command:

```
Switch(config-if)# glbp group priority level
```

GLBP group numbers range from 0 to 1023. The router priority can be 1 to 255 (255 is the highest priority), defaulting to 100.

As with HSRP, another router cannot take over an active role until the current active router fails. GLBP does allow a router to preempt and become the AVG if it has a higher priority than the current AVG. Use the following command to enable preempting and to set a time delay before preempting begins:

```
Switch(config-if)# glbp group preempt [delay minimum seconds]
```

Routers participating in GLBP must monitor each other's presence so that another router can assume the role of a failed router. To do this, the AVG sends periodic hello messages to each of the other GLBP peers. In addition, it expects to receive hello messages from each of them.

Hello messages are sent at *hellotime* intervals, with a default of 3 seconds. If hellos are not received from a peer within *a holdtime*, defaulting to 10 seconds, that peer is presumed to have failed. You can adjust the GLBP timers with the following interface configuration command:

```
Switch(config-if)# glbp group timers [msec] hellotime [msec] holdtime
```

The timer values normally are given in seconds, unless they are preceded by the **msec** keyword, to indicate milliseconds. The *hellotime* can range from 1 to 60 seconds or from 50 to 60,000 milliseconds. The *holdtime* must be greater than *the hellotime* and can go up to 180 seconds or 180,000 milliseconds. You always should make the *holdtime* at least three times greater than the *hellotime* to give some tolerance to missed or delayed hellos from a functional peer.

Tip Although you can use the previous command to configure the GLBP timers on each peer router, it is not necessary. Instead, just configure the timers on the router you have identified as the AVG. The AVG will advertise the timer values it is using, and every other peer will learn those values if they have not already been explicitly set.

Active Virtual Forwarder

Each router participating in the GLBP group can become an AVF, if the AVG assigns it that role, along with a virtual MAC address. The virtual MAC addresses always have the form 0007.b4xx.xxyy. The 16-bit value denoted by xx.xx represents six 0 bits followed by a 10-bit GLBP group number. The 8-bit yy value is the virtual forwarder number.

By default, GLBP uses the periodic hello messages to detect AVF failures, too. Each router within a GLBP group must send hellos to every other GLBP peer. Hellos also are expected from every other peer. For example, if hellos from the AVF are not received by the AVG before its Hold-Time timer expires, the AVG assumes that the current AVF has failed. The AVG then assigns the AVF role to another router.

Naturally, the router that is given the new AVF role might already be an AVF for a different virtual MAC address. Although a router can masquerade as two different virtual MAC addresses to support the two AVF functions, it does not make much sense to continue doing that for a long period of time. The AVG maintains two timers that help resolve this condition.

The *redirect* timer is used to determine when the AVG will stop using the old virtual MAC address in ARP replies. The AVF corresponding to the old address continues to act as a gateway for any clients that try to use it.

When the *timeout* timer expires, the old MAC address and the virtual forwarder using it are flushed from all the GLBP peers. The AVG assumes that the previously failed AVF will not return to service, so the resources assigned to it must be reclaimed. At this point, clients still using the old MAC address in their ARP caches must refresh the entry to obtain the new virtual MAC address.

The *redirect* timer defaults to 600 seconds (10 minutes) and can range from 0 to 3600 seconds (1 hour). The timeout timer defaults to 14,400 seconds (4 hours) and can range from 700 to 64,800 seconds (18 hours). You can adjust these timers with the following interface configuration command:

```
Switch(config-if)# glbp group timers redirect redirect timeout
```

GLBP also can use a weighting function to determine which router becomes the AVF for a virtual MAC address in a group. Each router begins with a maximum weight value (1 to 254). As specific interfaces go down, the weight is decreased by a configured amount. GLBP uses thresholds to determine when a router can and cannot be the AVF. If the weight falls below the lower threshold, the router must give up its AVF role. When the weight rises above the upper threshold, the router can resume its AVF role.

By default, a router receives a maximum weight of 100. If you want to make a dynamic weighting adjustment, GLBP must know which interfaces to track and how to adjust the weight. You must first define an interface as a tracked object with the following global configuration command:

```
Switch(config)# track object-number interface type member/module/number {line-
protocol | ip  routing}
```

The *object-number* is an arbitrary index (1 to 500) that is used for weight adjustment. The condition that triggers an adjustment can be **line-protocol** (the interface line protocol is up) or **ip routing**. (IP routing is enabled, the interface has an IP address, and the interface is up.)

Next, you must define the weighting thresholds for the interface with the following interface configuration command:

```
Switch(config-if)# glbp group weighting maximum [lower lower] [upper upper]
```

The maximum weight can range from 1 to 254 (default 100). The upper (*default maximum*) and lower (default 1) thresholds define when the router can and cannot be the AVF, respectively.

Finally, you must configure GLBP to know which objects to track so that the weighting can be adjusted with the following interface configuration command:

```
Switch(config-if)# glbp group weighting track object-number [decrement value]
```

When the tracked object fails, the weighting is decremented by *value* (1 to 254, default 10).

Likewise, a router that might serve as an AVF cannot preempt another when it has a higher weight value.

GLBP Load Balancing

The AVG establishes load balancing by handing out virtual router MAC addresses to clients in a deterministic fashion. Naturally, the AVG first must inform the AVFs in the group of the virtual MAC address that each should use. Up to four virtual MAC addresses, assigned in sequential order, can be used in a group.

Key
Topic

You can use one of the following load-balancing methods in a GLBP group:

- **Round robin:** Each new ARP request for the virtual router address receives the next available virtual MAC address in reply. Traffic load is distributed evenly across all routers participating as AVFs in the group, assuming that each of the clients sends and receives the same amount of traffic. This is the default method used by GLBP.

- **Weighted:** The GLBP group interface's weighting value determines the proportion of traffic that should be sent to that AVF. A higher weighting results in more frequent ARP replies containing the virtual MAC address of that router. If interface tracking is not configured, the maximum weighting value configured is used to set the relative proportions among AVFs.

- **Host dependent:** Each client that generates an ARP request for the virtual router address always receives the same virtual MAC address in reply. This method is used if the clients have a need for a consistent gateway MAC address. (Otherwise, a client could receive replies with different MAC addresses for the router over time, depending on the load-balancing method in use.)

On the AVG router (or its successors), use the following interface configuration command to define the method:

```
Switch(config-if)# glbp group load-balancing [round-robin | weighted |
host-dependent]
```

Enabling GLBP

To enable GLBP, you must assign a virtual IP address to the group by using the following interface configuration command:

```
Switch(config-if)# glbp group ip [ip-address [secondary]]
```

If the *ip-address* is not given in the command, it is learned from another router in the group. However, if this router is to be the AVG, you must explicitly configure the IP address; otherwise, no other router knows what the value should be.

Note   GLBP can also be used with IPv6. Rather than specifying an IPv6 address, use the following command to autoconfigure the address:

```
Switch(config-if)# glbp group ipv6 autoconfigure
```

Figure 18-3 shows a typical network in which three multilayer switches are participating in a common GLBP group. Switch A is elected the AVG, so it coordinates the entire GLBP process. The AVG answers all ARP requests for the virtual router 192.168.1.1. It has identified itself, Switch B, and Switch C as AVFs for the group.

In this figure, round-robin load balancing is being used. Each of the client PCs sends an ARP request to look for the virtual router address (192.168.1.1) in turn, from left to right. Each time the AVG replies, the next sequential virtual MAC address is sent back to a client. After the fourth PC sends a request, all three virtual MAC addresses (and AVF routers) have been used, so the AVG cycles back to the first virtual MAC address.

Notice that only one GLBP group has been configured, and all clients know of only one gateway IP address: 192.168.1.1. However, all uplinks are being used, and all routers are proportionately forwarding traffic.

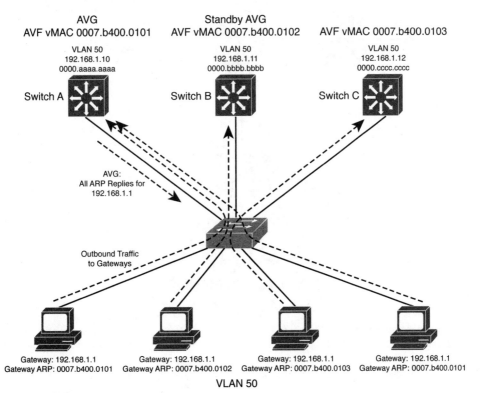

Figure 18-3   *Multilayer Switches in a GLBP Group*

Redundancy is also inherent in the GLBP group: Switch A is the AVG, but the next-highest priority router can take over if the AVG fails. All routers have been given an AVF role for a unique virtual MAC address in the group. If one AVF fails, some clients remember the last-known virtual MAC address that was handed out. Therefore, another of the routers also takes over the AVF role for the failed router, causing the virtual MAC address to remain alive at all times.

Figure 18-4 shows how these redundancy features react when the current active AVG fails. Before its failure, Switch A was the AVG because of its higher GLBP priority. After it failed, Switch B became the AVG, answering ARP requests with the appropriate virtual MAC address for gateway 192.168.1.1. Switch A also had been acting as an AVF, participating in the gateway load balancing. Switch B also picks up this responsibility, using its virtual MAC address 0007.b400.0102 along with the one Switch A had been using, 0007.b400.0101. Therefore, any hosts that know the gateway by any of its virtual MAC addresses still can reach a live gateway or AVF.

You can implement the scenario shown in Figures 18-3 and 18-4 with the configuration commands in Example 18-7 for Switch A, Switch B, and Switch C, respectively.

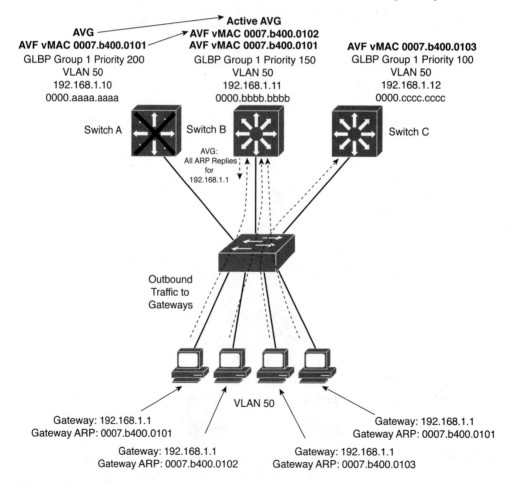

Figure 18-4   *How GLBP Reacts to a Component Failure*

Example 18-7 *Configuring GLBP Load Balancing*

```
Switch-A(config)# interface vlan 50
Switch-A(config-if)# ip address 192.168.1.10 255.255.255.0
Switch-A(config-if)# glbp 1 priority 200
Switch-A(config-if)# glbp 1 preempt
Switch-A(config-if)# glbp 1 ip 192.168.1.1


Switch-B(config)# interface vlan 50
Switch-B(config-if)# ip address 192.168.1.11 255.255.255.0
Switch-B(config-if)# glbp 1 priority 150
Switch-B(config-if)# glbp 1 preempt
Switch-B(config-if)# glbp 1 ip 192.168.1.1


Switch-C(config)# interface vlan 50
Switch-C(config-if)# ip address 192.168.1.12 255.255.255.0
Switch-C(config-if)# glbp 1 priority 100
Switch-C(config-if)# glbp 1 ip 192.168.1.1
```

You can verify GLBP operation with the **show glbp** [brief] command, as demonstrated in Example 18-8. With the **brief** keyword, the GLBP roles are summarized showing the interface, GLBP group number (Grp), virtual forwarder number (Fwd), GLBP priority (Pri), state, and addresses.

Example 18-8 *Verifying GLBP Operation*

```
Switch-A# show glbp brief
Interface   Grp  Fwd Pri State    Address         Active router   Standby router
Vl50        1    -   200 Active   192.168.1.1     local           192.168.1.11
Vl50        1    1   7   Active   0007.b400.0101  local           -
Vl50        1    2   7   Listen   0007.b400.0102  192.168.1.11    -
Vl50        1    3   7   Listen   0007.b400.0103  192.168.1.12    -
Switch-A#


Switch-B# show glbp brief
Interface   Grp  Fwd Pri State    Address         Active router   Standby router
Vl50        1    -   150 Standby  192.168.1.1     192.168.1.10    local
Vl50        1    1   7   Listen   0007.b400.0101  192.168.1.10    -
Vl50        1    2   7   Active   0007.b400.0102  local           -
Vl50        1    3   7   Listen   0007.b400.0103  192.168.1.12    -
Switch-B#


Switch-C# show glbp brief
Interface   Grp  Fwd Pri State    Address         Active router   Standby router
Vl50        1    -   100 Listen   192.168.1.1     192.168.1.10    192.168.1.11
Vl50        1    1   7   Listen   0007.b400.0101  192.168.1.10    -
```

```
Vl50        1    2    7    Listen   0007.b400.0102  192.168.1.11   -
Vl50        1    3    7    Active   0007.b400.0103  local          -
Switch-C#
```

Notice that Switch A is shown to be the AVG because it has a dash in the Fwd column and is in the Active state. It also is acting as AVF for virtual forwarder number 1. Because the GLBP group has three routers, there are three virtual forwarders and virtual MAC addresses. Switch A is in the Listen state for forwarders number 2 and 3, waiting to be given an active role in case one of those AVFs fails.

Switch B is shown to have the Standby role, waiting to take over in case the AVG fails. It is the AVF for virtual forwarder number 2.

Finally, Switch C has the lowest GLBP priority, so it stays in the Listen state, waiting for the active or standby AVG to fail. It is also the AVF for virtual forwarder number 3.

You also can display more detailed information about the GLBP configuration and status by omitting the **brief** keyword. Example 18-9 shows this output on the AVG router. Because this is the AVG, the virtual forwarder roles it has assigned to each of the routers in the GLBP group also are shown.

Example 18-9 *Displaying Detailed GLBP Configuration and Status Information*

```
Switch-A# show glbp
Vlan50 - Group 1
  State is Active
    7 state changes, last state change 03:28:05
  Virtual IP address is 192.168.1.1
  Hello time 3 sec, hold time 10 sec
    Next hello sent in 1.672 secs
  Redirect time 600 sec, forwarder time-out 14400 sec
  Preemption enabled, min delay 0 sec
  Active is local
  Standby is 192.168.1.11, priority 150 (expires in 9.632 sec)
  Priority 200 (configured)
  Weighting 100 (default 100), thresholds: lower 1, upper 100
  Load balancing: round-robin
  There are 3 forwarders (1 active)
  Forwarder 1
    State is Active
      3 state changes, last state change 03:27:37
    MAC address is 0007.b400.0101 (default)
    Owner ID is 00d0.0229.b80a
    Redirection enabled
    Preemption enabled, min delay 30 sec
    Active is local, weighting 100
  Forwarder 2
    State is Listen
```

```
    MAC address is 0007.b400.0102 (learnt)
    Owner ID is 0007.b372.dc4a
    Redirection enabled, 598.308 sec remaining (maximum 600 sec)
    Time to live: 14398.308 sec (maximum 14400 sec)
    Preemption enabled, min delay 30 sec
    Active is 192.168.1.11 (primary), weighting 100 (expires in 8.308 sec)
Forwarder 3
    State is Listen
    MAC address is 0007.b400.0103 (learnt)
    Owner ID is 00d0.ff8a.2c0a
    Redirection enabled, 599.892 sec remaining (maximum 600 sec)
    Time to live: 14399.892 sec (maximum 14400 sec)
    Preemption enabled, min delay 30 sec
    Active is 192.168.1.12 (primary), weighting 100 (expires in 9.892 sec)
Switch-A#
```

Verifying Gateway Redundancy

To verify the operation of the features discussed in this chapter, you can use the commands listed in Table 18-4. In particular, look for the active, standby, or backup routers in use.

Table 18-4 *Gateway Redundancy Verification Commands*

Task	Command Syntax
HSRP and VRRP	
Display HSRP status.	Switch# **show standby brief**
Display HSRP on an interface.	Switch# **show standby** *type member/module/number*
Display VRRP status.	Switch# **show vrrp brief all**
Display VRRP on an interface.	Switch# **show vrrp interface** *type member/module/ number*
GLBP	
Display status of a GLBP group.	Switch# **show glbp** [*group*] [**brief**]

Exam Preparation Tasks

Review All Key Topics

Review the most important topics in the chapter, noted with the Key Topic icon in the outer margin of the page. Table 18-5 lists a reference of these key topics and the page numbers on which each is found.

Table 18-5 *Key Topics for Chapter 18*

Key Topic Element	Description	Page Number
Paragraph	Explains HSRP active and standby routers	385
Paragraph	Describes the virtual MAC address used by HSRP	390
Paragraph	Discusses VRRP master and backup routers and the virtual MAC address	394
Paragraph	Describes the GLBP active virtual gateway and active virtual forwarder roles	397
List	Describes the methods GLBP uses for load balancing traffic within a GLBP group	400

Complete Tables and Lists from Memory

Print a copy of Appendix C, "Memory Tables" (found on the CD), or at least the section for this chapter, and complete the tables and lists from memory. Appendix D, "Memory Table Answer Key," also on the CD, includes completed tables and lists to check your work.

Define Key Terms

Define the following key terms from this chapter, and check your answers in the glossary:

HSRP active router, HSRP standby router, VRRP master router, VRRP backup router, active virtual gateway (AVG), active virtual forwarder (AVF)

Use Command Reference to Check Your Memory

This section includes the most important configuration and EXEC commands covered in this chapter. It might not be necessary to memorize the complete syntax of every command, but you should remember the basic keywords that are needed.

To test your memory of the configuration commands presented in this chapter, cover the right side of Tables 18-6 through 18-8 with a piece of paper, read the description on the left side, and then see how much of the command you can remember.

Table 18-6   *HSRP Configuration Commands*

Task	Command Syntax
Set the HSRP priority.	Switch(config-if)# **standby** *group* **priority** *priority*
Set the HSRP timers.	Switch(config-if)# **standby** *group* **timers** *hello holdtime*
Allow router preemption.	Switch(config-if)# **standby** *group* **preempt** [**delay** *seconds*]
Use group authentication.	Switch(config-if)# **standby** *group* **authentication** *string*
Adjust priority by tracking an interface.	Switch(config-if)# **standby** *group* **track** *type member/module/number decrementvalue*
Assign the virtual router address.	Switch(config-if)# **standby** *group* **ip** *ip address* [**secondary**]

Table 18-7   *VRRP Configuration Commands*

Task	Command Syntax
Assign a VRRP router priority (default 100).	Switch(config-if)# **vrrp** *group* **priority** *level*
Alter the advertisement timer (default 1 second).	Switch(config-if)# **vrrp** *group* **timers advertise** [**msec**] *interval*
Learn the advertisement interval from the master router.	Switch(config-if)# **vrrp** *group* **timers learn**
Disable preempting (default is to preempt).	Switch(config-if)# **no vrrp** *group* **preempt**
Change the preempt delay (default 0 seconds).	Switch(config-if)# **vrrp** *group* **preempt** [**delay** *seconds*]
Use authentication for advertisements.	Switch(config-if)# **vrrp** *group* **authentication** *string*
Assign a virtual IP address.	Switch(config-if)# **vrrp** *group* **ip** *ip-address* [**secondary**]

Table 18-8 *GLBP Configuration Commands*

Task	Command Syntax
Assign a GLBP priority.	Switch(config-if)# **glbp** *group* **priority** *level*
Allow GLBP preemption.	Switch(config-if)# **glbp** *group* **preempt** [**delay minimum** *seconds*]
Define an object to be tracked.	Switch(config)# **track** *object-number* **interface** *type member/module/number* {**line-protocol** | **ip routing**}
Define the weighting thresholds.	Switch(config-if)# **glbp** *group* **weighting** *maximum* [**lower** *lower*] [**upper** *upper*]
Track an object.	Switch(config-if)# **glbp** *group* **weighting track** *object-number* [**decrement** *value*]
Choose the load-balancing method.	Switch(config-if)# **glbp** *group* **load-balancing** [**round-robin** | **weighted** | **host-dependent**]
Assign a virtual router address.	Switch(config-if)# **glbp** *group* **ip** [*ip-address* [**secondary**]]

This chapter covers the following topics that you need to master for the CCNP SWITCH exam:

■ **Port Security:** This section explains how to configure switch ports to allow network access to only hosts with specific or learned MAC addresses.

■ **Port-Based Authentication:** This section discusses a method you can use to require user authentication before network access is offered to a client host.

■ **Using Storm Control:** This section explains how you can configure a method to limit the effects of traffic storms coming from devices that are connected to a switch.

■ **Best Practices for Securing Switches:** This section provides several guidelines for tightening control over Catalyst switches and the protocols they use for switch communication and maintenance.

CHAPTER 19

Securing Switch Access

Traditionally, users have been able to connect a PC to a switched network and gain immediate access to enterprise resources. As networks grow and as more confidential data and restricted resources become available, it is important to limit the access that users receive.

Catalyst switches have a variety of methods that can secure or control user access. Users can be authenticated as they connect to or through a switch and can be authorized to perform certain actions on a switch. User access can be recorded as switch accounting information. The physical switch port access also can be controlled based on the user's MAC address or authentication.

In addition, Catalyst switches can detect and prevent certain types of attacks. Several features can be used to validate information passing through a switch so that spoofed addresses cannot be used to compromise hosts.

"Do I Know This Already?" Quiz

The "Do I Know This Already?" quiz allows you to assess whether you should read this entire chapter thoroughly or jump to the "Exam Preparation Tasks" section. If you are in doubt based on your answers to these questions or your own assessment of your knowledge of the topics, read the entire chapter. Table 19-1 outlines the major headings in this chapter and the "Do I Know This Already?" quiz questions that go with them. You can find the answers in Appendix A, "Answers to the 'Do I Know This Already?' Quizzes."

Table 19-1 *"Do I Know This Already?" Foundation Topics Section-to-Question Mapping*

Foundation Topics Section	Questions Covered in This Section
Port Security	1–4
Port-Based Authentication	5–9
Using Storm Control	10-11
Best Practices for Securing Switches	12–13

1. Which switch feature can grant access through a port only if the host with MAC address 0005.0004.0003 is connected?

   a. SPAN

   b. MAC address ACL

   c. Port security

   d. Port-based authentication

2. Port security is being used to control access to a switch port. Which one of these commands will put the port into the errdisable state if an unauthorized station connects?

   a. **switchport port-security violation protect**

   b. **switchport port-security violation restrict**

   c. **switchport port-security violation errdisable**

   d. **switchport port-security violation shutdown**

3. If port security is enabled and left to its default configuration, how many different MAC addresses can be learned at one time on a switch port?

   a. 0

   b. 1

   c. 16

   d. 256

4. The following commands are configured on a Catalyst switch port. What happens when the host with MAC address 0001.0002.0003 tries to connect?

   ```
   switchport port-security
   switchport port-security maximum 3
   switchport port-security mac-address 0002.0002.0002
   switchport port-security violation shutdown
   ```

   a. The port shuts down.

   b. The host is allowed to connect.

   c. The host is denied a connection.

   d. The host can connect only when 0002.0002.0002 is not connected.

5. What protocol is used for port-based authentication?

   a. 802.1D

   b. 802.1Q

   c. 802.1X

   d. 802.1w

6. When 802.1X802.1X is used for a switch port, where must it be configured?

   a. Switch port and client PC

   b. Switch port only

   c. Client PC only

   d. Switch port and a RADIUS server

7. When port-based authentication is enabled globally, what is the default behavior for all switch ports?

   a. Authenticate users before enabling the port.

   b. Allow all connections without authentication.

   c. Do not allow any connections.

   d. There is no default behavior.

8. When port-based authentication is enabled, what method is available for a user to authenticate?

   a. Web browser

   b. Telnet session

   c. 802.1X client

   d. DHCP

9. The users in a department are using a variety of host platforms, some old and some new. All of them have been approved with a user ID in a RADIUS server database. Which one of these features should be used to restrict access to the switch ports in the building?

   a. AAA authentication

   b. AAA authorization

   c. Port security

   d. Port-based authentication

10. Which of the following are types of frames that Storm Control can limit before they can cause problems for hosts that are connected to a switch? (Choose all that apply.)

    a. Unicast frames

    b. Broadcast frames

    c. Multicast frames

    d. Unknown unicast frames

11. Suppose that an interface receives the following configuration command:

```
storm-control broadcast level 10
```

Storm control will be triggered when which one of the following rising thresholds is reached?

    a. At least 10 broadcast frames are received

    b. At least 10 hosts are connected to a VLAN that will receive a flooded broadcast frame

    c. Broadcast frames exceed 10 percent of the interface bandwidth

    d. Broadcast frames exceed 10 percent of the interface MTU size

12. Which two of the following methods should you use to secure inbound CLI sessions to a switch?

    a. Disable all inbound CLI connections.

    b. Use SSH only.

    c. Use Telnet only.

    d. Apply an access list to the vty lines.

13. Suppose that you need to disable CDP and LLDP advertisements on a switch port so that untrusted devices cannot learn anything about your switch. Which one of the following answers contains the interface configuration commands that should be used?

    a. cdp disable

        lldp disable

    b. no cdp

        no lldp

    c. no cdp enable

        no lldp transmit

    d. no cdp transmit

        no lldp transmit

Foundation Topics

Port Security

In some environments, a network must be secured by controlling what stations can gain access to the network itself. Where user workstations are stationary, their MAC addresses always can be expected to connect to the same access layer switch ports. If stations are mobile, their MAC addresses can be learned dynamically or added to a list of addresses to expect on a switch port.

Catalyst switches offer the port security feature to control port access based on MAC addresses. To configure port security on an access layer switch port, begin by enabling it on a per-interface basis with the following interface-configuration command:

```
Switch(config-if)# switchport port-security
```

Next, you must identify a set of allowed MAC addresses so that the port can grant them access. You can explicitly configure addresses or they can be learned dynamically from port traffic. On each interface that uses port security, specify the maximum number of MAC addresses that will be allowed access using the following interface configuration command:

```
Switch(config-if)# switchport port-security maximum max-addr
```

By default, port security will make sure that only one MAC address will be allowed access on each switch port. You can set the maximum number of addresses in the range of 1 to 1024.

Key Topic

Each interface using port security dynamically learns MAC addresses by default and expects those addresses to appear on that interface in the future. MAC addresses are learned as hosts transmit frames on an interface. The interface learns up to the maximum number of addresses allowed. Learned addresses also can be aged out of the table if those hosts are silent for a period of time. By default, no aging occurs.

For example, to set the maximum number of MAC addresses that can be active on a switch port at any time to two, you could use the following command:

```
Switch(config-if)# switchport port-security maximum 2
```

By default, port security learns MAC addresses dynamically and stores them in the CAM table and also in the running configuration. If the switch reboots for some reason, port security will have to relearn a new set of MAC addresses. To make the learned addresses persistent across a switch reboot, you can enable "sticky" MAC address learning with the following command:

```
Switch(config-if)# switchport port-security mac-address sticky
```

You also can statically define one or more MAC addresses on an interface. Any of these addresses are allowed to access the network through the port. Use the following interface configuration command to define a static address:

```
Switch(config-if)# switchport port-security mac-address mac-addr
```

The MAC address is given in dotted-triplet format. If the number of static addresses configured is less than the maximum number of addresses secured on a port, the remaining addresses are learned dynamically. Be sure to set the maximum number appropriately.

As an example, you could use the following command to configure a static address entry on an interface, so that 0006.5b02.a841 will be expected:

```
Switch(config-if)# switchport port-security mac-address 0006.5b02.a841
```

Finally, you must define how each interface using port security should react if a MAC address is in violation by using the following interface-configuration command:

```
Switch(config-if)# switchport port-security violation {shutdown | restrict | protect}
```

A violation occurs if more than the maximum number of MAC addresses are learned or if an unknown (not statically defined) MAC address attempts to transmit on the port. The switch port takes one of the following configured actions when a violation is detected:

- **Shutdown:** The port immediately is put into the errdisable state, which effectively shuts it down. It must be reenabled manually or through errdisable recovery to be used again.

- **Restrict:** The port is allowed to stay up, but all packets from violating MAC addresses are dropped. The switch keeps a running count of the number of violating packets and can send an SNMP trap and a syslog message as an alert of the violation.

- **Protect:** The port is allowed to stay up, as in the restrict mode. Although packets from violating addresses are dropped, no record of the violation is kept.

As an example of the restrict mode, a switch interface has received the following configuration commands:

```
interface GigabitEthernet1/0/11
 switchport access vlan 991
 switchport mode access
 switchport port-security
 switchport port-security violation restrict
 spanning-tree portfast
```

When the default maximum of one MAC address is exceeded on this interface, the condition is logged but the interface stays up. This is shown by the following syslog message:

```
Jun  3 17:18:41.888 EDT: %PORT_SECURITY-2-PSECURE_VIOLATION: Security violation occurred, caused by MAC address 0000.5e00.0101 on port GigabitEthernet1/0/11.
```

Tip   If an interface is undergoing the **restrict** or **protect** condition, you might need to clear the learned MAC addresses so that a specific host can use the switch port. You can clear a MAC address or the complete port cache with the following command:

```
Switch# clear port-security {all | configured | dynamic | sticky}
[address mac-addr | interface type member/mod/num]
```

In the shutdown mode, the port security action is much more drastic. When the maximum number of MAC addresses is exceeded, the following syslog messages indicate that the port has been shut down in the errdisable state:

```
Jun  3 17:14:19.018 EDT: %PM-4-ERR_DISABLE: psecure-violation error detected on
Gi1/0/11, putting Gi1/0/11 in err-disable state

Jun  3 17:14:19.022 EDT: %PORT_SECURITY-2-PSECURE_VIOLATION: Security violation
occurred, caused by MAC address 0003.a089.efc5 on port GigabitEthernet1/0/11.

Jun  3 17:14:20.022 EDT: %LINEPROTO-5-UPDOWN: Line protocol on Interface
GigabitEthernet1/0/11, changed state to down

Jun  3 17:14:21.023 EDT: %LINK-3-UPDOWN: Interface GigabitEthernet1/0/11, changed
state to down
```

You also can show the port status with the **show port-security interface** command, as demonstrated in Example 19-1.

Example 19-1   *Displaying Port Security Port Status*

```
Switch# show port-security interface gigabitethernet 1/0/11
Port Security               : Enabled
Port Status                 : Secure-shutdown
Violation Mode              : Shutdown
Aging Time                  : 0 mins
Aging Type                  : Absolute
SecureStatic Address Aging  : Disabled
Maximum MAC Addresses       : 1
Total MAC Addresses         : 0
Configured MAC Addresses    : 0
Sticky MAC Addresses        : 0
Last Source Address         : 0003.a089.efc5
Security Violation Count    : 1
Switch#
```

To see a quick summary of only ports in the errdisable state, along with the reason for errdisable, you can use the **show interfaces status err-disabled** command, as demonstrated in Example 19-2.

Example 19-2 *Displaying Summary Information for Ports in the Errdisable State*

```
Switch# show interfaces status err-disabled
Port        Name                 Status        Reason
Gi1/0/11    Test port            err-disabled psecure-violation
Switch#
```

Tip   When a port is moved to the errdisable state, you must either manually cycle it or configure the switch to automatically re-enable ports after a prescribed delay. To manually cycle a port and return it to service, use the following commands:

```
Switch(config)# interface type member/mod/num
Switch(config-if)# shutdown
Switch(config-if)# no shutdown
```

Finally, you can display a summary of the port-security status with the **show port-security** command, as demonstrated in Example 19-3.

Example 19-3 *Displaying Port Security Status Summary Information*

```
Switch# show port-security
Secure Port  MaxSecureAddr  CurrentAddr  SecurityViolation  Security Action
             (Count)        (Count)      (Count)

-----------------------------------------------------------------------------

   Gi1/0/11          5            1               0           Restrict
   Gi1/0/12          1            0               0           Shutdown

-----------------------------------------------------------------------------
Total Addresses in System (excluding one mac per port)   : 0
Max Addresses limit in System (excluding one mac per port) : 6176
Switch#
```

Port-Based Authentication

Catalyst switches can support port-based authentication, a combination of AAA authentication and port security. This feature is based on the IEEE 802.1X standard. When it is enabled, a switch port will not pass any traffic until a user has authenticated with the switch. If the authentication is successful, the user can use the port normally.

For port-based authentication, both the switch and the end user's PC must support the 802.1X standard, using the Extensible Authentication Protocol over LANs (EAPOL). The 802.1X standard is a cooperative effort between the client and the switch offering network service. If the client PC is configured to use 802.lx but the switch does not support it, the PC abandons the protocol and communicates normally. However, if the switch is configured for 802.1X but the PC does not support it, the switch port remains in the unauthorized state so that it will not forward any traffic to the client PC.

Note   802.1X EAPOL is a Layer 2 protocol. At the point that a switch detects the presence of a device on a port, the port remains in the unauthorized state. Therefore, the client PC cannot communicate with anything other than the switch by using EAPOL. If the PC does not already have an IP address, it cannot request one. The PC also has no knowledge of the switch or its IP address, so any means other than a Layer 2 protocol is not possible. This is why the PC must also have an 802.1X-capable application or client software.

An 802.1X switch port begins in the unauthorized state so that no data other than the 802.1X protocol itself is allowed through the port. Either the client or the switch can initiate an 802.1X session. The authorized state of the port ends when the user logs out, causing the 802.1X client to inform the switch to revert back to the unauthorized state. The switch can also time out the user's authorized session. If this happens, the client must reauthenticate to continue using the switch port.

802.1X Configuration

Port-based authentication can be handled by one or more external Remote Authentication Dial-In User Service (RADIUS) servers. Although many Cisco switch platforms allow other authentication methods to be configured, only RADIUS is supported for 802.1X.

The actual RADIUS authentication method must be configured first, followed by 802.1X, as shown in the following steps:

Step 1.   Enable AAA on the switch.By default, AAA is disabled. You can enable AAA for port-based authentication by using the following global configuration command:

```
Switch(config)# aaa new-model
```

The **new-model** keyword refers to the use of method lists, by which authentication methods and sources can be grouped or organized. The new model is much more scalable than the "old model," in which the authentication source was explicitly configured.

Step 2.   Define external RADIUS servers.

First, define each server along with its secret shared password. This string is known only to the switch and the server, and provides a key for encrypting the authentication session. Use the following global configuration command:

```
Switch(config)# radius-server host {hostname | ip-address} [key string]
```

This command can be repeated to define additional RADIUS servers.

Step 3.   Define the authentication method for 802.1X.

Using the following command causes all RADIUS authentication servers that are defined on the switch to be used for 802.1X authentication:

```
Switch(config)# aaa authentication dot1x default group radius
```

Step 4.   Enable 802.1X on the switch:

```
Switch(config)# dot1x system-auth-control
```

Step 5.   Configure each switch port that will use 802.1X:

```
Switch(config)# interface type mod/num
Switch(config-if)# dot1x port-control {force-authorized | force-
unauthorized | auto}
```

Here, the 802.1X state is one of the following:

- **force-authorized:** The port is forced to always authorize any connected client. No authentication is necessary. This is the default state for all switch ports when 802.1X is enabled.

- **force-unauthorized:** The port is forced to never authorize any connected client. As a result, the port cannot move to the authorized state to pass traffic to a connected client.

- **Auto:** The port uses an 802.1X exchange to move from the unauthorized to the authorized state, if successful. This requires an 802.1X-capable application on the client PC.

Tip   After 802.1X is globally enabled on a switch, all switch ports default to the **force-authorized** state. This means that any PC connected to a switch port can immediately start accessing the network. Ideally, you should explicitly configure each port to use the **auto** state so that connected PCs are forced to authenticate through the 802.1X exchange.

Step 6.   Allow multiple hosts on a switch port.

It might be obvious that port-based authentication is tailored to controlling access to a single host PC that is connected to a switch port. However, 802.1X also supports cases in which multiple hosts are attached to a single switch port through an Ethernet hub or another access layer switch.

If the switch should expect to find multiple hosts present on the switch port, use the following interface configuration command:

```
Switch(config-if)# dot1x host-mode multi-host
```

Tip   You can use the **show dot1x all** command to verify the 802.1X operation on each switch port that is configured to use port-based authentication.

802.1X Port-Based Authentication Example

In Example 19-4, two RADIUS servers are located at 10.1.1.1 and 10.1.1.2. Switch ports Gigabit Ethernet 1/0/1 through 1/0/40 will use 802.1X for port-based authentication. When authenticated, the end users will be associated with VLAN 10.

Example 19-4   *Configuring 802.1X Port-Based Authentication*

```
Switch(config)# aaa new-model
Switch(config)# radius-server host 10.1.1.1 key BigSecret
Switch(config)# radius-server host 10.1.1.2 key AnotherBigSecret
Switch(config)# aaa authentication dot1x default group radius
Switch(config)# dot1x system-auth-control
Switch(config)# interface range gigabitethernet1/0/1 - 40
Switch(config-if)# switchport access vlan 10
Switch(config-if)# switchport mode access
Switch(config-if)# dot1x port-control auto
```

Using Storm Control

Recall from Chapter 2, "Switch Operation," that a LAN switch makes a network operate more efficiently by breaking it up into many isolated portions. A single host can connect to a single switch port, forming a tiny collision domain. More importantly, a switch uses a destination MAC address to deliver a frame to the switch port where the corresponding host is connected. For the most part, each host receives only the frames that are meant to reach it. Frame delivery is streamlined and hosts are spared spending their resources receiving and discarding unnecessary and unrelated frames.

Three exceptions apply to this idealized scenario:

- Broadcast frames
- Multicast frames
- Unknown unicast frames

In each of these cases, frames have a destination MAC address that is not specific or one that cannot be located. Therefore, the frames must be flooded or delivered to multiple hosts over multiple switch ports. Some amount of flooded traffic is normal and should be expected. After all, hosts must rely on broadcasts like ARP requests to find other hosts. Until a host transmits a frame and the switch learns its MAC address, the switch must flood frames destined for the host.

However, it is entirely possible to have an excessive amount of flooded traffic on a network. For example, a host might have a runaway process or malicious software that sends a broadcast storm into its local VLAN. Another host might set aside one network interface card (NIC) to receive traffic and another one to transmit traffic. The receiving NIC will never send a frame, so the switch will never learn its MAC address. As a result, all traffic destined for the receiving NIC will be flooded to all hosts on the VLAN as unknown unicast frames.

By default, frames will be flooded at the same rate they are received by a switch. Under normal conditions, the volume of flooded frames should not be too great for hosts to handle. Under extreme conditions, flooded frames can overwhelm many hosts. You can leverage the Storm Control feature to set limits on flooded traffic before it can cause problems on your network.

Storm Control is configured on a per-interface basis to monitor traffic that is arriving or being received at the interface, as shown in Figure 19-1. The idea is to take action on frames as they enter the switch and arrive at the internal switching bus, *before* they are flooded to multiple switch ports. You can configure thresholds for the amount of broadcast, multicast, or unknown unicast traffic and an action to be taken when the thresholds are exceeded.

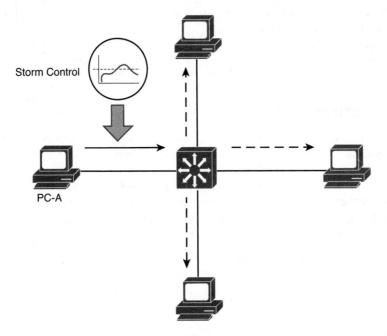

Figure 19-1   *Using Storm Control to Limit Received Frames Before They Are Flooded*

First, select an interface where frames might be received and flooded. Then configure a threshold using the following interface configuration command:

```
Switch(config-if)# storm-control {broadcast | multicast | unicast}
level {level [level-low] | bps bps [bps-low] | pps pps [pps-low]}
```

Select the type of threshold with the **broadcast**, **multicast**, or **unicast** keyword. Keep in mind that "unicast" actually means unknown unicast; otherwise, the threshold would limit the volume of normal unicast frames passing through the interface.

You can set the traffic threshold with the **level** keyword and one of the following keywords and values:

- *level [level-low]*: The threshold is set to a percentage of the interface bandwidth. The *level* and *level-low* percentages can be a value with two decimal places from 0.00 to 100.00.

- **bps** *bps [bps-low]*: The threshold is set to a specific bits per second rate. The *bps* and *bps-low* values can range from 0.0 to 10000000000.0 (10 Gbps), with one decimal place.

■ **pps** *pps* [*pps-low*]: The threshold is set to a specific packets per second rate. The *pps* and *pps-low* values can range from 0.0 to 10000000000.0 (10 Gbps), with one decimal place.

Storm Control will take action when the flooded traffic rises to the first value, then will stop the action when the traffic falls below that value. You can set a different falling threshold by specifying the second *-low* value.

> **Tip**   Rather than counting zeroes for large bps and pps values, you can use k, m, and g to designate kilo-, mega-, and giga- units.

You can repeat the **storm control** command to define separate thresholds for broadcast, multicast, and unknown unicast traffic.

Next, specify the action to be taken when the threshold is exceeded. By default, the excessive frames are simply dropped as they are received. In addition, you can use the following interface configuration command to shut down the interface in errdisable mode or to send an SNMP trap as an alert of a storm condition in progress:

```
Switch(config-if)# storm-control action {shutdown | trap}
```

In Example 19-5, Storm Control is enabled for traffic received on interface Gigabit Ethernet 1/0/1. Because there is no **storm control action** command entered, the default action to drop excessive frames will be taken. When broadcast frames exceed 50 percent of the interface bandwidth, they will be dropped. When the rate of multicast frames exceeds 50,000 packets per second, they will be dropped. Finally, when the volume of unknown unicast frames rises above 20 percent and then stays above 10 percent of the interface bandwidth, they will be dropped.

Example 19-5   *Enabling Storm Control*

```
Switch(config)# interface gigabitethernet1/0/1
Switch(config-if)# storm control broadcast level 50
Switch(config-if)# storm control multicast level pps 50k
Switch(config-if)# storm control unicast level 20 10
```

You can display the rising and falling Storm Control thresholds, in addition to the current rate, with the following EXEC command:

```
Switch# show storm-control [interface-id] [broadcast | multicast | unicast]
```

Best Practices for Securing Switches

Although you can configure and use many different features on Cisco Catalyst switches, you should be aware of some common weaknesses that can be exploited. In other words, do not become complacent and assume that everyone connected to your network will be good citizens and play by the rules. Think ahead and try to prevent as many things as possible that might be leveraged to assist an attacker.

This section presents a brief overview of many best-practice suggestions that can help secure your switched network:

- **Configure secure passwords:** Whenever possible, you should use the **enable secret** command to set the privileged-level password on a switch. This command uses a stronger encryption than the normal **enable password** command.

  You also should use external AAA servers to authenticate administrative users whenever possible. The usernames and passwords are maintained externally, so they are not stored or managed directly on the switch. In addition, having a centralized user management is much more scalable than configuring and changing user credentials on many individual switches and routers.

  Finally, you always should use the **service password-encryption** configuration command to automatically encrypt password strings that are stored in the switch configuration. Although the encryption is not excessively strong, it can prevent casual observers from seeing passwords in the clear.

- **Use system banners:** When users successfully access a switch, they should be aware of any specific access or acceptable use policies that are pertinent to your organization. You should configure system banners so that this type of information is displayed when users log in to a switch. The idea is to warn unauthorized users (if they gain access) that their activities could be grounds for prosecution—or that they are unwelcome, at the very least.

  You should use the **banner motd** command to define the text that is displayed to authenticated users. Try to avoid using other banner types that display information about your organization or the switch before users actually log in. Never divulge any extra information about your network that malicious users could use.

- **Secure the web interface:** Decide whether you will use the web interface to manage or monitor a switch. Some network professionals use the command line interface exclusively, so the web interface is not needed in a production environment. In this case, you should disable the web interface with the **no ip http server** global configuration command.

  If you do decide to use the web interface, be sure to use the HTTPS interface, if it is supported on the switch platform. The standard HTTP web interface has some glaring weaknesses, mainly because none of the traffic is encrypted or protected. Enable the HTTPS interface with the **ip http secure server** global configuration command instead of the **ip http server** command.

  In addition, try to limit the source addresses that can access the HTTPS interface. First, create an access list that permits only approved source addresses; then apply the access list to the HTTPS interface with the **ip http access-class** configuration command. As an example, the following configuration commands permit HTTPS connections that are sourced from the 10.100.50.0/24 network:

```
Switch(config)# ip http secure server
Switch(config)# access-list 1 permit 10.100.50.0 0.0.0.255
Switch(config)# ip http access-class 1
```

- **Secure the switch console:** In many environments, switches are locked away in wiring closets where physical security is used to keep people from connecting to the switch console. Even so, you always should configure authentication on any switch console. It is usually appropriate to use the same authentication configuration on the console as the virtual terminal (vty) lines.

- **Secure virtual terminal access:** You always should configure user authentication on *all* the vty lines on a switch. In addition, you should use access lists to limit the source IP addresses of potential administrative users who try to use Telnet or Secure Shell (SSH) to access a switch.

  You can use a simple IP access list to permit inbound connections only from known source addresses, as in the following example:

```
Switch(config)# access-list 10 permit 192.168.199.10
Switch(config)# access-list 10 permit 192.168.201.100
Switch(config)# line vty 0 15
Switch(config-line)# access-class 10 in
```

  Be sure you apply the access list to all the **line vty** entries in the switch configuration. Many times, the vty lines are separated into groups in the configuration. You can use the **show user all** command to see every possible line that can be used to access a switch.

- **Use SSH whenever possible:** Although Telnet access is easy to configure and use, Telnet is not secure. Every character you type in a Telnet session is sent to and echoed from a switch in the clear, with no encryption. Therefore, it is very easy to eavesdrop on Telnet sessions to overhear usernames and passwords.

  Instead, you should use SSH whenever possible. SSH uses strong encryption to secure session data. Therefore, you need a strong-encryption IOS image running on a switch before SSH can be configured and used. You should use the highest SSH version that is available on a switch. The early SSHv1 and SSHv1.5 have some weaknesses, so you should choose SSHv2 with the **ip ssh version 2** global configuration command whenever possible.

- **Secure SNMP access:** As a best practice, you should always leverage the secure features of SNMPv3. You should also prevent unauthorized users from making changes to a switch configuration by disabling any SNMPv1 or SNMPv2C read-write SNMP access. These are commands of the form **snmp-server community** *string* **rw**.

  Instead, you should have only read-only commands in the configuration. In addition, you should use access lists to limit the source addresses that have read-only access. Do not depend on the SNMPv1 or SNMPv2c community strings for security because these are passed in the clear in SNMP packets.

■ **Secure unused switch ports:** Every unused switch port should be disabled so that unexpected users cannot connect and use them without your knowledge. You can do this with the **shutdown** interface configuration command.

In addition, you should configure every user port as an access port with the **switch-port mode access** interface configuration command. Otherwise, a malicious user might connect and attempt to negotiate trunking mode on a port. You also should consider associating every unused access port with a bogus or isolated VLAN. If an unexpected user does gain access to a port, he will have access only to a VLAN that is isolated from every other resource on your network.

Tip You might consider using the **switchport host** interface configuration command as a quick way to force a port to support only a single PC. This command is actually a macro, as shown in the following example:

```
Switch(config)# interface gigabitethernet 1/0/1
Switch(config-if)# switchport host
switchport mode will be set to access
spanning-tree portfast will be enabled
channel group will be disabled
Switch(config-if)#
```

■ **Secure STP operation:** A malicious user can inject STP bridge protocol data units (BPDUs) into switch ports or VLANs, and can disrupt a stable, loop-free topology. You always should enable the BPDU Guard feature so that access switch ports automatically are disabled if unexpected BPDUs are received.

■ **Secure the use of CDP and LLDP:** By default, Cisco Discovery Protocol (CDP) advertisements are sent on every switch port at 60-second intervals. If Link Layer Discovery Protocol (LLDP) is enabled, its advertisements are sent at 30-second intervals. Although CDP and LLDP are very handy tools for discovering neighboring network devices, you should not allow those protocols to advertise unnecessary information about your switch to listening attackers.

For example, the following information is sent in a CDP advertisement in the clear. An attacker might use the device ID to physically locate the switch, its IP address to target Telnet, SSH, or Simple Network Management Protocol (SNMP) attacks, or the native VLAN and switch port ID to attempt a VLAN hopping attack:

```
Device ID: nyc-bldgA-dist1.mycompany.com
Entry address(es):
  IP address: 10.1.76.2
Platform: cisco WS-C6509-E,  Capabilities: Router Switch IGMP
Interface: TenGigabitEthernet1/1/1,  Port ID (outgoing port):
TenGigabitEthernet1/5
Holdtime : 137 sec
Version :
```

```
Cisco IOS Software, s72033_rp Software (s72033_rp-ADVIPSERVICESK9_WAN-M), Version
12.2(33)SXI4, RELEASE SOFTWARE (fc3)
Technical Support: http://www.cisco.com/techsupport
Copyright (c) 1986-2010 by Cisco Systems, Inc.
Compiled Sat 29-May-10 17:54 by prod_rel_team
advertisement version: 2
VTP Management Domain: 'MyCompany'
Native VLAN: 101
Duplex: full
Management address(es):
  IP address: 10.1.76.2
```

CDP should be enabled only on switch ports that connect to other trusted Cisco devices. Do not forget that CDP must be enabled on access switch ports where Cisco IP phones are connected. When the CDP messages reach the IP phone, they will not be relayed on to a PC connected to the phone's data port. You can disable CDP on a port-by-port basis with the **no cdp enable** interface configuration command.

Exam Preparation Tasks

Review All Key Topics

Review the most important topics in the chapter, noted with the Key Topic icon in the outer margin of the page. Table 19-2 lists a reference of these key topics and the page numbers on which each is found.

Table 19-2 *Key Topics for Chapter 19*

Key Topic Element	Description	Page Number
Paragraph	Discusses port security and MAC address control using sticky MAC addresses	415
List	Explains the actions port security can take when the MAC address limits are violated	416
Paragraph	Discusses port based authentication using IEEE 802.1X and EAPOL	418
Paragraph	Explains how to configure Storm Control	422

Complete Tables and Lists from Memory

There are no memory tables in this chapter.

Define Key Terms

Define the following key terms from this chapter, and check your answers in the glossary:

sticky MAC address, IEEE 802.1X

Use Command Reference to Check Your Memory

This section includes the most important configuration and EXEC commands covered in this chapter. It might not be necessary to memorize the complete syntax of every command, but you should remember the basic keywords that are needed.

To test your memory of the STP configuration commands, cover the right side of Tables 19-3 through 19-5 with a piece of paper, read the description on the left side, and then see how much of the command you can remember.

Table 19-3 *Port Security Configuration Commands*

Task	Command Syntax
Enable port security on an interface.	Switch(config-if)# **switchport port-security**
Set the maximum number of learned addresses.	Switch(config-if)# **switchport port-security** *maximum max-addr*
Define a static MAC address.	Switch(config-if)# **switchport port-security mac-address** *mac-addr*
Define an action to take.	Switch(config-if)# **switchport port-security violation {shutdown	restrict	protect}**
Display port security status.	Switch# **show port-security** [interface *type member/module/number*]

Table 19-4 *Port-Based Authentication Configuration Commands*

Task	Command Syntax
Define a method list for 802.1X.	Switch(config)# **aaa authentication dot1x default group radius**
Globally enable 802.1X.	Switch(config)# **dot1x system-auth-control**
Define the 802.1X behavior on a port.	Switch(config-if)# **dot1x port-control {force-authorized	force- unauthorized	auto}**
Support more than one host on a port.	Switch(config-if)# **dot1x host-mode multi-host**
Display 802.1X interface status.	Switch# **show dot1x** [all] [interface *type member/ module/number*]

Table 19-5 *Storm Control Configuration Commands*

Task	Command Syntax
Enable a Storm Control threshold on an interface.	Switch(config-if)# **storm-control {broadcast	multicast	unicast} level** {*level* [*level-low*]	**bps** *bps* [*bps-low*]	**pps** *pps* [*pps-low*]}
Define an action for Storm Control. (By default, frames are dropped if this command is not present.)	Switch(config-if)# **storm-control action {shutdown	trap}**
Display Storm Control status.	Switch# **show storm-control** [*interface-id*] [**broadcast	multicast	unicast**]

This chapter covers the following topics that you need to master for the CCNP SWITCH exam:

■ **VLAN Access Lists:** This section discusses how traffic can be controlled within a VLAN. You can use VLAN access control lists (ACL) to filter packets even as they are bridged or switched.

■ **Private VLANs:** This section explains the mechanisms that you can use to provide isolation within a single VLAN. Private VLANs have a unidirectional nature; several of them can be isolated yet share a common subnet and gateway.

■ **Securing VLAN Trunks:** This section covers two types of attacks that can be leveraged against a VLAN trunk link. If a trunk link is extended to or accessible from an attacker, any VLAN carried over the trunk can be compromised in turn.

CHAPTER 20

Securing VLANs

Traditionally, traffic has been filtered only at router boundaries, where packets naturally are inspected before being forwarded. This is true within Catalyst switches because access lists can be applied as a part of multilayer switching. Catalysts also can filter packets even if they stay within the same VLAN; VLAN access control lists, or VACLs, provide this capability.

Catalyst switches also have the capability to logically divide a single VLAN into multiple partitions. Each partition can be isolated from others, with all of them sharing a common IP subnet and a common gateway address. Private VLANs make it possible to offer up a single VLAN to many disparate customers or organizations without any interaction between them.

VLAN trunks are commonly used on links between switches to carry data from multiple VLANs. If the switches are all under the same administrative control, it is easy to become complacent about the security of the trunks. A few known attacks can be used to gain access to the VLANs that are carried over trunk links. Therefore, network administrators should be aware of the steps that can be taken to prevent any attacks.

"Do I Know This Already?" Quiz

The "Do I Know This Already?" quiz allows you to assess whether you should read this entire chapter thoroughly or jump to the "Exam Preparation Tasks" section. If you are in doubt based on your answers to these questions or your own assessment of your knowledge of the topics, read the entire chapter. Table 20-1 outlines the major headings in this chapter and the "Do I Know This Already?" quiz questions that go with them. You can find the answers in Appendix A, "Answers to the 'Do I Know This Already?' Quizzes."

Table 20-1 *"Do I Know This Already?" Foundation Topics Section-to-Question Mapping*

Foundation Topics Section	Questions Covered in This Section
VLAN Access Lists	1–4
Private VLANs	5–8
Securing VLAN Trunks	9–12

1. Which one of the following can filter packets even if they are not routed to another Layer 3 interface?

   a. IP extended access lists

   b. MAC address access lists

   c. VLAN access lists

   d. Port-based access lists

2. In what part of a Catalyst switch are VLAN ACLs implemented?

   a. NVRAM

   b. CAM

   c. RAM

   d. TCAM

3. Which one of the following commands can implement a VLAN ACL called test?

   a. access-list vlan test

   b. vacl test

   c. switchport vacl test

   d. vlan access-map test

4. After a VACL is configured, where is it applied?

   a. Globally on a VLAN

   b. On the VLAN interface

   c. In the VLAN configuration

   d. On all ports or interfaces mapped to a VLAN

5. Which of the following private VLANs is the most restrictive?

   a. Community VLAN

   b. Isolated VLAN

   c. Restricted VLAN

   d. Promiscuous VLAN

6. The vlan 100 command has just been entered. What is the next command needed to configure VLAN 100 as a secondary isolated VLAN?

   a. private-vlan isolated

   b. private-vlan isolated 100

   c. pvlan secondary isolated

   d. No further configuration necessary

7. What type of port configuration should you use for private VLAN interfaces that connect to a router?

   a. Host

   b. Gateway

   c. Promiscuous

   d. Transparent

8. Promiscuous ports must be _____ to primary and secondary VLANs, and host ports must be _____.

   a. Mapped, associated

   b. Mapped, mapped

   c. Associated, mapped

   d. Associated, associated

9. In a switch spoofing attack, an attacker makes use of which one of the following?

   a. The switch management IP address

   b. CDP message exchanges

   c. Spanning Tree Protocol

   d. DTP to negotiate a trunk

10. Which one of the following commands enables you to prevent a switch spoofing attack on an end-user port?

   a. switchport mode access

   b. switchport mode trunk

   c. no switchport spoof

   d. spanning-tree spoof-guard

11. Which one of the following represents the spoofed information an attacker sends in a VLAN hopping attack?

   a. 802.1Q tags

   b. DTP information

   c. VTP information

   d. 802.1x information

12. Which one of the following methods can be used to prevent a VLAN hopping attack?

    a. Use VTP throughout the network.

    b. Set the native VLAN to the user access VLAN.

    c. Remove the native VLAN from a trunk link.

    d. Avoid using EtherChannel link bundling.

Foundation Topics

VLAN Access Lists

Access lists can manage or control traffic as it passes through a switch. When normal access lists are configured on a Catalyst switch, they filter traffic through the use of the ternary content-addressable memory (TCAM). Recall from Chapter 2, "Switch Operation," that access lists (also known as *router access lists*, or RACLs) are merged or compiled into the TCAM. Each ACL is applied to an interface according to the direction of traffic—inbound or outbound. Packets then can be filtered in hardware with no switching performance penalty. However, only packets that pass *between* VLANs can be filtered this way.

Packets that stay in the same VLAN do not cross a VLAN or interface boundary and do not necessarily have a direction in relation to an interface. These packets also might be non-IP or completely bridged; therefore, they never pass through the multilayer switching mechanism. VLAN access lists (VACLs) are filters that directly can affect how packets are handled *within* a VLAN.

VACLs are somewhat different from RACLs or traditional access control lists. Although they, too, are merged into the TCAM, they can permit, deny, or redirect packets as they are matched. VACLs also are configured in a route map fashion, with a series of matching conditions and actions to take.

VACL Configuration

VACLs are configured as a VLAN access map in much the same format as a route map. A VLAN access map consists of one or more statements, each having a common map name. First, you define the VACL with the following global configuration command:

```
Switch(config)# vlan access-map map-name [sequence-number]
```

Access map statements are evaluated in sequence according to the sequence number. Each statement can contain one or more matching conditions, followed by an action.

Next, define the matching conditions that identify the traffic to be filtered. Matching is performed by access lists (IP or MAC address ACLs), which you must configure independently. Configure a matching condition with one of the following access map configuration commands:

```
Switch(config-access-map)# match ip address {acl-number | acl-name}
Switch(config-access-map)# match mac address acl-name
```

You can repeat these commands to define several matching conditions; the first match encountered triggers an action to take. Define the action with the following access map configuration command:

```
Switch(config-access-map)# action {drop | forward [capture] | redirect type mod/
num}
```

A VACL can either drop a matching packet, forward it, or redirect it to another interface. The TCAM performs the entire VACL match and action as packets are switched or bridged within a VLAN or routed into or out of a VLAN.

Finally, you must apply the VACL to a VLAN using the following global configuration command:

```
Switch(config)# vlan filter map-name vlan-list vlan-list
```

Notice that the VACL is applied globally to one or more VLANs listed and not to a VLAN interface switch virtual interface (SVI). Recall that VLANs can be present in a switch as explicit interfaces or as inherent Layer 2 entities. The VLAN interface is the point where packets enter or leave a VLAN, so it does not make sense to apply a VACL there. Instead, the VACL needs to function within the VLAN itself, where there is no inbound or outbound direction.

For example, suppose that you need to filter traffic within VLAN 99 so that host 192.168.99.17 is not allowed to contact any other host on its local subnet. Access list local-17 is created to identify traffic between this host and anything else on its local subnet. Then a VLAN access map is defined: If the local-17 access list matches (permits) the IP address, the packet is dropped; otherwise, the packet is forwarded. Example 20-1 shows the commands necessary for this example.

Example 20-1   *Filtering Traffic Within the Local Subnet*

```
Switch(config)# ip access-list extended local-17
Switch(config-acl)# permit ip host 192.168.99.17 192.168.99.0  0.0.0.255
Switch(config-acl)# exit
Switch(config)# vlan access-map block-17 10
Switch(config-access-map)# match ip address local-17
Switch(config-access-map)# action drop
Switch(config-access-map)# vlan access-map block-17 20
Switch(config-access-map)# action forward
Switch(config-access-map)# exit
Switch(config)# vlan filter block-17 vlan-list 99
```

Private VLANs

Normally, traffic is allowed to move unrestricted within a VLAN. Packets sent from one host to another normally are heard only by the destination host because of the nature of Layer 2 switching.

However, if one host broadcasts a packet, all hosts on the VLAN must listen. You can use a VACL to filter packets between a source and destination in a VLAN if both connect to the local switch.

Sometimes it would be nice to have the capability to segment traffic within a single VLAN, without having to use multiple VLANs and a router. For example, in a single-VLAN server farm, all servers should be capable of communicating with the router or gateway, but the servers should not have to listen to each other's broadcast traffic. Taking this a step further, suppose that each server belongs to a separate organization. Now each server should be isolated from the others but still be capable of reaching the gateway to find clients not on the local network.

Another application is a service provider network. Here, the provider might want to use a single VLAN to connect to several customer networks. Each customer needs to be able to contact the provider's gateway on the VLAN. Clearly, the customer sites do not need to interact with each other.

Private VLANs (PVLANs) solve this problem on Catalyst switches. In a nutshell, a normal, or *primary*, VLAN can be logically associated with special unidirectional, or secondary, VLANs. Hosts associated with a secondary VLAN can communicate with ports on the primary VLAN (a router, for example), but not with another secondary VLAN. A secondary VLAN is configured as one of the following types:

- **Isolated:** Any switch ports associated with an isolated VLAN can reach the primary VLAN but not any other secondary VLAN. In addition, hosts associated with the same isolated VLAN cannot reach each other. They are, in effect, isolated from everything except the primary VLAN.

- **Community:** Any switch ports associated with a common community VLAN can communicate with each other and with the primary VLAN but not with any other secondary VLAN. This provides the basis for server farms and workgroups within an organization, while giving isolation between organizations.

All secondary VLANs must be associated with one primary VLAN to set up the unidirectional relationship. Private VLANs are configured using special cases of regular VLANs. However, the VLAN Trunking Protocol (VTP) does not pass any information about the private VLAN configuration. Therefore, private VLANs are only locally significant to a switch. Each of the private VLANs must be configured locally on each switch that interconnects them.

You must configure each physical switch port that uses a private VLAN with a VLAN association. You also must define the port with one of the following modes:

- **Promiscuous:** The switch port connects to a router, firewall, or other common gateway device. This port can communicate with anything else connected to the primary or any secondary VLAN. In other words, the port is in promiscuous mode, in which the rules of private VLANs are ignored.

- **Host:** The switch port connects to a regular host that resides on an isolated or community VLAN. The port communicates only with a promiscuous port or ports on the same community VLAN.

Figure 20-1 shows the basic private VLAN operation. Some host PCs connect to a secondary community VLAN. The two community VLANs associate with a primary VLAN, where the router connects. The router connects to a promiscuous port on the primary VLAN. A single host PC connects to a secondary isolated VLAN, so it can communicate only with the router's promiscuous port.

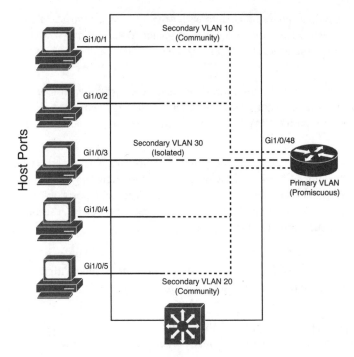

Figure 20-1   *Private VLAN Functionality Within a Switch*

Private VLAN Configuration

Defining a private VLAN involves several configuration steps. These steps are described in the sections that follow.

Configure the Private VLANs

To configure a private VLAN, begin by defining any secondary VLANs that are needed for isolation using the following configuration commands:

```
Switch(config)# vlan vlan-id
Switch(config-vlan)# private-vlan {isolated | community}
```

The secondary VLAN can be an isolated VLAN (no connectivity between isolated ports) or a community VLAN (connectivity between member ports).

Now define the primary VLAN that will provide the underlying private VLAN connectivity using the following configuration commands:

```
Switch(config)# vlan vlan-id
Switch(config-vlan)# private-vlan primary
Switch(config-vlan)# private-vlan association {secondary-vlan-list | add  second-
ary-vlan-list | remove secondary-vlan-list}
```

Be sure to associate the primary VLAN with all its component secondary VLANs using the **association** keyword. If the primary VLAN already has been configured, you can add (**add**) or remove (**remove**) secondary VLAN associations individually.

These VLAN configuration commands set up only the mechanisms for unidirectional connectivity from the secondary VLANs to the primary VLAN. You also must associate the individual switch ports with their respective private VLANs.

Associate Ports with Private VLANs

First, define the function of the port that will participate on a private VLAN using the following configuration command:

```
Switch(config-if)# switchport mode private-vlan {host | promiscuous}
```

If the host connected to this port is a router, firewall, or common gateway for the VLAN, use the **promiscuous** keyword. This allows the host to reach all other promiscuous, isolated, or community ports associated with the primary VLAN. Otherwise, any isolated or community port must receive the **host** keyword.

For a nonpromiscuous port (using the **switchport mode private-vlan host** command), you must associate the switch port with the appropriate primary and secondary VLANs. Remember, only the private VLANs themselves have been configured until now. The switch port must know how to interact with the various VLANs using the following interface configuration command:

```
Switch(config-if)# switchport private-vlan host-association primary-vlan-id
secondary-vlan-id
```

Note When a switch port is associated with private VLANs, you do not have to configure a static access VLAN. Instead, the port takes on membership in the primary and secondary VLANs simultaneously. This does not mean that the port has a fully functional assignment to multiple VLANs. Instead, it takes on only the unidirectional behavior between the secondary and primary VLANs.

For a promiscuous port (using the **switchport mode private-vlan promiscuous** command), you must map the port to primary and secondary VLANs. Notice that promiscuous mode ports, or ports that can communicate with any other private VLAN device, are mapped, whereas other secondary VLAN ports are associated. One (promiscuous mode port) exhibits bidirectional behavior, whereas the other (secondary VLAN ports) exhibits unidirectional or logical behavior.

Use the following interface configuration command to map promiscuous mode ports to primary and secondary VLANs:

```
Switch(config-if)# switchport private-vlan mapping primary-vlan-id secondary-vlan-
list | {add secondary-vlan-list} | {remove secondary-vlan-list}
```

Assume, for example, that the switch in Figure 20-1 is configured as in Example 20-2. Host PCs on ports Gigabit Ethernet 1/0/1 and 1/0/2 are in community VLAN 10, hosts on ports Gigabit Ethernet 1/0/4 and 1/0/5 are in community VLAN 20, and the host on port Gigabit Ethernet 1/0/3 is in isolated VLAN 30. The router on port Gigabit Ethernet 1/0/48 is in promiscuous mode on primary VLAN 100. Each VLAN is assigned a role, and the primary VLAN is associated with its secondary VLANs. Then each interface is associated with a primary and secondary VLAN (if a host is attached) or mapped to the primary and secondary VLANs (if a promiscuous host is attached).

Example 20-2 *Configuring Ports with PVLANs*

```
Switch(config)# vlan 10
Switch(config-vlan)# private-vlan community
Switch(config-vlan)# vlan 20
Switch(config-vlan)# private-vlan community
Switch(config-vlan)# vlan 30
Switch(config-vlan)# private-vlan isolated
Switch(config-vlan)# vlan 100
Switch(config-vlan)# private-vlan primary
Switch(config-vlan)# private-vlan association 10,20,30
Switch(config-vlan)# exit
Switch(config)# interface range gigabitethernet 1/0/1 - 1/0/2
Switch(config-if)# switchport mode private-vlan host
Switch(config-if)# switchport private-vlan host-association 100 10
Switch(config-if)# exit
Switch(config)# interface range gigabitethernet 1/0/4 - 1/0/5
Switch(config-if)# switchport mode private-vlan host
Switch(config-if)# switchport private-vlan host-association 100 20
Switch(config-if)# exit
Switch(config)# interface gigabitethernet 1/0/3
Switch(config-if)# switchport mode private-vlan host
Switch(config-if)# switchport private-vlan host-association 100 30
Switch(config-if)# exit
Switch(config)# interface gigabitethernet 1/0/48
Switch(config-if)# switchport mode private-vlan promiscuous
Switch(config-if)# switchport private-vlan mapping 100 10,20,30
```

Associate Secondary VLANs to a Primary VLAN SVI

On switched virtual interfaces, or VLAN interfaces configured with Layer 3 addresses, you must configure some additional private VLAN mapping. Consider a different example, where the SVI for the primary VLAN, VLAN 200, has an IP address and participates in routing traffic. Secondary VLANs 40 (an isolated VLAN) and 50 (a community VLAN) are associated at Layer 2 with primary VLAN 200 using the configuration in Example 20-3.

Example 20-3 *Associating Secondary VLANs to a Primary VLAN SVI*

```
Switch(config)# vlan 40
Switch(config-vlan)# private-vlan isolated
Switch(config-vlan)# vlan 50
Switch(config-vlan)# private-vlan community
Switch(config-vlan)# vlan 200
Switch(config-vlan)# private-vlan primary
Switch(config-vlan)# private-vlan association 40,50
Switch(config-vlan)# exit
Switch(config)# interface vlan 200
Switch(config-if)# ip address 192.168.199.1 255.255.255.0
```

Primary VLAN 200 can forward traffic at Layer 3, but the secondary VLAN associations with it are good at only Layer 2. To allow Layer 3 traffic switching coming from the secondary VLANs as well, you must add a private VLAN mapping to the primary VLAN (SVI) interface, using the following interface configuration command:

```
Switch(config-if)# private-vlan mapping {secondary-vlan-list | add secondary-vlan-
list | remove secondary-vlan-list}
```

The primary VLAN SVI function is extended to the secondary VLANs instead of requiring SVIs for each of them. If some mapping already has been configured for the primary VLAN SVI, you can add (**add**) or remove (**remove**) secondary VLAN mappings individually.

Continuing with Example 20-3, you would map the private VLAN by adding the following commands:

```
Switch(config)# interface vlan 200
Switch(config-if)# private-vlan mapping 40,50
```

Securing VLAN Trunks

Because trunk links usually are bounded between two switches, you might think that they are more or less secure. Each end of the trunk is connected to a device that is under your control, VLANs carried over the trunk remain isolated, and so on.

Some attacks or exploits can be leveraged to gain access to a trunk or to the VLANs carried over a trunk. Therefore, you should become familiar with how the attacks work and what steps you can take to prevent them in the first place.

Switch Spoofing

Recall from Chapter 4, "VLANs and Trunks," that two switches can be connected by a common trunk link that can carry traffic from multiple VLANs. The trunk does not have to exist all the time. The switches dynamically can negotiate its use and its encapsulation mode by exchanging Dynamic Trunking Protocol (DTP) messages.

Although DTP can make switch administration easier, it also can expose switch ports to be compromised. Suppose that a switch port is left to its default configuration, in which the trunking mode is auto. Normally, the switch port would wait to be asked by another switch in the auto or on mode to become a trunk.

Now suppose that an end user's PC is connected to that port. A well-behaved end user would not use DTP at all, so the port would come up in access mode with a single-access VLAN. A malicious user, however, might exploit the use of DTP and attempt to negotiate a trunk with the switch port. This makes the PC appear to be another switch; in effect, the PC is spoofing a switch.

After the trunk is negotiated, the attacker has access to any VLAN that is permitted to pass over the trunk. If the switch port has been left to its default configuration, all VLANs configured on the switch are allowed onto the trunk. Figure 20-2 shows this scenario. The attacker can receive any traffic being sent over the trunk on any VLAN. In addition, he can send traffic into any VLAN of his choice.

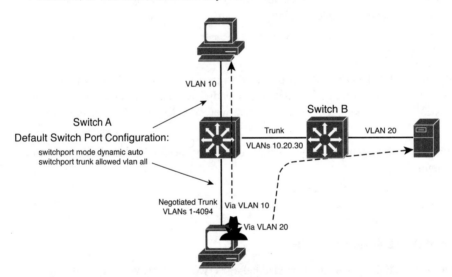

Figure 20-2   *An Example of Switch Spoofing to Gain Access to a Trunk*

To demonstrate this further, consider the output in Example 20-4, which shows the default access switch port configuration. Notice that trunking is possible because the port is set to dynamic auto mode, awaiting DTP negotiation from a connected device. If a trunk is negotiated, all VLANs are permitted to be carried over it.

Example 20-4   *Displaying the Default Switch Port Configuration*

```
Switch# show interfaces gigabitethernet 1/0/46 switchport
Name: Gi1/0/46
Switchport: Enabled
Administrative Mode: dynamic auto
Operational Mode: trunk
Administrative Trunking Encapsulation: negotiate
```

```
Negotiation of Trunking: On
Access Mode VLAN: 1 (default)
Trunking Native Mode VLAN: 1 (default)
Administrative Native VLAN tagging: enabled
Voice VLAN: none
Administrative private-vlan host-association: none
Administrative private-vlan mapping: none
Administrative private-vlan trunk native VLAN: none
Administrative private-vlan trunk Native VLAN tagging: enabled
Administrative private-vlan trunk encapsulation: dot1q
Administrative private-vlan trunk normal VLANs: none
Administrative private-vlan trunk private VLANs: none
Operational private-vlan: none
Trunking VLANs Enabled: ALL
Pruning VLANs Enabled: 2-1001
Capture Mode Disabled Capture VLANs Allowed: ALL
Protected: false
Unknown unicast blocked: disabled
Unknown multicast blocked: disabled
Appliance trust: none
Switch#
```

The solution to this situation is to configure every switch port to have an expected and controlled behavior. For example, instead of leaving an end-user switch port set to use DTP in auto mode, configure it to static access mode with the following commands:

```
Switch(config)# interface type member/mod/num
Switch(config-if)# switchport access vlan vlan-id
Switch(config-if)# switchport mode access
```

This way, an end user never will be able to send any type of spoofed traffic that will make the switch port begin trunking.

In addition, you might be wise to disable any unused switch ports to prevent someone from discovering a live port that might be exploited.

VLAN Hopping

When securing VLAN trunks, also consider the potential for an exploit called *VLAN hopping*. Here, an attacker positioned on one access VLAN can craft and send frames with spoofed 802.1Q tags so that the packet payloads ultimately appear on a totally different VLAN, all without the use of a router.

For this exploit to work, the following conditions must exist in the network configuration:

- The attacker is connected to an access switch port.

- The same switch must have an 802.1Q trunk.

- The trunk must have the attacker's access VLAN as its native VLAN.

Figure 20-3 shows how VLAN hopping works. The attacker, situated on VLAN 10, sends frames that are doubly tagged as if an 802.1Q trunk were being used. Naturally, the attacker is not connected to a trunk; he is spoofing the trunk encapsulation to trick the switch into making the frames hop over to another VLAN.

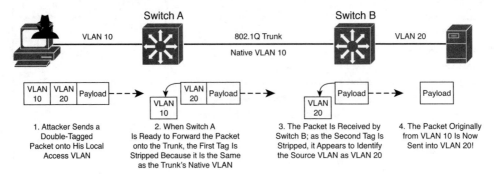

Figure 20-3   *VLAN Hopping Attack Process*

The regular frame—or malicious payload, in this case—is first given an 802.1Q tag with the VLAN ID of the target VLAN. Then a second bogus 802.1Q tag is added with the attacker's access VLAN ID.

When the local switch Switch A receives a doubly tagged frame, it decides to forward it out the trunk interface. Because the first (outermost) tag has the same VLAN ID as the trunk's native VLAN, that tag is removed as the frame is sent on the trunk. The switch believes that the native VLAN should be untagged, as it should. Now the second (inner-most) tag is exposed on the trunk.

When Switch B receives the frame, it examines any 802.1Q tag it finds. The spoofed tag for VLAN 20 is found, so the tag is removed and the frame is forwarded onto VLAN 20. Now the attacker successfully has sent a frame on VLAN 10 and gotten the frame inject-ed onto VLAN 20—all through Layer 2 switching.

Clearly, the key to this type of attack revolves around the use of untagged native VLANs. Therefore, to thwart VLAN hopping, you always should carefully configure trunk links with the following steps:

Key Topic

Step 1.   Set the native VLAN of a trunk to a bogus or unused VLAN ID.

Step 2.   Prune the native VLAN off both ends of the trunk.

For example, suppose that an 802.1Q trunk should carry only VLANs 10 and 20. You should set the native VLAN to an unused value, such as 800. Then you should remove VLAN 800 from the trunk so that it is confined to the trunk link itself. Example 20-5 demonstrates how to accomplish this.

Example 20-5   *Configuring the 802.1Q Trunk to Carry Only VLANs 10 and 20*

```
Switch(config)# vlan 800
Switch(config-vlan)# name bogus_native
Switch(config-vlan)# exit
```

```
Switch(config)# interface gigabitethernet 1/0/1
Switch(config-if)# switchport trunk encapsulation dot1q
Switch(config-if)# switchport trunk native vlan 800
Switch(config-if)# switchport trunk allowed vlan remove 800
Switch(config-if)# switchport mode trunk
```

Tip Although maintenance protocols such as Cisco Discovery Protocol (CDP), Port Aggregation Protocol (PAgP), and Dynamic Trunking Protocol (DTP) normally are carried over the native VLAN of a trunk, they will not be affected if the native VLAN is removed or manually pruned from the trunk. They still will be sent and received on the native VLAN as a special case even if the native VLAN ID is not in the list of allowed VLANs.

One alternative is to force all 802.1Q trunks to add tags to frames for the native VLAN, too. The double-tagged VLAN hopping attack will not work because the switch will not remove the first tag with the native VLAN ID (VLAN 10 in the example). Instead, that tag will remain on the spoofed frame as it enters the trunk. At the far end of the trunk, the same tag will be examined, and the frame will stay on the original access VLAN (VLAN 10).

To force a switch to tag the native VLAN on all its 802.1Q trunks, you can use the following command:

```
Switch(config)# vlan dot1q tag native
```

Exam Preparation Tasks

Review All Key Topics

Review the most important topics in the chapter, noted with the Key Topic icon in the outer margin of the page. Table 20-2 lists a reference of these key topics and the page numbers on which each is found.

Key Topic

Table 20-2 *Key Topics for Chapter 20*

Key Topic Element	Description	Page Number
Paragraph	Explains VLAN ACLs and how they are configured	435
Paragraph	Discusses private VLANs, primary and secondary VLANs, and isolated and community VLANs	437
List	Discusses promiscuous and host ports within a private VLAN	437
Paragraph	Explains the switch spoofing attack	442
Paragraph	Explains the VLAN hopping attack	443
List	Explains the steps necessary to prevent a VLAN hopping attack	444

Complete Tables and Lists from Memory

There are no memory tables in this chapter.

Define Key Terms

Define the following key terms from this chapter, and check your answers in the glossary:

VACL, private VLAN, primary VLAN, secondary VLAN, isolated VLAN, community VLAN, promiscuous port, host port, switch spoofing, VLAN hopping

Use Command Reference to Check Your Memory

This section includes the most important configuration and EXEC commands covered in this chapter. It might not be necessary to memorize the complete syntax of every command, but you should remember the basic keywords that are needed.

To test your memory of the VLAN ACL and private VLAN configuration, cover the right side of Tables 20-3 and 20-4 with a piece of paper, read the description on the left side, and then see how much of the command you can remember.

Table 20-3   *VLAN ACL Configuration Commands*

Task	Command Syntax
Define a VACL.	Switch(config)# **vlan access-map** *map-name* [*sequence-number*]
Define a matching condition.	Switch(config-access-map)# **match** {**ip address** {*acl-number* / *acl-name*}} / {**mac address** *acl-name*}}
Define an action.	Switch(config-access-map)# **action** {**drop** | **forward** [**capture**] | **redirect** *type mod/num*}
Apply the VACL to VLANs.	Switch(config)# **vlan filter** *map-name* **vlan-list** *vlan-list*

Table 20-4   *Private VLAN Configuration Commands*

Task	Command Syntax
Define a secondary VLAN.	Switch(config)# **vlan** *vlan-id* Switch(config-vlan)# **private-vlan** {**isolated** | **community**}
Define a primary VLAN; associate it with secondary VLANs.	Switch(config)# **vlan** *vlan-id* Switch(config-vlan)# **private-vlan primary** Switch(config-vlan)# **private-vlan association** {*secondary-vlan-list* | **add** *secondary-vlan-list* | **remove** *secondary-vlan-list*}
Associate ports with private VLANs.	Switch(config-if)# **switchport mode private-vlan** {**host** | **promiscuous**}
Associate nonpromiscuous ports with private VLANs.	Switch(config-if)# **switchport private-vlan host-association** *primary-vlan-id secondary-vlan-id*
Associate promiscuous ports with private VLANs.	Switch(config-if)# **switchport private-vlan mapping** {*primary-vlan-id*} {*secondary-vlan-list*} | {**add** *secondary-vlan-list*} | {**remove** *secondary-vlan-list*}
Associate secondary VLANs with a primary VLAN Layer 3 SVI.	Switch(config-if)# **private-vlan mapping** {*secondary-vlan-list* | **add** *secondary-vlan-list* | **remove** *secondary-vlan-list*}

This chapter covers the following topics that you need to master for the CCNP SWITCH exam:

■ **DHCP Snooping:** This section covers a method to prevent rogue DHCP servers from appearing on your network and disrupting service to your users.

■ **IP Source Guard:** This section discusses a mechanism you can leverage to detect and suppress hosts that use spoofed IP addresses to attack a network.

■ **Dynamic ARP Inspection:** This section explains how you can configure a switch to detect and mitigate ARP spoofing attacks.

CHAPTER 21

Preventing Spoofing Attacks

Catalyst switches can detect and prevent certain types of attacks. This chapter discusses several features that you can use to validate information passing through a switch so that spoofed addresses cannot be used to compromise hosts.

"Do I Know This Already?" Quiz

The "Do I Know This Already?" quiz allows you to assess whether you should read this entire chapter thoroughly or jump to the "Exam Preparation Tasks" section. If you are in doubt based on your answers to these questions or your own assessment of your knowledge of the topics, read the entire chapter. Table 21-1 outlines the major headings in this chapter and the "Do I Know This Already?" quiz questions that go with them. You can find the answers in Appendix A, "Answers to the 'Do I Know This Already?' Quizzes."

Table 21-1 *"Do I Know This Already?" Foundation Topics Section-to-Question Mapping*

Foundation Topics Section	Questions Covered in This Section
DHCP Snooping	1–2
IP Source Guard	3–4
Dynamic ARP Inspection	5–6

1. DHCP snooping helps mitigate which one of the following spoofed parameters?

   a. Subnet mask

   b. Gateway address

   c. DNS address

   d. DHCP request

2. With DHCP snooping, an untrusted port filters out which one of the following?

   a. DHCP replies from legitimate DHCP servers

   b. DHCP replies from rogue DHCP servers

   c. DHCP requests from legitimate clients

   d. DHCP requests from rogue clients

3. Which two of the following methods does a switch use to detect spoofed addresses when IP Source Guard is enabled?

    a. ARP entries

    b. DHCP database

    c. DHCP snooping database

    d. Static IP source binding entries

    e. Reverse path-forwarding entries

4. Which one of the following commands should you use to enable IP Source Guard on a switch interface?

    a. **ip source-guard**

    b. **ip guard source**

    c. **ip verify source**

    d. **ip source spoof**

5. Dynamic ARP Inspection helps mitigate an attack based on which one of the following parameters within an ARP reply packet?

    a. Source IP address

    b. MAC address

    c. Destination IP address

    d. Sequence number

6. Which one of the following should be configured as a trusted port for dynamic ARP inspection?

    a. The port where the ARP server is located.

    b. The port where an end-user host is located.

    c. The port where another switch is located.

    d. None; all ports are untrusted.

Foundation Topics

Malicious users sometimes can send spoofed—information to trick switches or other hosts into using a rogue machine as a gateway. The attacker's goal is to become the man in the middle, with a naive user sending packets to the attacker as if it were a router. The attacker can glean information from the packets sent to it before it forwards them normally. This section describes three Cisco Catalyst features—DHCP snooping, IP Source Guard, and dynamic ARP inspection—that prevent certain types of spoofing attacks.

DHCP Snooping

A Dynamic Host Configuration Protocol (DHCP) server normally provides all the basic information a client PC needs to operate on a network. For example, the client might receive an IP address, a subnet mask, a default gateway address, DNS addresses, and so on.

Suppose that an attacker could bring up a rogue DHCP server on a machine in the same subnet as that same client PC. Now when the client broadcasts its DHCP request, the rogue server could send a carefully crafted DHCP reply with its own IP address substituted as the default gateway.

When the client receives the reply, it begins using the spoofed gateway address. Packets destined for addresses outside the local subnet then go to the attacker's machine first. The attacker can forward the packets to the correct destination, but in the meantime, it can examine every packet that it intercepts. In effect, this becomes a type of man-in-the-middle attack; the attacker is wedged into the path and the client does not realize it.

Cisco Catalyst switches can use the DHCP snooping feature to help mitigate this type of attack. When DHCP snooping is enabled, switch ports are categorized as trusted or untrusted. Legitimate DHCP servers can be found on trusted ports, whereas all other hosts sit behind untrusted ports.

A switch intercepts all DHCP requests coming from untrusted ports before flooding them throughout the VLAN. Any DHCP replies coming from an untrusted port are discarded because they must have come from a rogue DHCP server. In addition, the offending switch port automatically is shut down in the errdisable state.

DHCP snooping also keeps track of the completed DHCP bindings as clients receive legitimate replies. This database contains the client MAC address, IP address offered, lease time, and so on.

You can configure DHCP snooping first by enabling it globally on a switch with the following configuration command:

```
Switch(config)# ip dhcp snooping
```

Next identify the VLANs where DHCP snooping should be implemented with the following command:

```
Switch(config)# ip dhcp snooping vlan vlan-id [vlan-id]
```

You can give a single VLAN number as *vlan-id* or a range of VLAN numbers by giving the start and end VLAN IDs of the range.

By default, all switch ports are assumed to be untrusted so that DHCP replies are not expected or permitted. Only trusted ports are allowed to send DHCP replies. Therefore, you should identify only the ports where known, trusted DHCP servers are located. You can do this with the following interface configuration command:

```
Switch(config)# interface type member/module/number
Switch(config-if)# ip dhcp snooping trust
```

For untrusted ports, an unlimited rate of DHCP requests is accepted. If you want to rate-limit DHCP traffic on an untrusted port, use the following interface configuration command:

```
Switch(config)# interface type member/module/number
Switch(config-if)# ip dhcp snooping limit rate rate
```

The rate can be 1 to 2048 DHCP packets per second.

You also can configure the switch to use DHCP option-82, the DHCP Relay Agent Information option, which is described in RFCs 3046 and 6607. When a DHCP request is intercepted on an untrusted port, the switch adds its own MAC address and the switch port identifier into the option-82 field of the request. The request then is forwarded normally so that it can reach a trusted DHCP server.

Adding option-82 provides more information about the actual client that generated the DHCP request. In addition, the DHCP reply (if any) echoes back the option-82 information. The switch intercepts the reply and compares the option-82 data to confirm that the request came from a valid port on itself. This feature is enabled by default. You can enable or disable option-82 globally with the following configuration command:

```
Switch(config)# [no] ip dhcp snooping information option
```

When DHCP snooping is configured, you can display its status with the following command:

```
Switch# show ip dhcp snooping [binding]
```

You can use the **binding** keyword to display all the known DHCP bindings that have been overheard. The switch maintains these in its own database. Otherwise, only the switch ports that are trusted or that have rate limiting applied are listed. All other ports are considered to be untrusted with an unlimited DHCP request rate.

As an example, interfaces Gigabit Ethernet 1/0/35 and 1/0/36 use access VLAN 104, are considered untrusted, and have DHCP rate limiting applied at three per second. A known

DHCP server is located on the Gigabit Ethernet 1/1/1 uplink. Example 21-1 shows the configuration for this scenario.

Example 21-1 *DHCP Snooping Configuration*

```
Switch(config)# ip dhcp snooping
Switch(config)# ip dhcp snooping vlan 104
Switch(config)# interface range gigabitethernet 1/0/35 - 36
Switch(config-if)# ip dhcp snooping limit rate 3
Switch(config-if)# interface gigabitethernet 1/1/1
Switch(config-if)# ip dhcp snooping trust
```

Example 21-2 shows the resulting DHCP snooping status.

Example 21-2 *DHCP Snooping Status Display*

```
Switch# show ip dhcp snooping
Switch DHCP snooping is enabled
DHCP snooping is configured on following VLANs:
104
Insertion of option 82 is enabled
Interface               Trusted      Rate limit (pps)
----------------------  -------      ----------------
GigabitEthernet1/0/35     no         3
GigabitEthernet1/0/36     no         3
GigabitEthernet1/1/1      yes        unlimited
Switch#
```

IP Source Guard

Address spoofing is one type of attack that can be difficult to mitigate. Normally, a host is assigned an IP address and is expected to use that address in all the traffic it sends out. IP addresses are effectively used on the honor system, where hosts are trusted to behave themselves and use their own legitimate source addresses.

A rogue or compromised host PC does not necessarily play by those rules. It can use its legitimate address, or it can begin to use spoofed addresses—borrowed from other hosts or used at random. Spoofed addresses are often used to disguise the origin of denial-of-service attacks. If the source address does not really exist, no return traffic will find its way back to the originator.

Routers or Layer 3 devices can perform some simple tests to detect spoofed source addresses in packets passing through. For example, if the 10.10.0.0 network is known to exist on VLAN 10, packets entering from VLAN 20 should never have source addresses in that subnet.

However, it is difficult to detect spoofed addresses when they are used *inside* the VLAN or subnet where they should already exist. For example, within the 10.10.0.0 network on

VLAN 10, as shown in Figure 21-1, a rogue host begins to send packets with a spoofed source address of 10.10.10.10. The 10.10.10.10 address is certainly within the 10.10.0.0/16 subnet, so it does not stand out as an obvious spoof. Therefore, the rogue host might be very successful in attacking other hosts in its own subnet or VLAN.

Cisco Catalyst switches can use the IP source guard feature to detect and suppress address spoofing attacks—even if they occur within the same subnet. A Layer 2 switch, and a Layer 2 port in turn, normally learns and stores MAC addresses. The switch must have a way to look up MAC addresses and find out what IP address are associated with them.

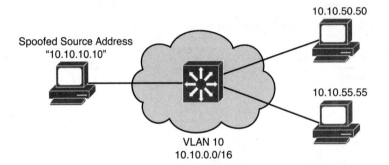

Figure 21-1 *Using a Spoofed Address Within a Subnet*

IP Source Guard does this by making use of the DHCP snooping database and static IP source binding entries. If DHCP snooping is configured and enabled, the switch learns the MAC and IP addresses of hosts that use DHCP. Packets arriving on a switch port can be tested for one of the following conditions:

- The source IP address must be identical to the IP address learned by DHCP snooping or a static entry. A dynamic port access control list (ACL) is used to filter traffic. The switch automatically creates this ACL, adds the learned source IP address to the ACL, and applies the ACL to the interface where the address is learned.

- The source MAC address must be identical to the MAC address learned on the switch port and by DHCP snooping. Port security is used to filter traffic.

If the address is something other than the one learned or statically configured, the switch drops the packet.

To configure IP Source Guard, first configure and enable DHCP snooping, as presented in the previous section. If you want IP Source Guard to detect spoofed MAC addresses, you also need to configure and enable port security.

For the hosts that do not use DHCP, you can configure a static IP source binding with the following configuration command:

```
Switch(config)# ip source binding mac-address vlan vlan-id ip-address interface
type member/module/number
```

Here, the host's MAC address is bound to a specific VLAN and IP address, and is expected to be found on a specific switch interface.

Next, enable IP source guard on one or more switch interfaces with the following configuration commands:

```
Switch(config)# interface type member/module/number
Switch(config-if)# ip verify source [port-security]
```

The **ip verify source** command inspects the source IP address only. You can add the **port-security** keyword to inspect the source MAC address, too.

To verify the IP source guard status, you can use the following EXEC command:

```
Switch# show ip verify source [interface type member/module/number]
```

If you need to verify the information contained in the IP source binding database, either learned or statically configured, you can use the following EXEC command:

```
Switch# show ip source binding [ip-address] [mac-address] [dhcp-snooping | static]
[interface type member/mod/num] [vlan vlan-id]
```

Dynamic ARP Inspection

Hosts normally use the Address Resolution Protocol (ARP) to resolve an unknown MAC address when the IP address is known. If a MAC address is needed so that a packet can be forwarded at Layer 2, a host broadcasts an ARP request that contains the IP address of the target in question. If any other host is using that IP address, it responds with an ARP reply containing its MAC address.

The ARP process works well among trusted and well-behaved users. However, suppose that an attacker could send its own crafted ARP reply when it overhears an ARP request being broadcast. The reply could contain its own MAC address, causing the original requester to think that it is bound to the IP address in question. The requester would add the bogus ARP entry into its own ARP cache, only to begin forwarding packets to the spoofed MAC address.

In effect, this scheme places the attacker's machine right in the middle of an otherwise legitimate path. Packets will be sent to the attacker instead of another host or the default gateway. The attacker can intercept packets and (perhaps) forward them on only after examining the packets' contents.

Key Topic

This attack is known as *ARP poisoning* or *ARP spoofing*, and it is considered to be a type of man-in-the-middle attack. The attacker wedges into the normal forwarding path, transparent to the end users. Cisco Catalyst switches can use the dynamic ARP inspection (DAI) feature to help mitigate this type of attack.

DAI works much like DHCP snooping. All switch ports are classified as trusted or untrusted. The switch intercepts and inspects all ARP packets that arrive on an untrusted port; no inspection is done on trusted ports.

When an ARP reply is received on an untrusted port, the switch checks the MAC and IP addresses reported in the reply packet against known and trusted values. A switch can gather trusted ARP information from statically configured entries or from dynamic entries in the DHCP snooping database. In the latter case, DHCP snooping must be enabled in addition to DAI.

If an ARP reply contains invalid information or values that conflict with entries in the trusted database, it is dropped and a log message is generated. This action prevents invalid or spoofed ARP entries from being sent and added to other machines' ARP caches.

You can configure DAI by first enabling it on one or more client VLANs with the following configuration command:

```
Switch(config)# ip arp inspection vlan vlan-range
```

The VLAN range can be a single VLAN ID, a range of VLAN IDs separated by a hyphen, or a list of VLAN IDs separated by commas.

By default, all switch ports associated with the VLAN range are considered to be untrusted. You should identify trusted ports as those that connect to other switches. In other words, the local switch will not inspect ARP packets arriving on trusted ports; it will assume that the neighboring switch also is performing DAI on all of its ports in that VLAN. Configure a trusted port with the following interface configuration command:

```
Switch(config)# interface type member/module/number
Switch(config-if)# ip arp inspection trust
```

If you have hosts with statically configured IP address information, there will be no DHCP message exchange that can be inspected. Instead, you can configure an ARP access list that defines static MAC-IP address bindings that are permitted. Use the following configuration commands to define the ARP access list and one or more static entries:

```
Switch(config)# arp access-list acl-name
Switch(config-acl)# permit ip host sender-ip mac host sender-mac [log]
[Repeat the previous command as needed]
Switch(config-acl)# exit
```

Now the ARP access list must be applied to DAI with the following configuration command:

```
Switch(config)# ip arp inspection filter arp-acl-name vlan vlan-range [static]
```

When ARP replies are intercepted, their contents are matched against the access list entries first. If no match is found, the DHCP snooping bindings database is checked next. You can give the **static** keyword to prevent the DHCP bindings database from being checked at all. In effect, this creates an implicit deny statement at the end of the ARP access list; if no match is found in the access list, the ARP reply is considered invalid.

Finally, you can specify further validations on the contents of ARP reply packets. By default, only the MAC and IP addresses contained within the ARP reply are validated. This does not take the actual MAC addresses contained in the Ethernet header of the ARP reply.

To validate that an ARP reply packet is really coming from the address listed inside it, you can enable DAI validation with the following configuration command:

```
Switch(config)# ip arp inspection validate {[src-mac] [dst-mac] [ip]}
```

Be sure to specify at least one of the options:

- **src-mac:** Check the source MAC address in the Ethernet header against the sender MAC address in the ARP reply.

- **dst-mac:** Check the destination MAC address in the Ethernet header against the target MAC address in the ARP reply.

- **ip:** Check the sender's IP address in all ARP requests; check the sender's IP address against the target IP address in all ARP replies.

Example 21-3 demonstrates where DAI is enabled for all switch ports associated with VLAN 104 on an access layer switch. The uplink to a distribution switch (Gigabit Ethernet 1/0/49) is considered to be trusted.

Example 21-3 *Configuring DAI to Validate ARP Replies*

```
Switch(config)# ip arp inspection vlan 104
Switch(config)# arp access-list StaticARP
Switch(config-acl)# permit ip host 192.168.1.10 mac host 0006.5b02.a841
Switch(config-acl)# exit
Switch(config)# ip arp inspection filter StaticARP vlan 104
Switch(config)# interface gigabitethernet 1/0/49
Switch(config-if)# ip arp inspection trust
```

You can display DAI status information with the **show ip arp inspection** command.

Exam Preparation Tasks

Review All Key Topics

Review the most important topics in the chapter, noted with the Key Topic icon in the outer margin of the page. Table 21-2 lists a reference of these key topics and the page numbers on which each is found.

Table 21-2 *Key Topics for Chapter 21*

Key Topic Element	Description	Page Number
Paragraph	Explains DHCP snooping	451
List	Lists IP Source Guard conditions	454
Paragraph	Describes ARP poisoning, ARP spoofing attacks, and dynamic ARP inspection	455

Complete Tables and Lists from Memory

There are no memory tables in this chapter.

Define Key Terms

Define the following key terms from this chapter, and check your answers in the glossary:

DHCP snooping, ARP poisoning (also known as ARP spoofing), dynamic ARP inspection (DAI)

Use Command Reference to Check Your Memory

This section includes the most important configuration and EXEC commands covered in this chapter. It might not be necessary to memorize the complete syntax of every command, but you should remember the basic keywords that are needed.

To test your memory of the configuration commands presented in this chapter, cover the right side of Tables 21-3 through 21-5 with a piece of paper, read the description on the left side, and then see how much of the command you can remember.

Table 21-3   *DHCP Snooping Configuration Commands*

Task	Command Syntax
Globally enable DHCP snooping.	Switch(config)# ip dhcp snooping
Define a trusted interface.	Switch(config-if)# **ip dhcp snooping trust**
Limit the interface DHCP packet rate.	Switch(config-if)# **ip dhcp snooping limit rate** *rate*
Display DHCP snooping status.	Switch# **show ip dhcp snooping** [**binding**]

Table 21-4   *IP Source Guard Configuration Commands*

Task	Command Syntax
Define a static IP source binding entry.	Switch(config)# **ip source binding** *mac-address* **vlan** *vlan-id ip-address* **interface** *type member/module/number*
Enable IP source guard on an interface.	Switch(config-if)# **ip verify source** [**port-security**]
Display IP source guard status.	Switch# **show ip verify source** [**interface** *type member/module/number*]
Display IP source binding database.	Switch# **show ip source binding** [*ip-address*] [*mac-address*] [**dhcp-snooping** | **static**] [**interface** *type member/module/number*] [**vlan** *vlan-id*]

Table 21-5   *Dynamic ARP Inspection Configuration Commands*

Task	Command Syntax
Enable DAI on a VLAN.	Switch(config)# **ip arp inspection vlan** *vlan-range*
Define a trusted interface.	Switch(config-if)# **ip arp inspection trust**
Define a static ARP inspection binding.	Switch(config)# **arp access-list** *acl-name* **permit ip host** *sender-ip* **mac host** *sender-mac* [**log**]
Apply static ARP inspection bindings.	Switch(config)# **ip arp inspection filter** *arp-acl-name* **vlan** *vlan-range* [**static**]
Validate addresses within ARP replies.	Switch(config)# **ip arp inspection validate** {[**src-mac**] [**dst-mac**] [**ip**]}
Display DAI status.	Switch# **show ip arp inspection**

This chapter covers the following topics that you need to master for the CCNP SWITCH exam:

■ **Configuring Authentication:** This section describes methods you can use to authenticate users when they need to connect to and manage a switch.

■ **Configuring Authorization:** This section covers methods that can authorize or grant privilege to administrative users on a switch.

■ **Configuring Accounting:** This section discusses methods that you can use to record events that occur while an administrative user is connected to a switch.

CHAPTER 22

Managing Switch Users

Catalyst switches have a variety of methods that can secure or control user access. Users can be authenticated as they connect to or through a switch, and can be authorized to perform certain actions on a switch. User access can also be recorded as switch accounting information. This chapter discusses methods you can use to control who has access to a switch and what they can do once they are logged in.

"Do I Know This Already?" Quiz

The "Do I Know This Already?" quiz allows you to assess whether you should read this entire chapter thoroughly or jump to the "Exam Preparation Tasks" section. If you are in doubt based on your answers to these questions or your own assessment of your knowledge of the topics, read the entire chapter. Table 22-1 outlines the major headings in this chapter and the "Do I Know This Already?" quiz questions that go with them. You can find the answers in Appendix A, "Answers to the 'Do I Know This Already?' Quizzes."

Table 22-1   *"Do I Know This Already?" Foundation Topics Section-to-Question Mapping*

Foundation Topics Section	Questions Covered in This Section
Configuring Authentication	1–6
Configuring Authorization	7–9
Configuring Accounting	10

1. The acronym AAA represents which three of the following functions?

   a. Analysis

   b. Authentication

   c. Accounting

   d. Administration

   e. Authorization

   f. Accounts

2. If the **username** command is used in a switch configuration, which one of the following authentication methods is implied?

   a. Remote

   b. Local

   c. RADIUS

   d. TACACS+

3. Which two external methods of authentication do Catalyst switches support?

   a. Pre-shared key

   b. Active Directory

   c. RADIUS

   d. KERBEROS

   e. TACACS+

4. Which one of the following commands should be used to configure a vty line to use the myservers authentication method list?

   a. line authentication myservers

   b. authentication myservers

   c. authentication method myservers

   d. login authentication myservers

5. A RADIUS server is located at IP address 192.168.199.10. Which one of the following commands configures a Catalyst switch to find the server?

   a. authentication radius 192.168.199.10

   b. aaa radius 192.168.199.10

   c. radius-server host 192.168.199.10

   d. radius server 192.168.199.10

6. Suppose that the following configuration command has been entered on a Catalyst switch. Which one answer correctly identifies the authentication method that will be used first when a user tries to connect to the switch?

   ```
   Switch(config)# aaa authentication login default radius tacacs+ local
   ```

   a. RADIUS servers

   b. Locally defined usernames

   c. TACACS+ servers

   d. Default line passwords

   e. None of the these answers; all methods are tried simultaneously

7. If a user needs to be in privileged EXEC or enable mode, which part of AAA must succeed? (Choose one correct answer.)

   a. Authentication

   b. Authorization

   c. Accounting

   d. Administration

8. What happens if authorization is not configured on a switch? (Choose one correct answer.)

   a. Authenticated users cannot use any switch commands.

   b. Authenticated users must authenticate themselves to move to a higher privilege level.

   c. Authenticated users can use any switch command.

   d. Authorization cannot be disabled or omitted.

9. Which two of the following commands will begin a configuration that will authorize users to run any switch command and to make configuration changes?

   a. aaa authorization commands ...

   b. aaa authorization exec ...

   c. aaa authorization config-commands ...

   d. aaa authorization config all ...

   e. aaa authorization any any

10. Suppose you would like to configure AAA accounting to keep a record of switch commands that are entered by users. Which one of the following commands should you enter to accomplish your goal?

   a. aaa accounting exec default start-stop mymethods

   b. aaa accounting commands 15 default start-stop mymethods

   c. aaa accounting system commands start-stop mymethods

   d. aaa accounting commands 15 default none mymethods

Foundation Topics

You can manage user activity to and through a switch with authentication, authorization, and accounting (AAA) features. AAA uses standardized methods to challenge users for their credentials before access is allowed or authorized. Accounting protocols also can record user activity on a switch.

In a nutshell, you can think of AAA in the following manner:

- **Authentication:** Who is the user?

- **Authorization:** What is the user allowed to do?

- **Accounting:** What did the user do?

As a network administrator, you have several methods to manage users who might try to log in to one of your switches to perform some operation. At the most basic level, you could avoid any authentication other than simple passwords configured on the switch console and vty lines. Authorization can be equally simple: When users successfully log in, they are authorized for EXEC level privileges. By entering the correct enable secret password, users can be authorized for a higher privilege level.

Under the simple scenario, if a user knows the correct password, he can connect to the switch. But who is that user? You might never know who actually logged in and changed the configuration or rebooted the switch! Instead, you could use the **username** command to configure individual usernames and passwords on the switch. That would solve the user anonymity problem, but your network might consist of many administrative users and many switches, requiring quite a bit of username configuration and maintenance.

A more scalable solution is to leverage AAA functions that are centralized, standardized, resilient, and flexible. For example, a centralized authentication server can contain a database of all possible users and their passwords, as well as policies to authorize user activities. As users come and go, their accounts can be easily updated in one place. All switches and routers query the AAA server to get up-to-date information about a user.

Cisco switches can use the following two protocols to communicate with AAA servers:

- **TACACS+:** A Cisco proprietary protocol that separates each of the AAA functions; communication is secure and encrypted over TCP port 49.

- **RADIUS:** A standards-based protocol that combines authentication and authorization into a single resource; communication uses UDP ports 1812 and 1813 (accounting), but is not completely encrypted.

Both TACACS+ and RADIUS are arranged as a client/server model, where a switch acts as a client talking to a AAA server. Figure 22-1 shows a simplified view of the process. In the AAA client role, a switch is often called a *network access device* (NAD) or *network access server* (NAS). When a user tries to connect to a switch, the switch challenges the user for credentials, then passes the credentials along to the AAA server. In simple terms, if the user passes authentication, the AAA server returns an "accept" message to the switch. Otherwise, a "reject" message is returned.

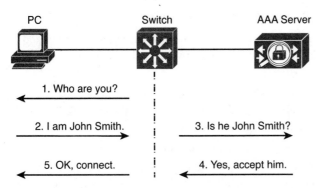

PC   Switch   AAA Server

1. Who are you?

2. I am John Smith.   3. Is he John Smith?

5. OK, connect.   4. Yes, accept him.

Figure 22-1 *A Simplified View of AAA*

Cisco implements AAA services in its Identity Services Engine (ISE) and Cisco Secure Access Control Server (ACS).

Configuring Authentication

Switch access can be granted only after a user's identity has been validated. User authentication is commonly used on switches and routers to permit remote access to the network administration staff only. In this case, when someone uses Telnet or Secure Shell (SSH) to log in to a switch, that individual is challenged to provide a username and password. The individual's credentials are then submitted to a device that can grant the user access.

User authentication can be handled by several methods:

■ Usernames and passwords configured locally on the switch

■ One or more external Remote Authentication Dial-In User Service (RADIUS) servers

■ One or more external Terminal Access Controller Access Control System+ (TACACS+) servers

Any combination of these methods can be used. In fact, authentication must be defined by grouping the desired methods into a method list. The list contains the types or protocols that will be used, in the sequential order that they will be tried.

To use authentication on a Catalyst switch, you must configure several things in the following order:

Step 1. Enable AAA on the switch.By default, AAA is disabled. Therefore, all user authentication is handled locally by configuring usernames and passwords on the switch itself. To enable AAA, use the following global configuration command:

```
Switch(config)# aaa new-model
```

The **new-model** refers to the use of method lists, by which authentication methods and sources can be grouped or organized. The new model is much more scalable than the "old model," in which the authentication source was explicitly configured.

Step 2.   Define the source of authentication.

You can compare user credentials against locally configured usernames and passwords, or against a database managed by external RADIUS or TACACS+ servers.

Use locally configured usernames and passwords as a last resort, when no other authentication servers are reachable or in use on the network. To define a username, use the following global configuration command:

```
Switch(config)# username username password password
```

RADIUS or TACACS+ servers are defined in groups. First, define each server along with its secret shared password. This string is known only to the switch and the server, and provides a key for encrypting the authentication session. Use one of the following global configuration commands:

```
Switch(config)# radius-server host {hostname | ip-address} [key
string]
Switch(config)# tacacs-server host {hostname | ip-address} [key
string]
```

Then define a group name that will contain a list of servers, using the following global configuration command:

```
Switch(config)# aaa group server {radius | tacacs+} group-name
```

Define each server of the group type with the following server-group configuration command:

```
Switch(config-sg)# server ip-address
```

You can define multiple RADIUS or TACACS+ servers by repeating the commands in this step.

Step 3.   Define a list of authentication methods to try.

You can list switch login authentication methods by giving the method a descriptive name or using the unnamed "default" method. List each method or protocol type in the order that it should be tried. If none of the servers for the first method responds, the switch will try the servers in the next method listed.

Use the following global configuration command to define a method list:

```
Switch(config)# aaa authentication login {default | list-name}
method1 [method2 ...]
```

Here the methods refer to the following keywords:

- **tacacs+:** Each of the TACACS+ servers configured on the switch is tried, in the order that it was configured.

- **radius:** Each of the RADIUS servers configured on the switch is tried, in the order that it was configured.

- **local:** The user's credentials are compared against all the **username** commands configured on the local switch.

- **line:** The line passwords authenticate any connected user. No usernames can be used.

Tip   Be sure to add either the **local** or **line** methods at the end of the list, as a last resort. This way, if all the RADIUS or TACACS+ servers are unavailable or the switch is completely isolated from the rest of the network, a locally configured authentication method will eventually be used. Otherwise, you will never be able to access the switch until at least one of the servers comes back online.

Step 4.   Apply a method list to a switch line.

First, select a line (console or vty for Telnet/SSH access) using the **line** *line* command. Then trigger the user authentication on that line to use an AAA method list. Use the following line-configuration command:

```
Switch(config-line)# login authentication {default | list-name}
```

You can use the default method list only if one list is sufficient for all circumstances on the switch. Otherwise, if you have configured named method lists, you can reference one of them here.

Step 5.   After authentication is configured on a switch, it is a good idea to stay logged in on one session so that the authentication can be tested. If you exit the configuration session, you will not be able to log in again if the authentication is misconfigured. While you stay logged in on the original session, bring up a new Telnet session to the switch. If you can authenticate successfully, everything is configured properly.

Example 22-1 lists the commands necessary to configure a switch to use two TACACS+ servers to authenticate management users. The servers are 192.168.10.10 and 192.168.10.11, also known as the AAA group named myauthservers. AAA authentication group myauth is configured to try the TACACS+ server group; if none of the servers is available, local authentication will be used instead. Notice that a username lastresort is configured for that case. Finally, the myauth method is used to authenticate users on lines vty 0 through 15 for Telnet or SSH access.

Example 22-1   *An Example AAA Authentication Configuration*

```
Switch(config)# aaa new-model
Switch(config)# username lastresort  password  MySecretP@ssw0rd
Switch(config)# tacacs-server host 192.168.10.10 key t@c@csk3y
Switch(config)# tacacs-server host 192.168.10.11 key t@c@csk3y
Switch(config)# aaa group server tacacs+ myauthservers
Switch(config-sg)# server 192.168.10.10
Switch(config-sg)# server 192.168.10.11
Switch(config-sg)# exit
Switch(config)# aaa authentication login myauth group myauthservers local
Switch(config)# line vty 0 15
Switch(config-line)# login authentication myauth
```

Configuring Authorization

After a user is authenticated, the switch allows access to certain services or switch commands based on the user's privilege level. Authenticated users are put at the EXEC level by default.

Certain commands, such as **show interface**, are available at the EXEC level. Other commands, such as **configure terminal**, are accessible only if the user is able to move into the privileged EXEC or enable mode.

Authorization provides a means of granting specific users the ability to perform certain tasks. As with authentication, authorization is performed by querying external RADIUS or TACACS+ servers. If the authorization server has an entry for a user and a service or command, the switch allows the user to perform that task.

Configure authorization by first defining any RADIUS or TACACS+ servers that will be used. These normally are defined as part of the authentication configuration and do not need to be redefined for authorization.

Next, define a method list of authorization methods that will be tried in sequence using the following global configuration command:

```
Switch(config)# aaa authorization {commands | config-commands
| configuration | exec | network | reverse-access} {default |
list-name} method1 [method2 ...]
```

Here you specify the function or service needing authorization with one of the following keywords:

■ **commands:** The server must return permission to use any switch command at any privilege level.

■ **config-commands:** The server must return permission to use any switch configuration command.

- **configuration:** The server must return permission to enter the switch configuration mode.

- **exec:** The server must return permission for the user to run a switch EXEC session. The server also can return the privilege level for the user so that the user immediately can be put into privileged EXEC (enable) mode without having to type in the **enable** command.

- **network:** The server must return permission to use network-related services.

- **reverse-access:** The server must return permission for the user to access a reverse Telnet session on the switch.

You can identify the method with a descriptive name (*list-name*) if you are configuring more than one list. Otherwise, a single unnamed list is called the *default* list. Each authorization method then is listed in the order it will be tried. The methods can be any of the following values:

- **group** *group-name*: Requests are sent to the servers in a specific group.

- **group** {radius | tacacs+}: Requests are sent to all servers of this type.

- **if-authenticated:** Requests are granted if the user already is authenticated.

- **none:** No external authorization is used; every user is authorized successfully.

Tip   Only TACACS+ servers can authorize users with permission to use specific commands. RADIUS servers offer more of an all-or-nothing approach.

Next, you can apply an authorization method list to a specific line on the switch. Users accessing the switch through that line will be subject to authorization. Use the following line configuration command:

```
Switch(config-line)# authorization {commands level | exec | reverse-access}
{default | list-name}
```

If you do not use this command, the default group is used for all lines. To configure a switch to use AAA authorization for all lines, you enter the following:

```
Switch(config)# aaa authorization exec default group myauthservers none
```

The AAA servers contained in the group myauthservers (configured previously in Example 22-1) are used as a default method to allow authenticated users into the EXEC mode or any other privilege level granted.

Configuring Accounting

Catalyst switches also support the capability to use AAA for producing accounting information of user activity. This accounting information can be collected by RADIUS and

TACACS+ servers. Again, the RADIUS and TACACS+ servers must already be configured and grouped as part of the authentication configuration.

As usual, you must define a method list giving a sequence of accounting methods by using the following global configuration command:

```
Switch(config)# aaa accounting {system | exec | commands level} {default
| list-name} {start-stop | stop-only | wait-start | none} method1 [method2
...]
```

The function triggering the accounting can be one of the following keywords:

- **system:** Major switch events such as a reload are recorded.

- **exec:** User authentication into an EXEC session is recorded, along with information about the user's address and the time and duration of the session.

- **commands** *level*: Information about any command running at a specific privilege level is recorded, along with the user who issued the command.

You can specify that certain types of accounting records be sent to the accounting server using the following keywords:

- **start-stop:** Events are recorded when they start and stop.

- **stop-only:** Events are recorded only when they stop.

- **none:** No events are recorded.

Next, you can apply an accounting method list to a specific line (console or vty) on the switch. Users accessing the switch through that line will have their activity recorded. Use the following line-configuration command to accomplish this:

```
Switch(config-line)# accounting {commands level | connection | exec}
{default | list-name}
```

If you do not use this command, the default group will be used for all lines. In Example 22-2, AAA accounting is configured for all lines on the switch, using the AAA servers contained in the myauthservers group (configured in Example 22-1). User EXEC sessions will be recorded as they start and stop, along with user information. Any commands that are entered while a user is in privilege level 15 (enable mode) will be recorded, too.

Example 22-2 *Configuring AAA Accounting*

```
Switch(config)# aaa accounting exec default start-stop group myauthservers
Switch(config)# aaa accounting commands 15 default start-stop group myauthservers
```

Exam Preparation Tasks

Review All Key Topics

Review the most important topics in the chapter, noted with the Key Topic icon in the outer margin of the page. Table 22-2 lists a reference of these key topics and the page numbers on which each is found.

Key Topic

Table 22-2 *Key Topics for Chapter 22*

Key Topic Element	Description	Page Number
List	Lists AAA protocols	464
List	Lists authentication methods	465

Complete Tables and Lists from Memory

There are no memory tables in this chapter.

Define Key Terms

Define the following key terms from this chapter, and check your answers in the glossary:

AAA, NAS, RADIUS, TACACS+

Use Command Reference to Check Your Memory

This section includes the most important configuration and EXEC commands covered in this chapter. It might not be necessary to memorize the complete syntax of every command, but you should remember the basic keywords that are needed.

To test your memory of the configuration commands presented in this chapter, cover the right side of Table 22-3 with a piece of paper, read the description on the left side, and then see how much of the command you can remember.

Table 22-3 *AAA Configuration Commands*

Task	Command Syntax
Enable AAA on a switch.	Switch(config)# **aaa new-model**
Use local authentication.	Switch(config)# **username** *username* **password** *password*

Task	Command Syntax
Define individual authentication servers.	Switch(config)# **radius-server host** {*hostname* | *ip-address*} [**key** *string*] Switch(config)# **tacacs-server host** {*hostname* | *ip-address*} [**key** *string*]
Define a group of authentication servers.	Switch(config)# **aaa group server** {**radius** | **tacacs+**} *group-name* Switch(config-sg)# **server** *ip-address*
Define a list of authentication methods to try.	Switch(config)# **aaa authentication login** {**default** | *list-name*} *method1* [*method2* ...]
Apply an authentication method list to a line.	Switch(config-line)# **login authentication** {**default** | *list-name*}
Define a list of authorization methods to try.	Switch(config)# **aaa authorization** {**commands** | **config-commands** | **configuration** | **exec** | **network** | **reverse-access**} {**default** | *list-name*} *method1* [*method2* ...]
Apply an authorization method list to a line.	Switch(config)# **authorization** {**commands** *level* | **exec** | **reverse-access**} {**default** | *list-name*}
Define a list of accounting methods to try.	Switch(config)# **aaa accounting** {**system** | **exec** | **commands** *level*} {**default** | *list-name*} {**start-stop** | **stop-only** | **wait-start** | **none**} *method1* [*method2*...]
Apply an accounting method list to a line.	Switch(config-line)# **accounting** {**commands** *level* | **connection** | **exec**} {**default** | *list-name*}

CHAPTER 23

Final Preparation

The first 22 chapters of this book cover the technologies, protocols, commands, and features required to be prepared to pass the CCNP SWITCH exam. Although these chapters supply the detailed information, most people need more preparation than just reading alone. This chapter details a set of tools and a study plan to help you complete your preparation for the exam.

This short chapter has two main sections. The first section explains how to install the exam engine and practice exams from the CD that accompanies this book. The second section lists some suggestions for a study plan, now that you have completed all the earlier chapters in this book.

Note Appendixes C, D, and E exist as soft-copy appendixes on the CD included in the back of this book.

Tools for Final Preparation

This section lists some information about exam preparation tools and how to access the tools.

Exam Engine and Questions on the CD

The CD in the back of the book includes the Pearson Cert Practice Test (PCPT) engine. This software presents you with a set of multiple-choice questions, covering the topics you will be likely find on the real exam. The PCPT engine lets you study the exam content (using study mode) or take a simulated exam (in practice exam mode).

The CD in the back of the book contains the exam engine. Once installed, you can then activate and download the current SWITCH practice exam from Pearson's website. Installation of the exam engine takes place in two steps:

Step 1. Install the exam engine from the CD.

Step 2. Activate and download the SWITCH practice exam.

Install the Exam Engine

The following are the steps you should perform to install the software:

Step 1.   Insert the CD into your computer.

Step 2.   The software that automatically runs is the Cisco Press software to access and use all CD-based features, including the exam engine and the CD-only appendixes. From the main menu, click the option to **Install the Exam Engine**.

Step 3.   Respond to the prompt windows as you would with any typical software installation process.

The installation process gives you the option to activate your exam with the activation code supplied on the paper in the CD sleeve. This process requires that you establish a Pearson website login. You will need this login to activate the exam. Therefore, please register when prompted. If you already have a Pearson website login, you do not need to register again; just use your existing login.

Activate and Download the Practice Exam

Once the exam engine is installed, you should then activate the exam associated with this book (if you did not do so during the installation process), as follows:

Step 1.   Start the PCPT software.

Step 2.   To activate and download the exam associated with this book, from the **My Products** or **Tools** tab, click the **Activate** button.

Step 3.   At the next screen, enter the Activation Key from the paper inside the cardboard CD holder in the back of the book. Once entered, click the **Activate** button.

Step 4.   The activation process will download the practice exam. Click **Next**; then click **Finish**.

Once the activation process is completed, the **My Products** tab should list your new exam. If you do not see the exam, make sure that you selected the **My Products** tab on the menu. At this point, the software and practice exam are ready to use. Simply select the exam, and click the **Use** button.

To update a particular exam you have already activated and downloaded, select the **Tools** tab, and then click the **Update Products** button. Updating your exams will ensure that you have the latest changes and updates to the exam data.

If you want to check for updates to the PCPT exam engine software, select the **Tools** tab, and then click the **Update Application** button. This will ensure that you are running the latest version of the software engine.

Activating Other Exams

The exam software installation process, and the registration process, only has to happen once. Then, for each new exam, only a few steps are required. For instance, if you buy another new Cisco Press Official Cert Guide or Pearson IT Certification Cert Guide, remove the activation code from the CD sleeve in the back of that book—you do not even need the CD at this point. From there, all you have to do is start the exam engine (if not still up and running), and perform Steps 2 through 4 from the previous list.

Premium Edition

In addition to the free practice exam provided on the CD-ROM, you can purchase additional exams with expanded functionality directly from Pearson IT Certification. The Premium Edition of this title contains an additional two full practice exams as well as an eBook (in both PDF and ePub format). In addition, the Premium Edition title also has remediation for each question to the specific part of the eBook that relates to that question.

Because you have purchased the print version of this title, you can purchase the Premium Edition at a deep discount. You will find a coupon code in the CD sleeve that contains a one-time-use code, in addition to instructions for where you can purchase the Premium Edition.

To view the Premium Edition product page, go to www.ciscopress.com/title/9781587205606.

The Cisco Learning Network

Cisco provides a wide variety of CCNP preparation tools at a Cisco website called the *Cisco Learning Network*. Resources found here include sample questions, forums on each Cisco exam, learning video games, and information about each exam.

To reach the Cisco Learning Network, go to learningnetwork.cisco.com, or just search for "Cisco Learning Network." To access some of the features/resources, you need to use the login you created at Cisco.com. If you do not have such a login, you can register for free. To register, just go to Cisco.com, click **Register** at the top of the page, and supply some information.

Memory Tables

Like most Certification Guides from Cisco Press, this book purposefully organizes information into tables and lists for easier study and review. Rereading these tables can be very useful before the exam. However, it is easy to skim over the tables without paying attention to every detail, especially when you remember having seen the table's contents when reading the chapter.

Instead of simply reading the tables in the various chapters, this book's Appendixes C and D give you another review tool. Appendix C, "Memory Tables," lists partially completed versions of many of the tables from the book. You can open Appendix C (a PDF on the CD that comes with this book) and print the appendix. For review, you can attempt to complete the tables. This exercise can help you focus during your review. It also exercises the memory connectors in your brain; plus it makes you think about the information without as much information, which forces a little more contemplation about the facts.

Appendix D, "Memory Table Answer Key," also a PDF located on the CD, lists the completed tables to check yourself. You can also just refer to the tables as printed in the book.

Chapter-Ending Review Tools

Chapters 1 through 22 each have several features in the "Exam Preparation Tasks" section at the end of the chapter. You might have used some or all of these tools at the end of each chapter, but it can also be useful to use these tools again as you make your final preparations for the exam.

Study Plan

With plenty of resources at your disposal, you should approach studying for the CCNP SWITCH exam with a plan. Consider the following ideas as you move from reading this book to preparing for the exam.

Recall the Facts

As with most exams, many facts, concepts, and definitions must be recalled to do well on the test. If you do not work with every Cisco LAN switching feature on a daily basis, you might have trouble remembering everything that might appear on the CCNP SWITCH exam.

You can refresh your memory and practice recalling information by reviewing the activities in the "Exam Preparation Tasks" section at the end of each chapter. These sections will help you study key topics, memorize the definitions of important LAN switching terms, and recall the basic command syntax of configuration and verification commands.

Practice Configurations

The CCNP exams include an emphasis on practical knowledge. You need to be familiar with switch features and the order in which configuration steps should be implemented. You also need to know how to plan a LAN switching project and how to verify your results.

This means that hands-on experience is going to take you over the top to confidently and accurately build or verify configurations (and pass the exam). If at all possible, try to gain access to some Cisco Catalyst switches and spend some time working with various features.

If you have access to a lab provided by your company, take advantage of it. You might also have some Cisco equipment in a personal lab at home. Otherwise, there are a number of sources for lab access, including online rack rentals from trusted Cisco Partners and the Cisco Partner E-Learning Connection (PEC), if you work for a Partner. Nothing beats hands-on experience.

In addition, you can review the key topics in each chapter and follow the example configurations in this book. At the least, you will see the command syntax and the sequence in which the configuration commands should be entered.

Using the Exam Engine

The PCPT engine on the CD lets you access a database of questions created specifically for this book. The PCPT engine can be used either in study mode or practice exam mode, as follows:

- **Study mode:** Study mode is most useful when you want to use the questions for learning and practicing. In study mode, you can select options like randomizing the order of the questions and answers, automatically viewing answers to the questions as you go, testing on specific topics, and many other options.

- **Practice exam mode:** This mode presents questions in a timed environment, providing you with a more exam-realistic experience. It also restricts your ability to see your score as you progress through the exam and view answers to questions as you are taking the exam. These timed exams not only allow you to study for the actual 300-115 SWITCH Exam, they also help you simulate the time pressure that can occur on the actual exam.

When doing your final preparation, you can use study mode, practice exam mode, or both. However, after you have seen each question a couple of times, you will likely start to remember the questions, and the usefulness of the exam database may go down. So, consider the following options when using the exam engine:

- Use the question database for review. Use study mode to study the questions by chapter, just as with the other final review steps listed in this chapter. Consider upgrading to the Premium Edition of this book if you want to take additional simulated exams.

- Save the question database, not using it for review during your review of each book part. Save it until the end so that you will not have seen the questions before. Then, use practice exam mode to simulate the exam.

To select the exam engine mode, click the **My Products** tab. Select the exam you want to use from the list of available exams, and then click the **Use** button. The engine should display a window from which you can choose **Study Mode** or **Practice Exam Mode**. When in study mode, you can further choose the book chapters, limiting the questions to those explained in the specified chapters of the book.

Answers to the "Do I Know This Already?" Quizzes

Chapter 1

1. A
2. C
3. B
4. C
5. C
6. C
7. C
8. D
9. C
10. C
11. A, B
12. A, C, E
13. D
14. A, C
15. C, D, E
16. B
17. B, C

Chapter 2

1. B
2. B
3. B
4. C
5. C
6. B
7. C
8. D
9. B
10. C
11. D
12. B

Chapter 3

1. C

2. B. All forms of Ethernet share a common operation at the data link layer.

3. A. All forms of Ethernet are different at the physical layer.

4. B

5. B

6. B

7. C

8. C

9. D. Even though you will probably want to disable and reenable the port to get it back in operation, you should begin by figuring out what caused the port to become errdisabled in the first place. Otherwise, if you reenable the port, the same error condition may cause it to fail again.

10. E

11. D

12. B

13. B

14. D

Chapter 4

1. C

2. B

3. B

4. B

5. B

6. C

7. D

8. C

9. B

10. A

11. C

12. A

13. B, C. Interface Gig1/0/33 is not listed as a member of VLAN 10, so it could be configured for a different VLAN. The interface could also be configured as a trunk carrying one or more VLANs. In that case, it would not be listed as a member of VLAN 10 only.

14. C. Because the interfaces begin with their default configurations, each one uses native VLAN 1. Even though the interfaces are not configured with a consistent list of allowed VLANs, that will not prevent the trunk link from being negotiated. The real reason the trunk is not working is that both switches are configured with dynamic auto mode, causing neither switch to actively negotiate a trunk. Instead, each switch is waiting for the other one to ask for a trunk link.

15. A

16. D

17. E

18. A

Chapter 5

1. C

2. A

3. C

4. B

5. B

6. B, C

7. A

8. C

9. B

10. C

11. B

12. D

Chapter 6

1. C
2. C
3. B
4. B
5. C
6. A
7. B
8. D
9. B
10. B
11. C

Chapter 7

1. C
2. C
3. C
4. D
5. C
6. C
7. C
8. B
9. D
10. C
11. A
12. A
13. D
14. C

Chapter 8

1. B
2. C
3. C
4. B
5. B
6. A
7. B
8. B
9. C
10. C
11. C
12. B
13. B

Chapter 9

1. A
2. C
3. A
4. C
5. A
6. B
7. C
8. D
9. C
10. D
11. B
12. C

Chapter 10

1. E
2. C
3. C
4. D
5. C
6. C
7. A
8. D
9. B
10. C
11. C
12. C
13. C

Chapter 11

1. D
2. A
3. A
4. B
5. C
6. C
7. C
8. D
9. C
10. C
11. C

Chapter 12

1. B
2. C
3. A
4. A
5. C
6. D
7. B
8. D

Chapter 13

1. E
2. D
3. C
4. A
5. B
6. B
7. C
8. B

Chapter 14

1. A
2. C
3. D
4. C
5. B
6. D
7. C
8. E

Chapter 15

1. B. The IP SLA feature may be configured on Cisco switches from the CLI. A third-party platform is not necessary, but may be used to ease the configuration and analysis if you need to set up many IP SLA tests.

2. A, C, F

3. D

4. B

5. B

6. D

Chapter 16

1. C

2. A, B, D, E

3. C

4. D

5. A

6. B

7. B, C

8. B, D

Chapter 17

1. C

2. D

3. A

4. C

5. B

6. B

7. B

Chapter 18

1. D

2. D

3. C

4. B

5. B

6. B

7. C

8. C

9. C

10. B

Chapter 19

1. C

2. D

3. B

4. B. The trick is in the **maximum 3** keywords. This sets the maximum number of addresses that can be learned on a port. If only one static address is configured, two more addresses can be learned dynamically.

5. C

6. A

7. B

8. C

9. C. Because of the variety of user host platforms, port-based authentication (802.1X) cannot be used. The problem also states that the goal is to restrict access to physical switch ports, so AAA is of no benefit. Port security can do the job by restricting access according to the end users' MAC addresses.

10. B, C, D

11. C

12. B, D

13. C

Chapter 20

1. C
2. D
3. D
4. A
5. B
6. A
7. C
8. A
9. D
10. A
11. A
12. C

Chapter 21

1. B
2. B
3. C, D
4. C
5. B
6. C

Chapter 22

1. B, C, E
2. B
3. C, E
4. D
5. C
6. A
7. B
8. B
9. A, C. The **aaa authorization** command separates the switch command and configuration command functions so that each can have its own method list. The respective keywords are **aaa authorization commands** and **aaa authorization config-commands**.
10. B

Exam Updates

Over time, reader feedback allows Cisco Press to gauge which topics give our readers the most problems when taking the exams. To assist readers with those topics, the authors create new materials clarifying and expanding upon those troublesome exam topics. As mentioned in the Introduction, the additional content about the exam is contained in a PDF document on this book's companion website, at http://www.ciscopress.com/title/9781587205606.

This appendix is intended to provide you with updated information if Cisco makes minor modifications to the exam upon which this book is based. When Cisco releases an entirely new exam, the changes are usually too extensive to provide in a simple update appendix. In those cases, you might need to consult the new edition of the book for the updated content.

This appendix attempts to fill the void that occurs with any print book. In particular, this appendix does the following:

- Mentions technical items that might not have been mentioned elsewhere in the book

- Covers new topics if Cisco adds new content to the exam over time

- Provides a way to get up-to-the-minute current information about content for the exam

Always Get the Latest at the Companion Website

You are reading the version of this appendix that was available when your book was printed. However, given that the main purpose of this appendix is to be a living, changing document, it is important that you look for the latest version online at the book's companion website. To do so, follow these steps:

Step 1. Browse to http://www.ciscopress.com/title/9781587205606.

Step 2. Select the **Appendix** option under the More Information box.

Step 3. Download the latest "Appendix B" document.

Note   Note that the downloaded document has a version number. Comparing the version of the print Appendix B (Version 1.0) with the latest online version of this appendix, you should do the following:

- **Same version:** Ignore the PDF that you downloaded from the companion website.
- **Website has a later version:** Ignore this Appendix B in your book and read only the latest version that you downloaded from the companion website.

Technical Content

The current version of this appendix does not contain any additional technical coverage.

GLOSSARY

20/80 rule   Network traffic pattern where 20 percent of traffic stays in a local area, while 80 percent travels to or from a remote resource.

802.1Q   A method of passing frames and their VLAN associations over a trunk link, based on the IEEE 802.1Q standard.

AAA   Authentication, authorization, and accounting services used to control user access to a switch or a switch port.

access layer   The layer of the network where end users are connected.

active virtual forwarder (AVF)   A GLBP router that takes on a virtual MAC address and forwards traffic received on that address.

active virtual gateway (AVG)   The GLBP router that answers all ARP requests for the virtual router address and assigns virtual MAC addresses to each router in the GLBP group.

adjacency table   A table used by CEF to collect the MAC addresses of nodes that can be reached in a single Layer 2 hop.

alternate port   In RSTP, a port other than the root port that has an alternative path to the root bridge.

ARP poisoning   Also known as ARP spoofing. An attack whereby an attacker sends specially crafted ARP replies so that its own MAC address appears as the gateway or some other targeted host. From that time on, unsuspecting clients unknowingly send traffic to the attacker.

Auto-QoS   An automated method to configure complex QoS parameters with a simple IOS macro command.

autonegotiation   A mechanism used by a device and a switch port to automatically negotiate the link speed and duplex mode.

autonomous mode AP   An access point that operates in a standalone mode, such that it is autonomous and can offer a functioning WLAN cell itself.

BackboneFast   An STP feature that can detect an indirect link failure and shorten the STP convergence time to 30 seconds by bypassing the Max Age timeout period.

backup port   In RSTP, a port that provides a redundant (but less desirable) connection to a segment where another switch port already connects.

best effort delivery   Packets are forwarded in the order in which they are received, regardless of any policy or the packet contents.

BPDU   Bridge protocol data unit; the data message exchanged by switches participating in the Spanning Tree Protocol.

BPDU filtering   Prevents BPDUs from being sent or processed on a switch port.

BPDU Guard   An STP feature that disables a switch port if any BPDU is received there.

bridging loop   A condition where Ethernet frames are forwarded endlessly around a Layer 2 loop formed between switches.

broadcast domain   The extent of a network where a single broadcast frame or packet will be seen.

CAM   Content-addressable memory; the high-performance table used by a switch to correlate MAC addresses with the switch interfaces where they can be found.

CDP   Cisco Discovery Protocol; a Cisco proprietary protocol used to advertise and discover directly connected devices automatically

CEF   Cisco Express Forwarding; an efficient topology-based system for forwarding IP packets.

collapsed core   A network design where the core and distribution layers are collapsed or combined into a single layer of switches.

collision domain   The extent within a network that an Ethernet collision will be noticed or experienced.

Common Spanning Tree (CST)   A single instance of STP defined in the IEEE 802.1Q standard.

community VLAN   A type of secondary private VLAN; switch ports associated with a community VLAN can communicate with each other.

Control and Provisioning Wireless Access Point (CAPWAP)   A standards-based tunneling protocol used to transport control messages and data packets between a wireless LAN controller (WLC) and a lightweight access point (LAP). CAPWAP is defined in RFC 4118.

core layer   The "backbone" layer of the network where all distribution layer switches are aggregated.

CoS marking   Class of service marking; a method of marking frames with a QoS value as they cross a trunk link between two switches.

CSMA/CA   Carrier sense multiple access collision avoidance. The mechanism used in 802.11 WLANs by which clients attempt to avoid collisions.

CSMA/CD   Carrier sense multiple access collision detect. A mechanism used on Ethernet networks to detect collisions and cause transmitting devices to back off for a random time.

delay   The amount of time required for a packet to be forwarded across a network.

designated port   One nonroot port selected on a network segment, such that only one switch forwards traffic to and from that segment.

DHCP   Dynamic Host Configuration Protocol; a protocol used to negotiate IP address assignment between a client and a server. The client and server must reside on the same VLAN.

DHCP relay   A multilayer switch that intercepts and relays DHCP negotiation messages between a client and a DHCP server, even if they exist on different VLANs.

DHCP snooping   A security feature that enables a switch to intercept all DHCP requests coming from untrusted switch ports before they are flooded to unsuspecting users.

DHCPv6   A DHCP service that is compatible with IPv6 clients; a switch can assign IPv6 addresses and advertise DHCP-related options.

DHCPv6 Lite   A DHCP service that is compatible with IPv6 clients; IPv6 addresses are obtained through stateless autoconfiguration, but DHCP-related options are advertised through the DHCPv6 Lite server.

differentiated services (DiffServ) model   Packet forwarding is handled according to local QoS policies on a per-device or per-hop basis.

discarding state   In RSTP, incoming frames are dropped and no MAC addresses are learned.

distribution layer   The layer of the network where access layer switches are aggregated and routing is performed.

DTP   Dynamic Trunking Protocol; a Cisco proprietary method of negotiating a trunk link between two switches.

dual core   A network design that has a distinct core layer made up of a redundant pair of switches.

duplex mismatch   A condition where the devices on each end of a link use conflicting duplex modes.

duplex mode   The Ethernet mode that governs how devices can transmit over a connection. Half-duplex mode forces only one device to transmit at a time, as all devices share the same media. Full-duplex mode is used when only two devices share the media, such that both devices can transmit simultaneously.

Dynamic ARP inspection (DAI)   A security feature that can mitigate ARP-based attacks. ARP replies received on untrusted switch ports are checked against known, good values contained in the DHCP snooping database.

edge port   In RSTP, a port at the "edge" of the network, where only a single host connects.

end-to-end VLAN   A single VLAN that spans the entire switched network, from one end to the other.

EtherChannel   A logical link made up of bundled or aggregated physical links.

EtherChannel Guard   A feature that can detect errors in the EtherChannel configuration on a switch.

expedited forwarding (EF)   The DSCP value used to mark time-critical packets for premium QoS handling. EF is usually reserved for voice bearer traffic.

FIB   Forwarding Information Base; a CEF database that contains the current routing table.

flooding   An Ethernet frame is replicated and sent out every available switch port.

forward delay   The time interval that a switch spends in the Listening and Learning states; default 15 seconds.

hello time   The time interval between configuration BPDUs sent by the root bridge; defaults to 2 seconds.

hierarchical network design   A campus network that is usually organized into an access layer, a distribution layer, and a core layer.

host port   A switch port mapped to a private VLAN such that a connected device can communicate with only a promiscuous port or ports within the same community VLAN.

HSRP active router   The router in a Hot Standby Router Protocol (HSRP) group that forwards traffic sent to the virtual gateway IP and MAC address.

HSRP standby router   A router in an HSRP group that waits until the active router fails before taking over that role.

IEEE 802.1X   The standard that defines port-based authentication between a network device and a client device.

IEEE 802.3   The standard upon which all generations of Ethernet (Ethernet, Fast Ethernet, Gigabit Ethernet, 10-Gigabit Ethernet) are based.

inter-VLAN routing   The function performed by a Layer 3 device that connects and forwards packets between multiple VLANs.

IP Service Level Agreement (IP SLA)   A feature within Cisco IOS that can be used to test how specific types of traffic are being handled end to end across a network.

IP SLA responder   A network device that responds to and participates in IP SLA tests.

ISL   Inter-Switch Link; a Cisco proprietary method of tagging frames passing over a trunk link.

isolated VLAN   A type of secondary private VLAN; switch ports associated with an isolated VLAN are effectively isolated from each other.

IST instance   Internal spanning-tree instance; used by Multiple Spanning Tree (MST) to represent an entire region as a single virtual bridge to a common spanning tree.

jitter   The variation in packet delivery delay times.

LACP   Link Aggregation Control Protocol; a standards-based method for negotiating EtherChannels automatically.

Layer 2 roaming   Movement of a WLAN client from one AP to another, while keeping its same IP address.

Layer 3 roaming   Movement of a WLAN client from one AP to another, where the APs are located across IP subnet boundaries.

lightweight access point (LAP)   An access point that runs a lightweight code image that performs real-time 802.11 operations. An LAP cannot offer a fully functioning WLAN cell by itself; instead, it must coexist with a wireless LAN controller.

Lightweight Access Point Protocol (LWAPP)   The tunneling protocol developed by Cisco that is used to transport control messages and data packets between a WLC and an LAP.

link-local address   An IPv6 address used by a device for neighbor discovery; link-local addresses begin with the prefix FE80::/10 followed by an interface identifier in the EUI-64 format. Packets sent from a link-local address must stay on the local link and not be forwarded elsewhere.

LLDP   Link Layer Discovery Protocol; a standards-based protocol used to advertise and discover directly connected devices.

local SPAN   A Switched Port Analyzer (SPAN) session configured to mirror traffic from a source interface or VLAN onto a different interface for monitoring or analysis purposes.

local VLAN   A single VLAN that is bounded by a small area of the network, situated locally with a group of member devices.

Loop Guard   An STP feature that disables a switch port if expected BPDUs suddenly go missing.

Management Information Base (MIB)   A collection of information and data that a network device maintains about itself and its operation. MIB variables can be read or written through SNMP.

Max Age time   The time interval that a switch stores a BPDU before discarding it or aging it out; the default is 20 seconds.

MST   Multiple Spanning Tree protocol, used to map one or more VLANs to a single STP instance, reducing the total number of STP instances.

MST instance (MSTI)   A single instance of STP running within an MST region; multiple VLANs can be mapped to the MST instance.

MST region   A group of switches running compatible MST configurations.

multichassis EtherChannel (MEC)   An EtherChannel made up of links that are bundled across multiple switches that are organized as a single logical or virtual switch.

native VLAN   On an 802.1Q trunk link, frames associated with the native VLAN are not tagged at all.

network access server (NAS)   The function a switch performs as it intervenes between end users and AAA servers.

Network Time Protocol (NTP)   A mechanism used to synchronize a device's time clock with another, more reliable source.

nonstop forwarding (NSF)   A redundancy method that quickly rebuilds routing information after a redundant Catalyst switch supervisor takes over.

object identifier (OID)   A unique string of digits that identifies a variable or a tree of variables in a MIB.

packet loss   Packets are simply dropped without delivery for some reason.

packet rewrite   Just before forwarding a packet, a multilayer switch has to change several fields in the packet to reflect the Layer 3 forwarding operation.

PAgP   Port Aggregation Protocol; a Cisco-developed method for negotiating EtherChannels automatically.

point-to-point port   In the Cisco implementation of RSTP, a full-duplex port that connects to another switch and becomes a designated port.

PortFast   An STP feature used on a host port, where a single host is connected, that shortens the Listening and Learning states so that the host can gain quick access to the network.

power class   Categories of PoE devices based on the maximum amount of power required; power classes range from 0 to 4.

Power over Ethernet (PoE)   Electrical power supplied to a networked device over the network cabling itself.

primary VLAN   A normal Layer 2 VLAN used as the basis for a private VLAN when it is associated with one or more secondary VLANs.

private VLAN   A special purpose VLAN, designated as either primary or secondary, which can restrict or isolate traffic flow with other private VLANs.

promiscuous port   A switch port mapped to a private VLAN such that a connected device can communicate with any other switch port in the private VLAN.

PVST   Per-VLAN Spanning Tree; a Cisco proprietary version of STP where one instance of STP runs on each VLAN present in a Layer 2 switch.

PVST+   Per-VLAN Spanning Tree Plus; a Cisco proprietary version of PVST that enables PVST, PVST+, and CST to interoperate on a switch.

quality of service (QoS)   The overall method used in a network to protect and prioritize time-critical or important traffic.

Remote Authentication Dial-In User Service (RADIUS)   A standards-based protocol used to communicate with AAA servers.

root bridge   The single STP device that is elected as a common frame of reference for working out a loop-free topology.

Root Guard   An STP feature that controls where candidate root bridges can be found on a switch.

root path cost   The cumulative cost of all the links leading to the root bridge.

root port   Each switch selects one port that has the lowest root path cost leading toward the root bridge.

Route Processor Redundancy (RPR)   A redundancy mode where a redundant supervisor partially boots and waits to become active after the primary supervisor fails.

Route Processor Redundancy Plus (RPR+)   A redundancy mode where a redundant supervisor boots up and waits to begin Layer 2 or Layer 3 functions.

RPVST+   Also known as Rapid PVST+, where RSTP is used on a per-VLAN basis; in effect, RSTP replaces traditional 802.1D STP in the PVST+ operation.

RSPAN   Also known as Remote Switched Port Analyzer, where a SPAN session is split across two independent switches and mirrored data is transported over a special purpose VLAN between them.

RSTP   The Rapid Spanning Tree Protocol, based on the IEEE 802.1w standard.

SDM   Switching Database Manager: A Cisco IOS Software function that configures or tunes memory table space on a LAN switch platform

secondary VLAN   A unidirectional VLAN that can pass traffic to and from its associated primary VLAN, but not with any other secondary VLAN.

Simple Network Management Protocol (SNMP)   A protocol used between an SNMP manager and an SNMP agent to obtain data about device operation or to set configuration parameters.

SNMP agent   A process that runs on the network device being monitored and uses SNMP to provide data to an SNMP manager.

SNMP inform   A message that a network device sends to alert an SNMP manager about an event or a failure. The SNMP manager must acknowledge receipt of the inform by echoing the message back to the SNMP agent in the device.

SNMP manager   A network management system that uses SNMP to poll network devices for operational and configuration data.

SNMP trap   A message that a network device sends to alert an SNMP manager about an event or a failure. The SNMP manager does not need to acknowledge a trap that it receives.

SPAN   Also known as Switched Port Analyzer, where a switch mirrors traffic from a source interface or VLAN onto a different interface for monitoring or analysis purposes.

Spanning Tree Protocol (STP)   A protocol communicated between Layer 2 switches that attempts to detect a loop in the topology before it forms, thus preventing a bridging loop from occurring.

Split-MAC architecture   Normal Media Access Control (MAC) operations are divided into two distinct locations, the LAP and the WLC, such that the two form a completely functioning WLAN cell.

SSID   Service set identifier; a text string that identifies a service set, or a group of WLAN devices, that can communicate with each other.

StackWise   Cisco method to connect multiple switches together to form one logical switch. The switch stack is controlled by one of the member switches, while others can take over the role if needed. Member switches are connected to each other through a dual ring of StackWise cables.

stateful switchover (SSO)   A redundancy mode where a redundant supervisor fully boots and initializes, allowing configurations and Layer 2 tables to be synchronized between an active supervisor and a redundant one.

sticky MAC address   MAC addresses dynamically learned by the port security feature are remembered and expected to appear on the same switch ports.

stratum   A number that indicates in which layer of the NTP hierarchy a time source is located; stratum 1 represents the most authoritative and accurate time source.

superior BPDU   A received BPDU that contains a better bridge ID than the current root bridge.

SVI   Switched virtual interface; a logical interface used to assign a Layer 3 address to an entire VLAN.

switch block   A network module or building block that contains a group of access layer switches, together with the pair of distribution switches that connect them.

switch spoofing   A malicious host uses DTP to masquerade as a switch, with the goal of negotiating a trunk link and gaining access to additional VLANs.

synchronization   In RSTP, the process by which two switches exchange a proposal-agreement handshake to make sure neither will introduce a bridging loop.

syslog   System message logs that are generated by a switch and can be collected locally or sent to and collected on a remote server.

syslog severity level   An indicator of how important or severe a logged event is.

TACACS+ (Terminal Access Controller Access-Control System Plus)   A Cisco proprietary protocol used to communicate with AAA servers.

TCAM   Ternary content-addressable memory; a switching table found in Catalyst switches that is used to evaluate packet forwarding decisions based on policies or access lists. TCAM evaluation is performed simultaneously with the Layer 2 or Layer 3 forwarding decisions.

TCN   Topology Change Notification; a message sent out the root port of a switch when it detects a port moving into the Forwarding state or back into the Blocking state. The TCN is sent toward the root bridge, where it is reflected and propagated to every other switch in the Layer 2 network.

TLV   An attribute formed by type, length, and value parameters; used in LLDP advertisements.

transparent bridge   A network device that isolates two physical LANs but forwards Ethernet frames between them.

trust boundary A perimeter in a network, formed by switches and routers, where QoS decisions take place. QoS information found inside incoming traffic is evaluated at the trust boundary; either it is trusted or it is not trusted. In the latter case, the QoS information can be altered or overridden. All devices inside the trust boundary can assume that QoS information is correct and trusted, such that the QoS information already conforms to enterprise policies.

UDLD Unidirectional Link Detection; a feature that enables a switch to confirm that a link is operating bidirectionally. If not, the port can be disabled automatically.

unknown unicast flooding The action taken by a switch when the destination MAC address cannot be found; the frame is flooded or replicated out all switch ports except the receiving port.

UplinkFast An STP feature that enables access layer switches to unblock a redundant uplink when the primary root port fails.

VACL VLAN access control list; a filter that can control traffic passing within a VLAN.

Virtual Switching System (VSS) Cisco method to join two separate physical switch chassis together as one logical switch. The two chassis are managed by one supervisor, while the other can take over if needed. The switch chassis are connected with VSS links and can be geographically separated.

VLAN Virtual LAN; a logical network existing on one or more Layer 2 switches, forming a single broadcast domain.

VLAN hopping A malicious host sends specially crafted frames that contain extra, spoofed 802.1Q trunking tags into an access port, while the packet payloads appear on a totally different VLAN.

VLAN number A unique index number given to a VLAN on a switch, differentiating it from other VLANs on the switch.

VLAN trunk A physical link that can carry traffic on more than one VLAN through logical tagging.

voice VLAN The VLAN used between a Cisco IP Phone and a Catalyst switch to carry voice traffic.

VRRP backup router A router in a VRRP group that waits until the master router fails before taking over that role.

VRRP master router The router in a VRRP group that forwards traffic sent to the virtual gateway IP and MAC address.

VSPAN Also known as VLAN-based Switched Port Analyzer, where a switch mirrors traffic from a source VLAN onto a different interface for monitoring or analysis purposes.

VTP VLAN Trunking Protocol; used to communicate VLAN configuration information among a group of switches.

VTP configuration revision number   An index that indicates the current version of VLAN information used in the VTP domain; a higher number is more preferable.

VTP domain   A logical grouping of switches that share a common set of VLAN requirements.

VTP pruning   VTP reduces unnecessary flooded traffic by pruning or removing VLANs from a trunk link, only when there are no active hosts associated with the VLANs.

VTP synchronization problem   An unexpected VTP advertisement with a higher configuration revision number is received, overriding valid information in a VTP domain.

wireless LAN controller (WLC)   A Cisco device that provides management functions to lightweight access points and aggregates all traffic to and from the LAPs.

Index

Numbers

10GBASE-CX4, 66
10GBASE-ER, 66
10GBASE-LR, 66
10GBASE-LRM, 66
10GBASE-LX4, 66
10GBASE-SR, 66
10GE (10Gigabit Ethernet) links, 245
10GEC (10-Gigabit Etherchannel) links, 245
10-Gigabit Ethernet
  10GBASE-CX4, 66
  10GBASE-ER, 66
  10GBASE-LR, 66
  10GBASE-LRM, 66
  10GBASE-LX4, 66
  10GBASE-SR, 66
  bandwidth, 60
  PMD interfaces, 62
  PMD types, 62
20/80 rule, 493
40-Gigabit Ethernet, 63
  bandwidth, 60
100-Gigabit Ethernet, 63
  bandwidth, 60
802.1.x switch port
  authentication example, 420-421
  configuration, 419-420
802.IQ, 493
1000BASE-LX/LH, 65
1000BASE-SX, 65
1000BASE-T, 66
1000BASE-ZX, 66

A

AAA (authentication, authorization, accounting), 493
  enabling, 465-466
  overview, 464
  servers
    RADIUS protocol, 464
    TACACS+ protocol, 464
accelerated CEF (aCEF), 276
access keyword, 328
access layer, 12, 493
  independent switches, 369
  switch platforms, 25
  switches, 12
access maps (VACLs), 435
access vlan command, 98
accounting
  configuration, 460, 469-470
  See also AAA (authentication, authorization, accounting)
aCEF (accelerated CEF), 276
ACK message (DHCP), 292

ACLs (access control lists), 36

  QoS, 36, 39

  VLAN (*See* VACLs (VLAN access lists))

ACS (Access Control Server), 465

Activation Key for practice exam, 476

address keyword, 45

addresses

  gateway, HSRP, 390

  leases, 294

  link-local addresses, 497

  manual binding, 294-295

  See also MAC addresses

adjacency table, 276-279, 493

after keyword, 341

ageout keyword, 341

aggregation

  EtherChannel, 240, 245-247

    bundling ports, 247

    LACP, 240, 252

    load balancing, 249-251

    negotiation protocols, 251

    PAgP, 240, 251-252

    traffic distribution, 247-249

  LACP (Link Aggregation Control Protocol), 240

  PAgP (Port Aggregation Protocol), 240

aggressive keyword, 212

alternate port, 493

answers to quizzes, 481-486

any keyword, 44

APs (access points), lightweight mode, 118

ARP inspection, 448

ARP poisoning, 493

ASN.1 (Abstract Syntax Notation 1), 324

auth keyword, 328-329

authentication

  802.1x, 419

    example, 420-421

  configuration, 460, 465-468

  HSRP, 388

    MD5, 388-389

    plain text, 388

  method list, 466

  port-based, Catalyst switches, 418

  RADIUS, 419

  session encryption, 466

  source, 466

  See also AAA (authentication, authorization, accounting)

authorization

  configuration, 460, 468-469

  See also AAA (authentication, authorization, accounting)

auto keyword, 80

autonegotiation, 64, 493

autonomous mode AP, 493

Auto-QoS, 493

AVF (active virtual forwarder), 398-400, 493

AVG (active virtual gateway), 397-398, 493

B

Backbone Fast, 493

backup port, 493

bandwidth
Ethernet segments, 60
scaling, 245
link bundles, 246
throwing bandwidth, 7
VTP pruning and, 139

banner motd command, 424

best effort delivery, 494

Blocking state, 162, 223

BPDUs (bridge protocol data units), 155, 355, 494
BPDU Guard, 208-209, 494
Configuration BPDU, 155
messages, 155-156
filtering, 494
STP disabling, 213-214
Loop Guard and, 210-211
PortFast, enabling, 208-209
root bridges and, 157
Root Guard, 207-208
RSTP and, 224-225
sudden loss, 210
suprerior, 500
TCN (Topology Change Notification) BPDU, 155
topology change messages, 167

bridging
Bridge Priority field, 156
frames and, 151-152
loops, 494
preventing, 154-155
MAC address, 156-157
redundant, 152
root bridges, 156-158
election example, 157
transparent
Layer 2 and, 32-35
STP and, 151-154
switches and, 152

broadcast domain, 494

broadcast keyword, 422

broadcast traffic, 8

building distribution switches, 12

C

cabling
Fast Ethernet, 60
Gigabit Ethernet, 61
port cables, connecting switches and devices, 65-66

caching, route caching, multilayer switching, 37

CAM (content-addressable memory) table, 40-41, 494
command syntax, 41
table operation, 45-48
table size, 47-50
TCAM, 41
example, 43-44
port operations, 44-45
value patterns, 42

campus networks, 7

core size, 24

CAPWAP (control and provisioning wireless access point), 494

Catalyst switch, 28

See also switches

catalyst switches, 37

CD accompanying book

exam engine, 475-476

Memory Tables, 477-478

Premium Edition of book, 477

CDP (Cisco Discovery Protocol), 355, 494

connected devices, 73-75

neighbor information display, 74-75

securing, 426

CEF (Cisco Express Forwarding), 37, 272-273, 494

CEF punt, 275

configuration, 280

multilayer switching and, 264, 272

table entry updates, 275

verification, 283-284

Cisco hierarchical design, 24-26

Cisco IP phone, 112-113

voice VLAN trunking mode, 114

Cisco Learning Network, 477

client mode (VTP), 127

client-identifier command, 295

clocks, synchronization, 313-315

collapsed core, 23-24, 494

collision domains, 494

limiting size, 8

collisions, switched Ethernet and, 59

command-line interface, 33

commands

access vlan, 98

banner motd, 424

CAM tables, 41

client-identifier, 295

debug ip dhcp server, 295

default-router, 293

enable secret, 424

ip dhcp excluded-address, 293

ip dhcp pool, 293

ip helper-address, 297

ip http access-class configuration, 425

ip http server, 424

ip sla key-chain, 339

ip sla schedule, 341

key, 389

key chain, 389

key-string, 389

lacp port-priority, 255

lease, 294

line line, 467

logging host, 311

macro, 186

monitor session filter, 358

MST configuration, 237

name, 98

network, 293

no cdp run, 75

no ip cef interface configuration, 280

no ip route-cache cef, 280

no shutdown, 213

no switchport, 270

no vlan vlan-num, 98

ntp access-group, 316

ntp associations, 315

ntp server, 315

ntp status, 315

PoE, 83

show adjacency summary, 276

show cdp neighbors, 73

show cef not-cef-switched, 279

show clock, 312

show dotlx all, 420

show etherchannel load-balance, 250

show etherchannel port-channel, 250

show etherchannel summary, 257

show interface, 72

show interface switchport, 115

show interfaces, 71

show interfaces status, 71

show interfaces status err-disabled, 417

show ip arp, 278

show ip arp inspection, 457

show ip cef, 274

show ip dhcp binding, 294

show ip interface, 281

show ip interface brief, 282

show ip sla configuration, 342

show lldp, 75

show logging, 311

show mac address-table count, 47

show mac address-table EXEC, 45

show port-security, 418

show port-security interface, 417

show spanning-tree interface, 116, 191

show spanning-tree vlan vlan-id, 230

show vlan, 99, 281

show vlan brief, 99

show vlan id vlan-id EXEC, 110

show vtp status, 133, 137

shutdown, 70, 213

snmp-server group, 328

snmp-server host, 327

snmp-server user, 328

snmp-server view, 328

spanning-tree mode, 231

spanning-tree vlan vlan-id priority
bridge-priority, 188

spanning-tree vlan vlan-id root, 188

STP protection and, 214

summer-time recurring, 313

switchport, 98

switchport interface, 269

switchport mode, 107

switchport nonegotiate, 108

switchport trunk allowed vlan,
106-107, 140

switchport trunk encapsulation, 106

switchport trunk native vlan, 106

terminal monitor, 310

track, 343

udp-jitter, 340

username, 464

VTP configuration troubleshooting,
142

commands keyword, 468

commands level keyword, 470

community VLAN, 494

companion website, exam updates,
489-490

config-commands keyword, 468

configuration

accounting, 460, 469-470

authentication, 460, 465-468

authorization, 460, 468-469

autoconfiguration, stateless, 298

CEF (Cisco Express Forwarding), 280

EtherChannel, 253-257

    EtherChannel Guard, 255-257

    LACP, 254-255

    PAgP, 253-254

inter-VLAN routing, 269

    Layer 2, 270

    Layer 3, 270-271

    SVI port, 271-272

local SPAN, 354-356

MST (Multiple Spanning Tree), 236-237

PoE, 80-81

PVLANs, 438-439

RSPAN, 357-359

RSTP, 229-230

SNMPv1, 327

SNMPv2C, 327

SNMPv3, 328-329

static VLANs, 97-99

study plan, 478-479

switch ports

    duplex mode, 69

    link mode, 69

    port description, 68

    port selection, 66-68

    port speed, 68

VACLs, 435-436

VLAN trunks, 106-110

voice VLANs, 113-115

VRRP, 394-395

VTP, 132-133

    example, 136-137

    management domain, 134-135

    modes, 135-136

    version, 133-134

Configuration BPDU, 155

message content, 155-156

configuration keyword, 469

connections

device discovery, 73-77

    CDP (Cisco Discovery Protocol), 73-75

    LLDP, 75-77

Ethernet

    Gigabit Ethernet, 65-66

    port cables, 65-66

connectivity, troubleshooting, 71

convergence, RSTP, 225

sequence of events, 228

core layer, 10, 20-23, 494

campus networks, 24

collapsed core, 23-24

switches, 12-13

CoS marking, 494

CST (Common Spanning Tree), 173, 494

D

DAI (Dynamic ARP Inspection), 495

dCEF (distributed CEF), 276

debug ip dhcp server command, 295

default keyword, 214

default-router command, 293

delay, 494

delay keyword, 387

deployment, VLANs, 99-100

devices

connected, 54

discovery, 73-77

Ethernet port cables, 65-66

PoE and, detecting, 79-80

power for operation, 54

(See also PoE (Power over Ethernet))

DHCP (Dynamic Host Configuration Protocol), 495

ACK message, 292

Discover message, 292

IPv4, server configuration, 288, 293-294

IPv6, configuration, 288

IPv6 support, 297

DHCPv6 server, 298-299

stateless autoconfiguration, 298

manual address binding, 294-295

MLS and, 292-293

DHCPv6 Lite, 299-300

DHCPv6 relay agent, 300

IPv4 server configuration, 293-294

IPv6 operation, 300

manual address binding, 294-295

options configuration, 296

relays, 296-297

Offer message, 292

relay, 495

Request message, 292

snooping, 448, 495

DHCP relay agent, 300

DHCPv6, 298-299, 495

DHCPv6 Lite, 299-300, 495

DiffServ model, 495

direct topology changes, 168-169

disable keyword, 212

Disabled state, 162, 223

discard adjacency, 279

Discarding state, 224

discarding state, 495

Discover message (DHCP), 292

distributed CEF (dCEF), 276

distribution layer, 12, 495

switch platforms, 26

switches

building, 12

redundant, 14

distribution switches, 18

"Do I Know This Already?" Quiz answers, 481-486

domains, collision domains, limiting size, 8

dotlq keyword, 355

DP (designated port), 495

DPs (designated ports), electing, 160-162

DRM (dual-router mode), 374

drop adjacency, 279

DTP (Dynamic Trunking Protocol), 355, 495

spoofing and, 441-443

dual core, 495

duplex mismatch, 495

duplex mode, 495

duplex operation

Ethernet, 63-65

speed/duplex mismatches, 72-73

switch ports, configuration, 69

dynamic trunking protocol, 105-106

dynamic VLANs, 99

E

EAPOL (Extensible Authentication Protocol over LANs), 418-419

edge port, 226, 495

EF (expedited forwarding), 496

enable keyword, 212

enable secret command, 424

end-to-end VLANs, 100-101, 495

errdisable state, 69-70

  ports, 417-418

  re-enabling ports, 70-71

error detection, switch ports, 69-70

error management, switch ports, 69

error recovery, 70-71

EtherChannel, 495

  aggregation, 245-247

    bundling ports, 247

    LACP, 252

    negotiation protocols, 251

    PAgP, 251-252

    traffic distribution, 247-249

  configuration, 240, 253

    EtherChannel Guard, 255-257

    LACP, 254-255

    PAgP, 253-254

  frame distribution, 248

  LACP (Link Aggregation Channel), 240

  load balancing, 249-251

  logical switches, 369-370

  Multichassis, 247

  negotiation protocols, 251

  PAgP (Port Aggregation Protocol), 240

  ports, bundling, 247

  traffic distribution, 247-249

  troubleshooting, 240, 257-259

EtherChannel Guard, 255-257, 496

Ethernet, 54

  10-Gigabit Ethernet

    bandwidth, 60

    PMD interfaces, 62

    PMD types, 62

  40-Gigabit Ethernet, 63

    bandwidth, 60

  100-Gigabit Ethernet, 63

    bandwidth, 60

  duplex operation, 63-65

  Fast Ethernet, bandwidth, 60

  Gigabit Ethernet

    bandwidth, 60

    cabling, 61

    link bundling, 62

    modular connectivity, 65-66

  overview, 59

  ports, 67

  scaling, 60

  segments

    bandwidth, 60

    crowded, 59

  switches, 59

    collisions, 59

Ethernet switches, 28

exam engine, 475

  installation, 476

  mode selection, 479

  study plan, 479

Exam Preparation Tasks, 478

exams

  study plan, 478-479

  updates, 489

    companion website, 489-490

EXEC, authenticated users, 468

exec keyword, 469-470

F

Fast EtherChannel, 62
Fast Ethernet
    bandwidth, 60
    cabling specifications, 60
    link bundling, 61
FE (Fast Ethernet) links, 245
FEC (Fast EtherChannel) links, 245
FHRP (first-hop redundancy protocols),
    384
FIB (Forwarding Information Base), 37,
    496
    aCEF (accelerated CEF), 276
    dCEF (distributed CEF), 276
    MLS (multilayer switching) and,
        273-276
filters, BPDU, 494
flat networks, 95
    switched networks and, 95
flooding, 496
FM (Feature Manager), 41
forward delay, 496
Forward Delay timer (STP), 165
forwarding packets, 384-385
Forwarding state, 163, 223-224
frames
    bridging and, 151-152
    EtherChannel, 248
    forwarding, MAC addresses and, 33
    mirrored, 354
    Storm Control and, 421-423
    VLAN trunks, 103

G

GARP (VLAN Registration Protocol),
    122
gateway addresses, HSRP, 390
gateway redundancy, verification, 405
GBIC (gigabit bidrectional link), 211
GE (Gigabit Ethernet) links, 245
GEC (Gigabit EtherChannel) links, 245
Gigabit Ethernet
    1000BASE-LX/LH, 65
    1000BASE-SX, 65
    1000BASE-T, 66
    1000BASE-ZX, 66
    bandwidth, 60
    cabling specifications, 61
    link bundling, 62
    modular connectivity, 65-66
GLBP (Gateway Load Balancing
    Protocol), 373, 380, 384, 397
    AVF (active virtual forwarder),
        398-400
    AVG (active virtual gateway), 397-398
    enabling, 400-405
    load balancing, 400
GVRP (VLAN Registration Protocol),
    122

H

half-duplex ports, 226
hello time, 496
Hello timer (STP), 165
hierarchical design, 7-13, 496
    access layer, 12
    Cisco products, 24-26

core layer, 10
> *switches, 12-13*

distribution layer, 12

switches, 10

traffic flow paths, 10

two-layer networks, 9

host dependent balancing (GLBP), 400

host keyword, 44

host port, 496

HSRP (Hot Standby Router Protocol), 373, 380, 384-386

active router, 496

election, 386-388
> *conceding, 389*

gateway addressing, 390

load balancing, 391-394

MD5 authentication, 388-389

plain-text authentication, 388

standby router, 496

I

ICMP (Internet Control Message Protocol), 336

IEEE 802.1D protocol, 146

STP (Spanning Tree Protocol), bridging loops, 151-154

IEEE 802.1Q protocol, VLAN trunks, 104-105

IEEE 802.1X, 496

IEEE 802.3 standard, 496

bandwidth, 60

Ethernet generations, 60

IEEE (Institute of Electrical and Electronics Engineers) 802.3 standard, 59

independent switches, access layer, 369

indirect topology chages, 169-171

informational keyword, 310

informs keyword, 327

insignificant topology changes, 171-172

interfaces

hosts
> *active, 46*
> *finding many, 46-47*

inter-VLAN routing, 268-269

internal time clock, 312-313

synchronization, 313-315

inter-VLAN routing, 268, 496

adjacency table, 276-279

configuration, 269
> *Layer 2, 270*
> *Layer 3, 270-271*
> *SVI port, 271-272*

connections, examples, 268

interfaces, 268-269

verification, 280-283

IP addresses

manual binding, 294-295

virtual terminal access security, 425

ip dhcp excluded-address command, 293

ip dhcp pool command, 293

ip helper-address command, 297

ip http access-class configuration command, 425

ip http server command, 424

IP SLA (IP Service Level Agreement), 336, 496

configuration, 338-341
> *displaying, 342*
> *verification, 341*

HSRP pairs, 344

MD5 (message digest 5), 339

operations, defining, 339

responder, 496

setup, 338

statistics display, 342-343

test operations, 337

test type, 339

parameters, 340

UDP Jitter test, 337

ip sla key-chain command, 339

ip sla schedule command, 341

IP Source Guard, 448

ipa sla schedule command, 341

IPv4 DHCP server, configuration, 293-294

IPv6 DHCP, 297

DHCPv6, 298-299

DHCPv6 Lite, 299-300

DHCPv6 relay agent, 300

stateless autoconfiguration, 298

verification, 300

ISE (Identity Services Engine), 465

isl keyword, 355

ISL (Inter-Switch Link) protocol, 103-104, 355, 496

isolated VLAN, 496

IST (Internal Spanning Tree), 234-235

instance, 496

J

jitter, 496

K

key chain command, 389

key command, 389

key-string command, 389

keywords

access, 328

address, 45

after, 341

ageout, 341

aggressive, 212

any, 44

auth, 328-329

auto, 80

broadcast, 422

Cisco IP phone trunking modes, 114

commands, 468

commands level, 470

config-commands, 468

configuration, 469

default, 214

delay, 387

disable, 212

dotlq, 355

enable, 212

exec, 469-470

host, 44

informational, 310

informs, 327

isl, 355

level, 422

life, 341

line, 467

local, 467

localtime, 317

mac address-table, 41

minimum, 387

msec, 317

multicast, 422

network, 469

new-model, 419

noauth, 328

none, 470

notify, 328

now, 341

ntp, 317

peer, 316

prefer, 315

priv, 328-329

query-only, 316

radius, 467

read, 328

recurring, 341

reload, 388

reverse-access, 469

ro, 327

rw, 327

SDM template type, 50

serve, 316

serve-only, 316

severity level and, 310

show-timezone, 317

start-stop, 470

start-time, 341

state, 343

stop-only, 470

system, 470

tacacs+, 467

unicast, 422

vlan, 45

write, 328

year, 317

L

LACP (Link Aggregation Control Protocol), 240, 251-252, 496

configuration, 254-255

lacp port-priority command, 255

LAN PHY (PMD interface), 62-63

LAP (lightweight access point), 494, 497

Layer 2 roaming, 497

Layer 3 roaming, 497

layers, distribution, 495

Learning state, 163, 223-224

lease command, 294

level keyword, 422

life keyword, 341

line keyword, 467

line line command, 467

link-local address, 497

links

bandwidth, scaling, 245

bundling

Fast Ethernet, 61

Gigabit Ethernet, 62

mode, switch ports, 69

Listening state, 223

Listening state (STPs), 163

LLDP (Link Layer Discovery Protocol), 426, 497

connected devices, 75-77

neighbor information display, 76-77

LLDP-MED (LLDP Media Endpoint Device), 75

load balancing

EtherChannel, 249-251

GLBP, 400

HSRP, 391-394

VRRP, 395-396

local keyword, 467

local SPAN, 352, 497

configuration, 354-356

traffic, monitoring, 352-353

local VLANs, 101, 497

localtime keyword, 317

logging host command, 311

logical switches, 364

building

StackWise, 371-372

VSS (Virtual Switching System), 372

EtherChannel, connection, 369-370

redundant switched network architecture, 370

Loop Guard, 210-211, 497

loops

preventing, STP and, 154-155

root bridges and, 156-158

LWAPP (Lightweight Access Point Protocol), 497

M

MAC addresses

AVG and, 397

bridging, 156-157

frame forwarding and, 33

port security, 415-418

sticky, 500

mac address-table keywords, 41

MAC (Media Access Control) layer, 60

mac-address-table keywords, 41

macro command, 186

macros, defining, 67

manual address bindings, 294-295

Max Age timer (STP), 166, 497

MD5, authentication, HSRP and, 388-389

MEC (multichassis EtherChannel), 497

Memory Tables, 477-478

MIB (Management Information Base), 324, 497

structure, 324

minimum keyword, 387

mirrored frames, 354

MLS (multilayer switching), 28

catalyst switches, 37

CEF (Cisco Express Forwarding) and, 264, 272-273

configuration, 280

verification, 283-284

DHCP and, 292-293

IPv4 server configuration, 293-294

IPv6 support, 297-300

manual address binding, 294-295

options configuration, 296

relays, 296-297

exceptions, 39-40

FIB (Forwarding Information Base), 273-276

inter-VLAN routing, 264

configuration, 269-272

connection examples, 268

interface types, 268-269

L2 forwarding table, 38

L3 forwarding table, 38

MSFC (Multilayer Switch Feature), 272

NetFlow switching, 272

overview, 272

packets, 37-39

rewrites, 279-280

QoS ACLs, 39

route caching, 37

RP (route processor), 272

RSFC (Route Switch Feature), 272

RSM (Route Switch Module), 272

SE (switching engine), 272

security ACLs, 39

switch interface information, 282

topology based, 37

types, 37

verification, 264

inter-VLAN routing, 280-283

modular connectivity, Gigabit Ethernet, 65-66

modular network desgin, 13-16

switches, 13

monitor session filter command, 358

msec keyword, 317

MSFC (Multilayer Switch Feature Card), 272

MST (Multiple Spanning Tree), 223, 497

802.IQ, 231

configuration, 236-237

implementation, 233

PVST+, 231

regions, 233-234, 497

spanning tree instances, 234

MSTI (Multiple Spanning Tree instances), 235-236, 497

MSTP (Multiple STP), 218

multicast keyword, 422

Multichassis EtherChannel, 247

N

NAD (network access device), 465

name command, 98

NAS (network access server), 465, 497

negotiation, EtherChannel, 251

NetFlow LAN switching, 37, 272

network analyzers, 348

See also sniffers

network command, 293

network keyword, 469

networks

campus networks, 7

core size, 24

disorganized growth, 15

flat, 95

hierarchies

access layer, 12

core layer, 10, 12-13

distribution layer, 12

traffic flow paths, 10

two-layer, 9

models, predictable, 9-11

modular design, 13-16

physical size, 166

segmented, expanding, 7-8

service types, 10

switched, flat networks and, 95

VLANS, 8

new-model keyword, 419

no cdp run command, 75

no ip cef interface configuration command, 280

no ip route-cache cef command, 280

no shutdown command, 213

no switchport command, 270

no vlan vlan-num command, 98

noauth keyword, 328

none keyword, 470

notify keyword, 328

now keyword, 341

NSF (nonstop forwarding), 364, 498

NTP (Network Time Protocol), 498

  securing, 316

  time source synchronization, 313-315

ntp access-group command, 316

ntp associations command, 315

ntp keyword, 317

ntp server command, 315

ntp status command, 315

null adjacency, 278

O

off mode (VTP), 128

Offer message (DHCP), 292

OID (object identifier), 498

P

packet forwarding, 384-385

packet loss, 498

packet rewrite, 498

packet rewrite engine, 279-280

packets

  CEF and, 273

  MLS, rewrites, 279-280

  multilayer switching, 37-39

PAgP (Page Aggregation Protocol), 240, 251-252, 355, 498

  configuration, 253-254

passwords, secure, 424

PCPT (Pearson Cert Practice Test)

  exam activation, 477

  exam engine, 475

    installation, 476

    mode selection, 479

    practice exam mode, 479

    study mode, 479

  practice exam

    activating, 476

    downloading, 476

PMD (Physical Media Dependent) interfaces, 62

  10-Gigabit Ethernet, 62

  transceiver types, 63

PoE (Power over Ethernet), 77-79, 498

  commands, 83

  configuration, 80-81

  detail information display, 83

  device detection, 79-80

  disabling on switch interface, 81

  limit setting, 80-81

  methods, 79

  power classes, 79

  status, switch ports, 81-82

  verification, 81-83

  See also PoE (Power over Ethernet)

point-to-point port, 226, 498

port cables, connecting switches and devices, 65-66

port operations, TCAM, 44-45

port security, 410, 415-418

  802.1X switch port, 419

  errdisable state, 417-418

  port status display, 417

  status summary, 418

port-based authentication, 410
  Catalyst switches, 418
PortFast, 498
  enabling, 208-209
ports
  alternate, 493
  bundling, aggregation, 247
  description, 68
  designated (DPs), 495
      electing, 160-162
  Discarding state, 224
  edge port, 495
  Ethernet type, 67
  Forwarding state, 224
  Learning state, 224
  promiscuous, 498
  root ports, electing, 158-160
  RSTP
      alternate port, 224
      backup port, 224
      designated port, 224
      Edge port, 226
      half-duplex, 226
      Point-to-point port, 226
      Root port, 226
      root port, 224
      synchronization, 227-229
  speed, 68
  STP disabling, 213-214
  STP states, 164
power class, 498
power for device operation, 54
  See also PoE (Power over Ethernet)
practice exam
  activating, 476
  downloading, 476

predictable network models, 9-11
prefer keyword, 315
Premium Edition of title, 477
primary VLAN, 498
priv keyword, 328-329
promiscuous ports, 498
punt adjacency, 279
PVLANs (private VLANs), 436-437,
  498
  configuration, 438-439
  functionality within a switch, 437
  port associations, 439-440
  port configuration, 440
PVST (Per-VLAN Spanning Tree), 146,
  173, 498
PVST+ (Per-VLAN Spanning Tree Plus),
  146, 173-174, 498
  RSTP and, 223

Q

QoS (quality of service), 498
  ACLs, 36, 39

R

RACLs (router access lists), 435
RADIUS (Remote Authentication Dial-
  In User Service), 419, 498
  protocol, 464
      server definition, 466
  server, authorization configuration,
      468
radius keyword, 467
read keyword, 328
recovering from errors, 70-71

recurring keyword, 341

redundancy, 14-15, 368

  bridging, 152

  gateway, verification, 405

  GLBP (Gateway Loading Balancing Protocol), 380

  HSRP (Hot Standby Router Protocol), 373, 380

  mode configuration, 374-376

  NSF (nonstop forwarding), 364, 377

  redundant switch supervisors, 373-374

  redundant switched network architecture, 370

  RIB (Routing Information Base), 377

  RPR (route processor redundancy), 373

  RPR+ (route processor redundancy plus), 373

  SSO (stateful switchover), 364, 374

  switch blocks, 18-20

  VRRP (Virtual Router Redundancy Protocol), 373, 380

Redundant Link Convergence, 176

redundant switch supervisors, 373-374

reload keyword, 388

Request message (DHCP), 292

reverse-access keyword, 469

ro keyword, 327

root bridges, 156-158, 498

  BPDUs and, 157

  election example, 157

  STP, 176

Root Guard, 498

  alternate port, 207

  blocking port, 207

  designated port, 207

  forwarding port, 207

  root port, 207

root path cost, 158-160, 499

root port, 226, 499

  electing, 158-160

round robin load balancing (GLBP), 400

route caching, multilayer switching, 37

RPR (route processor redundancy), 364, 373, 499

RPR+ (route processor redundancy plus), 364, 373, 499

RPVST+ (Rapid PVST+), 223, 230-231, 499

RSFC (Route Switch Feature Card), 272

RSM (Route Switch Module), 272

RSPAN (remote SPAN), 352, 499

  configuration, 357-359

  RSPAN VLAN, 357

  source, 356

  traffic mirroring, multiple switches, 357

RSTP (Rapid STP), 218, 499

  alternate port, 224

  backup port, 224

  BPDUs in, 224-225

  configuration, 229-230

  convergence, 225

    sequence of events, 228

  designated port, 224

  Edge port, 226

  Point-to-point port, 226

  ports

    half-duplex, 226

    roles, 223

    synchronization, 227-229

  PVST+ and, 223

Root port, 226
root port, 224
topology changes, 229
RTR (Response Time Reporter), 336
RTT (round-trip transit), 336
rw keyword, 327

S

SAA (Service Assurance Agent), 336
scaling, Ethernet, 60
SDM (Switching Database Manager), 41, 499
  templates, 49-50
secondary VLAN, 499
segmented networks, expanding, 7-8
server mode (VTP), 127
SFP (small form factor pluggable) module, 211
show adjacency summary command, 276
show cdp neighbors command, 73
show cef not-cef-switched command, 279
show clock command, 312
show dotlx all command, 420
show etherchannel load-balance command, 250
show etherchannel port-channel command, 250
show etherchannel summary command, 257
show interface command, 72
show interface switchport command, 115
show interfaces command, 71
show interfaces status command, 71

show interfaces status err-disabled command, 417
show ip arp command, 278
show ip arp inspection command, 457
show ip cef command, 274
show ip dhcp binding command, 294
show ip interface brief command, 282
show ip interface command, 281
show ip sla configuration command, 342
show lldp command, 75
show logging command, 311
show mac address-table count command, 47
show mac address-table EXEC command, 45
show port-security command, 418
show port-security interface command, 417
show spanning-tree interface command, 116, 191
show spanning-tree vlan vlan-id command, 230
show vlan brief command, 99
show vlan command, 99, 281
show vlan id vlan-id EXEC command, 110
show vtp status command, 137
show-timezone keyword, 317
shutdown command, 70, 213
sniffers, 348
SNMP (Simple Network Management Protocol), 499
  configuration
    SNMPv1, 327
    SNMPv2C, 327
    SNMPv3, 328-329
  packets, 326

polls, 324-325

securing access, 425

SNMP agent, 324, 499

SNMP inform, 499

SNMP manager, 324, 499

trap, 499

versions, 325-326

    comparisons, 326

snmp-server group command, 328

snmp-server host command, 327

snmp-server user command, 328

snmp-server view command, 328

snooping, 448

DHCP, 495

SNTP (Simplified Network Time Protocol), 316-317

SPAN (Switch Port Analysis), 499

catalyst switches, 348

local, 348, 352

    configuration, 354-356

    traffic monitoring, 352-353

packets, copying, 355

remote, 348, 352

sessions, 348

    deleting, 360

    management, 359-360

    numbering, 354-355

spanning-tree mode command, 231

spanning-tree vlan vlan-id priority bridge-priority command, 188

spanning-tree vlan vlan-id root command, 188

split-MAC architecture, 499

spoofing switches, 441-443

SRM (single-router mode), 374

SSH, 425

SSID (service-set identifier), 500

SSO (stateful switchover), 364, 374, 500

StackWise, 500

logical switches, 371-372

start-stop keyword, 470

start-time keyword, 341

state keyword, 343

static VLANs, 96-97

configuration, 97-99

sticky MAC address, 500

stop-only keyword, 470

Storm Control, 421-423

enabling, 423

storm control, 410

STP (Spanning Tree Protocol), 35, 140, 355, 499

BPDUs (bridge-protocol data units), 155

    Configuration BPDU, 155-156

    TCN BPDU, 155

bridging loops, 151-154

convergence,

    Redundant Link, 176

CST (Common Spanning Tree), 146, 173

customization, 176

disabling, BPDU filtering and, 213-214

Loop Guard, 210-211

loops, preventing, 154-155

manual computation, 165

monitoring, 176

MSTP (Multiple STP), 218

port activity, 163

PVST (Per-VLAN Spanning Tree), 146, 173

PVST+ (Per-VLAN Spanning Tree Plus), 146, 173-174

root bridge, 176

root path cost, 158-160

RSTP (Rapid STP), 218

secure operation, 426

states, 163

    Blocking, 162

    Disabled, 162

    Forwarding, 163

    Learning, 163

    Listening, 163

    port progression, 164

switch type determination, 231

timers, 165

    default values, 166

    Forward Delay timer, 165

    functions, 166

    Hello timer, 165

    Max Age timer, 166

topology

    designated ports, 162

    VLANs, 232

troubleshooting protection, 214

UDLDs and, 211-212

stratum, 500

study plan, 478-479

summer-time recurring command, 313

superior BPDU, 500

supervisors

redundant, 373-374

synchronization, 376

SVI (switch virtual interface), 269, 500

inter-VLAN configuration, 271-272

VLAN association, 440-441

switch blocks, 15, 500

distribution switches, 18

redundancy, 18-20

sizing, 16-17

switch console

securing, 425

syslog and, 310

switch lines, method list, 467

switch ports

Blocking state, 223

configuration, 54

    duplex mode, 69

    link mode, 69

    port description, 68

    port selection, 66-68

    port speed, 68

connectivity, troubleshooting, 71

Disabled state, 223

enabling, 71

errdisable state, 69-70

    re-enabling ports, 70-71

error detection, 69-70

error management, 69

errors, recovery, 70-71

Forwarding state, 223

Learning state, 223

Listening state, 223

PoE limit setting, 80-81

PoE status display, 81-82

port state, 71-72

speed/duplex mismatches, 72-73

unused, 426

switch spoofing, 500

switched networks, flat networks and, 95

switches, 8-9

access layer, 12, 25

authentication, 465-466

Catalyst switch, 28

command-line interface, 33

connecting, 54
    Ethernet port cables, 65-66
distribution layer, 26
Ethernet, 28, 59
    collisions, 59
flooding, 139
hierarchical design and, 10
independent, access layer, 369
internal memory buffer, 310-311
Layer 2, transparent bridging, 32-35
logical (*See* logical switches)
MIB database, 324
port-based authentication, 418
redundancy and, 14-15
redundancy modes, 373-374
securing, best practices, 410, 423-427
SNMP polls, 324
SPAN, 348
spoofing, 441-443
supervisors, redundant, 373-374
switch interfaces, 8
syslog message format, 308
transparent bridging, 152
switching
Layer 2, 28, 32
logs, syslog messages, 308-311
multilayers, 28
    catalyst switches, 37
    exceptions, 39-40
    L2 forwarding table, 38
    L3 forwarding table, 38
    packets, 37-39
    QoS ACLs, 39
    route caching, 37
    security ACLs, 39

    topology based, 37
    types, 37
tables, 28
    CAM (content-addressable memory), 40-41
    CAM table operation, 45-48
    sizes, managing, 49-50
    TCAM (ternary content-addressable memory), 41-45
switchport command, 98
switchport interface command, 269
switchport mode command, 107
switchport nonegotiate command, 108
switchport trunk allowed vlan command, 106-107, 140
switchport trunk encapsulation command, 106
switchport trunk native vlan command, 106
synchronization, 500
syslog, 500
remote server login, 311
syslog messages
Catalyst switch
    internal memory buffer, 310-311
    message format, 308
fields, 308
severity levels, 309-310
switch console, 310
time stamps, 312, 317
    internal time clock, 312-313
syslog severity level, 500
system banners, 424
system keyword, 470

T

tables
  CAM, size, 47-50
  switches and, 28
    CAM (content-addressable memory), 40-41
    CAM table operation, 45-48
    size management, 49-50
    TCAM (ternary content-addressable memory), 41-45
TACACS+ (Terminal Access Controller Access-Control System Plus), 500
  protocol, 464
    server definition, 466
  server, authorization configuration, 468
tacacs+ keyword, 467
TCAM (ternary content-addressable memory), 41, 500
  example, 43-44
  operation, 48
  port operations, 44-45
  value patterns, 42
  VLAN access lists, 435
TCN (Topology Change Notification) BPDU, 155, 167, 500
templates, SDM (Switching Database Manager), 49
terminal access, virtual, securing, 425
terminal monitor command, 310
throwing bandwidth, 7
time stamps
  clock synchronization
    NTP, 313-315
    SNTP, 316-317
  syslog messages, 312, 317
    internal time clock, 312-313

timers, STP, 165
  default values, 166
  Forward Delay timer, 165
  functions, 166
  Hello timer, 165
  Max Age timer, 166
TLV (Type-Length-Value), 75, 500
topology
  changes, 167
    direct changes, 168-169
    indirect, 169-171
    insignificant, 171-172
    RSTP and, 229
  multilayer switching, 37
  STP, VLANs, 232
track command, 343
traffic
  broadcast traffic, 8
  EtherChannel, 247-249
  flow paths, 10
  local SPAN, 352-353
  Storm Control and, 421-423
transparent bridging, 500
  Layer 2 and, 32-35
  STP and, 151-154
  switches and, 152
transparent mode (VTP), 128
troubleshooting
  EtherChannel, 257-259
  STP protection, 214
  switch port connectivity, 71
  VLAN trunks, 110-112
  VLANs, 110-112
trust boundary, 501
two-layer networks, 9

U

UDLD (Unidirectional Link Detection), 210-213, 501

Aggressive mode, 212

Normal mode, 212

UDP Jitter test, 337

udp-jitter command, 340

Unicast, flooding, 34

unicast keyword, 422

unknown unicast flooding, 501

UplinkFast, 223, 501

username command, 464

usernames, defining, 466

V

VACLs (VLAN access lists), 435, 501

access maps, 435

configuration, 435-436

virtual terminal access, securing, 425

vlan keyword, 45

VLANs (virtual LANs), 8, 501

ACLs (access lists) (*See* VACLs (VLAN access lists))

community VLAN, 494

CST (Common Spanning Tree), 173

deploying, 99-100

dynamic, 99

end-to-end, 100-101, 495

flat networks, 95

hopping, 443-445, 501

inter-VLAN routing, 496

isolated, 496

listing configured, 281

local, 101

membership methods, 96

native, 497

numbers, 501

primary, 498

private VLANs, 430, 498

PVLANs (private VLANs), 436-437

RSPAN, 357

secondary, 437, 499

static, 96-97

configuration, 97-99

STP topologies, 232

SVI association, 440-441

switch ports, assigning, 98

switches, configuration, 110

traffic monitoring, 354

troubleshooting, 110-112

trucks, 430

trunks, 101-103, 501

configuration, 106-110

dynamic trunking protocol, 105-106

frames, 103

IEEE 802.1Q protocol, 104-105

ISL (Inter-Switch Link) protocol, 103-104

securing, 441-445

switch port trunking status, 108

troubleshooting, 110-112

voice, 112-113, 501

configuration, 113-115

verification, 115-116

VTP (VLAN Trunking Protocol), 97

wireless, 117-118

See also inter-VLAN routing

VMPS (VLAN Membership Policy Server), 99

voice VLANs, 112-113, 501
  configuration, 113-115
  verification, 115-116
VRRP (Virtual Router Redundancy
  Protocol), 373, 380, 384, 394-396
  backup router, 501
  configuration commands, 394
  load balancing, 395-396
  master router, 501
  multiple group status, 396
VSPAN (VLAN-based Switched Port
  Analayzer), 501
VSS (Virtual Switching System), 364,
  372, 501
VTP (VLAN Trunking Protocol), 97,
  127, 355, 501
  advertisements, 128-131
    client requests, 130
    subset, 129
    summary, 129
  configuration, 122, 132-133
    example, 136-137
    management domain, 134-135
    modes, 135-136
    revision number, 502
    VTP version, 133-134
  configuration revision number, 128
  domains, 127, 502
  features supported, 134

  modes
    client, 127
    off, 128
    server, 127
    transparent, 128, 137-138
  pruning, 122, 138-140, 502
    enabling, 140-141
  status, display, 137-138
  switches, attributes, 127
  synchronization, 131-132, 502
  troubleshooting, 122, 141-142
VTP (VLAN trunking protocol), 122

W

WAN PHY (PMD interface), 62-63
web interface, securing, 424-425
weighted load balancing (GLBP), 400
wireless VLANs, 117-118
wiring. See cabling
WLC (wireless LAN controller), 494,
  502
write keyword, 328

Y

year keyword, 317